SACRED BOOKS OF THE EAST

SACRED BOOKS OF THE EAST

INCLUDING SELECTIONS FROM THE VEDIC HYMNS, ZEND-AVESTA, DHAMMAPADA, UPANISHADS, THE KORAN, AND THE LIFE OF BUDDHA

WITH CRITICAL AND BIOGRAPHICAL SKETCHES BY

EPIPHANIUS WILSON, A. M.

GYAN

Published by

GYAN

Gyan Publishing House
5, Ansari Road
Daryaganj, New Delhi-110002
Phone: 011-47034999, 9811692060
E-mail: books@gyanbooks.com

Distribution Network
gyanbooks.com
India, USA, Canada, UK, Australia, France

ISBN : 978-81-212-3975-2 (PB)
First Published, 1945

2nd Impression 2020

Printed at: Gyan Press, Delhi.

Sacred Books of the East

INCLUDING SELECTIONS FROM

THE VEDIC HYMNS, ZEND-AVESTA,
DHAMMAPADA, UPANISHADS,
THE KORAN, AND THE
LIFE OF BUDDHA

WITH CRITICAL AND BIOGRAPHICAL SKETCHES BY
EPIPHANIUS WILSON, A.M.

REVISED EDITION

NEW YORK AND LONDON
THE CO-OPERATIVE PUBLICATION SOCIETY

The Muezzin

Photogravure from a painting by J. F. Gerome

"NOW the Muezzin's call is heard, sonorous clanging
Through thronged bazaar, concealed harem, and cool kiosk:
'In the Prophet's name, God is God, and there is no other.'
On roofs, in streets, alone, or close beside his brother,
Each Moslem kneels, his forehead turned towards Mecca's shrine,
And all the world forgotten in one thought divine."

CONTENTS

VEDIC HYMNS

THE ZEND-AVESTA

THE DHAMMAPADA

THE UPANISHADS

SELECTIONS FROM THE KORAN

LIFE OF BUDDHA

VEDIC HYMNS

[*Translation by F. Max Müller.*]

INTRODUCTION

THE Vedic Hymns are among the most interesting portions of Hindoo literature. In form and spirit they resemble both the poems of the Hebrew psalter and the lyrics of Pindar. They deal with the most elemental religious conceptions and are full of the imagery of nature. It would be absurd to deny to very many of them the possession of the truest poetic inspiration. The scenery of the Himalayas, ice and snow, storm and tempest, lend their majesty to the strains of the Vedic poet. He describes the storm sweeping over the white-crested mountains till the earth, like a hoary king, trembles with fear. The Maruts, or storm-gods, are terrible, glorious, musical, riding on strong-hoofed, never-wearying steeds. There is something Homeric, Pindaric in these epithets. Yet Soma and Rudra are addressed, though they wield sharp weapons; and sharp bolts, *i.e.*, those of the lightning, are spoken of as kind friends. "Deliver us," says the poet, "from the snare of Varuna, and guard us, as kind-hearted gods." One of the most remarkable of these hymns is that addressed to the Unknown God. The poet says: "In the beginning there arose the Golden Child. As soon as he was born he alone was the lord of all that is. He established the earth and this heaven." The hymn consists of ten stanzas, in which the Deity is celebrated as the maker of the snowy mountains, the sea and the distant river, who made fast the awful heaven, He who alone is God above all gods, before whom heaven and earth stand trembling in their mind. Each stanza concludes with the refrain, "Who is the God to whom we shall offer sacrifice?"

We have in this hymn a most sublime conception of the Supreme Being, and while there are many Vedic hymns whose tone is pantheistic and seems to imply that the wild forces of nature are Gods who rule the world, this hymn to the Unknown God is as purely monotheistic as a psalm of David, and shows a spirit of religious awe as profound as any we find in the Hebrew Scriptures.

It is very difficult to arrive at the true date of the Vedas. The word Veda means knowledge, and is applied to unwritten literature. The Vedas are therefore the oldest Sanscrit writings which exist, and stand in the same class with regard to Hindoo literature as Homer does with regard to Greek literature. Probably the earliest Vedas were recited a thousand years before Christ, while the more recent of the hymns date about five hundred before Christ. We must therefore consider them to be the most primitive form of Aryan poetry in existence.

There is in the West a misunderstanding as to the exact meaning of "Vedic" and "Sanscrit"; for the latter is often used as if it were synonymous with Indian; whereas, only the later Indian literature can be classed under that head, and "Vedic" is often used to indicate only the Vedic Hymns, whereas it really denotes Hymns, Bráhmanas, Upanishads, and Sutras; in fact, all literature which orthodox Hindoos regard as sacred. The correct distinction then between the Vedic and the Sanscrit writings is that of holy writ and profane literature.

E. W.

VEDIC HYMNS

TO THE UNKNOWN GOD

IN the beginning there arose the Golden Child. As soon as born, he alone was the lord of all that is. He established the earth and this heaven:—Who is the God to whom we shall offer sacrifice?

He who gives breath, he who gives strength, whose command all the bright gods revere, whose shadow is immortality, whose shadow is death:—Who is the God to whom we shall offer sacrifice?

He who through his might became the sole king of the breathing and twinkling world, who governs all this, man and beast:—Who is the God to whom we shall offer sacrifice?

He through whose might these snowy mountains are, and the sea, they say, with the distant river; he of whom these regions are indeed the two arms:—Who is the God to whom we shall offer sacrifice?

He through whom the awful heaven and the earth were made fast, he through whom the ether was established, and the firmament; he who measured the air in the sky:—Who is the God to whom we shall offer sacrifice?

He to whom heaven and earth, standing firm by his will, look up, trembling in their mind; he over whom the risen sun shines forth:—Who is the God to whom we shall offer sacrifice?

When the great waters went everywhere, holding the germ, and generating light, then there arose from them the breath of the gods:—Who is the God to whom we shall offer sacrifice?

He who by his might looked even over the waters which held power and generated the sacrifice, he who alone is God above all gods:—Who is the God to whom we shall offer sacrifice?

May he not hurt us, he who is the begetter of the earth, or he, the righteous, who begat the heaven; he who also begat the bright and mighty waters:—Who is the God to whom we shall offer sacrifice?

Pragâpati, no other than thou embraces all these created things. May that be ours which we desire when sacrificing to thee: may we be lords of wealth!

TO THE MARUTS*

I

COME hither, Maruts, on your chariots charged with lightning, resounding with beautiful songs, stored with spears, and winged with horses! Fly to us like birds, with your best food, you mighty ones! They come gloriously on their red, or, it may be, on their tawny horses which hasten their chariots. He who holds the axe is brilliant like gold;—with the tire of the chariot they have struck the earth. On your bodies there are daggers for beauty; may they stir up our minds as they stir up the forests. For yourselves, O well-born Maruts, the vigorous among you shake the stone for distilling Soma. Days went round you and came back, O hawks, back to this prayer, and to this sacred rite; the Gotamas making prayer with songs, pushed up the lid of the cloud to drink. No such hymn was ever known as this which Gotama sounded for you, O Maruts, when he saw you on golden wheels, wild boars rushing about with iron tusks. This comforting speech rushes sounding towards you, like the speech of a suppliant: it rushed freely from our hands as our speeches are wont to do.

II

Let us now proclaim for the robust host, for the herald of the powerful Indra, their ancient greatness! O ye strong-voiced Maruts, you heroes, prove your powers on your march, as with a torch, as with a sword! Like parents bringing a dainty to their own son, the wild Maruts play playfully at the sacrifices. The Rudras reach the worshipper with their protection, strong in themselves, they do not fail the sacrificer. For him to whom the immortal guardians have given fulness of wealth, and who is himself a giver of oblations, the Maruts,

* The Maruts are the "Storm-Gods."

who gladden men with the milk of rain, pour out, like friends, many clouds. You who have stirred up the clouds with might, your horses rushed forth, self-guided. All beings who dwell in houses are afraid of you, your march is brilliant with your spears thrust forth. When they whose march is terrible have caused the rocks to tremble, or when the manly Maruts have shaken the back of heaven, then every lord of the forest fears at your racing, each shrub flies out of your way, whirling like chariot-wheels. You, O terrible Maruts, whose ranks are never broken, favorably fulfil our prayer! Wherever your glory-toothed lightning bites, it crunches cattle, like a well-aimed bolt. The Maruts whose gifts are firm, whose bounties are never ceasing, who do not revile, and who are highly praised at the sacrifices, they sing their song for to drink the sweet juice: they know the first manly deeds of the hero Indra. The man whom you have guarded, O Maruts, shield him with hundredfold strongholds from injury and mischief—the man whom you, O fearful, powerful singers, protect from reproach in the prosperity of his children. On your chariots, O Maruts, there are all good things, strong weapons are piled up clashing against each other. When you are on your journeys, you carry the rings on your shoulders, and your axle turns the two wheels at once. In their manly arms there are many good things, on their chests golden chains, flaring ornaments, on their shoulders speckled deer-skins, on their fellies sharp edges; as birds spread their wings, they spread out splendors behind. They, mighty by might, all-powerful powers, visible from afar like the heavens with the stars, sweet-toned, soft-tongued singers with their mouths, the Maruts, united with Indra, shout all around. This is your greatness, O well-born Maruts!—your bounty extends far, as the sway of Aditi. Not even Indra in his scorn can injure that bounty, on whatever man you have bestowed it for his good deeds. This is your kinship with us, O Maruts, that you, immortals, in former years have often protected the singer. Having through this prayer granted a hearing to man, all these heroes together have become well known by their valiant deeds. That we may long flourish, O Maruts, with your wealth, O ye racers, that our men may spread in the camp, therefore let me achieve the rite with these offerings. May this praise, O Maruts, this song of Mândârya, the son of Mâna, the poet, ask you with food for offspring for ourselves! May we have an invigorating autumn, with quickening rain!

III

For the manly host, the joyful, the wise, for the Maruts bring thou, O Nodhas, a pure offering. I prepare songs, like as a handy priest, wise in his mind, prepares the water, mighty at sacrifices. They are born, the tall bulls of heaven, the manly youths of Rudra, the divine, the blameless, pure, and bright like suns; scattering raindrops, full of terrible designs, like giants. The youthful Rudras, they who never grow old, the slayers of the demon, have grown irresistible like mountains. They throw down with their strength all beings, even the strongest, on earth and in heaven. They deck themselves with glittering ornaments for a marvellous show; on their chests they fastened gold chains for beauty; the spears on their shoulders pound to pieces; they were born together by themselves, the men of Dyu. They who confer power, the roarers, the devourers of foes, they made winds and lightnings by their powers. The shakers milk the heavenly udders, they sprinkle the earth all round with milk. The bounteous Maruts pour forth water, mighty at sacrifices, the fat milk of the clouds. They seem to lead about the powerful horse, the cloud, to make it rain; they milk the thundering, unceasing spring. Mighty they are, powerful, of beautiful splendor, strong in themselves like mountains, yet swiftly gliding along;—you chew up forests, like wild elephants, when you have assumed your powers among the red flames. Like lions they roar, the wise Maruts, they are handsome like gazelles, the all-knowing. By night with their spotted rain-clouds and with their spears—lightnings—they rouse the companions together, they whose ire through strength is like the ire of serpents. You who march in companies, the friends of man, heroes, whose ire through strength is like the ire of serpents, salute heaven and earth! On the seats on your chariots, O Maruts, the lightning stands, visible like light. All-knowing, surrounded with wealth, endowed with powers, singers, men of endless prowess, armed with strong rings, they, the archers, have taken the arrow in their fists. The Maruts who with the golden tires of their wheels increase the rain, stir up the clouds like wanderers on the road. They are brisk, indefatigable, they move by themselves; they throw down what is firm, the Maruts with their brilliant spears make everything to reel. We invoke with prayer the offspring of Rudra, the brisk, the pure, the worshipful, the active. Cling for happiness-sake to the strong company of the Maruts, the chasers of the sky, the powerful, the impetuous. The mortal whom ye, Maruts, protected, he indeed surpasses people in strength through your protection. He carries off booty with his horses, treasures with his men; he acquires honorable wisdom, and he prospers. Give, O Maruts, to our lords strength glorious, invincible in battle, brilliant, wealth-acquiring, praiseworthy, known to all men. Let us foster our kith and kin during a hundred winters. Will you then, O Maruts, grant unto us wealth, durable, rich in men, defying all onslaughts?—wealth a hundred and a thousand-fold, always increasing?—May he who is rich in prayers come early and soon!

IV

Sing forth, O Kanvas, to the sportive host of your Maruts, brilliant on their chariots, and unscathed,—they who were born together, self-luminous, with the spotted deer, the spears, the daggers, the glittering ornaments. I hear their whips, almost close by, when they crack them in their hands; they gain splendor on their way. Sing forth the god-given prayer to the wild host of your Maruts, endowed with terrible vigor and strength. Celebrate the bull among the cows, for it is the sportive host of the Maruts; he grew as he tasted the rain. Who, O ye men, is the strongest among you here, ye shakers of heaven and earth, when you shake them like the hem of a garment? At your approach the son of man holds himself down; the gnarled cloud fled at your fierce anger. They at whose racings the earth, like a hoary king, trembles for fear on their ways, their birth is strong indeed: there is strength to come forth from their mother, nay, there is vigor twice enough for it. And these sons, the singers, stretched out the fences in their racings; the cows had to walk knee-deep. They cause this long and broad unceasing rain to fall on their ways. O Maruts, with such strength as yours, you have caused men to tremble, you have caused the mountains to tremble. As the Maruts pass along, they talk together on the way: does anyone hear them? Come fast on your quick steeds! there are worshippers for you among the Kanvas: may you well rejoice among them. Truly there is enough for your rejoicing. We always are their servants, that we may live even the whole of life.

V

To every sacrifice you hasten together, you accept prayer after prayer, O quick Maruts! Let me therefore bring you hither by my prayers from heaven and earth, for our welfare, and for our great protection; the shakers who were born to bring food and light, self-born and self-supported, like springs, like thousandfold waves of water, aye, visibly like unto excellent bulls, those Maruts, like Soma-drops, which squeezed from ripe stems dwell, when drunk, in the hearts of the worshipper—see how on their shoulders there clings as if a clinging wife; in their hands the quoit is held and the sword. Lightly they have come down from heaven of their own accord: Immortals, stir yourselves with the whip! The mighty Maruts on dustless paths, armed with brilliant spears, have shaken down even the strong places. O ye Maruts, who are armed with lightning-spears, who stirs you from within by himself, as the jaws are stirred by the tongue? You shake the sky, as if on the search for food; you are invoked by many, like the solar horse of the day. Where, O Maruts, is the top, where the bottom of the mighty sky where you came? When you throw down with the thunderbolt what is strong, like brittle things, you fly across the terrible sea! As your conquest is violent, splendid, terrible, full and crushing, so, O Maruts, is your gift delightful, like the largess of a liberal worshipper, wide-spreading, laughing like heavenly lightning. From the tires of their chariot-wheels streams gush forth, when they send out the voice of the clouds; the lightnings smiled upon the earth, when the Maruts shower down fatness. Prisni brought forth for the great fight the terrible train of the untiring Maruts: when fed they produced the dark cloud, and then looked about for invigorating food. May this praise, O Maruts, this song of Mândârya, the son of Mâna, the poet, ask you with food for offspring for ourselves! May we have an invigorating autumn, with quickening rain!

VI

The Maruts charged with rain, endowed with fierce force, terrible like wild beasts, blazing in their strength, brilliant like fires, and impetuous, have uncovered the rain-giving cows by blowing away the cloud. The Maruts with their rings appeared like the heavens with their stars, they shone wide like streams from clouds as soon as Rudra, the strong man, was born for you, O golden-breasted Maruts, in the bright lap of Prisni. They wash their horses like racers in the courses, they hasten with the points of the reed on their quick steeds. O golden-jawed Maruts, violently shaking your jaws, you go quick with your spotted deer, being friends of one mind. Those Maruts have grown to feed all these beings, or, it may be, they have come hither for the sake of a friend, they who always bring quickening rain. They have spotted horses, their bounties cannot be taken away, they are like headlong charioteers on their ways. O Maruts, wielding your brilliant spears, come hither on smooth roads with your fiery cows whose udders are swelling; being of one mind, like swans toward their nests, to enjoy the sweet offering. O one-minded Maruts, come to our prayers, come to our libations like Indra praised by men! Fulfil our prayer, like the udder of a barren cow, and make the prayer glorious by booty to the singer. Grant us this strong horse for our chariot, a draught that rouses our prayers, from day to day, food to the singers, and to the poet in our homesteads luck, wisdom, inviolable and invincible strength. When the gold-breasted Maruts harness the horses to their chariots, bounteous in wealth, then it is as if a cow in the folds poured out to her calf copious food, to every man who has offered libations. Whatever mortal enemy may have placed us among wolves, shield us from hurt, ye Vasus! Turn the wheels with burning heat against him, and strike down the weapon of the impious fiend, O Rudras! Your march, O Maruts, appears brilliant, whether even friends have milked the udder of Prisni, or whether, O sons of Rudra, you mean to blame him who praises you, and to weaken those who are weakening Trita, O unbeguiled heroes. We invoke you, the great Maruts, the constant wanderers, at the offering of the rapid Vishnu; holding ladles and prayerful we ask the golden-colored and exalted Maruts for glorious wealth. The Dasagvas carried on the sacrifice first; may they rouse us at the break of dawn. Like the dawn, they uncover the dark nights with the red rays, the strong ones, with their brilliant light, as with a sea of milk. With the morning clouds, as if with glittering red ornaments, these Maruts have grown great in the sacred places. Streaming down with rushing splendor, they have assumed their bright and brilliant color. Approaching them for their great protection to help us, we invoke them with this worship, they whom Trita may bring near, like the five Hotri priests for victory, descending on their chariot to help. May that grace of yours by which you help the wretched across all anguish, and by which you deliver the worshipper from the reviler, come hither, O Maruts; may your favor approach us like a cow going to her calf!

VII

I come to you with this adoration, with a hymn I implore the favor of the quick Maruts. O Maruts, you have rejoiced in it clearly, put down then all anger and unharness your horses! This reverent praise of yours, O Maruts, fashioned in the heart, has been offered by the mind, O gods! Come to it, pleased in your mind, for you give increase to our worship. May the Maruts when they have been praised be gracious to us, and likewise Indra, the best giver of happiness, when he has been praised. May our lances through our valor stand always erect, O Maruts! I am afraid of this powerful one, and trembling in fear of Indra. For you the offerings were prepared—we have now put them away, forgive us! Thou through whom the Mânas see the mornings, whenever the eternal dawns flash forth with power, O Indra, O strong hero, grant thou glory to us with the Maruts, terrible with the terrible ones, strong and a giver of victory. O Indra, protect thou these bravest of men, let thy anger be turned away from the Maruts, for thou hast become victorious together with those brilliant heroes. May we have an invigorating autumn, with quickening rain!

VIII

O Maruts, that man in whose dwelling you drink the Soma, ye mighty sons of heaven, he indeed has the best guardians. You who are propitiated either by sacrifices or from the prayers of the sage, hear the call, O Maruts! Aye, the powerful man to whom you have granted a sage, he will live in a stable rich in cattle. On the altar of this strong man Soma is poured out in daily sacrifices; praise and joy are sung. To him let the mighty Maruts listen, to him who surpasses all men, as the flowing rain-clouds pass over the sun. For we, O Maruts, have sacrificed at many harvests, through the mercies of the storm-gods. May that mortal be blessed, O chasing Maruts, whose offerings you carry off. You take notice either of the sweat of him who praises you, ye men of true strength, or of the desire of the suppliant. O ye of true strength, make this manifest with might! strike the fiend with your lightning! Hide the hideous darkness, destroy every tusky fiend. Make the light which we long for!

IX

Endowed with exceeding vigor and power, the singers, the never flinching, the immovable, the impetuous, the most beloved and most manly, have decked themselves with their glittering ornaments, a few only, like the heavens with the stars. When you have seen your way through the clefts, like birds, O Maruts, on whatever road it be, then the clouds on your chariots trickle everywhere, and you pour out the honey-like fatness for him who praises you. At their racings the earth shakes, as if broken, when on the heavenly paths they harness their deer for victory. They the sportive, the roaring, with bright spears, the shakers of the clouds have themselves glorified their greatness. That youthful company, with their spotted horses, moves by itself; hence it exercises lordship, invested with powers. Thou indeed art true, thou searchest out sin, thou art without blemish. Therefore the manly host will help this prayer. We speak after the kind of our old father, our tongue goes forth at the sight of the Soma: when the singers had joined Indra in deed, then only they took their holy names;—these Maruts, armed with beautiful rings, obtained splendors for their glory, they obtained rays, and men to celebrate them; nay, armed with daggers, speeding along, and fearless, they found the beloved domain of the Maruts.

X

What then now? When will you take us as a dear father takes his son by both hands, O ye gods, for whom the sacred grass has been trimmed? Where now? On what errand of yours are you going, in heaven, not on earth? Where are your cows sporting? Where are your newest favors, O Maruts? Where the blessings? Where all delights? If you, sons of Prisni, were mortals, and your praiser an immortal, then never should your praiser be unwelcome, like a deer in pasture grass, nor should he go on the path of Yama. Let not one sin after another, difficult to be conquered, overcome us; may it depart together with greed. Truly they are terrible and powerful; even to the desert the Rudriyas bring rain that is never dried up. The lightning lows like a cow, it follows as a mother follows after her young, when the shower of the Maruts has been let loose. Even by day the Maruts create darkness with the water-bearing cloud, when they drench the earth. Then from the shouting of the Maruts over the whole space of the earth, men reeled forward. Maruts on your strong-hoofed, never-wearying steeds go after those bright ones, which are still locked up. May your fellies be strong, the chariots, and their horses, may your reins be well-fashioned. Speak forth forever with thy voice to praise the Lord of prayer, Agni, who is like a friend, the bright one. Fashion a hymn in thy mouth! Expand like the cloud! Sing a song of praise. Worship the host of the Maruts, the terrible, the glorious, the musical. May they be magnified here among us.

XI

Let your voice-born prayers go forth to the great Vishnu, accompanied by the Maruts, Evayâmarut, and to the chasing host, adorned with good rings, the strong, in their jubilant throng, to the shouting power of the Maruts. O Maruts, you who are born great, and proclaim it yourselves by knowledge,

Evayâmarut, that power of yours cannot be approached by wisdom, that power of theirs cannot be approached by gift or might; they are like unapproachable mountains. They who are heard with their voice from the high heaven, the brilliant and strong, Evayâmarut, in whose council no tyrant reigns, the rushing chariots of these roaring Maruts come forth, like fires with their own lightning. The wide-striding Vishnu strode forth from the great common seat, Evayâmarut. When he has started by himself from his own place along the ridges, O ye striving, mighty Maruts, he goes together with the heroes, conferring blessings. Impetuous, like your own shout, the strong one made everything tremble, the terrible, the wanderer, the mighty, Evayâmarut; strong with him you advanced self-luminous, with firm reins, golden colored, well armed, speeding along. Your greatness is infinite, ye Maruts, endowed with full power, may that terrible power help, Evayâmarut. In your raid you are indeed to be seen as charioteers; deliver us therefore from the enemy, like shining fires. May then these Rudras, lively like fires and with vigorous shine, help, Evayâmarut. The seat of the earth is stretched out far and wide, when the hosts of these faultless Maruts come quickly to the races. Come kindly on your path, O Maruts, listen to the call of him who praises you, Evayâmarut. Confidants of the great Vishnu, may you together, like charioteers, keep all hateful things far, by your wonderful skill. Come zealously to our sacrifice, ye worshipful, hear our guileless call, Evayâmarut. Like the oldest mountains in the sky, O wise guardians, prove yourselves for him irresistible to the enemy.

XII

O Syâvâsva, sing boldly with the Maruts, the singers who, worthy themselves of sacrifice, rejoice in their guileless glory according to their nature. They are indeed boldly the friends of strong power; they on their march protect all who by themselves are full of daring. Like rushing bulls, these Maruts spring over the dark cows, and then we perceive the might of the Maruts in heaven and on earth. Let us boldly offer praise and sacrifice to your Maruts, to all them who protect the generation of men, who protect the mortal from injury. They who are worthy, bounteous, men of perfect strength, to those heavenly Maruts who are worthy of sacrifice, praise the sacrifice! The tall men, coming near with their bright chains, and their weapon, have hurled forth their spears. Behind these Maruts there came by itself the splendor of heaven, like laughing lightnings. Those who have grown up on earth, or in the wide sky, or in the realm of the rivers, or in the abode of the great heaven, praise that host of the Maruts, endowed with true strength and boldness, whether those rushing heroes have by themselves harnessed their horses for triumph, or whether these brilliant Maruts have in the speckled cloud clothed themselves in wool, or whether by their strength they cut the mountain asunder with the tire of their chariot; call them comers, or goers, or enterers, or followers, under all these names, they watch on the straw for my sacrifice. The men watch, and their steeds watch. Then, so brilliant are their forms to be soon, that people say, Look at the strangers! In measured steps and wildly shouting the gleemen have danced towards the cloud. They who appeared one by one like thieves, were helpers to me to see the light. Worship, therefore, O seer, that host of Maruts, and keep and delight them with your voice, they who are themselves wise poets, tall heroes armed with lightning-spears. Approach, O seer, the host of Maruts, as a woman approaches a friend, for a gift; and you, Maruts, bold in your strength, hasten hither, even from heaven, when you have been praised by our hymns. If he, after perceiving them, has approached them as gods with an offering, then may he for a gift remain united with the brilliant Maruts, who by their ornaments are glorious on their march. They, the wise Maruts, the lords, who, when there was inquiry for their kindred, told me of the cow, they told me of Prisni as their mother, and of the strong Rudra as their father. The seven and seven heroes gave me each a hundred. On the Yamunâ I clear off glorious wealth in cows, I clear wealth in horses.

XIII

Those who glance forth like wives and yoke-fellows, the powerful sons of Rudra on their way, they, the Maruts, have indeed made heaven and earth to grow; they, the strong and wild, delight in the sacrifices. When grown up, they attained to greatness; the Rudras have established their seat in the sky.

While singing their song and increasing their vigor, the sons of Prisni have clothed themselves in beauty. When these sons of the cow adorn themselves with glittering ornaments, the brilliant ones put bright weapons on their bodies. They drive away every adversary; fatness streams along their paths;—when you, the powerful, who shine with your spears, shaking even what is unshakable by strength—when you, O Maruts, the manly hosts, had yoked the spotted deer, swift as thought, to your chariots;—when you had yoked the spotted deer before your chariots, hurling thunderbolt in the fight, then the streams of the red-horse rush forth: like a skin with water they water the earth. May the swiftly-gliding, swift-winged horses carry you hither! Come forth with your arms! Sit down on the grass-pile; a wide seat has been made for you. Rejoice, O Maruts, in the sweet food. Strong in themselves, they grew with might; they stepped to the firmament, they made their seat wide. When Vishnu saved the enrapturing Soma, the Maruts sat down like birds on their beloved altar. Like heroes indeed thirsting for fight they rush about; like combatants eager for glory they have striven in battles. All beings are afraid of the Maruts; they are men terrible to behold, like kings. When the clever Tvashtar had turned the well-made, golden, thousand-edged thunderbolt, Indra takes it to perform his manly deeds; he slew Vritra, he forced out the stream of water. By their power they pushed the well aloft, they clove asunder the rock, however strong. Blowing forth their voice the bounteous Maruts performed, while drunk of Soma, their glorious deeds. They pushed the cloud athwart this way, they poured out the spring to the thirsty Gotama. The Maruts with beautiful splendor approach him with help, they in their own ways satisfied the desire of the sage. The shelters which you have for him who praises you, grant them threefold to the man who gives! Extend the same to us, O Maruts! Give us, ye heroes, wealth with valiant offspring!

XIV

Who are these resplendent men, dwelling together, the boys of Rudra, also with good horses? No one indeed knows their births, they alone know each other's birthplace. They plucked each other with their beaks; the hawks, rushing like the wind, strove together. A wise man understands these secrets, that Prisni, the great, bore an udder. May that clan be rich in heroes by the Maruts, always victorious, rich in manhood! They are quickest to go, most splendid with splendor, endowed with beauty, strong with strength. Strong is your strength, steadfast your powers, and thus by the Maruts is this clan mighty. Resplendent is your breath, furious are the minds of the wild host, like a shouting maniac. Keep from us entirely your flame, let not your hatred reach us here. I call on the dear names of your swift ones, so that the greedy should be satisfied, O Maruts, the well-armed, the swift, decked with beautiful chains, who themselves adorn their bodies. Bright are the libations for you, the bright ones, O Maruts, a bright sacrifice I prepare for the bright. In proper order came those who truly follow the order, the bright born, the bright, the pure. On your shoulders, O Maruts, are the rings, on your chests the golden chains are fastened; far-shining like lightnings with showers, you wield your weapons, according to your wont. Your hidden splendors come forth; spread out your powers, O racers! Accept, O Maruts, this thousandfold, domestic share, as an offering for the house-gods. If you thus listen, O Maruts, to this praise, at the invocation of the powerful sage, give him quickly a share of wealth in plentiful offspring, which no selfish enemy shall be able to hurt. The Maruts, who are fleet like racers, the manly youths, shone like Yakshas; they are beautiful like boys standing round the hearth, they play about like calves who are still sucking. May the bounteous Maruts be gracious to us, opening up to us the firm heaven and earth. May that bolt of yours which kills cattle and men be far from us! Incline to us, O Vasus, with your favors. The Hotri priest calls on you again and again, sitting down and praising your common gift, O Maruts. O strong ones, he who is the guardian of so much wealth, he calls on you with praises, free from guile. These Maruts stop the swift, they bend strength by strength, they ward off the curse of the plotter, and turn their heavy hatred on the enemy. These Maruts stir up even the sluggard, even the vagrant, as the gods pleased. O strong ones, drive away the darkness, and grant us all our kith and kin. May we not fall away from your bounty, O Maruts, may we not stay behind, O charioteers, in the distribution of your gifts. Let us share in the brilliant wealth, the well-acquired, that belongs to you, O strong ones. When valiant men fiercely fight together, for rivers, plants, and houses, then, O Maruts, sons of Rudra, be in battles our protectors from the enemy. O Maruts, you have valued the praises which our fathers have formerly recited to you; with the Maruts the victor is terrible in battle, with the Maruts alone the racer wins the prize. O Maruts, may we have a strong son, who is lord among men, a ruler, through whom we may cross the waters to dwell in safety, and then obtain our own home for you. May Indra then, Varuna, Mitra, Agni, the waters, the plants, the trees of the forest be pleased with us. Let us be in the keeping, in the lap of the Maruts; protect us always with your favors.

XV

Sing to the company of the Maruts, growing up together, the strong among the divine host: they stir heaven and earth by their might, they mount up to the firmament from the abyss of Nirriti. Even your birth was with fire and fury, O Maruts! You, terrible, wrathful, never tiring! You who stand forth with might and strength; everyone who sees the sun, fears at your coming. Grant mighty strength to our lords, if the Maruts are pleased with our praise. As a trodden path furthers a man, may they further us; help us with your brilliant favors. Favored by you, O Maruts, a wise man wins a hundred, favored by you a strong racer wins a thousand, favored by you a king also kills his enemy: may that gift of yours prevail, O ye shakers. I invite these bounteous sons of Rudra, will these Maruts turn again to us? Whatever they hated secretly or openly, that sin we pray the swift ones to forgive. This praise of our lords has been spoken: may the Maruts be pleased with this hymn. Keep far from us, O strong ones, all hatred, protect us always with your favors!

XVI

Come hither, do not fail, when you march forward! Do not stay away, O united friends, you who can bend even what is firm. O Maruts, Ribhukshans, come hither on your flaming strong fellies, O Rudras, come to us to-day with food, you much-desired ones, come to the sacrifice, you friends of the Sobharis. For we know indeed the terrible strength of the sons of Rudra, of the vigorous Maruts, the liberal givers of rain. The clouds were scattered, but the monster remained, heaven and earth were joined together. O you who are armed with bright rings, the tracts of the sky expanded, whenever you stir, radiant with your own splendor. Even things that cannot be thrown down resound at your race, the mountains, the lord of the forest—the earth quivers on your marches. The upper sky makes wide room, to let your violence pass, O Maruts, when these strong-armed heroes display their energies in their own bodies. According to their wont these men, exceeding terrible, impetuous, with strong and unbending forms, bring with them beautiful light. The arrow of the Sobharis is shot from the bowstrings at the golden chest on the chariot of the Maruts. They, the kindred of the cow, the well-born, should enjoy their food, the great ones should help us. Bring forward, O strongly-anointed priests, your libations to the strong host of the Maruts, the strongly advancing. O Maruts, O heroes, come quickly hither, like winged hawks, on your chariot with strong horses, of strong shape, with strong naves, to enjoy our libations. Their anointing is the same, the golden chains shine on their arms, their spears sparkle. These strong, manly, strong-armed Maruts, do not strive among themselves; firm are the bows, the weapons on your chariot, and on your faces are splendors. They whose terrible name, wide-spreading like the ocean, is the one of all that is of use, whose strength is like the vigor of their father, worship these Maruts, and praise them! Of these shouters, as of moving spokes, no one is the last; this is theirs by gift, by greatness is it theirs. Happy is he who was under your protection, O Maruts, in former mornings, or who may be so even now. Or he, O men, whose libations you went to enjoy; that mighty one, O shakers, will obtain your favors with brilliant riches and booty. As the sons of Rudra, the servants of the divine Dyu, will it, O youths, so shall it be. Whatever liberal givers may worship the Maruts, and move about together as generous benefactors, even from them turn towards us with a kinder heart, you youths! O Sobhari, call loud with your newest song the young, strong, and pure Maruts, as the plougher calls the cows. Worship the Maruts with a song, they who are strong like a boxer, called in to assist those who call for him in all fights; worship them the most glorious, like bright-shining bulls. Yes, O united friends, kindred, O Maruts, by a common birth, the oxen lick one another's humps. O ye dancers, with golden ornaments on your chests, even a mortal comes to ask for your brotherhood; take care of us, ye Maruts, for your friendship lasts forever. O bounteous Maruts, bring us some of your Marut-medicine, you friends, and steeds. With the favors whereby you favor the Sindhu, whereby you save, whereby you help Krivi, with those propitious favors be our delight, O delightful ones, ye who never hate your followers. O Maruts, for whom we have prepared good altars, whatever medicine there is on the Sindhu, on the Asiknî, in the seas, on the mountains, seeing it, you carry it all on your bodies. Bless us with it! Down to the earth, O Maruts, with what hurts our sick one—straighten what is crooked!

XVII

Full of devotion like priests with their prayers, wealthy like pious men, who please the gods with their offerings, beautiful to behold like brilliant kings, without a blemish like the youths of our hamlets—they who are gold-breasted like Agni with his splendor, quick to help like self-harnessed winds, good leaders like the oldest experts, they are to the righteous man like Somas, that yield the best protection. They who are roaring and hasting like winds, brilliant like the tongues of fires, powerful like mailed soldiers, full of blessings like the prayers of our fathers, who hold together like the spokes of chariot-wheels, who glance forward like victorious heroes, who scatter ghrita like wooing youths, who chant beautifully like singers, intoning a hymn of praise, who are swift like the best of horses, who are bounteous like lords of chariots on a suit, who are hastening on like water with downward floods, who are like the manifold Angiras with their numerous songs. These noble sons of Sindhu are like grinding-stones, they are always like Soma-stones, tearing everything to pieces; these sons of a good mother are like playful children, they are by their glare like a great troop on its march. Illumining the sacrifice like the rays of the dawn, they shone forth in their ornaments like triumphant warriors; the Maruts with bright spears seem like running rivers, from afar they measure many miles. O gods, make us happy and rich, prospering us, your praisers, O Maruts! Remember our praise and our friendship, for from of old there are always with you gifts of treasures.

XVIII

O Indra, a thousand have been thy helps accorded to us, a thousand, O driver of the bays, have been thy most delightful viands. May thousands of treasures richly to enjoy, may goods come to us a thousandfold. May the Maruts come towards us with their aids, the mighty ones, or with their best aids from the great heaven, now that their furthest steeds have rushed forth on the distant shore of the sea; there clings to the Maruts one who moves in secret, like a man's wife,[1] and who is like a spear carried behind, well grasped, resplendent, gold-adorned; there is also with them Vâk,[2] like unto a courtly, eloquent woman. Far away the brilliant, untiring Maruts cling to their young maid, as if she belonged to them all; but the terrible ones did not drive away Rodasî, for they wished her to grow their friend. When the divine Rodasî with dishevelled locks, the manly-minded, wished to follow them, she went, like Sûryâ,[3] to the chariot of her servant, with terrible look, as with the pace of a cloud. As soon as the poet with the libations, O Maruts, had sung his song at the sacrifice, pouring out Soma, the youthful men placed the young maid in their chariot as their companion for victory, mighty in assemblies. I praise what is the praiseworthy true greatness of those Maruts, that the manly-minded, proud, and strong one drives with them towards the blessed mothers. They protect Mitra and Varuna from the unspeakable, and Aryaman also finds out the infamous. Even what is firm and unshakable is being shaken; but he who dispenses treasures, O Maruts, has grown in strength. No people indeed, whether near to us, or from afar, have ever found the end of your strength, O Maruts! The Maruts, strong in daring strength, have, like the sea, boldly surrounded their haters. May we to-day, may we tomorrow in battle be called the most beloved of Indra. We were so formerly, may we truly be so day by day, and may the

[1] The lightning. [2] The voice of thunder. [3] The dawn.

lord of the Maruts be with us. May this praise, O Maruts, this song of Mândârya, the son of Mâna, the poet, ask you with food for offspring for ourselves! May we have an invigorating autumn, with quickening rain!

XIX

Who knows their birth? or who was of yore in the favor of the Maruts, when they harnessed the spotted deer? Who has heard them when they had mounted their chariots, how they went forth? For the sake of what liberal giver did they run, and their comrades followed, as streams of rain filled with food? They themselves said to me when day by day they came to the feast with their birds: they are manly youths and blameless; seeing them, praise them thus; they who shine by themselves in their ornaments, their daggers, their garlands, their golden chains, their rings, going on their chariots and on dry land. O Maruts, givers of quickening rain, I am made to rejoice, following after your chariots, as after days going with rain. The bucket which the bounteous heroes shook down from heaven for their worshipper, that cloud they send along heaven and earth, and showers follow on the dry land. The rivers having pierced the air with a rush of water, went forth like milk-cows; when your spotted deer roll about like horses that have hasted to the resting-place on their road. Come hither, O Maruts, from heaven, from the sky, even from near; do not go far away! Let not the Rasâ, the Anitabhâ, the Kubhâ, the Krumu, let not the Sindhu delay you! Let not the marshy Sarayu prevent you! May your favor be with us alone! The showers come forth after the host of your chariots, after the terrible Marut-host of the ever-youthful heroes. Let us then follow with our praises and our prayers each host of yours, each troop, each company. To what well-born generous worshipper have the Maruts gone to-day on that march, on which you bring to kith and kin the never-failing seed of corn? Give us that for which we ask you, wealth and everlasting happiness! Let us safely pass through our revilers, leaving behind the unspeakable and the enemies. Let us be with you when in the morning you shower down health, wealth, water, and medicine, O Maruts! That mortal, O men, O Maruts, whom you protect, may well be always beloved by the gods, and rich in valiant offspring. May we be such! Praise the liberal Maruts, and may they delight on the path of this man here who praises them, like cows in fodder. When they go, call after them as for old friends, praise them who love you, with your song!

XX

You have fashioned this speech for the brilliant Marut-host which shakes the mountains: celebrate then the great manhood in honor of that host who praises the warm milk of the sacrifice, and sacrifices on the height of heaven, whose glory is brilliant. O Maruts, your powerful men came forth searching for water, invigorating, harnessing their horses, swarming around. When they aim with the lightning, Trita shouts, and the waters murmur, running around on their course. These Maruts are men brilliant with lightning, they shoot with thunderbolts, they blaze with the wind, they shake the mountains, and suddenly, when wishing to give water, they whirl the hail; they have thundering strength, they are robust, they are ever-powerful. When you drive forth the nights, O Rudras, the days, O powerful men, the sky, the mists, ye shakers, the plains, like ships, and the strongholds, O Maruts, you suffer nowhere. That strength of yours, O Maruts, that greatness extended as far as the sun extends its daily course, when you, like your deer on their march, went down to the western mountain with untouched splendor. Your host, O Maruts, shone forth when, O sages, you strip, like a caterpillar, the waving tree. Conduct then, O friends, our service to a good end, as the eye conducts the man in walking. That man, O Maruts, is not overpowered, he is not killed, he does not fail, he does not shake, he does not drop, his goods do not perish, nor his protections, if you lead him rightly, whether he be a seer or a king. The men with their steeds, like conquerors of clans, like Aryaman, the Maruts, carrying waterskins, fill the well; when the strong ones roar, they moisten the earth with the juice of sweetness. When the Maruts come forth this earth bows, the heaven bows, the paths in the sky bow, and the cloud-mountains with their quickening rain. When you rejoice at sunrise, O Maruts, toiling together, men of sunlight, men of heaven, your horses never tire in running, and you quickly reach the end of your journey. On your shoulders are the spears, on your feet rings, on your chests golden chains, O Maruts, on your chariot gems; fiery lightnings in your fists, and golden headbands tied round your heads. O Maruts, you shake the red apple from the firmament, whose splendor no enemy can touch; the hamlets bowed when the Maruts blazed, and the pious people intoned their far-reaching shout. O wise Maruts, let us carry off the wealth of food which you have bestowed on us; give us, O Maruts, such thousandfold wealth as never fails, like the star Tishya from heaven! O Maruts, you protect our wealth of excellent men, and the seer, clever in song; you give to the warrior a strong horse, you make the king to be obeyed. O you who are quickly ready to help, I implore you for wealth whereby we may overshadow all men, like the sky. O Maruts, be pleased with this word of mine, and let us speed by its speed over a hundred winters!

XXI

The chasing Maruts with gleaming spears, the golden-breasted, have gained great strength, they move along on quick, well-broken horses;—when they went in triumph, the chariots followed. You have yourselves, you know, acquired power; you shine bright and wide, you great ones. They have even measured the sky with their strength;—when they went in triumph, the chariots followed. The strong heroes, born together, and nourished together, have further grown to real beauty. They shine brilliantly like the rays of the sun;—when they went in triumph, the chariots followed. Your greatness, O Maruts, is to be honored, it is to be yearned for like the sight of the sun. Place us also in immortality;—when they went in triumph, the chariots followed. O Maruts, you raise the rain from the sea, and rain it down, O yeomen! Your milch-cows, O destroyers, are never destroyed;—when they went in triumph, the chariots followed. When you have joined the deer as horses to the shafts, and have clothed yourselves in golden garments, then, O Maruts, you scatter all enemies;—when they went in triumph, the chariots followed. Not mountains, not rivers have kept you back, wherever you see, O Maruts, there you go. You go even round heaven and earth;—when they went in triumph, the chariots followed. Be it old, O Maruts, or be it new, be it spoken, O Vasus, or be it recited, you take cognizance of it all;—when they went in triumph, the chariots followed. Have mercy on us, O Maruts, do not strike us, extend to us your manifold protection. Do remember the praise, the friendship;—when they went in triumph, the chariots followed. Lead us, O Maruts, towards greater wealth, and out of tribulations, when you have been praised. O worshipful Maruts, accept our offering, and let us be lords of treasures!

XXII

O Agni, on to the strong host of the Maruts, bedecked with golden chains and ornaments. To-day I call the folk of the Maruts down from the light of heaven. As thou, Agni, thinkest in thine heart, to the same object my wishes have gone. Strengthen thou these Maruts, terrible to behold, who have come nearest to thy invocations. Like a bountiful lady, the earth comes towards us, staggering, yet rejoicing; for your onslaught, O Maruts, is vigorous, like a bear, and fearful, like a wild bull. They who by their strength disperse wildly like bulls, impatient of the yoke, they by their marches make the heavenly stone, the rocky mountain cloud to shake. Arise, for now I call with my hymns the troop of these Maruts, grown strong together, the manifold, the incomparable, as if calling a drove of bulls. Harness the red mares to the chariot, harness the ruddy horses to the chariots, harness the two bays, ready to drive in the yoke, most vehement to drive in the yoke. And this red stallion too, loudly neighing, has been placed here, beautiful to behold; may it not cause you delay on your marches, O Maruts; spur him forth on your chariots.

We call towards us the glorious chariot of the Maruts, whereon there stands also Rodasi, carrying delightful gifts, among the Maruts.

I call hither this your host, brilliant on chariots, terrible and glorious, among which she, the well-born and fortunate, the bounteous lady, is also magnified among the Maruts.

XXIII

O Rudras, joined by Indra, friends on golden chariots, come hither for our welfare! This prayer from us is acceptable to you like the springs of heaven to a thirsty soul longing for water. O you sons of Prisni, you are armed with daggers and spears, you are wise, carrying good bows and arrows and quivers, possessed of good horses and chariots. With your good weapons, O Maruts, you go to triumph! You shake the sky and the mountains for wealth to the liberal giver; the forests bend down out of your way from fear. O sons of Prisni, you rouse the earth when you, O terrible ones, have harnessed the spotted deer for triumph! The Maruts, blazing with the wind, clothed in rain, are as like one another as twins, and well adorned. They have tawny horses, and red horses, they are faultless, endowed with exceeding vigor; they are in greatness wide as the heaven. Rich in rain-drops, well adorned, bounteous, terrible to behold, of inexhaustible wealth, noble by birth, golden-breasted, these singers of the sky have obtained their immortal name. Spears are on your two shoulders, in your arms are placed strength, power, and might. Manly thoughts dwell in your heads, on your chariots are weapons, and every beauty has been laid on your bodies. O Maruts, you have given us wealth of cows, horses, chariots, and heroes, golden wealth! O men of Rudra, bestow on us great praise, and may I enjoy your divine protection! Hark, O heroes, O Maruts! Be gracious to us! You who are of great bounty, immortal, righteous, truly listening to us, poets, young, dwelling on mighty mountains, and grown mighty.

XXIV

I praise now the powerful company of these ever-young Maruts, who drive violently along with quick horses; aye, the sovereigns are lords of Amrita the immortal. The terrible company, the powerful, adorned with quoits on their hands, given to roaring, potent, dispensing treasures, they who are beneficent, infinite in greatness, praise, O poet, these men of great wealth! May your water-carriers come here to-day, all the Maruts who stir up the rain. That fire which has been lighted for you, O Maruts, accept it, O young singers! O worshipful Maruts, you create for man an active king, fashioned by Vibhvan; from you comes the man who can fight with his fist, and is quick with his arm, from you the man with good horses and valiant heroes. Like the spokes of a wheel, no one is last, like the days they are born on and on, not deficient in might. The very high sons of Prisni are full of fury, the Maruts cling firmly to their own will. When you have come forth with your speckled deer as horses on strong-fellied chariots, O Maruts, the waters gush, the forests go asunder;—let Dyu roar down, the bull of the Dawn. At their approach, even the earth opened wide, and they placed their own strength as a husband the germ. Indeed they have harnessed the winds as horses to the yoke, and the men of Rudra have changed their sweat into rain. Hark, O heroes, O Maruts! Be gracious to us! You who are of great bounty, immortal, righteous, truly listening to us, poets, young, dwelling on mighty mountains, and grown mighty.

XXV

They truly tried to make you grant them welfare. Do thou sing praises to Heaven, I offer sacrifice to the Earth. The Maruts wash their horses and race to the air, they soften their splendor by waving mists. The earth trembles with fear from their onset. She sways like a full ship, that goes rolling. The heroes who appear on their marches, visible from afar, strive together within the great sacrificial assembly. Your horn is exalted for glory, as the horns of cows; your eye is like the sun, when the mist is scattered. Like strong racers, you are beautiful, O heroes, you think of glory, like manly youths. Who could reach, O Maruts, the great wise thoughts, who the great manly deeds of you, great ones? You shake the earth like a speck of dust, when you are carried forth for granting welfare. These kinsmen are like red horses, like heroes eager for battle, and they have rushed forward to fight. They are like well-grown manly youths, and the men have grown strong, with streams of rain they dim the eye of the sun. At their outbreak there is none among them who is the eldest, or the youngest, or the middle: they have grown by their own might, these sons of Prisni, noble by birth, the boys of Dyaus; come hither to us!

Those who like birds flew with strength in rows from the ridge of the mighty heaven to its ends, their horses shook the springs of the mountain cloud, so that people on both sides knew it. May Dyaus Aditi roar for our feast, may the dew-lighted Dawns come striving together; these, the Maruts, O poet, the sons of Rudra, have shaken the heavenly bucket cloud, when they had been praised.

TO THE MARUTS AND INDRA

The Prologue

THE sacrificer speaks:

To what splendor do the Maruts all equally cling, they who are of the same age, and dwell in the same nest? With what thoughts?—from whence are they come? Do these heroes sing forth their own strength, wishing for wealth? Whose prayers have the youths accepted? Who has turned the Maruts to his own sacrifice? By what strong desire may we arrest them, they who float through the air like hawks?

The Dialogue

The Maruts speak:

From whence, O Indra, dost thou come alone, thou who art mighty? O lord of men, what has thus happened to thee? Thou greetest us when thou comest together with us. Tell us then, thou with thy bay horses, what thou hast against us!

Indra speaks:

The sacred songs are mine, the prayers; sweet are the libations! My strength rises, my thunderbolt is hurled forth. They call for me, the hymns yearn for me. Here are my horses, they carry me hither.

The Maruts speak:

From thence, in company with our strong friends, having adorned our bodies, we now harness our fallow deer with all our might;—for, Indra, according to custom, thou hast come to be with us.

Indra speaks:

Where, O Maruts, was that custom with you, when you left

me alone in the killing of Ahi? I indeed am terrible, powerful, strong,—I escaped from the blows of every enemy.

The Maruts speak:

Thou hast achieved much with us as companions. With equal valor, O hero! let us achieve then many things, O thou most powerful, O Indra! whatever we, O Maruts, wish with our mind.

Indra speaks:

I slew Vritra, O Maruts, with Indra's might, having grown powerful through my own vigor; I, who hold the thunderbolt in my arms, have made these all-brilliant waters to flow freely for man.

The Maruts speak:

Nothing, O mighty lord, is strong before thee: no one is known among the gods like unto thee. No one who is now born comes near, no one who has been born. Do what thou wilt do, thou who art grown so strong.

Indra speaks:

Almighty strength be mine alone, whatever I may do, daring in my heart; for I indeed, O Maruts, am known as terrible: of all that I threw down, I, Indra, am the lord.

O Maruts, now your praise has pleased me, the glorious hymn which you have made for me, ye men!—for me, for Indra, for the joyful hero, as friends for a friend, for your own sake, and by your own efforts.

Truly, there they are, shining towards me, bringing blameless glory, bringing food. O Maruts, wherever I have looked for you, you have appeared to me in bright splendor: appear to me also now!

The Epilogue

The sacrificer speaks:

Who has magnified you here, O Maruts? Come hither, O friends, towards your friends. Ye brilliant Maruts, welcoming these prayers, be mindful of these my rites. The wisdom of Mânya has brought us hither, that he should help as the poet helps the performer of a sacrifice: turn hither quickly! Maruts, on to the sage! the singer has recited these prayers for you. May this your praise, O Maruts, this song of Mândârya, the son of Mâna, the poet, bring offspring for ourselves with food. May we have an invigorating autumn, with quickening rain.

TO INDRA AND THE MARUTS

THOSE who stand around him while he moves on, harness the bright red steed; the lights in heaven shine forth. They harness to the chariot on each side his two favorite bays, the brown, the bold, who can carry the hero. Thou who createst light where there was no light, and form, O men! where there was no form, hast been born together with the dawns. Thereupon they (the Maruts), according to their wont, assumed again the form of new-born babes, taking their sacred name. Thou, O Indra, with the swift Maruts, who break even through the stronghold, hast found even in their hiding-place the bright ones. The pious singers have, after their own mind, shouted towards the giver of wealth, the great, the glorious Indra. Mayest thou, host of the Maruts, be verily seen coming together with Indra, the fearless: you are both happy-making, and of equal splendor. With the beloved hosts of Indra, with the blameless, hasting (Maruts), the sacrificer cries aloud. From yonder, O traveller, Indra, come hither, or from the light of heaven; the singers all yearn for it;—or we ask Indra for help from here, or from heaven, or from above the earth, or from the great sky.

TO AGNI* AND THE MARUTS

THOU art called forth to this fair sacrifice for a draught of milk; with the Maruts come hither, O Agni! No god indeed, no mortal, is beyond the might of thee, the mighty one; with the Maruts come hither, O Agni! They who know of the great sky, the Visve Devas without guile; with those Maruts come hither, O Agni! The strong ones who sing their song, unconquerable by force; with the Maruts come hither, O Agni! They who are brilliant, of terrible designs, powerful, and devourers of foes; with the Maruts come hither, O Agni! They who in heaven are enthroned as gods, in the light of the firmament; with the Maruts come

*Agni is the "God of Fire."

hither, O Agni! They who toss the clouds across the surging sea; with the Maruts come hither, O Agni! They who shoot with their darts across the sea with might; with the Maruts come hither, O Agni! I pour out to thee for the early draught the sweet juice of Soma; with the Maruts come hither, O Agni!

TO RUDRA*

WE offer these prayers to Rudra, the strong, whose hair is braided, who rules over heroes that he may be a blessing to man and beast, that everything in this our village may be prosperous and free from disease. Be gracious to us, O Rudra, and give us joy, and we shall honor thee, the ruler of heroes, with worship. What health and wealth father Manu acquired by his sacrifices, may we obtain the same, O Rudra, under thy guidance. O bounteous Rudra, may we by sacrifice obtain the good-will of thee, the ruler of heroes; come to our clans, well-disposed, and, with unarmed men, we shall offer our libation to thee. We call down for our help the fierce Rudra, who fulfils our sacrifice, the swift, the wise; may he drive far away from us the anger of the gods; we desire his good-will only. We call down with worship the red boar of the sky, the god with braided hair, the blazing form; may he who carries in his hand the best medicines grant us protection, shield, and shelter! This speech is spoken for the father of the Maruts, sweeter than sweet, a joy to Rudra; grant to us also, O immortal, the food of mortals, be gracious to us and to our kith and kin! Do not slay our great or our small ones, our growing or our grown ones, our father or our mother, and do not hurt our own bodies, O Rudra! O Rudra, hurt us not in our kith and kin, nor in our own life, not in our cows, nor in our horses! Do not slay our men in thy wrath: carrying libations, we call on thee always. Like a shepherd, I have driven these praises near to thee; O father of the Maruts, grant us thy favor! For thy good-will is auspicious, and most gracious, hence we desire thy protection alone. Let thy cow-slay-

* Rudra is the "Father of the Maruts."

ing and thy man-slaying be far away, and let thy favor be with us, O ruler of heroes! Be gracious to us, and bless us, O god, and then give us twofold protection. We have uttered our supplication to him, desiring his help; may Rudra with the Maruts hear our call. May Mitra, Varuna, Aditi, the River, Earth, and the Sky, grant us this!

TO RUDRA

O FATHER of the Maruts, let thy favor come near, and do not deprive us of the sight of the sun; may the hero (Rudra) be gracious to our horse, and may we increase in offspring, O Rudra! May I attain to a hundred winters through the most blissful medicines which thou hast given! Put away far from us all hatred, put away anguish, put away sickness in all directions! In beauty thou art the most beautiful of all that exists, O Rudra, the strongest of the strong, thou wielder of the thunderbolt! Carry us happily to the other shore of our anguish, and ward off all assaults of mischief. Let us not incense thee, O Rudra, by our worship, not by bad praise, O hero, and not by divided praise! Raise up our men by thy medicines, for I hear thou art the best of all physicians. He who is invoked by invocations and libations, may I pay off that Rudra with my hymns of praise. Let not him who is kind-hearted, who readily hears our call, the tawny, with beautiful cheeks, deliver us to this wrath! The manly hero with the Maruts has gladdened me, the suppliant, with more vigorous health. May I without mischief find shade, as if from sunshine, may I gain the favor of Rudra! O Rudra, where is thy softly stroking hand which cures and relieves? Thou, the remover of all heaven-sent mischief, wilt thou, O strong hero, bear with me? I send forth a great, great hymn of praise to the bright tawny bull. Let me reverence the fiery god with prostrations; we celebrate the flaring name of Rudra. He, the fierce god, with strong limbs, assuming many forms, the tawny Rudra, decked himself with brilliant golden ornaments. From Rudra, who is lord of this wide world, divine power will never depart. Worthily thou bearest arrows and bow, worthily, O worshipful, the golden, variegated chain; worthily thou cuttest every fiend here to pieces, for there is nothing indeed stronger than thou, O Rudra. Praise him, the famous, sitting in his chariot, the youthful, who is fierce and attacks like a terrible lion. And when thou hast been praised, O Rudra, be gracious to him who magnifies thee, and let thy armies mow down others than us! O Rudra, a boy indeed makes obeisance to his father who comes to greet him: I praise the lord of brave men, the giver of many gifts, and thou, when thou hast been praised, wilt give us thy medicines. O Maruts, those pure medicines of yours, the most beneficent and delightful, O heroes, those which Manu, our father, chose, those I crave from Rudra, as health and wealth. May the weapon of Rudra avoid us, may the great anger of the flaring one pass us by. Unstring thy strong bows for the sake of our liberal lords, O bounteous Rudra, be gracious to our kith and kin. Thus, O tawny and manly god, showing thyself, so as neither to be angry nor to kill, be mindful of our invocations, and, rich in brave sons, we shall magnify thee in the congregation.

TO AGNI AND THE MARUTS

I IMPLORE Agni, the gracious, with salutations, may he sit down here, and gather what we have made. I offer him sacrifice as with racing chariots; may I, turning to the right, accomplish this hymn to the Maruts. Those who approached on their glorious deer, on their easy chariots, the Rudras, the Maruts—through fear of you, ye terrible ones, the forests even bend down, the earth shakes, and also the mountain cloud. At your shouting, even the mountain cloud, grown large, fears, and the ridge of heaven trembles. When you play together, O Maruts, armed with spears, you run together like waters. Like rich suitors the Maruts have themselves adorned their bodies with golden ornaments; more glorious for glory, and powerful on their chariots, they have brought together splendors on their bodies. As brothers, no one being the eldest or the youngest, they have grown up together to happiness.

Young is their clever father Rudra, flowing with plenty is Prisni, always kind to the Maruts. O happy Maruts, whether you are in the highest, or in the middle, or in the lowest heaven, from thence, O Rudras, or thou also, O Agni, take notice of this libation which we offer. When Agni, and you, wealthy Maruts, drive down from the higher heaven over the ridges, give then, if pleased, you roarers, O destroyers of enemies, wealth to the sacrificer who prepares Soma-juice. Agni, be pleased to drink Soma with the brilliant Maruts, the singers, approaching in companies, with the men, who brighten and enliven everything; do this, Agni, thou who art always endowed with splendor.

TO VÂYU

COME hither, O Vâyu, thou beautiful one! These Somas are ready, drink of them, hear our call! O Vâyu, the praisers celebrate thee with hymns, they who know the feast-days, and have prepared the Soma. O Vâyu, thy satisfying stream goes to the worshipper, wide-reaching, to the Soma-draught. O Indra and Vâyu, these libations of Soma are poured out; come hither for the sake of our offerings, for the drops of Soma long for you. O Indra and Vâyu, you perceive the libations, you who are rich in booty; come then quickly hither! O Vâyu and Indra, come near to the work of the sacrificer, quick, thus is my prayer, O ye men! I call Mitra, endowed with holy strength, and Varuna, who destroys all enemies; who both fulfil a prayer accompanied by fat offerings. On the right way, O Mitra and Varuna, you have obtained great wisdom, you who increase the right and adhere to the right; These two sages, Mitra and Varuna, the mighty, wide-ruling, give us efficient strength.

TO VÂYU

O VÂYU, may the quick racers bring thee towards the offerings, to the early drink here, to the early drink of Soma! May the Dawn stand erect, approving thy mind! Come near on thy harnessed chariot to share, O Vâyu, to share in the sacrifice! May the delightful drops of Soma delight thee, the drops made by us, well-made, and heaven-directed, yes, made with milk, and heaven-directed. When his performed aids assume strength for achievement, our prayers implore the assembled steeds for gifts, yes, the prayers implore them. Vâyu yokes the two ruddy, Vâyu yokes the two red horses, Vâyu yokes to the chariot the two swift horses to draw in the yoke, the strongest to draw in the yoke. Awake Purandhi (the morning) as a lover wakes a sleeping maid, reveal heaven and earth, brighten the dawn, yes, for glory brighten the dawn. For thee the bright dawns spread out in the distance beautiful garments, in their houses, in their rays, beautiful in their new rays. To thee the juice-yielding cow pours out all treasures. Thou hast brought forth the Maruts from the flanks, yes, from the flanks of heaven. For thee the white, bright, rushing Somas, strong in raptures, have rushed to the whirl, they have rushed to the whirl of the waters. The tired hunter asks luck of thee in the chase; thou shieldest by thy power from every being, yes, thou shieldest by thy power from powerful spirits. Thou, O Vâyu, art worthy as the first before all others to drink these our Somas, thou art worthy to drink these poured-out Somas. Among the people also who invoke thee and have turned to thee, all the cows pour out the milk, they pour out butter and milk for the Soma.

INDRA AND AGASTYA*: A DIALOGUE

INDRA: There is no such thing to-day, nor will it be so to-morrow. Who knows what strange thing this is? We must consult the thought of another, for even what we once knew seems to vanish.

Agastya: Why dost thou wish to kill us, O Indra? the Maruts are thy brothers; fare kindly with them, and do not strike us in battle.

The Maruts: O Brother Agastya, why, being a friend, dost thou despise us? We know quite well what thy mind was. Dost thou not wish to give to us?

Agastya: Let them prepare the altar, let them light the fire in front! Here we two will spread for thee the sacrifice, to be seen by the immortal.

Agastya: Thou rulest, O lord of treasures; thou, lord of friends, art the most generous. Indra, speak again with the Maruts, and then consume our offerings at the right season.

TO SOMA AND RUDRA

SOMA and Rudra, may you maintain your divine dominion, and may the oblations reach you properly. Bringing the seven treasures to every house, be kind to our children and our cattle. Soma and Rudra, draw far away in every direction the disease which has entered our house. Drive far away Nirriti, and may auspicious glories belong to us! Soma and Rudra, bestow all these remedies on our bodies. Tear away and remove from us whatever evil we have committed, which clings to our bodies. Soma and Rudra, wielding sharp weapons and sharp bolts, kind friends, be gracious unto us here! Deliver us from the snare of Varuna, and guard us, as kind-hearted gods!

* Agastya is a worshipper of Indra.

TO RUDRA

OFFER ye these songs to Rudra whose bow is strong, whose arrows are swift, the self-dependent god, the unconquered conqueror, the intelligent, whose weapons are sharp—may he hear us! For, being the lord, he looks after what is born on earth; being the universal ruler, he looks after what is born in heaven. Protecting us, come to our protecting doors, be without illness among our people, O Rudra! May that thunderbolt of thine, which, sent from heaven, traverses the earth, pass us by! A thousand medicines are thine, O thou who art freely accessible; do not hurt us through out kith and kin! Do not strike us, O Rudra, do not forsake us! May we not be in thy way when thou rushest forth furiously. Let us have our altar and a good report among men—protect us always with your favors!

TO VÂTA

NOW for the greatness of the chariot of Vâta. Its roar goes crashing and thundering. It moves touching the sky, and creating red sheens, or it goes scattering the dust of the earth. Afterwards there rise the gusts of Vâta, they go towards him, like women to a feast. The god goes with them on the same chariot, he, the king of the whole of this world. When he moves on his paths along the sky, he rests not even a single day; the friend of the waters, the first-born, the holy, where was he born, whence did he spring? The breath of the gods, the germ of the world, that god moves wherever he listeth; his roars indeed are heard, not his form —let us offer sacrifice to that Vâta!

TO VÂTA

MAY Vâta waft medicine, healthful, delightful to our heart; may he prolong our lives! Thou, O Vâta, art our father, and our brother, and our friend; do thou grant us to live! O Vâta, from that treasure of the immortal which is placed in thy house yonder, give us to live!

I

I magnify Agni, the Purohita, the divine ministrant of the sacrifice, the Hotri priest, the greatest bestower of treasures. Agni, worthy to be magnified by the ancient Rishis and by the present ones—may he conduct the gods hither. May one obtain through Agni wealth and welfare day by day, which may bring glory and high bliss of valiant offspring. Agni, whatever sacrifice and worship thou encompassest on every side, that indeed goes to the gods. May Agni the thoughtful Hotri, he who is true and most splendidly renowned, may the god come hither with the gods. Whatever good thou wilt do to thy worshipper, O Agni, that work verily is thine, O Angiras. Thee, O Agni, we approach day by day, O god who shinest in the darkness; with our prayer, bringing adoration to thee who art the king of all worship, the guardian of Rita, the shining one, increasing in thy own house. Thus, O Agni, be easy of access to us, as a father is to his son. Stay with us for our happiness.

II

We implore with well-spoken words the vigorous Agni who belongs to many people, to the clans that worship the gods, whom other people also magnify. Men have placed Agni on the altar as the augmenter of strength. May we worship thee, rich in sacrificial food. Thus be thou here to-day gracious to us, a helper in our striving for gain, O good one! We choose thee, the all-possessor, as our messenger and as our Hotri. The flames of thee, who art great, spread around; thy rays touch the heaven. The gods, Varuna, Mitra, Aryaman, kindle thee, the ancient messenger. The mortal, O Agni, who worships thee, gains through thee every prize. Thou art the cheerful Hotri and householder, O Agni, the messenger of the clans. In thee all the firm laws are comprised which the gods have made. In thee, the blessed one, O Agni, youngest god, all sacrificial food is offered. Sacrifice then thou who art gracious to us to-day and afterwards, to the gods that we may be rich in valiant men. Him, the king, verily the adorers approach reverentially. With oblations men kindle Agni, having overcome all failures. Destroying the foe, they victoriously got through Heaven and Earth and the waters; they have made wide room for their dwelling. May the manly Agni, after he has received the oblations, become brilliant at the side of Kanva; may he neigh as a horse in battles. Take thy seat; thou art great. Shine forth, thou who most excellently repairest to the gods. O Agni, holy god, emit thy red, beautiful smoke, O glorious one! Thou whom the gods have placed here for Manu as the best performer of the sacrifice, O carrier of oblations, whom Kanva and Medhyâtithi, whom Vrishan and Upastuta have worshipped, the winner of prizes. That Agni's nourishment has shone brightly whom Medhyâtithi and Kanva have kindled on behalf of Rita. Him do these hymns, him do we extol. Fill us with wealth, thou self-dependent one, for thou, O Agni, hast companionship with the gods. Thou art lord over glorious booty. Have mercy upon us; thou art great. Stand up straight for blessing us, like the god Savitri, straight a winner of booty, when we with our worshippers and with ointments call thee in emulation with other people. Standing straight, protect us by thy splendor from evil; burn down every ghoul. Let us stand straight that we may walk and live. Find out our worship among the gods. Save us, O Agni, from the sorcerer, save us from mischief, from the niggard. Save us from him who does us harm or tries to kill us, O youngest god with bright splendor! As with a club smite the niggards in all directions, and him who deceives us, O god with fiery jaws. The mortal who makes his weapons very sharp by night, may that impostor not rule over us. Agni has won abundance in heroes. Agni and the two Mitras have blessed Medhyâtithi. Agni has blessed Upastuta in the acquirement of wealth. Through Agni we call hither from afar Turvasa, Yadu, and Ugradeva. May Agni, our strength against the Dasyu, conduct hither Navavâstva, Brihadratha. and Turviti.

Manu has established thee, O Agni, as a light for all people. Thou hast shone forth with Kanva, born from Rita, grown strong, thou whom the human races worship. Agni's flames are impetuous and violent; they are terrible and not to be withstood. Always burn down the sorcerers, and the allies of the Yâtus, every ghoul.

III

We choose Agni as our messenger, the all-possessor, as the Hotri of this sacrifice, the highly wise. Agni and Agni! again they constantly invoked with their invocations, the lord of the clans, the bearer of oblations, the beloved of many. Agni, when born, conduct the gods hither for him who has strewn the sacrificial grass; thou art our Hotri, worthy of being magnified. Awaken them, the willing ones, when thou goest as messenger, O Agni. Sit down with the gods on the Barhis. O thou to whom Ghrita oblations are poured out, resplendent god, burn against the mischievous, O Agni, against the sorcerers. By Agni Agni is kindled, the sage, the master of the house, the young one, the bearer of oblations, whose mouth is the sacrificial spoon. Praise Agni the sage, whose ordinances for the sacrifice are true, the god who drives away sickness. Be the protector, O Agni, of a master of sacrificial food who worships thee, O god, as his messenger. Be merciful, O purifier, unto the man who is rich in sacrificial food, and who invites Agni to the feast of the gods. Thus, O Agni, resplendent purifier, conduct the gods hither to us, to our sacrifice and to our food. Thus praised by us with our new Gâyatra hymn, bring us wealth of valiant men and food. Agni with thy bright splendor be pleased, through all our invocations of the gods, with this our praise.

IV

With reverence I shall worship thee who art long-tailed like a horse, Agni, king of worship. May he, our son of strength, proceeding on his broad way, the propitious, become bountiful to us. Thus protect us always, thou who hast a full life, from the mortal who seeks to do us harm, whether near or afar. And mayest thou, O Agni, announce to the gods this our newest efficient Gâyatra song. Let us partake of all booty that is highest and that is middle; help us to the wealth that is nearest.

O god with bright splendor, thou art the distributor. Thou instantly flowest for the liberal giver in the wave of the river, near at hand. The mortal, O Agni, whom thou protectest in battles, whom thou speedest in the races, he will command constant nourishment: Whosoever he may be, no one will overtake him, O conqueror Agni! His strength is glorious. May he, known among all tribes, win the race with his horses; may he with the help of his priests become a gainer. O Garâbodha! Accomplish this task for every house: a beautiful song of praise for worshipful Rudra. May he, the great, the immeasurable, the smoke-bannered, rich in splendor, incite us to pious thoughts and to strength. May he hear us, like the rich lord of a clan, the banner of the gods, on behalf of our hymns, Agni with bright light. Reverence to the great ones, reverence to the lesser ones! Reverence to the young, reverence to the old! Let us sacrifice to the gods, if we can. May I not, O gods, fall as a victim to the curse of my better.

V

I press on for you with my prayer to the all-possessing messenger, the immortal bearer of offerings, the best sacrificer. He, the great one, knows indeed the place of wealth, the ascent to heaven; may he conduct the gods hither. He, the god, knows how to direct the gods for the righteous worshipper, in his house. He gives us wealth dear to us. He is the Hotri; he who knows the office of a messenger, goes to and fro, knowing the ascent to heaven. May we be of those who have worshipped Agni with the gift of offerings, who cause him to thrive and kindle him. The men who have brought worship to Agni, are renowned as successful by wealth and by powerful offspring. May much-desired wealth come to us day by day; may gains arise among us. He, the priest of the tribes, the priest of men, pierces all hostile powers by his might as with a tossing bow.

VI

He has brought down the wisdom of many a worshipper, he who holds in his hand all manly power. Agni has become the lord of treasures, he who brought together all powers of immortality. All the clever immortals when seeking did not find the calf though sojourning round about us. The attentive gods, wearying themselves, following his footsteps, stood at the highest, beautiful standing-place of Agni. When the bright ones had done service to thee, the bright one, Agni, with Ghrita through three autumns, they assumed worshipful names; the well-born shaped their own bodies. Acquiring for themselves the two great worlds, the worshipful ones brought forward their Rudra-like powers. The mortal, when beings were in discord, perceived and found out Agni standing in the highest place. Being like-minded they reverentially approached him on their knees. Together with their wives they venerated the venerable one. Abandoning their bodies they made them their own, the one friend waking when the other friend closed his eyes. When the worshipful gods have discovered the thrice seven secret steps laid down in thee, they concordantly guard with them immortality. Protect thou the cattle and that which remains steadfast and that which moves. Knowing, O Agni, the established orders of human dwellings, distribute in due order gifts that they may live. Knowing the ways which the gods do, thou hast become the unwearied messenger, the bearer of oblations. They who knew the right way and were filled with good intentions, beheld from heaven the seven young rivers and the doors of riches. Saramâ found the strong stable of the cows from which human clans receive their nourishment. The Earth has spread herself far and wide with them who are great in their greatness, the mother Aditi, for the refreshment of the bird, with her sons who have assumed all powers of their own dominion, preparing for themselves the way to immortality. When the immortals created the two eyes of heaven, they placed fair splendor in him. Then they rush down like streams let loose. The red ones have recognized, O Agni, those which are directed downwards.

VII

Forward goes your strength tending heavenward, rich in offerings, with the ladle full of ghee. To the gods goes the worshipper desirous of their favor. I magnify with prayer Agni who has knowledge of prayers, the accomplisher of sacrifice, who hears us, and in whom manifold wealth has been laid down. O Agni, may we be able to bridle thee the strong god;

may we overcome all hostile powers. Agni, inflamed at the sacrifice, the purifier who should be magnified, whose hair is flame—him we approach with prayers. With his broad stream of light the immortal Agni, clothed in ghee, well served with oblations, is the carrier of offerings at the sacrifice. Holding the sacrificial ladles, performing the sacrifice they have with right thought, pressingly brought Agni hither for help. The Hotri, the immortal god goes in front with his secret power, instigating the sacrifices. The strong is set at the races. He is led forth at the sacrifices, the priest, the accomplisher of sacrifice. He has been produced by prayer, the excellent one. I have established him, the germ of beings, forever the father of Daksha. I have laid thee down, the excellent one, with the nourishment of Daksha, O thou who art produced by power, O Agni, thee the resplendent one, O Usig. The priests, eager to set to work the Rita, kindle with quick strength Agni the governor, him who crosses the waters. I magnify the child of vigor at this sacrifice, who shines under the heaven, the thoughtful Agni. He who should be magnified and adored, who is visible through the darkness, Agni, the manly, is kindled. Agni, the manly, is kindled, he who draws hither the gods like a horse. The worshippers rich in offerings magnify him. We the manly ones will kindle thee the manly god, O manly Agni, who shinest mightily.

VIII

Produce thy stream of flames like a broad onslaught. Go forth impetuous like a king with his elephant, thou art an archer; shoot the sorcerers with thy hottest arrows. Thy whirls fly quickly. Fiercely flaming touch them. O Agni, send forth with the ladle thy heat, thy winged flames; send forth unfettered thy firebrands all around. Being the quickest, send forth thy spies against all evildoers. Be an undeceivable guardian of this clan. He who attacks us with evil spells, far or near, may no such foe defy thy track. Rise up, O Agni! Spread out against all foes! Burn down the foes, O god with the sharp weapon! When kindled, O Agni, burn down like dry brushwood, the man who exercises malice against us. Stand upright, strike the foes away from us! Make manifest thy divine powers, O Agni! Unbend the strong bows of those who incite demons against us. Crush all enemies, be they relations or strangers. He knows thy favor, O youngest one, who makes a way for a sacred speech like this. Mayest thou beam forth to his doors all auspicious days and the wealth and the splendor of the niggard. Let him, O Agni, be fortunate and blessed with good rain, who longs to gladden thee with constant offerings and hymns through his life in his house. May such longing ever bring auspicious days to him. I praise thy favor; it resounded here. May this song, which is like a favorite wife, awaken for thee. Let us brighten thee, being rich in horses and chariots. Mayest thou maintain our knightly power day by day. May the worshipper here frequently of his own accord approach thee, O god who shinest in darkness, resplendent day by day. Let us worship thee sporting and joyous, surpassing the splendor of other people. Whoever, rich in horses and rich in gold, approaches thee, O Agni, with his chariot full of wealth—thou art the protector and the friend of him who always delights in showing thee hospitality. Through my kinship with thee I break down the great foes by my words. That kinship has come down to me from my father Gotama. Be thou attentive to this our word, O youngest, highly wise Hotri, as the friend of our house. May those guardians of thine, infallible Agni, sitting down together protect us, the never sleeping, onward-pressing, kind, unwearied ones, who keep off the wolf, who never tire. Thy guardians, O Agni, who seeing have saved the blind son of Mamatâ from distress—He the possessor of all wealth has saved them who have done good deeds. The impostors, though trying to deceive, could not deceive. In thy companionship we dwell, protected by thee. Under thy guidance let us acquire gain. Accomplish both praises, O thou who art the truth! Do so by thy present power, O fearless one! May we worship thee, O Agni, with this log of wood. Accept the hymn of praise which we recite. Burn down those who curse us, the sorcerers. Protect us, O god who art great like Mitra, from guile, from revilement, and from disgrace.

IX

Bright, flaming, like the lover of the Dawn,* he has, like the light of the sky, filled the two worlds of Heaven and Earth which are turned towards each other. As soon as thou wert born thou hast excelled by thy power of mind; being the son of the gods thou hast become their father. Agni is a worshipper of the gods, never foolish, always discriminating; he is like the udder of the cows; he is the sweetness of food. Like a kind friend to men, not to be led astray, sitting in the midst, the lovely one, in the house; like a child when born, he is delightful in the house; like a race-horse which is well cared for, he has wandered across the clans. When I call to the sacrifice the clans who dwell in the same nest with the heroes, may Agni then attain all divine powers. When thou hast listened to these heroes, no one breaks those laws of thine. That verily is thy wonderful deed that thou hast killed, with thy companions, all foes; that, joined by the heroes, thou hast accomplished thy works. Like the lover of the Dawn, resplendent and bright, of familiar form: may he thus pay attention to this sacrificer. Carrying him they opened by themselves the doors of heaven. They all shouted at the aspect of the sun.

X

Like unto excellent wealth, like unto the shine of the sun, like unto living breath, like unto one's own son, like unto a quick takvan Agni holds the wood, like milk, like a milch cow, bright and shining. He holds safety, pleasant like a homestead, like ripe barley, a conqueror of men; like a Rishi uttering sacred shouts, praised among the clans; like a well-cared-for race-horse, Agni bestows vigor. He to whose flame men do not grow accustomed, who is like one's own mind, like a wife on a couch, enough for all happiness. When the bright Agni has shone forth, he is like a white horse among people, like a chariot with golden ornaments, impetuous in fights. Like an army which is sent forward he shows his vehemence, like an archer's shaft with sharp point. He who is born is one twin; he who will be born is the other twin—the lover of

* The sun.

maidens, the husband of wives. As cows go to their stalls, all that moves and we, for the sake of a dwelling, reach him who has been kindled. Like the flood of the Sindhu he has driven forward the downward-flowing waters. The cows lowed at the sight of the sun.

XI

The Hotri goes forward in order to fufil his duty by his wonderful power, directing upwards the brightly adorned prayer. He steps towards the sacrificial ladles which are turned to the right, and which first kiss his foundation. They have greeted with shouts the streams of Rita which were hidden at the birthplace of the god, at his seat. When He dwelt dispersed in the lap of the waters, he drank the draughts by the power of which he moves. Two beings of the same age try to draw that wonderful shape towards themselves, progressing in turns towards a common aim. Then he is to be proclaimed by us like a winner in a contest. The charioteer governs all things as if pulling in the reins of a draught-horse. He whom two beings of the same age serve, two twins dwelling together in one common abode, the gray one has been born as a youth by night as by day, the ageless one who wanders through many generations of men. The prayers, the ten fingers stir him up. We, the mortals, call him, the god, for his protection. From the dry land he hastens to the declivities. With those who approached him he has established new rules. Thou indeed, O Agni, reignest by thy own nature over the heavenly and over the terrestrial world as a shepherd takes care of his cattle. These two variegated, great goddesses striving for gloriousness, the golden ones who move crookedly, have approached thy sacrificial grass. Agni! Be gratified and accept graciously this prayer, O joy-giver, independent one, who art born in the Rita, good-willed one, whose face is turned towards us from all sides, conspicuous one, gay in thy aspect, like a dwelling-place rich in food.

SELECTIONS FROM THE ZEND-AVESTA

[*Translation by James Darmestetter*]

INTRODUCTION

THE study of religion, like the study of poetry, brings us face to face with the fundamental principles of human nature. Religion, whether it be natural religion or that which is formulated in a book, is as universal as poetry, and like poetry, existed before letters and writing. It is only in a serious and sympathetic frame of mind that we should approach the rudest forms of these two departments of human activity. A general analysis of the "Zend-Avesta" suggests to us the mind of the Persian sage Zarathustra, or Zoroaster, fixed upon the phenomena of nature and life, and trying to give a systematized account of them. He sees good and evil, life and death, sickness and health, right and wrong, engaged in almost equal conflict. He sees in the sun the origin of light and heat, the source of comfort and life to man. Thus he institutes the doctrine of Dualism and the worship of Fire. The evil things that come unexpectedly and irresistibly, he attributes to the Devas: the help and comfort that man needs and often obtains by means which are beyond his control, he attributes to the "Holy Immortal Ones," who stand around the Presence of Ormuzd. As he watches the purity of the flame, of the limpid stream, and of the sweet smelling ground, he connects it with the moral purity which springs from innocence and rectitude, and in his code it is as reprehensible to pollute the fire by burning the dead, or the stream by committing the corpse to its waves, or the earth by making it a burial-place, as it is to cheat or lie or commit an act of violence. The wonders of Nature furnish abundant imagery for his hymns or his litanies, and he relies for his cosmogony on the faint traditions of the past gathered from whatever nation, and reduced into conformity with his Dualistic creed.

"Zend-Avesta" is the religious book of the Persians who professed the creed of Zarathustra, known in classic and modern times as Zoroaster. Zoroaster is to be classed with such great religious leaders as Buddha and Mohammed. He was the predecessor of Mohammed and the worship and belief which he instituted were trampled out in Persia by the forces of Islam in the seventh century of our era. The Persian Zoroastrians fled to India, where they are still found as Parsis on the west coast of Hindostan. The religion of Zoroaster was a Dualism. Two powerful and creative beings, the one good the one evil, have control of the universe. Thus, in the account of the creation, the two deities are said to have equal though opposite share in the work. This is indicated by the following passage—

> The third of the good lands and countries which I, Ahura Mazda (Ormuzd) created, was the strong, holy Môuru (Merv).
>
> Thereupon came Angra Mainyu (Ahriman), who is all death, and he counter-created plunder and sin.

This constant struggle of the two divinities with their armies of good and bad spirits formed the background of Zoroastrian supernaturalism. The worship of the Persians was the worship of the powers of Nature, and especially of fire, although water, earth, and air, are also addressed in the litanies of the "Zend-Avesta." The down-falling water and the uprising mist are thus spoken of in one passage:—

> As the sea (Vouru-kasha) is the gathering place of the waters, rising up and going down, up the aërial way and down the earth, down the earth and up the aërial way: thus rise up and roll along! thou in whose rising and growing Ahura Mazda made the aërial way.

The sun is also invoked:—

> Up! rise up and roll along! thou swift-horsed Sun, above Hara Berezaiti, and produce light for the world.

The earth was considered to be polluted by the burial of the dead, who are to be exposed in high places to be devoured by the birds of the air and swept away by the streams into which the rain should wash their remains. But the principal subjects of Zoroaster's teaching was the struggle between Ormuzd and Ahriman and their hosts "The Holy Immortal Ones" and the Devas, or evil spirits. This is the basis of all the activities of the world and, according to Zoroaster, is to result in a triumph of the good.

Zoroaster taught that the life of man has two parts, that on earth and that beyond the grave. After his earthly life each one should be punished or rewarded according to his deeds.

The "Zend-Avesta" cannot be dated earlier than the first century before our era. It consists of four books, of which the chief one is the Vendidâd; the other three are the liturgical and devotional works, consisting of hymns, litanies, and songs of praise, addressed to the Deities and angels of Goodness.

The Vendidâd contains an account of the creation and counter-creation of Ormuzd and Ahriman, the author of the good things and of the evil things in the world. After this follows what we may call a history of the beginnings of civilization under Yima, the Persian Noah. The revelation is described as being made directly to Zoroaster, who, like Moses, talked with God. Thus, in the second fargard, or chapter, we read:—

> Zarathustra (Zoroaster) asked Ahura Mazda (Ormuzd):—
>
> "O Ahura Mazda (Ormuzd), most beneficent Spirit, Maker of the material world, thou Holy One! Who was the first mortal, before myself, Zarathustra, with whom thou, Ahura Mazda, didst converse, whom thou didst teach the religion of Ahura, the Religion of Zarathustra?"
>
> Ahura Mazda answered:—
>
> "The fair Yima, the good shepherd, O holy Zarathustra! he was the first mortal before thee, Zarathustra, with whom I, Ahura Mazda, did converse, whom I taught the Religion of Ahura, the Religion of Zarathustra. Unto him, O Zarathustra, I, Ahura Mazda, spake, saying: 'Well, fair Yima, son of Vîvanghat, be thou the Preacher and the bearer of my Religion!' And the fair Yima, O Zarathustra, replied unto me, saying: 'I was not born, I was not taught to be the preacher and the bearer of thy Religion.'"

The rest of the Vendidâd is taken up with the praises of agriculture, injunctions as to the care and pity due to the dog, the guardian of the home and flock, the hunter and the scavenger. It includes an elaborate code of ceremonial purification, resembling on this point the Leviticus of the Bible, and it prescribes also the gradations of penance for sins of various degrees of heinousness.

E. W.

DISCOVERY OF THE ZEND-AVESTA

THE "Zend-Avesta" is the sacred book of the Parsis; that is to say, of the few remaining followers of that religion which reigned over Persia at the time when the second successor of Mohammed overthrew the Sassanian dynasty (A.D. 642), and which has been called Dualism, or Mazdeism, or Magism, or Zoroastrianism, or Fire-worship, according as its main tenet, or its supreme God, or its priests, or its supposed founder, or its apparent object of worship has been most kept in view. In less than a century after their defeat, most of the conquered people were brought over to the faith of their new rulers, either by force, or policy, or the attractive power of a simpler form of creed. But many of those who clung to the faith of their fathers, went and sought abroad for a new home, where they might freely worship their old gods, say their old prayers, and perform their old rites. That home they found at last among the tolerant Hindoos, on the western coast of India and in the peninsula of Guzerat. There they throve and there they live still, while the ranks of their co-religionists in Persia are daily thinning and dwindling away.[1]

As the Parsis are the ruins of a people, so are their sacred books the ruins of a religion. There has been no other great belief in the world that ever left such poor and meagre monuments of its past splendor. Yet great is the value which that small book, the "Avesta," and the belief of that scanty people, the Parsis, have in the eyes of the historian and theologian, as they present to us the last reflex of the ideas which prevailed in Iran during the five centuries which preceded and the seven which followed the birth of Christ, a period which gave to the world the Gospels, the Talmud, and the Qur'ân. Persia, it is known, had much influence on each of the movements which

[1] A century ago, it is said, they still numbered nearly 100,000 souls; but there now remain no more than 8,000 or 9,000, scattered in Yazd and the surrounding villages. Houtum-Schindler gave 8,499 in 1879; of that number there were 6,483 in Yazd, 1,756 in Kirmân, 150 in Teherân.

produced, or proceeded from, those three books; she lent much to the first heresiarchs, much to the Rabbis, much to Mohammed. By help of the Parsi religion and the "Avesta," we are enabled to go back to the very heart of that most momentous period in the history of religious thought, which saw the blending of the Aryan mind with the Semitic, and thus opened the second stage of Aryan thought.

Inquiries into the religion of ancient Persia began long ago, and it was the old enemy of Persia, the Greek, who first studied it. Aristotle, Hermippus, and many others wrote of it in books of which, unfortunately, nothing more than a few fragments or merely the titles have come down to us. We find much valuable information about it, scattered in the accounts of historians and travellers, extending over ten centuries, from Herodotos down to Agathias and Procopius (from B.C. 450 to A.D. 550). The clearest and most faithful account of the Dualist doctrine is found in the treatise *De Iside et Osiride*, ascribed to Plutarch. But Zoroastrianism was never more eagerly studied than in the first centuries of the Christian era, though without anything of the disinterested and almost scientific curiosity of the earlier times. Religious and philosophic sects, in search of new dogmas, eagerly received whatever came to them bearing the name of Zoroaster. As Xanthos the Lydian, who is said to have lived before Herodotos, had mentioned Zoroastrianism, there came to light, in those later times, scores of oracles, styled "Oracula Chaldaïca sive Magica," the work of Neo-Platonists who were but very remote disciples of the Median sage. As his name had become the very emblem of wisdom, they would cover with it the latest inventions of their ever-deepening theosophy. Zoroaster and Plato were treated as if they had been philosophers of the same school, and Hierocles expounded their doctrines in the same book. Proclus collected seventy Tetrads of Zoroaster and wrote commentaries on them; but we need hardly say that Zoroaster commented on by Proçlus was nothing more or less than Proclus commented on by himself. Prodicus, the Gnostic, possessed secret books of Zoroaster; and, upon the whole, it may be said that in the first centuries of Christianity, the religion of Persia was more studied and less understood than it had ever been before. The real object aimed at, in studying the old religion, was to form a new one.

Throughout the Middle Ages nothing was known of Mazdeism but the name of its founder, who from a Magus was converted into a magician and master of the hidden sciences. It was not until the Renaissance that real inquiry was resumed. The first step was to collect all the information that could be gathered from Greek and Roman writers. That task was undertaken and successfully completed by Barnabé Brisson. A nearer approach to the original source was made in the following century by Italian, English, and French travellers in Asia. Pietro della Valle, Henry Lord, Mandelslo, Ovington, Chardin, Gabriel du Chinon, and Tavernier, found Zoroaster's last followers in Persia and India, and made known their existence, their manners, and the main features of their belief to Europe. Gabriel du Chinon saw their books and recognized that they were not all written in the same language, their original holy writ being no longer understood except by means of translations and commentaries in another tongue.

In the year 1700, a professor at Oxford, Thomas Hyde, the greatest Orientalist of his time in Europe, made the first systematic attempt to restore the history of the old Persian religion by combining the accounts of the Mohammedan writers with "the true and genuine monuments of ancient Persia." Unfortunately the so-called genuine monuments of ancient Persia were nothing more than recent Persian compilations or refacimenti. But notwithstanding this defect, which could hardly be avoided then, and a distortion of critical acumen, the book of Thomas Hyde was the first complete and true picture of modern Parsîism, and it made inquiry into its history the order of the day. A warm appeal made by him to the zeal of travellers, to seek for and procure at any price the sacred books of the Parsis, did not remain ineffectual, and from that time scholars bethought themselves of studying Parsîism in its own home.

Eighteen years later, a countryman of Hyde, George Boucher, received from the Parsis in Surat a copy of the Vendîdâd Sâda, which was brought to England in 1723 by Richard Cobbe. But the old manuscript was a sealed book, and the most that could then be made of it was to hang it by an iron chain to the wall of the Bodleian Library, as a curiosity to be shown to foreigners. A few years later, a Scotchman, named Fraser, went to Surat, with the view of obtaining from the

Parsis, not only their books, but also a knowledge of their contents. He was not very successful in the first undertaking, and utterly failed in the second.

In 1754 a young man, twenty years old, Anquetil Duperron, a scholar of the *École des Langues Orientales* in Paris, happened to see a fac-simile of four leaves of the Oxford Vendîdâd, which had been sent from England, a few years before, to Etienne Fourmont, the Orientalist. He determined at once to give to France both the books of Zoroaster and the first European translation of them. Too impatient to set off to wait for a mission from the government which had been promised to him, he enlisted as a private soldier in the service of the French East India Company; he embarked at Lorient on February 24, 1755, and after three years of endless adventures and dangers through the whole breadth of Hindostan, at the very time when war was waging between France and England, he arrived at last in Surat, where he stayed among the Parsis for three years more. Here began another struggle, not less hard, but more decisive, against the same mistrust and ill-will which had disheartened Fraser; but he came out of it victorious, and prevailed at last on the Parsis to part both with their books and their knowledge. He came back to Paris on March 14, 1764, and deposited on the following day at the *Bibliothèque Royale* the whole of the "Zend-Avesta," and copies of several traditional books. He spent ten years in studying the material he had collected, and published in 1771 the first European translation of the "Zend-Avesta."

A violent dispute broke out at once, as half the learned world denied the authenticity of this "Avesta," which it pronounced a forgery. It was the future founder of the Royal Asiatic Society, William Jones, a young Oxonian then, who opened the war. He had been wounded to the quick by the scornful tone adopted by Anquetil towards Hyde and a few other English scholars: the "Zend-Avesta" suffered for the fault of its introducer, Zoroaster for Anquetil. In a pamphlet written in French, with a *verve* and in a style which showed him to be a good disciple of Voltaire, William Jones pointed out, and dwelt upon, the oddities and absurdities with which the so-called sacred books of Zoroaster teemed. It is true that Anquetil had given full scope to satire by the style he had adopted: he cared very little for literary elegance, and did not mind writing

Zend and Persian in French; so the new and strange ideas he had to express looked stranger still in the outlandish garb he gave them. Yet it was less the style than the ideas that shocked the contemporary of Voltaire. His main argument was that books, full of such silly tales, of laws and rules so absurd, of descriptions of gods and demons so grotesque, could not be the work of a sage like Zoroaster, nor the code of a religion so much celebrated for its simplicity, wisdom, and purity. His conclusion was that the "Avesta" was a rhapsody of some modern Guebre. In fact, the only thing in which Jones succeeded was to prove in a decisive manner that the ancient Persians were not equal to the *lumières* of the eighteenth century, and that the authors of the "Avesta" had not read the "Encyclopédie."

Jones's censure was echoed in England by Sir John Chardin and Richardson, in Germany by Meiners. Richardson tried to give a scientific character to the attacks of Jones by founding them on philological grounds. That the "Avesta" was a fabrication of modern times was shown, he argued, by the number of Arabic words he fancied he found both in the Zend and Pahlavi dialects, as no Arabic element was introduced into the Persian idioms earlier than the seventh century; also by the harsh texture of the Zend, contrasted with the rare euphony of the Persian; and, lastly, by the radical difference between the Zend and Persian, both in words and grammar. To these objections, drawn from the form, he added another derived from the uncommon stupidity of the matter.

In Germany, Meiners, to the charges brought against the newly-found books, added another of a new and unexpected kind, namely, that they spoke of ideas unheard of before, and made known new things. "Pray, who would dare ascribe to Zoroaster books in which are found numberless names of trees, animals, men, and demons, unknown to the ancient Persians; in which are invoked an incredible number of pure animals and other things, which, as appears from the silence of ancient writers, were never known, or at least never worshipped, in Persia? What Greek ever spoke of Hôm, of Jemshîd, and of such other personages as the fabricators of that rhapsody exalt with every kind of praise, as divine heroes?"

Anquetil and the "Avesta" found an eager champion in the person of Kleuker, professor in the University of Riga. As soon as the French version of the "Avesta" appeared, he published a German translation of it, and also of Anquetil's historical dissertations. Then, in a series of dissertations of his own, he vindicated the authenticity of the Zend books. Anquetil had already tried to show, in a memoir on Plutarch, that the data of the "Avesta" fully agree with the account of the Magian religion given in the treatise on "Isis and Osiris." Kleuker enlarged the circle of comparison to the whole of ancient literature.

In the field of philology, he showed, as Anquetil had already done, that Zend has no Arabic elements in it, and that Pahlavi itself, which is more modern than Zend, does not contain any Arabic, but only Semitic words of the Aramean dialect, which are easily accounted for by the close relations of Persia with Aramean lands in the time of the Sassanian kings. He showed, lastly, that Arabic words appear only in the very books which Parsi tradition itself considers modern.

Another stanch upholder of the "Avesta" was the numismatologist Tychsen, who, having begun to read the book with a prejudice against its authenticity, quitted it with a conviction to the contrary. "There is nothing in it," he writes, "but what befits remote ages, and a man philosophizing in the infancy of the world. Such traces of a recent period as they fancy to have found in it, are either due to misunderstandings, or belong to its later portions. On the whole there is a marvellous accordance between the "Zend-Avesta" and the accounts of the ancients with regard to the doctrine and institutions of Zoroaster. Plutarch agrees so well with the Zend books that I think no one will deny the close resemblance of doctrines and identity of origin. Add to all this the incontrovertible argument to be drawn from the language, the antiquity of which is established by the fact that it was necessary to translate a part of the Zend books into Pahlavi, a language which was growing obsolete as early as the time of the Sassanides. Lastly, it cannot be denied that Zoroaster left books which were, through centuries, the groundwork of the Magic religion, and which were preserved by the Magi, as shown by a series of documents from the time of Hermippus. Therefore I am unable to see why we should not trust the Magi of our days when they ascribe to Zoroaster those traditional books of their ancestors, in which nothing is found to indicate fraud or a modern hand."

Two years afterwards, in 1793, was published in Paris a book which, without directly dealing with the "Avesta," was the first step taken to make its authenticity incontrovertible. It was the masterly memoir by Sylvestre de Sacy, in which the Pahlavi inscriptions of the first Sassanides were deciphered for the first time and in a decisive manner. De Sacy, in his researches, had chiefly relied on the Pahlavi lexicon published by Anquetil, whose work vindicated itself thus—better than by heaping up arguments—by promoting discoveries. The Pahlavi inscriptions gave the key, as is well-known, to the Persian cuneiform inscriptions, which were in return to put beyond all doubt the genuineness of the Zend language.

Tychsen, in an appendix to his Commentaries, pointed to the importance of the new discovery: "This," he writes, "is a proof that the Pahlavi was used during the reign of the Sassanides, for it was from them that these inscriptions emanated, as it was by them—nay, by the first of them, Ardeshîr Bâbagân—that the doctrine of Zoroaster was revived. One can now understand why the Zend books were translated into Pahlavi. Here, too, everything agrees, and speaks loudly for their antiquity and genuineness."

About the same time Sir William Jones, then president of the Royal Asiatic Society, which he had just founded, resumed in a discourse delivered before that society the same question he had solved in such an off-hand manner twenty years before. He was no longer the man to say, "*Sied-il à un homme né dans ce siècle de s'infatuer de fables indiennes?*" and although he had still a spite against Anquetil, he spoke of him with more reserve than in 1771. However, his judgment on the "Avesta" itself was not altered on the whole, although, as he himself declared, he had not thought it necessary to study the text. But a glance at the Zend glossary published by Anquetil suggested to him a remark which makes Sir William Jones, in spite of himself, the creator of the comparative grammar of Sanscrit and Zend. "When I perused the Zend glossary," he writes, "I was inexpressibly surprised to find that six or seven words in ten are pure Sanscrit, and even some of their inflexions formed by the rules of the Vyácaran, as yushmácam, the genitive plural of yushmad. Now M. Anquetil most certainly, and the Persian compiler most probably, had no knowledge of Sanscrit, and could not, therefore, have invented a list of Sanscrit words; it is, therefore, an authentic list of Zend words, which has been preserved in books or by tradition; it follows that the language of the Zend was at least a dialect of the Sanscrit, approaching perhaps as nearly to it as the Prácrit, or other popular idioms, which we know to have been spoken in India two thousand years ago." This conclusion, that Zend is a Sanscrit dialect, was incorrect, the connection assumed being too close; but it was a great thing that the near relationship of the two languages should have been brought to light.

In 1798 Father Paulo de St. Barthélemy further developed Jones's remark in an essay on the antiquity of the Zend language. He showed its affinity with the Sanscrit by a list of such Zend and Sanscrit words as were least likely to have been borrowed, viz., those that designate the degrees of relationship, the limbs of the body, and the most general and essential ideas. Another list, intended to show, on a special topic, how closely connected the two languages are, contains eighteen words taken from the liturgic language used in India and Persia. This list was not very happily drawn up, as out of the eighteen instances there is not a single one that stands inquiry; yet it was a happy idea, and one which has not even yet yielded all that it promised. His conclusions were that in a far remote antiquity Sanscrit was spoken in Persia and Media, that it gave birth to the Zend language, and that the "Zend-Avesta" is authentic: "Were it but a recent compilation," he writes, "as Jones asserts, how is it that the oldest rites of the Parsis, that the old inscriptions of the Persians, the accounts of the Zoroastrian religion by the classical writers, the liturgic prayers of the Parsis, and, lastly, even their books do not reveal the pure Sanscrit, as written in the land wherein the Parsis live, but a mixed language, which is as different from the other dialects of India as French is from Italian?" This amounted, in fact, to saying that the Zend is not derived from the Sanscrit, but that both are derived from another and older language. The Carmelite had a dim notion of that truth, but, as he failed to express it distinctly, it was lost for years, and had to be rediscovered.

The first twenty-five years of this century were void of results, but the old and sterile discussions as to the authenticity of the texts continued in England. In 1808 John Leyden regarded Zend as a Prácrit dialect, parallel to Pali; Pali being identical with the Magadhi dialect and Zend with the Sauraseni. In the eyes of Erskine, Zend was a Sanscrit dialect, imported from India by the founders of Mazdeism, but never spoken in Persia. His main argument was that Zend is not mentioned among the seven dialects which were current in ancient Persia according to the Farhang-i Jehangiri, and that Pahlavi and Persian exhibit no close relationship with Zend.

In Germany, Meiners had found no followers. The theologians appealed to the "Avesta," in their polemics, and Rhode sketched the religious history of Persia after the translations of Anquetil.

Erskine's essay provoked a decisive answer from Emmanuel Rask, one of the most gifted minds in the new school of philology, who had the honor of being a precursor of both Grimm and Burnouf. He showed that the list of the Jehangiri referred to an epoch later than that to which Zend must have belonged, and to parts of Persia different from those where it must have been spoken; he showed further that modern Persian is not derived from Zend, but from a dialect closely connected with it; and, lastly, he showed what was still more important, that Zend was not derived from Sanscrit. As to the system of its sounds, Zend approaches Persian rather than Sanscrit; and as to its grammatical forms, if they often remind one of Sanscrit, they also often remind one of Greek and Latin, and frequently have a special character of their own. Rask also gave the paradigm of three Zend nouns, belonging to different declensions, as well as the right pronunciation of the Zend letters, several of which had been incorrectly given by Anquetil. This was the first essay on Zend grammar, and it was a masterly one.

The essay published in 1831 by Peter von Bohlen on the origin of the Zend language threw the matter forty years back. According to him, Zend is a Prácrit dialect, as it had been pronounced by Jones, Leyden, and Erskine. His mistake consisted in taking Anquetil's transcriptions of the words, which are often so incorrect as to make them look like corrupted forms when compared with Sanscrit. And, what was worse, he took the proper names in their modern Parsi forms, which often led him to comparisons that would have appalled Ménage. Thus Ahriman became a Sanscrit word ariman, which would have meant "the fiend"; yet Bohlen might have seen in Anquetil's work itself that Ahriman is nothing but the modern form of Angra Mainyu, words which hardly remind one of the Sanscrit ariman. Again, the angel Vohu-manô, or "good thought," was reduced, by means of the Parsi form Bahman, to the Sanscrit bâhumân, "a long-armed god."

At length came Burnouf. From the time when Anquetil had published his translation, that is to say during seventy years, no real progress had been made in knowledge of the Avesta texts. The notion that Zend and Sanscrit are two kindred languages was the only new idea that had been acquired, but no practical advantage for the interpretation of the texts had resulted from it. Anquetil's translation was still the only guide, and as the doubts about the authenticity of the texts grew fainter, the authority of the translation became greater, the trust reposed in the "Avesta" being reflected on to the work of its interpreter. The Parsis had been the teachers of Anquetil; and who could ever understand the holy writ of the Parsis better than the Parsis themselves? There was no one who even tried to read the texts by the light of Anquetil's translation, to obtain a direct understanding of them.

About 1825 Eugène Burnouf was engaged in a course of researches on the geographical extent of the Aryan languages in India. After he had defined the limits which divide the races speaking Aryan languages from the native non-brahmanical tribes in the south, he wanted to know if a similar boundary had ever existed in the northwest; and if it is outside of India that the origin of the Indian languages and civilization is to be sought for. He was thus led to study the languages of Persia, and, first of all, the oldest of them, the Zend. But as he tried to read the texts by help of Anquetil's translation, he was surprised to find that this was not the clue he had expected. He saw that two causes had misled Anquetil: on the one hand, his teachers, the Parsi dasturs, either knew little themselves or taught him imperfectly, not only the Zend, but even the Pahlavi intended to explain the meaning of the Zend; so that the tradition on which his work rested, being incorrect in itself, corrupted it from the very beginning; on the other hand, as Sanscrit was unknown to him and comparative grammar did not as yet exist, he could not supply the defects of tradition by their aid. Burnouf, laying aside tradition as found in Anquetil's translation, consulted it as found in a much older and purer form, in a Sanscrit translation of the Yasna made in the fifteenth century by the Parsi Neriosengh in accordance with the old Pahlavi version. The information given by Neriosengh he tested, and either confirmed or corrected, by a comparison of parallel passages and by the help of comparative grammar, which had just been founded by Bopp, and applied by him successfully to the explanation of Zend forms. Thus he succeeded in tracing the general outlines of the Zend lexicon and in fixing its grammatical forms, and founded the only correct method of interpreting the "Avesta." He also gave the first notions of a comparative mythology of the "Avesta" and the "Veda," by showing the identity of the "Vedic Yama" with the "Avesta Yima," and of Traitâna with Thraêtaona and Ferîdûn. Thus he made his "Commentaire sur le Yasna" a marvellous and unparalleled model of critical insight and steady good sense, equally opposed to the narrowness of mind which clings to matters of fact without rising to their cause and connecting them with the series of associated phenomena, and to the wild and uncontrolled spirit of comparison, which, by comparing everything, confounds everything. Never sacrificing either tradition to comparison or comparison to tradition he knew how to pass from the one to the other, and was so enabled both to discover facts and to explain them.

At the same time the ancient Persian inscriptions at Persepolis and Behistun were deciphered by Burnouf in Paris, by Lassen in Bonn, and by Sir Henry Rawlinson in Persia. Thus was revealed the existence, at the time of the first Achaemenian kings, of a language closely connected with that of the "Avesta," and the last doubts as to the authenticity of the Zend books were at length removed. It would have required more than an ordinary amount of scepticism to look still upon the Zend as an artificial language, of foreign importation, without root in the land where it was written, and in the conscience of the people for whom it was written, at the moment when a twin language, bearing a striking likeness to it in nearly every feature, was suddenly making itself heard from the mouth of Darius, and speaking from the very tomb of the first Achaemenian king. That unexpected voice silenced all controversies, and the last echoes of the loud discussion which had been opened in 1771 died away unheeded.

SELECTIONS FROM THE ZEND-AVESTA

THE CREATION*

AHURA MAZDA spake unto Spitama Zarathustra, saying:—

"I have made every land dear to its people, even though it had no charms whatever in it: had I not made every land dear to its people, even though it had no charms whatever in it, then the whole living world would have invaded the Airyana Vaêgô. The first of the good lands and countries which I, Ahura Mazda, created, was the Airyana Vaêgô, by the Vanguhi Dâitya. Thereupon came Angra Mainyu, who is all death, and he counter-created the serpent in the river and Winter, a work of the Devas. There are ten winter months there, two summer months; and those are cold for the waters, cold for the earth, cold for the trees. Winters fall there, the worst of all plagues. The second of the good lands and countries which I, Ahura Mazda, created, was the plain which the Sughdhas inhabit. Thereupon came Angra Mainyu, who is all death, and he counter-created the locust, which brings death unto cattle and plants. The third of the good lands and countries which I, Ahura Mazda, created, was the strong, holy Môuru. Thereupon came Angra Mainyu, who is all death, and he counter-created plunder and sin. The fourth of the good lands and countries which I, Ahura Mazda, created, was the beautiful Bâkhdhi with high-lifted banners. Thereupon came Angra Mainyu, who is all death, and he counter-created the ants and the ant-hills. The fifth of the good lands and countries which I, Ahura Mazda, created, was Nisâya, that lies

* This chapter is an enumeration of sixteen perfect lands created by Ahura Mazda, and of as many plagues created in opposition by Angra Mainyu. Many attempts have been made, not only to identify these sixteen lands, but also to draw historical conclusions from their order of succession, as representing the actual order of the migrations and settlements of the old Iranian tribes. But there is nothing in the text to support such wide inferences. We have here nothing more than a geographical description of Iran, seen from the religious point of view.

between Môuru and Bâkhdhi. Thereupon came Angra Mainyu, who is all death, and he counter-created the sin of unbelief. The sixth of the good lands and countries which I, Ahura Mazda, created, was the house-deserting Harôyu. Thereupon came Angra Mainyu, who is all death, and he counter-created tears and wailing. The seventh of the good lands and countries which I, Ahura Mazda, created, was Vaêkereta, of the evil shadows. Thereupon came Angra Mainyu, who is all death, and he counter-created the Pairika Knãthaiti, who clave unto Keresâspa. The eighth of the good lands and countries which I, Ahura Mazda, created, was Urva of the rich pastures. Thereupon came Angra Mainyu, who is all death, and he counter-created the sin of pride. The ninth of the good lands and countries which I, Ahura Mazda, created, was Khnenta which the Vehrkânas inhabit. Thereupon came Angra Mainyu, who is all death, and he counter-created a sin for which there is no atonement, the unnatural sin. The tenth of the good lands and countries which I, Ahura Mazda, created, was the beautiful Harahvaiti. Thereupon came Angra Mainyu, who is all death, and he counter-created a sin for which there is no atonement, the burying of the dead. The eleventh of the good lands and countries which I, Ahura Mazda, created, was the bright, glorious Haêtumant. Thereupon came Angra Mainyu, who is all death, and he counter-created the evil work of witchcraft. And this is the sign by which it is known, this is that by which it is seen at once: wheresoever they may go and raise a cry of sorcery, there the worst works of witchcraft go forth. From there they come to kill and strike at heart, and they bring locusts as many as they want. The twelfth of the good lands and countries which I, Ahura Mazda, created, was Ragha of the three races. Thereupon came Angra Mainyu, who is all death, and he counter-created the sin of utter unbelief. The thirteenth of the good lands and countries which I, Ahura Mazda, created, was the strong, holy Kakhra. Thereupon came Angra Mainyu, who is all death, and he counter-created a sin for which there is no atonement, the cooking of corpses. The fourteenth of the good lands and countries which I, Ahura Mazda, created, was the four-cornered Varena, for which was born Thraêtaona, who smote Azi Dahâka. Thereupon came Angra Mainyu, who is all death, and he counter-created abnormal issues in women and barbarian oppression. The fifteenth of the good lands and countries which I, Ahura Mazda, created, was the Seven Rivers. Thereupon came Angra Mainyu, who is all death, and he counter-created abnormal issues in women and excessive heat. The sixteenth of the good lands and countries which I, Ahura Mazda, created, was the land by the sources of the Rangha, where people live who have no chiefs. Thereupon came Angra Mainyu, who is all death, and he counter-created Winter, a work of the Devas. There are still other lands and countries, beautiful and deep, longing and asking for the good, and bright."

MYTH OF YIMA

Zarathustra asked Ahura Mazda:—

"O Ahura Mazda, most beneficent Spirit, Maker of the material world, thou Holy One! Who was the first mortal, before myself, Zarathustra, with whom thou, Ahura Mazda, didst converse, whom thou didst teach the Religion of Ahura, the Religion of Zarathustra?

Ahura Mazda answered:—

"The fair Yima, the good shepherd, O holy Zarathustra! he was the first mortal, before thee, Zarathustra, with whom I, Ahura Mazda, did converse, whom I taught the Religion of Ahura, the Religion of Zarathustra. Unto him, O Zarathustra, I, Ahura Mazda, spake, saying: 'Well, fair Yima, son of Vivanghat, be thou the preacher and the bearer of my Religion!' And the fair Yima, O Zarathustra, replied unto me, saying: 'I was not born, I was not taught to be the preacher and the bearer of thy Religion.' Then I, Ahura Mazda, said thus unto him, O Zarathustra, 'Since thou dost not consent to be the preacher and the bearer of my Religion, then make thou my world increase, make my world grow: consent thou to nourish, to rule, and to watch over my world.' And the fair Yima replied unto me, O Zarathustra, saying: 'Yes! I will make thy world increase, I will make thy world grow. Yes! I will nourish, and rule, and watch over thy world. There shall be, while I am king, neither cold wind nor hot wind, neither disease nor death.' Then I, Ahura Mazda, brought two implements unto him: a golden seal and a poniard inlaid with gold. Behold, here Yima bears the royal sway! Thus, under the sway of Yima, three hundred winters passed away, and the earth was replenished with flocks and herds, with men and dogs and birds and with red blazing fires, and there was room no more for flocks, herds, and men. Then I warned the fair Yima, saying: 'O fair Yima, son of Vîvanghat, the earth has become full of flocks and herds, of men and dogs and birds and of red blazing fires, and there is room no more for flocks, herds, and men.' Then Yima stepped forward, in light, southwards, on the way of the sun, and afterwards he pressed the earth with the golden seal, and bored it with the poniard, speaking thus: 'O Spenta Ârmaiti, kindly open asunder and stretch thyself afar, to bear flocks and herds and men.' And Yima made the earth grow larger by one-third than it was before, and there came flocks and herds and men, at their will and wish, as many as he wished. Thus, under the sway of Yima, six hundred winters passed away, and the earth was replenished with flocks and herds, with men and dogs and birds and with red blazing fires, and there was room no more for flocks, herds, and men. And I warned the fair Yima, saying: 'O fair Yima, son of Vîvanghat, the earth has become full of flocks and herds, of men and dogs and birds and of red blazing fires, and there is room no more for flocks, herds, and men.'

"Then Yima stepped forward, in light, southwards, on the way of the sun, and afterwards he pressed the earth with the golden seal, and bored it with the poniard, speaking thus: 'O Spenta Ârmaiti, kindly open asunder and stretch thyself afar, to bear flocks and herds and men.' And Yima made the earth grow larger by two-thirds than it was before, and there came flocks and herds and men, at their will and wish, as many as he wished. Thus, under the sway of Yima, nine hundred winters passed away, and the earth was replenished with flocks and herds, with men and dogs and birds and with red blazing fires, and there was room no more for flocks, herds, and men. And I warned the fair Yima, saying: 'O fair Yima, son of Vîvanghat, the earth has become full of flocks and herds, of men and dogs and birds and of red blazing fires, and there is room no more for flocks, herds, and men.' Then Yima stepped forward, in light, southwards, on the way of the sun, and afterwards he pressed the earth with the golden seal, and bored it with the poniard, speaking thus: 'O Spenta Ârmaiti, kindly open asunder and stretch thyself afar, to bear flocks and herds and men.' And Yima made the earth grow larger by three-thirds than it was before, and there came flocks and herds and men, at their will and wish, as many as he wished."

THE EARTH

O Maker of the material world, thou Holy One! Which is the first place where the Earth feels most happy? Ahura Mazda answered: "It is the place whereon one of the faithful steps forward, O Spitama Zarathustra! with the log in his hand, the Baresma in his hand, the milk in his hand, the mortar in his hand, lifting up his voice in good accord with religion, and beseeching Mithra, the lord of the rolling country-side, and Râma Hvâstra." O Maker of the material world, thou Holy One! Which is the second place where the Earth feels most happy? Ahura Mazda answered: "It is the place whereon one of the faithful erects a house with a priest within, with cattle, with a wife, with children, and good herds within; and wherein afterwards the cattle continue to thrive, virtue to thrive, fodder to thrive, the dog to thrive, the wife to thrive, the child to thrive, the fire to thrive, and every blessing of life to thrive." O Maker of the material world, thou Holy One! Which is the third place where the Earth feels most happy? Ahura Mazda answered: "It is the place where one of the faithful sows most corn, grass, and fruit, O Spitama Zarathustra! where he waters ground that is dry, or drains ground that is too wet." O Maker of the material world, thou Holy One! Which is the fourth place where the Earth feels most happy? Ahura Mazda answered: "It is the place where there is most increase of flocks and herds." O Maker of the material world, thou Holy One! Which is the fifth place where the Earth feels most happy? Ahura Mazda answered: "It is the place where flocks and herds yield most dung."

O Maker of the material world, thou Holy One! Which is the first place where the Earth feels sorest grief? Ahura Mazda answered: "It is the neck of Arezûra, whereon the hosts of fiends rush forth from the burrow of the Drug." O

Maker of the material world, thou Holy One! Which is the second place where the Earth feels sorest grief? Ahura Mazda answered: "It is the place wherein most corpses of dogs and of men lie buried." O Maker of the material world, thou Holy One! Which is the third place where the Earth feels sorest grief? Ahura Mazda answered: "It is the place whereon stand most of those Dakhmas on which the corpses of men are deposited." O Maker of the material world, thou Holy One! Which is the fourth place where the Earth feels sorest grief? Ahura Mazda answered: "It is the place wherein are most burrows of the creatures of Angra Mainyu." O Maker of the material world, thou Holy One! Which is the fifth place where the Earth feels sorest grief? Ahura Mazda answered: "It is the place whereon the wife and children of one of the faithful, O Spitama Zarathustra! are driven along the way of captivity, the dry, the dusty way, and lift up a voice of wailing."

O Maker of the material world, thou Holy One! Who is the first that rejoices the Earth with greatest joy? Ahura Mazda answered: "It is he who digs out of it most corpses of dogs and men." O Maker of the material world, thou Holy One! Who is the second that rejoices the Earth with greatest joy? Ahura Mazda answered: "It is he who pulls down most of those Dakhmas on which the corpses of men are deposited. Let no man alone by himself carry a corpse. If a man alone by himself carry a corpse, the Nasu rushes upon him. This Drug Nasu falls upon and stains him, even to the end of the nails, and he is unclean, thenceforth, forever and ever." O Maker of the material world, thou Holy One! What shall be the place of that man who has carried a corpse alone? Ahura Mazda answered: "It shall be the place on this earth wherein is least water and fewest plants, whereof the ground is the cleanest and the driest and the least passed through by flocks and herds, by the fire of Ahura Mazda, by the consecrated bundles of Baresma, and by the faithful." O Maker of the material world, thou Holy One! How far from the fire? How far from the water? How far from the consecrated bundles of Baresma? How far from the faithful? Ahura Mazda answered: "Thirty paces from the fire, thirty paces from the water, thirty paces from the consecrated bundles of Baresma, three paces from the faithful. There, on that place, shall the worshippers of Mazda erect an enclosure, and therein shall they establish him with food, therein shall they establish him with clothes, with the coarsest food and with the most worn-out clothes. That food he shall live on, those clothes he shall wear, and thus shall they let him live, until he has grown to the age of a Hana, or of a Zaurura, or of a Pairista-khshudra. And when he has grown to the age of a Hana, or of a Zaurura, or of a Pairista-khshudra, then the worshippers of Mazda shall order a man strong, vigorous, and skilful, to cut the head off his neck, in his enclosure on the top of the mountain: and they shall deliver his corpse unto the greediest of the corpse-eating creatures made by the beneficent Spirit, unto the vultures, with these words: 'The man here has repented of all his evil thoughts, words, and deeds. If he has committed any other evil deed, it is remitted by his repentance: if he has committed no other evil deed, he is absolved by his repentance, forever and ever.'" O Maker of the material world, thou Holy One! Who is the third that rejoices the Earth with greatest joy? Ahura Mazda answered: "It is he who fills up most burrows of the creatures of Angra Mainyu." O Maker of the material world, thou Holy One! Who is the fourth that rejoices the Earth with greatest joy? Ahura Mazda answered: "It is he who sows most corn, grass, and fruit, O Spitama Zarathustra! who waters ground that is dry, or drains ground that is too wet. Unhappy is the land that has long lain unsown with the seed of the sower and wants a good husbandman, like a well-shapen maiden who has long gone childless and wants a good husband. He who would till the earth, O Spitama Zarathustra! with the left arm and the right, with the right arm and the left, unto him will she bring forth plenty of fruit: even as it were a lover sleeping with his bride on her bed; the bride will bring forth children, the earth will bring forth plenty of fruit. He who would till the earth, O Spitama Zarathustra! with the left arm and the right, with the right arm and the left, unto him thus says the Earth: 'O thou man! who dost till me with the left arm and the right, with the right arm and the left, here shall I ever go on bearing, bringing forth all manner of food, bringing corn first to thee.' He who does not till the Earth, O Spitama Zarathustra! with the left arm and the right, with the right arm and the left, unto him thus says the Earth: 'O thou man! who dost not till me with the left arm and the right, with the right arm and the left, ever shalt thou stand at the door of the stranger, among those who beg for bread; the refuse and the crumbs of the bread are brought unto thee, brought by those who have profusion of wealth.' "

O maker of the material world, thou Holy One! What is the food that fills the Religion of Mazda?

Ahura Mazda answered:—

" It is sowing corn again and again, O Spitama Zarathustra! He who sows corn, sows righteousness: he makes the Religion of Mazda walk, he suckles the Religion of Mazda; as well as he could do with a hundred man's feet, with a thousand woman's breasts, with ten thousand sacrificial formulas. When barley was created, the Devas started up; when it grew, then fainted the Devas' hearts; when the knots came, the Devas groaned; when the ear came, the Devas flew away. In that house the Devas stay, wherein wheat perishes. It is as though red hot iron were turned about in their throats, when there is plenty of corn. Then let people learn by heart this holy saying: 'No one who does not eat, has strength to do heavy works of holiness, strength to do works of husbandry, strength to beget children. By eating every material creature lives, by not eating it dies away.' "

O Maker of the material world, thou Holy One! Who is the fifth that rejoices the Earth with greatest joy?

Ahura Mazda answered:—

" It is he who kindly and piously gives to one of the faithful who tills the earth, O Spitama Zarathustra! He who would not kindly and piously give to one of the faithful who tills the earth, O Spitama Zarathustra! Spenta Ârmaiti will throw him down into darkness, down into the world of woe, the world of hell, down into the deep abyss."

O Maker of the material world, thou Holy One! If a man shall bury in the earth either the corpse of a dog or the corpse of a man, and if he shall not disinter it within half a year, what is the penalty that he shall pay?

Ahura Mazda answered:—

" Five hundred stripes with the Aspahê-astra, five hundred stripes with the Sraoshô-karana."

O Maker of the material world, thou Holy One! If a man shall bury in the earth either the corpse of a dog or the corpse of a man, and if he shall not disinter it within a year, what is the penalty that he shall pay?

Ahura Mazda answered:—

"A thousand stripes with the Aspahê-astra, a thousand stripes with the Sraoshô-karana."

O Maker of the material world, thou Holy One! If a man shall bury in the earth either the corpse of a dog or the corpse of a man, and if he shall not disinter it within the second year, what is the penalty for it? What is the atonement for it? What is the cleansing from it?

Ahura Mazda answered:—

"For that deed there is nothing that can pay, nothing that can atone, nothing that can cleanse from it; it is a trespass for which there is no atonement, forever and ever."

When is it so?

"It is so, if the sinner be a professor of the Religion of Mazda, or one who has been taught in it. But if he be not a professor of the Religion of Mazda, nor one who has been taught in it, then his sin is taken from him, if he makes confession of the Religion of Mazda and resolves never to commit again such forbidden deeds.

"The Religion of Mazda indeed, O Spitama Zarathustra! takes away from him who makes confession of it the bonds of his sin; it takes away the sin of breach of trust; it takes away the sin of murdering one of the faithful; it takes away the sin of burying a corpse; it takes away the sin of deeds for which there is no atonement; it takes away the worst sin of usury; it takes away any sin that may be sinned. In the same way the Religion of Mazda, O Spitama Zarathustra! cleanses the faithful from every evil thought, word, and deed, as a swift-rushing mighty wind cleanses the plain. So let all the deeds he doeth be henceforth good, O Zarathustra! a full atonement for his sin is effected by means of the Religion of Mazda."

CONTRACTS AND OUTRAGES*

"He that does not restore a loan to the man who lent it, steals the thing and robs the man. This he doeth every day, every night, as long as he keep in his house his neighbor's property, as though it were his own."

O Maker of the material world, thou Holy One! How many in number are thy contracts, O Ahura Mazda?

Ahura Mazda answered:—

"They are six in number, O holy Zarathustra. The first is the word-contract; the second is the hand-contract; the third is the contract to the amount of a sheep; the fourth is the contract to the amount of an ox; the fifth is the contract to the amount of a man; the sixth is the contract to the amount of a field, a field in good land, a fruitful one, in good bearing. The word-contract is fulfilled by words of mouth. It is cancelled by the hand-contract; he shall give as damages the amount of the hand-contract. The hand-contract is cancelled by the sheep-contract; he shall give as damages the amount of the sheep-contract. The sheep-contract is cancelled by the ox-contract; he shall give as damages the amount of the ox-contract. The ox-contract is cancelled by the man-contract; he shall give as damages the amount of the man-contract. The man-contract is cancelled by the field-contract; he shall give as damages the amount of the field-contract.

O Maker of the material world, thou Holy One! If a man break the word-contract, how many are involved in his sin?

Ahura Mazda answered:—

"His sin makes his Nabânazdistas answerable for three hundred years."

O Maker of the material world, thou Holy One! If a man break the hand-contract, how many are involved in his sin?

Ahura Mazda answered:—

"His sin makes his Nabânazdistas answerable for six hundred years."

O Maker of the material world, thou Holy One! If a man break the sheep-contract, how many are involved in his sin?

* This chapter is the only one in the Vendidad that deals with legal subjects.

Ahura Mazda answered:—

"His sin makes his Nabânazdistas answerable for seven hundred years."

O Maker of the material world, thou Holy One! If a man break the ox-contract, how many are involved in his sin?

Ahura Mazda answered:—

"His sin makes his Nabânazdistas answerable for eight hundred years."

O Maker of the material world, thou Holy One! If a man break the man-contract, how many are involved in his sin?

Ahura Mazda answered:—

"His sin makes his Nabânazdistas answerable for nine hundred years."

O Maker of the material world, thou Holy One! If a man break the field-contract, how many are involved in his sin?

Ahura Mazda answered:—

"His sin makes his Nabânazdistas answerable for a thousand years."

O Maker of the material world, thou Holy One! If a man break the word-contract, what is the penalty that he shall pay?

Ahura Mazda answered:—

"Three hundred stripes with the Aspahê-astra, three hundred stripes with the Sraoshô-karana."

O Maker of the material world, thou Holy One! If a man break the hand-contract, what is the penalty that he shall pay?

Ahura Mazda answered:—

"Six hundred stripes with the Aspahê-astra, six hundred stripes with the Sraoshô-karana."

O Maker of the material world, thou Holy One! If a man break the sheep-contract, what is the penalty that he shall pay?

Ahura Mazda answered:—

"Seven hundred stripes with the Aspahê-astra, seven hundred stripes with the Sraoshô-karana."

O Maker of the material world, thou Holy One! If a man break the ox-contract, what is the penalty that he shall pay?

Ahura Mazda answered:—

"Eight hundred stripes with the Aspahê-astra, eight hundred stripes with the Sraoshô-karana."

O Maker of the material world, thou Holy One! If a man break the man-contract, what is the penalty that he shall pay?

Ahura Mazda answered:—

"Nine hundred stripes with the Aspahê-astra, nine hundred stripes with the Sraoshô-karana."

O Maker of the material world, thou Holy One! If a man break the field-contract, what is the penalty that he shall pay?

Ahura Mazda answered:—

"A thousand stripes with the Aspahê-astra, a thousand stripes with the Sraoshô-karana."

If a man rise up with a weapon in his hand, it is an Âgerepta. If he brandish it, it is an Avaoirista. If he actually smite a man with malicious aforethought, it is an Aredus. Upon the fifth Aredus he becomes a Peshôtanu.

O Maker of the material world, thou Holy One! He that committeth an Âgerepta, what penalty shall he pay?

Ahura Mazda answered:—

"Five stripes with the Aspahê-astra, five stripes with the Sraoshô-karana; on the second Âgerepta, ten stripes with the Aspahê-astra, ten stripes with the Sraoshô-karana; on the third, fifteen stripes with the Aspahê-astra, fifteen stripes with the Sraoshô-karana; on the fourth, thirty stripes with the Aspahê-astra, thirty stripes with the Sraoshô-karana; on the fifth, fifty stripes with the Aspahê-astra, fifty stripes with the Sraoshô-karana; on the sixth, sixty stripes with the Aspahê-astra, sixty stripes with the Sraoshô-karana; on the seventh, ninety stripes with the Aspahê-astra, ninety stripes with the Sraoshô-karana."

If a man commit an Âgerepta for the eighth time, without having atoned for the preceding, what penalty shall he pay?

Ahura Mazda answered:—

"He is a Peshôtanu: two hundred stripes with the Aspahê-astra, two hundred stripes with the Sraoshô-karana."

If a man commit an Âgerepta, and refuse to atone for it, what penalty shall he pay?

Ahura Mazda answered:—

"He is a Peshôtanu: two hundred stripes with the Aspahê-astra, two hundred stripes with the Sraoshô-karana."

O Maker of the material world, thou Holy One! If a man commit an Avaoirista, what penalty shall he pay?

Ahura Mazda answered:—

"Ten stripes with the Aspahê-astra, ten stripes with the Sraoshô-karana; on the second Avaoirista, fifteen stripes with the

Aspahê-astra, fifteen stripes with the Sraoshô-karana; on the third, thirty stripes with the Aspahê-astra, thirty stripes with the Sraoshô-karana; on the fourth, fifty stripes with the Aspahê-astra, fifty stripes with the Sraoshô-karana; on the fifth, seventy stripes with the Aspahê-astra, seventy stripes with the Sraoshô-karana; on the sixth, ninety stripes with the Aspahê-astra, ninety stripes with the Sraoshô-karana."

O Maker of the material world, thou Holy One! If a man commit an Avaoirista for the seventh time, without having atoned for the preceding, what penalty shall he pay?

Ahura Mazda answered:—

"He is a Peshôtanu: two hundred stripes with the Aspahê-astra, two hundred stripes with the Sraoshô-karana."

O Maker of the material world, thou Holy One! If a man commit an Avaoirista, and refuse to atone for it, what penalty shall he pay?

Ahura Mazda answered:—

"He is a Peshôtanu: two hundred stripes with the Aspahê-astra, two hundred stripes with the Sraoshô-karana."

O Maker of the material world, thou Holy One! If a man commit an Aredus, what penalty shall he pay?

Ahura Mazda answered:—

"Fifteen stripes with the Aspahê-astra, fifteen stripes with the Sraoshô-karana.

"On the second Aredus, thirty stripes with the Aspahê-astra, thirty stripes with the Sraoshô-karana; on the third, fifty stripes with the Aspahê-astra, fifty stripes with the Sraoshô-karana; on the fourth, seventy stripes with the Aspahê-astra, seventy stripes with the Sraoshô-karana; on the fifth, ninety stripes with the Aspahê-astra, ninety stripes with the Sraoshô-karana."

O Maker of the material world, thou Holy One! If a man commit an Aredus for the sixth time, without having atoned for the preceding, what penalty shall he pay?

Ahura Mazda answered:—

"He is a Peshôtanu: two hundred stripes with the Aspahê-astra, two hundred stripes with the Sraoshô-karana."

O Maker of the material world, thou Holy One! If a man commit an Aredus, and refuse to atone for it, what penalty shall he pay?

Ahura Mazda answered:—

"He is a Peshôtanu: two hundred stripes with the Aspahê-astra, two hundred stripes with the Sraoshô-karana."

O Maker of the material world, thou Holy One! If a man smite another and hurt him sorely, what is the penalty that he shall pay?

Ahura Mazda answered:—

"Thirty stripes with the Aspahê-astra, thirty stripes with the Sraoshô-karana; the second time, fifty stripes with the Aspahê-astra, fifty stripes with the Sraoshô-karana; the third time, seventy stripes with the Aspahê-astra, seventy stripes with the Sraoshô-karana; the fourth time, ninety stripes with the Aspahê-astra, ninety stripes with the Sraoshô-karana."

If a man commit that deed for the fifth time, without having atoned for the preceding, what is the penalty that he shall pay?

Ahura Mazda answered:—

"He is a Peshôtanu: two hundred stripes with the Aspahê-astra, two hundred stripes with the Sraoshô-karana."

If a man commit that deed and refuse to atone for it, what is the penalty that he shall pay?

Ahura Mazda answered:—

"He is a Peshôtanu: two hundred stripes with the Aspahê-astra, two hundred stripes with the Sraoshô-karana."

O Maker of the material world, thou Holy One! If a man smite another so that the blood come, what is the penalty that he shall pay?

Ahura Mazda answered:—

"Fifty stripes with the Aspahê-astra, fifty stripes with the Sraoshô-karana; the second time, seventy stripes with the Aspahê-astra, seventy stripes with the Sraoshô-karana; the third time, ninety stripes with the Aspahê-astra, ninety stripes with the Sraoshô-karana."

If he commit that deed for the fourth time, without having atoned for the preceding, what is the penalty that he shall pay?

Ahura Mazda answered:—

"He is a Peshôtanu: two hundred stripes with the Aspahê-astra, two hundred stripes with the Sraoshô-karana."

O Maker of the material world, thou Holy One! If a man smite another so that the blood come, and if he refuse to atone for it, what is the penalty that he shall pay?

Ahura Mazda answered:—

"He is a Peshôtanu: two hundred stripes with the Aspahê-astra, two hundred stripes with the Sraoshô-karana."

O Maker of the material world, thou Holy One! If a man smite another so that he break a bone, what is the penalty that he shall pay?

Ahura Mazda answered:—

"Seventy stripes with the Aspahê-astra, seventy stripes with the Sraoshô-karana; the second time, ninety stripes with the Aspahê-astra, ninety stripes with the Sraoshô-karana."

If he commit that deed for the third time, without having atoned for the preceding, what is the penalty that he shall pay?

Ahura Mazda answered:—

"He is a Peshôtanu: two hundred stripes with the Aspahê-astra, two hundred stripes with the Sraoshô-karana."

O Maker of the material world, thou Holy One! If a man smite another so that he break a bone, and if he refuse to atone for it, what is the penalty that he shall pay?

Ahura Mazda answered:—

"He is a Peshôtanu: two hundred stripes with the Aspahê-astra, two hundred stripes with the Sraoshô-karana."

O Maker of the material world, thou Holy One! If a man smite another so that he give up the ghost, what is the penalty that he shall pay?

Ahura Mazda answered:—

"Ninety stripes with the Aspahê-astra, ninety stripes with the Sraoshô-karana."

If he commit that deed again, without having atoned for the preceding, what is the penalty that he shall pay?

Ahura Mazda answered:—

"He is a Peshôtanu: two hundred stripes with the Aspahê-astra, two hundred stripes with the Sraoshô-karana."

O Maker of the material world, thou Holy One! If a man smite another so that he give up the ghost, and if he refuse to atone for it, what is the penalty that he shall pay?

Ahura Mazda answered:—

"He is a Peshôtanu: two hundred stripes with the Aspahê-astra, two hundred stripes with the Sraoshô-karana.

"And they shall thenceforth in their doings walk after the way of holiness, after the word of holiness, after the ordinance of holiness.

"If men of the same faith, either friends or brothers, come to an agreement together, that one may obtain from the other either goods, or a wife, or knowledge, let him who desires goods have them delivered to him; let him who desires a wife receive and wed her; let him who desires knowledge be taught the holy word, during the first part of the day and the last, during the first part of the night and the last, that his mind may be increased in intelligence and wax strong in holiness. So shall he sit up, in devotion and prayers, that he may be increased in intelligence: he shall rest during the middle part of the day, during the middle part of the night, and thus shall he continue until he can say all the words which former Aêthrapaitis have said.

"Before the boiling water publicly prepared, O Spitama Zarathustra! let no one make bold to deny having received from his neighbor the ox or the garment in his possession.

"Verily I say it unto thee, O Spitama Zarathustra! the man who has a wife is far above him who lives in continence; he who keeps a house is far above him who has none; he who has children is far above the childless man; he who has riches is far above him who has none. And of two men, he who fills himself with meat receives in him Vohu Manô much better than he who does not do so; the latter is all but dead; the former is above him by the worth of an Asperena, by the worth of a sheep, by the worth of an ox, by the worth of a man. This man can strive against the onsets of Astô-vîdhôtu; he can strive against the well-darted arrow; he can strive against the winter fiend, with thinnest garment on; he can strive against the wicked tyrant and smite him on the head; he can strive against the ungodly fasting Ashemaogha.

"On the very first time when that deed has been done, without waiting until it is done again, down there the pain for that deed shall be as hard as any in this world: even as if one should cut off the limbs from his perishable body with knives of brass, or still worse; down there the pain for that deed shall be as hard as any in this world: even as if one should nail his perishable body with nails of brass, or still worse; down there the pain for that deed shall be as hard as any in this world: even as if one should by force throw his perishable body headlong down a precipice a hundred times the height of a man, or still worse; down there the pain for that deed shall be as hard as any in this world: even as if one should by force impale his perishable body, or still worse; down there the pain for this deed shall be as hard as any in this world: to-wit, the deed of a man, who, knowingly lying, confronts the brimstoned, golden, truth-knowing water with an appeal unto Rashnu and a lie unto Mithra."

O Maker of the material world, thou Holy One! He who, knowingly lying, confronts the brimstoned, golden, truth-knowing water with an appeal unto Rashnu and a lie unto Mithra, what is the penalty that he shall pay?

Ahura Mazda answered:—

"Seven hundred stripes with the Aspahê-astra, seven hundred stripes with the Sraoshô-karana."

UNCLEANNESS*

O Maker of the material world, thou Holy One! Here is a man watering a corn-field. The water streams down the field; it streams again; it streams a third time; and the fourth time, a dog, a fox, or a wolf carries some Nasu into the bed of the stream: what is the penalty that this man shall pay?

Ahura Mazda answered:—

"There is no sin upon a man for any Nasu that has been brought by dogs, by birds, by wolves, by winds, or by flies. For were there sin upon a man for any Nasu that might have been brought by dogs, by birds, by wolves, by winds, or by flies, how soon all this material world of mine would be only one Peshôtanu, bent on the destruction of righteousness, and whose soul will cry and wail! so numberless are the beings that die upon the face of the earth."

O Maker of the material world, thou Holy One! Does water kill?

Ahura Mazda answered:—

"Water kills no man: Astô-vîdhôtu binds him, and, thus bound, Vayu carries him off; and the flood takes him up, the flood takes him down, the flood throws him ashore; then birds feed upon him. When he goes away, it is by the will of Fate he goes."

* This chapter deals chiefly with uncleanness arising from the dead, and with the means of removing it from men and things.

O Maker of the material world, thou Holy One! Does fire kill?

Ahura Mazda answered:—

"Fire kills no man: Astô-vidhôtu binds him, and, thus bound, Vayu carries him off; and the fire burns up life and limb. When he goes away, it is by the will of Fate he goes."

O Maker of the material world, thou Holy One! If the summer is past and the winter has come, what shall the worshippers of Mazda do?

Ahura Mazda answered:—

"In every house, in every borough, they shall raise three rooms for the dead."

O Maker of the material world, thou Holy One! How large shall be those rooms for the dead?

Ahura Mazda answered:—

"Large enough not to strike the skull of the man, if he should stand erect, or his feet or his hands stretched out: such shall be, according to the law, the rooms for the dead. And they shall let the lifeless body lie there, for two nights, or for three nights, or a month long, until the birds begin to fly, the plants to grow, the hidden floods to flow, and the wind to dry up the earth. And as soon as the birds begin to fly, the plants to grow, the hidden floods to flow, and the wind to dry up the earth, then the worshippers of Mazda shall lay down the dead on the Dakhma, his eyes towards the sun. If the worshippers of Mazda have not, within a year, laid down the dead on the Dakhma, his eyes towards the sun, thou shalt prescribe for that trespass the same penalty as for the murder of one of the faithful; until the corpse has been rained on, until the Dakhma has been rained on, until the unclean remains have been rained on, until the birds have eaten up the corpse."

O Maker of the material world, thou Holy One! Is it true that thou, Ahura Mazda, seizest the waters from the sea Vourukasha with the wind and the clouds? That thou, Ahura Mazda, takest them down to the corpses? that thou, Ahura Mazda, takest them down to the Dakhmas? that thou, Ahura Mazda, takest them down to the unclean remains? that thou, Ahura Mazda, takest them down to the bones? and that then thou, Ahura Mazda, makest them flow back unseen? that thou, Ahura Mazda, makest them flow back to the sea Pûitika?

Ahura Mazda answered:—

"It is even so as thou hast said, O righteous Zarathustra! I, Ahura Mazda, seize the waters from the sea Vouru-kasha with the wind and the clouds. I, Ahura Mazda, take them to the corpses; I, Ahura Mazda, take them down to the Dakhmas; I, Ahura Mazda, take them down to the unclean remains; I, Ahura Mazda, take them down to the bones; then I, Ahura Mazda, make them flow back unseen; I, Ahura Mazda, make them flow back to the sea Pûitika. The waters stand there boiling, boiling up in the heart of the sea Pûitika, and, when cleansed there, they run back again from the sea Pûitika to the sea Vouru-kasha, towards the well-watered tree, whereon grow the seeds of my plants of every kind by hundreds, by thousands, by hundreds of thousands. Those plants, I, Ahura Mazda, rain down upon the earth, to bring food to the faithful, and fodder to the beneficent cow; to bring food to my people that they may live on it, and fodder to the beneficent cow.

"This is the best, this is the fairest of all things, even as thou hast said, O pure Zarathustra!"

With these words the holy Ahura Mazda rejoiced the holy Zarathustra: "Purity is for man, next to life, the greatest good, that purity, O Zarathustra, that is in the Religion of Mazda for him who cleanses his own self with good thoughts, words, and deeds."

O Maker of the material world, thou Holy One! This Law, this fiend-destroying Law of Zarathustra, by what greatness, goodness, and fairness is it great, good, and fair above all other utterances?

Ahura Mazda answered:—

"As much above all other floods as is the sea Vouru-kasha, so much above all other utterances in greatness, goodness, and fairness is this Law, this fiend-destroying Law of Zarathustra. As much as a great stream flows swifter than a slender rivulet, so much above all other utterances in greatness, goodness, and fairness is this Law, this fiend-destroying Law of Zarathustra. As high as the great tree stands above the small plants it overshadows, so high above all other utterances in greatness, goodness, and fairness is this Law, this fiend-destroying Law of Zarathustra. As high as heaven is above the earth that it compasses around, so high above all other utterances is this Law, this fiend-destroying Law of Mazda.

Therefore, he will apply to the Ratu, he will apply to the Sraoshâ-varez; whether for a draona-service that should have been undertaken and has not been undertaken; or for a draona that should have been offered up and has not been offered up; or for a draona that should have been intrusted and has not been intrusted. The Ratu has power to remit him one-third of his penalty; if he has committed any other evil deed, it is remitted by his repentance; if he has committed no other evil deed, he is absolved by his repentance forever and ever."

How long shall the piece of ground lie fallow whereon dogs or men have died?

Ahura Mazda answered:—

"A year long shall the piece of ground lie fallow whereon dogs or men have died, O holy Zarathustra! A year long shall no worshipper of Mazda sow or water that piece of ground whereon dogs or men have died; he may sow as he likes the rest of the ground; he may water it as he likes. If within the year they shall sow or water the piece of ground whereon dogs or men have died, they are guilty of the sin of 'burying the dead' towards the water, towards the earth, and towards the plants."

O Maker of the material world, thou Holy One! If worshippers of Mazda shall sow or water, within the year, the piece of ground whereon dogs or men have died, what is the penalty that they shall pay?

Ahura Mazda answered:—

"They are Peshôtanus: two hundred stripes with the Aspahê-astra, two hundred stripes with the Sraoshô-karana."

O Maker of the material world, thou Holy One! If worshippers of Mazda want to till that piece of ground again, to water it, to sow it, and to plough it, what shall they do?

Ahura Mazda answered:—

"They shall look on the ground for any bones, hair, dung, urine, or blood that may be there."

O Maker of the material world, thou Holy One! If they shall not look on the ground for any bones, hair, dung, urine, or blood that may be there, what is the penalty that they shall pay?

Ahura Mazda answered:—

"They are Peshôtanus: two hundred stripes with the Aspahê-astra, two hundred stripes with the Sraoshô-karana."

O Maker of the material world, thou Holy One! If a man shall throw on the ground a bone of a dead dog, or of a dead man, as large as the top joint of the little finger, and if grease or marrow flow from it on to the ground, what penalty shall he pay?

Ahura Mazda answered:—

"Thirty stripes with the Aspahê-astra, thirty stripes with the Sraoshô-karana."

O Maker of the material world, thou Holy One! If a man shall throw on the ground a bone of a dead dog, or of a dead man, as large as the top joint of the fore-finger, and if grease or marrow flow from it on to the ground, what penalty shall he pay?

Ahura Mazda answered:—

"Fifty stripes with the Aspahê-astra, fifty stripes with the Sraoshô-karana."

O Maker of the material world, thou Holy One! If a man shall throw on the ground a bone of a dead dog, or of a dead man, as large as the top joint of the middle finger, and if grease or marrow flow from it on to the ground, what penalty shall he pay?

Ahura Mazda answered:—

"Seventy stripes with the Aspahê-astra, seventy stripes with the Sraoshô-karana."

O Maker of the material world, thou Holy One! If a man shall throw on the ground a bone of a dead dog, or of a dead man, as large as a finger or as a rib, and if grease or marrow flow from it on to the ground, what penalty shall he pay?

Ahura Mazda answered:—

"Ninety stripes with the Aspahê-astra, ninety stripes with the Sraoshô-karana."

O Maker of the material world, thou Holy One! If a man shall throw on the ground a bone of a dead dog, or of a dead man, as large as two fingers or as two ribs, and if grease or marrow flow from it on to the ground, what penalty shall he pay?

Ahura Mazda answered:—

"He is a Peshôtanu: two hundred stripes with the Aspahê-astra, two hundred stripes with the Sraoshô-karana."

O Maker of the material world, thou Holy One! If a man shall throw on the ground a bone of a dead dog, or of a dead man, as large as an arm-bone or as a thigh-bone, and if grease or marrow flow from it on to the ground, what penalty shall he pay?

Ahura Mazda answered:—

"Four hundred stripes with the Aspahê-astra, four hundred stripes with the Sraoshô-karana."

O Maker of the material world, thou Holy One! If a man shall throw on the ground a bone of a dead dog, or of a dead man, as large as a man's skull, and if grease or marrow flow from it on to the ground, what penalty shall he pay?

Ahura Mazda answered:—

"Six hundred stripes with the Aspahê-astra, six hundred stripes with the Sraoshô-karana."

O Maker of the material world, thou Holy One! If a man shall throw on the ground the whole body of a dead dog, or of a dead man, and if grease or marrow flow from it on to the ground, what penalty shall he pay?

Ahura Mazda answered:—

"A thousand stripes with the Aspahê-astra, a thousand stripes with the Sraoshô-karana."

O Maker of the material world, thou Holy One! If a worshipper of Mazda, walking, or running, or riding, or driving, come upon a corpse in a stream of running water, what shall he do?

Ahura Mazda answered:—

"Taking off his shoes, putting off his clothes, while the others wait, O Zarathustra! he shall enter the river, and take the dead out of the water; he shall go down into the water ankle-deep, knee-deep, waist-deep, or a man's full depth, till he can reach the dead body."

O Maker of the material world, thou Holy One! If, however, the body be already falling to pieces and rotting, what shall the worshipper of Mazda do?

Ahura Mazda answered:—

"He shall draw out of the water as much of the corpse as he can grasp with both hands, and he shall lay it down on the dry ground; no sin attaches to him for any bone, hair, grease, dung, urine, or blood, that may drop back into the water."

O Maker of the material world, thou Holy One! What part of the water in a pond does the Drug Nasu defile with corruption, infection, and pollution?

Ahura Mazda answered:—

"Six steps on each of the four sides. As long as the corpse has not been taken out of the water, so long shall that water be unclean and unfit to drink. They shall, therefore, take the corpse out of the pond, and lay it down on the dry ground. And of the water they shall draw off the half, or the third, or the fourth, or the fifth part, according as they are able or not; and after the corpse has been taken out and the water has been drawn off, the rest of the water is clean, and both cattle and men may drink of it at their pleasure, as before."

O Maker of the material world, thou Holy One! What part of the water in a well does the Drug Nasu defile with corruption, infection, and pollution?

Ahura Mazda answered:—

"As long as the corpse has not been taken out of the water, so long shall that water be unclean and unfit to drink. They shall, therefore, take the corpse out of the well, and lay it down on the dry ground. And of the water in the well they shall draw off the half, or the third, or the fourth, or the fifth part, according as they are able or not; and after the corpse has been taken out and the water has been drawn off, the rest of the water is clean, and both cattle and men may drink of it at their pleasure, as before."

O Maker of the material world, thou Holy One! What part of a sheet of snow or hail does the Drug Nasu defile with corruption, infection, and pollution?

Ahura Mazda answered:—

"Three steps on each of the four sides. As long as the corpse has not been taken out of the water, so long shall that water be unclean and unfit to drink. They shall, therefore, take the corpse out of the water, and lay it down on the dry ground. After the corpse has been taken out, and the snow or the hail has melted, the water is clean, and both cattle and men may drink of it at their pleasure, as before."

O Maker of the material world, thou Holy One! What part of the water of a running stream does the Drug Nasu defile with corruption, infection, and pollution?

Ahura Mazda answered:—

"Three steps down the stream, nine steps up the stream, six steps across. As long as the corpse has not been taken out of the water, so long shall the water be unclean and unfit to drink. They shall, therefore, take the corpse out of the water, and lay it down on the dry ground. After the corpse has been taken out and the stream has flowed three times, the water is clean, and both cattle and men may drink of it at their pleasure, as before."

O Maker of the material world, thou Holy One! Can the Haoma that has been touched with Nasu from a dead dog, or from a dead man, be made clean again?

Ahura Mazda answered:—

"It can, O holy Zarathustra! If it has been prepared for the sacrifice, there is to it no corruption, no death, no touch of any Nasu. If it has not been prepared for the sacrifice, the stem is defiled the length of four fingers: it shall be laid down on the ground, in the middle of the house, for a year long. When the year is past, the faithful may drink of its juice at their pleasure, as before."

O Maker of the material world, thou Holy One! Whither shall we bring, where shall we lay the bodies of the dead, O Ahura Mazda?

Ahura Mazda answered:—

"On the highest summits, where they know there are always corpse-eating dogs and corpse-eating birds, O holy Zarathustra! There shall the worshippers of Mazda fasten the corpse, by the feet and by the hair, with brass, stones, or clay, lest the corpse-eating dogs and the corpse-eating birds shall go and carry the bones to the water and to the trees."

If they shall not fasten the corpse, so that the corpse-eating dogs and the corpse-eating birds may go and carry the bones to the water and to the trees, what is the penalty that they shall pay?

Ahura Mazda answered:—

"They shall be Peshôtanus: two hundred stripes with the Aspahê-astra, two hundred stripes with the Sraoshô-karana."

O Maker of the material world, thou Holy One! Whither shall we bring, where shall we lay the bones of the dead, O Ahura Mazda?

Ahura Mazda answered:—

"The worshippers of Mazda shall make a receptacle out of the reach of the dog, of the fox, and of the wolf, and wherein rain-water cannot stay. They shall make it, if they can afford it, with stones, plaster, or earth; if they cannot afford it, they shall lay down the dead man on the ground, on his carpet and his pillow, clothed with the light of heaven, and beholding the sun."

FUNERALS AND PURIFICATION

If a dog or a man die under a hut of wood or a hut of felt, what shall the worshippers of Mazda do?

Ahura Mazda answered:—

"They shall search for a Dakhma, they shall look for a Dakhma all around. If they find it easier to remove the dead, they shall take out the dead, they shall let the house stand, and shall perfume it with Urvâsna or Vohû-gaona, or Vohû-kereti, or Hadhâ-naêpata, or any other sweet-smelling plant. If they find it easier to remove the house, they shall take away the house, they shall let the dead lie on the spot, and shall perfume the house with Urvâsna, or Vohû-gaona, or Vohû-kereti, or Hadhâ-naêpata, or any other sweet-smelling plant."

O Maker of the material world, thou Holy One! If in the house of a worshipper of Mazda a dog or a man happens to die, and it is raining, or snowing, or blowing, or it is dark, or the day is at its end, when flocks and men lose their way, what shall the worshippers of Mazda do?

Ahura Mazda answered:—

"The place in that house whereof the ground is the cleanest and the driest, and the least passed through by flocks and herds, by the fire of Ahura Mazda, by the consecrated bundles of Baresma, and by the faithful."

O Maker of the material world, thou Holy One! How far from the fire? How far from the water? How far from the consecrated bundles of Baresma? How far from the faithful?

Ahura Mazda answered:—

"Thirty paces from the fire; thirty paces from the water; thirty paces from the consecrated bundles of Baresma; three paces from the faithful;—on that place they shall dig a grave, half a foot deep if the earth be hard, half the height of a man if it be soft; they shall cover the surface of the grave with ashes or cow-dung; they shall cover the surface of it with dust of bricks, of stones, or of dry earth. And they shall let the lifeless body lie there, for two nights, or three nights, or a month long, until the birds begin to fly, the plants to grow, the hidden floods to flow, and the wind to dry up the earth. And when the birds begin to fly, the plants to grow, the hidden floods to flow, and the wind to dry up the earth, then the worshippers of Mazda shall make a breach in the wall of the house, and two men, strong and skilful, having stripped their clothes off, shall take up the body from the clay or the stones, or from the plastered house, and they shall lay it down on a place where they know there are always corpse-eating dogs and corpse-eating birds. Afterwards the corpse-bearers shall sit down, three paces from the dead, and the holy Ratu shall proclaim to the worshippers of Mazda thus: 'Worshippers of Mazda, let the urine be brought here wherewith the corpse-bearers there shall wash their hair and their bodies.'"

O Maker of the material world, thou Holy One! Which is the urine wherewith the corpse-bearers shall wash their hair and their bodies? Is it of sheep or of oxen? Is it of man or of woman?

Ahura Mazda answered:—

"It is of sheep or of oxen; not of man nor of woman, except a man or a woman who has married the next-of-kin: these shall therefore procure the urine wherewith the corpse-bearers shall wash their hair and their bodies."

O Maker of the material world, thou Holy One! Can the way, whereon the carcasses of dogs or corpses of men have been carried, be passed through again by flocks and herds, by men and women, by the fire of Ahura Mazda, by the consecrated bundles of Baresma, and by the faithful?

Ahura Mazda answered:—

"It cannot be passed through again by flocks and herds, nor by men and women, nor by the fire of Ahura Mazda, nor by the consecrated bundles of Baresma, nor by the faithful. They shall therefore cause a yellow dog with four eyes,* or a white dog with yellow ears, to go three times through that way. When either the yellow dog with four eyes, or the white dog with yellow ears, is brought there, then the Drug Nasu flies away to the regions of the north, in the shape of a raging fly, with knees and tail sticking out, droning without end, and like unto the foulest Khrafstras. If the dog goes unwillingly, O Spitama Zarathustra, they shall cause the yellow dog with four

* A dog with two spots above the eyes.

eyes, or the white dog with yellow ears, to go six times through that way. When either the yellow dog with four eyes, or the white dog with yellow ears, is brought there, then the Drug Nasu flies away to the regions of the north, in the shape of a raging fly, with knees and tail sticking out, droning without end, and like unto the foulest Khrafstras. If the dog goes unwillingly, they shall cause the yellow dog with four eyes, or the white dog with yellow ears, to go nine times through that way. When either the yellow dog with four eyes, or the white dog with yellow ears, has been brought there, then the Drug Nasu flies away to the regions of the north, in the shape of a raging fly, with knees and tail sticking out, droning without end, and like unto the foulest Khrafstras. An Âthravan shall first go along the way and shall say aloud these victorious words: 'Yathâ ahû vairyô:—The will of the Lord is the law of righteousness. The gifts of Vohu-manô to the deeds done in this world for Mazda. He who relieves the poor makes Ahura king. What protector hast thou given unto me, O Mazda! while the hate of the wicked encompasses me? Whom but thy Âtar and Vohu-manô, through whose work I keep on the world of righteousness? Reveal therefore to me thy Religion as thy rule! Who is the victorious who will protect thy teaching? Make it clear that I am the guide for both worlds. May Sraosha come with Vohu-manô and help whomsoever thou pleasest, O Mazda! Keep us from our hater, O Mazda and Spenta Ârmaiti! Perish, O fiendish Drug! Perish, O brood of the fiend! Perish, O creation of the fiend! Perish, O world of the fiend! Perish away, O Drug! Rush away, O Drug! Perish away, O Drug! Perish away to the regions of the north, never more to give unto death the living world of Righteousness!' Then the worshippers of Mazda may at their will bring by those ways sheep and oxen, men and women, and Fire, the son of Ahura Mazda, the consecrated bundles of Baresma, and the faithful. The worshippers of Mazda may afterwards prepare meals with meat and wine in that house; it shall be clean, and there will be no sin, as before."

O Maker of the material world, thou Holy One! If a man shall throw clothes, either of skin or woven, upon a dead body, enough to cover the feet, what is the penalty that he shall pay?

Ahura Mazda answered:—

"Four hundred stripes with the Aspahê-astra, four hundred stripes with the Sraoshô-karana."

O Maker of the material world, thou Holy One! If a man shall throw clothes, either of skin or woven, upon a dead body, enough to cover both legs, what is the penalty that he shall pay?

Ahura Mazda answered:—

"Six hundred stripes with the Aspahê-astra, six hundred stripes with the Sraoshô-karana."

O Maker of the material world, thou Holy One! If a man shall throw clothes, either of skin or woven, upon a dead body, enough to cover the whole body, what is the penalty that he shall pay?

Ahura Mazda answered:—

"A thousand stripes with the Aspahê-astra, a thousand stripes with the Sraoshô-karana."

O Maker of the material world, thou Holy One! If a man, by force, commits the unnatural sin, what is the penalty that he shall pay?

Ahura Mazda answered:—

"Eight hundred stripes with the Aspahê-astra, eight hundred stripes with the Sraoshô-karana."

O Maker of the material world, thou Holy One! If a man voluntarily commits the unnatural sin, what is the penalty for it? What is the atonement for it? What is the cleansing from it?

Ahura Mazda answered:—

"For that deed there is nothing that can pay, nothing that can atone, nothing that can cleanse from it; it is a trespass for which there is no atonement, forever and ever."

O Maker of the material world, thou Holy One! Who is the man that is a Deva? Who is he that is a worshipper of the Devas? that is a male paramour of the Devas? that is a female paramour of the Devas? that is a wife to the Deva? that is as bad as a Deva? that is in his whole being a Deva? Who is he that is a Deva before he dies, and becomes one of the unseen Devas after death?

Ahura Mazda answered:—

"The man that lies with mankind as man lies with womankind, or as woman lies with mankind, is the man that is a Deva;

this one is the man that is a worshipper of the Devas, that is a male paramour of the Devas, that is a female paramour of the Devas, that is a wife to the Deva; this is the man that is as bad as a Deva, that is in his whole being a Deva; this is the man that is a Deva before he dies, and becomes one of the unseen Devas after death: so is he, whether he has lain with mankind as mankind, or as womankind."

O Maker of the material world, thou Holy One! Shall the man be clean who has touched a corpse that has been dried up and dead more than a year?

Ahura Mazda answered:—

"He shall. The dry mingles not with the dry. Should the dry mingle with the dry, how soon all this material world of mine would be only one Peshôtanu, bent on the destruction of righteousness, and whose soul will cry and wail! so numberless are the beings that die upon the face of the earth."

CLEANSING THE UNCLEAN

Zarathustra asked Ahura Mazda:—

O most beneficent Spirit, Maker of the material world, thou Holy One! To whom shall they apply here below, who want to cleanse their body defiled by the dead?

Ahura Mazda answered:—

"To a pious man, O Spitama Zarathustra! who knows how to speak, who speaks truth, who has learned the Holy Word, who is pious, and knows best the rites of cleansing according to the law of Mazda. That man shall fell the trees off the surface of the ground on a space of nine Vîbâzus square; in that part of the ground where there is least water and where there are fewest trees, the part which is the cleanest and driest, and the least passed through by sheep and oxen, and by the fire of Ahura Mazda, by the consecrated bundles of Baresma, and by the faithful."

How far from the fire? How far from the water? How far from the consecrated bundles of Baresma? How far from the faithful?

Ahura Mazda answered:—

"Thirty paces from the fire, thirty paces from the water, thirty paces from the consecrated bundles of Baresma, three paces from the faithful. Then thou shalt dig a hole, two fingers deep if the summer has come, four fingers deep if the winter and ice have come." How far from one another? "One pace." How much is the pace? "As much as three feet. Then thou shalt dig three holes more, two fingers deep if the summer has come, four fingers deep if the winter and ice have come." How far from the former six? "Three paces." What sort of paces? "Such as are taken in walking." How much are those three paces? "As much as nine feet. Then thou shalt draw a furrow all around with a metal knife. Then thou shalt draw twelve furrows; three of which thou shalt draw to surround and divide from the rest the first three holes; three thou shalt draw to surround and divide the first six holes; three thou shalt draw to surround and divide the nine holes; three thou shalt draw around the three inferior holes, outside the six other holes. At each of the three times nine feet, thou shalt place stones as steps to the holes; or potsherds, or stumps, or clods, or any hard matter. Then the man defiled shall walk to the holes; thou, O Zarathustra! shalt stand outside by the furrow, and thou shalt recite, 'Nemaskâ yâ ârmaitis izâkâ'; and the man defiled shall repeat, 'Nemaskâ yâ ârmaitis izâkâ.' The Drug becomes weaker and weaker at every one of those words which are a weapon to smite the fiend Angra Mainyu, to smite Aêshma of the murderous spear, to smite the Mâzainya fiends, to smite all the fiends. Then thou shalt take for the gômêz a spoon of brass or of lead. When thou takest a stick with nine knots, O Spitama Zarathustra! to sprinkle the gômêz from that spoon, thou shalt fasten the spoon to the end of the stick. They shall wash his hands first. If his hands be not washed first, he makes his whole body unclean. When he has washed his hands three times, after his hands have been washed, thou shalt sprinkle the forepart of his skull; then the Drug Nasu rushes in front, between his brows. Thou shalt sprinkle him in front between the brows; then the Drug Nasu rushes upon the back part of the skull. Thou shalt sprinkle the back part of the skull; then the Drug Nasu rushes upon the jaws. Thou shalt sprinkle the jaws; then the Drug Nasu rushes upon the right ear. Thou shalt sprinkle the right ear; then the Drug Nasu rushes upon the left ear. Thou shalt sprinkle the left ear; then the Drug Nasu rushes upon the right shoulder. Thou shalt sprinkle the right shoulder; then the Drug Nasu rushes upon the left shoulder. Thou shalt sprinkle the left shoulder; then the Drug Nasu rushes upon the right arm-pit. Thou shalt sprinkle the right arm-pit; then the Drug Nasu rushes upon the left arm-pit. Thou shalt sprinkle the left arm-pit; then the Drug Nasu rushes upon the chest. Thou shalt sprinkle the chest; then the Drug Nasu rushes upon the back. Thou shalt sprinkle the back; then the Drug Nasu rushes upon the right nipple. Thou shalt sprinkle the right nipple; then the Drug Nasu rushes upon the left nipple. Thou shalt sprinkle the left nipple; then the Drug Nasu rushes upon the right rib. Thou shalt sprinkle the right rib; then the Drug Nasu rushes upon the left rib. Thou shalt sprinkle the left rib; then the Drug Nasu rushes upon the right hip. Thou shalt sprinkle the right hip; then the Drug Nasu rushes upon the left hip. Thou shalt sprinkle the left hip; then the Drug Nasu rushes upon the sexual parts. Thou shalt sprinkle the sexual parts. If the unclean one be a man, thou shalt sprinkle him first behind, then before; if the unclean one be a woman, thou shalt sprinkle her first before, then behind; then the Drug Nasu rushes upon the right thigh. Thou shalt sprinkle the right thigh; then the Drug Nasu rushes upon the left thigh. Thou shalt sprinkle the left thigh; then the Drug Nasu rushes upon the right knee. Thou shalt sprinkle the right knee; then the Drug Nasu rushes upon the left knee. Thou shalt sprinkle the left knee; then the Drug Nasu rushes upon the right leg. Thou shalt sprinkle the right leg; then the Drug Nasu rushes upon the left leg. Thou shalt sprinkle the left leg; then the Drug Nasu rushes upon the right ankle. Thou shalt sprinkle the right ankle; then the Drug Nasu rushes upon the left ankle. Thou shalt sprinkle the left ankle; then the Drug Nasu rushes upon the right instep. Thou shalt sprinkle the right instep; then the Drug Nasu rushes upon the left instep. Thou shalt sprinkle the left instep; then the Drug Nasu turns round under the sole of the foot; it looks like the wing of a fly. He shall press his toes upon the ground and shall raise up his heels; thou shalt sprinkle his right sole; then the Drug Nasu rushes upon the left sole. Thou shalt sprinkle the left sole; then the Drug Nasu turns round under the toes; it looks like the wing of a fly. He shall press his heels upon the ground and shall raise up his toes; thou shalt sprinkle his right toe; then the Drug Nasu rushes upon the left toe. Thou shalt sprinkle the left toe; then the Drug Nasu flies away to the regions of the north, in the shape of a raging fly, with knees and tail sticking out, droning without end, and like unto the foulest Khrafstras. And thou shalt say these victorious, most healing words: 'The will of the Lord is the law of righteousness. The gifts of Vohu-manô to deeds done in this world for Mazda. He who relieves the poor makes Ahura king. What protector hadst thou given unto me, O Mazda! while the hate of the wicked encompasses me? Whom, but thy Âtar and Vohu-manô, through whose work I keep on the world of Righteousness? Reveal therefore to me thy Religion as thy rule! Who is the victorious who will protect thy teaching? Make it clear that I am the guide for both worlds. May Sraosha come with Vohu-manô and help whomsoever thou pleasest, O Mazda! Keep us from our hater, O Mazda and Spenta Ârmaiti! Perish, O fiendish Drug! Perish, O brood of the fiend! Perish, O world of the fiend! Perish away, O Drug! Rush away, O Drug! Perish away, O Drug! Perish away to the regions of the north, never more to give unto death the living world of Righteousness.'

"Afterwards the man defiled shall sit down, inside the furrows, outside the furrows of the six holes, four fingers from those furrows. There he shall cleanse his body with thick handfuls of dust. Fifteen times shall they take up dust from the ground for him to rub his body, and they shall wait there until he is dry even to the last hair on his head. When his body is dry with dust, then he shall step over the holes containing water. At the first hole he shall wash his body once with water; at the second hole he shall wash his body twice with water; at the third hole he shall wash his body thrice with water. Then he shall perfume his body with Urvâsna, or Vohû-gaona, or Vohû-kereti, or Hadhâ-naêpata, or any other sweet-smelling plant; then he shall put on his clothes, and shall go back to his house. He shall sit down there in the place of infirmity, inside the house, apart from the other worshippers of Mazda. He shall not go near the fire, nor near the water, nor near the earth, nor near the cow, nor near the trees, nor near the faithful, either man or woman. Thus shall he continue until three nights have passed. When three nights have passed, he shall wash his body, he shall wash his clothes with gômêz and water to make them clean. Then he shall sit down again in the place of infirmity, inside the house, apart from the other worshippers of Mazda. He shall not go near the fire, nor near the water, nor near the earth, nor near the cow, nor near the trees, nor near the faithful, either man or woman. Thus shall he continue until six nights have passed. When six nights have passed, he shall wash his body, he shall wash his clothes with gômêz and water to make them clean. Then he shall sit down again in the place of infirmity, inside the house, apart from the other worshippers of Mazda. He shall not go near the fire, nor near the water, nor near the earth, nor near the cow, nor near the trees, nor near the faithful, either man or woman. Thus shall he continue, until nine nights have passed. When nine nights have passed, he shall wash his body, he shall wash his clothes with gômêz and water to make them clean. He may thenceforth go near the fire, near the water, near the earth, near the cow, near the trees, and near the faithful, either man or woman.

"Thou shalt cleanse a priest for a blessing of the just. Thou shalt cleanse the lord of a province for the value of a camel of high value. Thou shalt cleanse the lord of a town for the value of a stallion of high value. Thou shalt cleanse the lord of a borough for the value of a bull of high value. Thou shalt cleanse the master of a house for the value of a cow three years old. Thou shalt cleanse the wife of the master of a house for the value of a ploughing cow. Thou shalt cleanse a menial for the value of a draught cow. Thou shalt cleanse a young child for the value of a lamb. These are the heads of cattle—flocks or herds—that the worshippers of Mazda shall give to the man who has cleansed them, if they can afford it; if they cannot afford it, they shall give him any other value that may make him leave their houses well pleased with them, and free from anger. For if the man who has cleansed them leave their houses displeased with them, and full of anger, then the Drug Nasu enters them from the nose of the dead, from the eyes, from the tongue, from the jaws, from the sexual organs, from the hinder parts. And the Drug Nasu rushes upon them even to the end of the nails, and they are unclean thenceforth forever and ever. It grieves the sun indeed, O Spitama Zarathustra! to shine upon a man defiled by the dead; it grieves the moon, it grieves the stars. That man delights them, O Spitama Zarathustra! who cleanses from the Nasu the man defiled by the dead; he delights the fire, he delights the water, he delights the earth, he delights the cow, he delights the trees, he delights the faithful, both men and women."

Zarathustra asked Ahura Mazda:—

O Maker of the material world, thou Holy One! What shall be his reward, after his soul has parted from his body, who has cleansed from the Nasu the man defiled by the dead?

Ahura Mazda answered:—

"The welfare of Paradise thou canst promise to that man, for his reward in the other world."

Zarathustra asked Ahura Mazda:—

O Maker of the material world, thou Holy One! How shall I fight against that Drug who from the dead rushes upon the living? How shall I fight against that Nasu who from the dead defiles the living?

Ahura Mazda answered:—

"Say aloud those words in the Gâthas that are to be said twice. Say aloud those words in the Gâthas that are to be said thrice. Say aloud those words in the Gâthas that are to be said four times. And the Drug shall fly away like the well-darted arrow, like the felt of last year, like the annual garment of the earth."

O Maker of the material world, thou Holy One! If a man who does not know the rites of cleansing according to the law of Mazda, offers to cleanse the unclean, how shall I then fight against that Drug who from the dead rushes upon the living? How shall I fight against that Drug who from the dead defiles the living?"

Ahura Mazda answered:—

"Then, O Spitama Zarathustra! the Drug Nasu appears to wax stronger than she was before. Stronger then are sickness and death and the working of the fiend than they were before."

O Maker of the material world, thou Holy One! What is the penalty that he shall pay?

Ahura Mazda answered:—

"The worshippers of Mazda shall bind him; they shall bind his hands first; then they shall strip him of his clothes, they shall cut the head off his neck, and they shall give over his corpse unto the greediest of the corpse-eating creatures made by the beneficent Spirit, unto the vultures, with these words: 'The man here has repented of all his evil thoughts, words, and deeds. If he has committed any other evil deed, it is remitted by his repentance; if he has committed no other evil deed, he is absolved by his repentance forever and ever.'"

Who is he, O Ahura Mazda! who threatens to take away fulness and increase from the world, and to bring in sickness and death?

Ahura Mazda answered:—

"It is the ungodly Ashemaogha, O Spitama Zarathustra! who in this material world cleanses the unclean without knowing the rites of cleansing according to the law of Mazda. For until then, O Spitama Zarathustra! sweetness and fatness would flow out from that land and from those fields, with health and healing, with fulness and increase and growth, and a growing of corn and grass."

O Maker of the material world, thou Holy One! When are sweetness and fatness to come back again to that land and to those fields, with health and healing, with fulness and increase and growth, and a growing of corn and grass?

Ahura Mazda answered:—

"Sweetness and fatness will never come back again to that land and to those fields, with health and healing, with fulness and increase and growth, and a growing of corn and grass, until that ungodly Ashemaogha has been smitten to death on the spot, and the holy Sraosha of that place has been offered up a sacrifice for three days and three nights, with fire blazing, with Baresma tied up, and with Haoma prepared. Then sweetness and fatness will come back again to that land and to those fields, with health and healing, with fulness and increase and growth, and a growing of corn and grass."

SPELLS RECITED DURING THE CLEANSING

Zarathustra asked Ahura Mazda:—

O Ahura Mazda! most beneficent Spirit, maker of the material world, thou Holy One! How shall I fight against that Drug who from the dead rushes upon the living? How shall I fight against that Drug who from the dead defiles the living?

Ahura Mazda answered:—

"Say aloud those words in the Gâthas that are to be said twice. 'I drive away Angra Mainyu from this house, from this borough, from this town, from this land; from the very body of the man defiled by the dead, from the very body of the woman defiled by the dead; from the master of the house, from the lord of the borough, from the lord of the town, from the lord of the land; from the whole of the world of Righteousness. I drive away the Nasu, I drive away direct defilement, I drive away indirect defilement, from this house, from this borough, from this town, from this land; from the very body of the man defiled by the dead, from the very body of the woman defiled by the dead; from the master of the house, from the lord of the borough, from the lord of the town, from the lord of the land; from the whole of the world of Righteousness.'"

O Maker of the material world, thou Holy One! Which are those words in the Gâthas that are to be said thrice?

Ahura Mazda answered:—

"'I drive away Indra, I drive away Sauru, I drive away the Deva Naunghaithya from this house, from this borough, from this town, from this land; from the very body of the man defiled by the dead, from the very body of the woman defiled by the dead; from the master of the house, from the lord of the borough, from the lord of the town, from the lord of the land; from the whole of the world of Righteousness. I drive away Tauru, I drive away Zairi, from this house, from this borough, from this town, from this land; from the very body of the man defiled by the dead, from the very body of the woman defiled by the dead; from the master of the house, from the lord of the borough, from the lord of the town, from the lord of the land; from the whole of the holy world.' "

O Maker of the material world, thou Holy One! Which are those words in the Gâthas that are to be said four times?

Ahura Mazda answered:—

" These are the words in the Gâthas that are to be said four times, and thou shalt four times say them aloud: 'I drive away Aêshma, the fiend of the murderous spear, I drive away the Deva Akatasha, from this house, from this borough, from this town, from this land; from the very body of the man defiled by the dead, from the very body of the woman defiled by the dead; from the master of the house, from the lord of the borough, from the lord of the town, from the lord of the land; from the whole of the world of Righteousness. I drive away the Varenya Devas, I drive away the Wind-Deva, from this house, from this borough, from this town, from this land; from the very body of the man defiled by the dead, from the very body of the woman defiled by the dead; from the master of the house, from the lord of the borough, from the lord of the town, from the lord of the land; from the whole of the world of Righteousness.' "

TO FIRES, WATERS, PLANTS

We worship thee, the Fire, O Ahura Mazda's son! We worship the fire Berezi-savangha (of the lofty use), and the fire Vohu-fryâna (the good and friendly), and the fire Urvâzista (the most beneficial and most helpful), and the fire Vâzista (the most supporting), and the fire Spenista (the most bountiful), and Nairya-sangha the Yazad of the royal lineage, and that fire which is the house-lord of all houses and Mazda-made, even the son of Ahura Mazda, the holy lord of the ritual order, with all the fires. And we worship the good and best waters Mazda-made, holy, all the waters Mazda-made and holy, and all the plants which Mazda made, and which are holy. And we worship the Māthra-spenta (the bounteous word-of-reason), the Zarathustrian law against the Devas, and its long descent. And we worship Mount Ushidarena which is Mazda-made and shining with its holiness, and all the mountains shining with holiness, and of abundant glory, and which Mazda made. And we worship the good and pious prayer for blessings, and these waters and these lands, and all the greatest chieftains, lords of the ritual order; and I praise, invoke, and glorify the good, heroic, bountiful Fravashis of the saints, those of the house, the Vîs, the Zantuma, the Dahvyuma, and the Zarathustrôtema, and all the holy Yazads!

TO THE EARTH AND THE SACRED WATERS

And now we worship this earth which bears us, together with Thy wives, O Ahura Mazda! yea, those Thy wives do we worship which are so desired from their sanctity. We sacrifice to their zealous wishes, and their capabilities, their inquiries, and their wise acts of pious reverence, and with these their blessedness, their full vigor and good portions, their good fame and ample wealth. O ye waters! now we worship you, you that are showered down, and you that stand in pools and vats, and you that bear forth our loaded vessels, ye female Ahuras of Ahura, you that serve us in helpful ways, well forded and full-flowing, and effective for the bathings, we will seek you and for both the worlds! Therefore did Ahura Mazda give you names, O ye beneficent ones! when He who made the good bestowed you. And by these names we worship you, and by them we would ingratiate ourselves with you, and with them would we bow before you, and direct our prayers to you with free confessions of our debt. O waters, ye who are productive, and ye maternal ones, ye with heat that suckles the frail and needy before birth, ye waters that have once been rulers of us all, we will now address you as the best, and the most bountiful; those are yours, those good objects of our offerings, ye long of arm to reach our sickness, or misfortune, ye mothers of our life!

PRAYER FOR HELPERS

And now in these Thy dispensations, O Ahura Mazda! do Thou wisely act for us, and with abundance with Thy bounty and Thy tenderness as touching us; and grant that reward which Thou hast appointed to our souls, O Ahura Mazda! Of this do Thou Thyself bestow upon us for this world and the spiritual; and now as part thereof do Thou grant that we may attain to fellowship with Thee, and Thy Righteousness for all duration. And do Thou grant us, O Ahura! men who are righteous, and both lovers and producers of the Right as well. And give us trained beasts for the pastures, broken in for riding, and for bearing, that they may be in helpful companionship with us, and as a source of long enduring vigor, and a means of rejoicing grace to us for this. So let there be a kinsman lord for us, with the laborers of the village, and so likewise let there be the clients. And by the help of those may we arise. So may we be to You, O Ahura Mazda! holy and true, and with free giving of our gifts.

A PRAYER FOR SANCTITY AND ITS BENEFITS

I pray with benedictions for a benefit, and for the good, even for the entire creation of the holy and the clean; I beseech for them the generation which is now alive, for that which is just coming into life, and for that which shall be hereafter. And I pray for that sanctity which leads to prosperity, and which has long afforded shelter, which goes on hand in hand with it, which joins it in its walk, and of itself becoming its close companion as it delivers forth its precepts, bearing every form of healing virtue which comes to us in waters, appertains to cattle, or is found in plants, and overwhelming all the harmful malice of the Devas, and their servants who might harm this dwelling and its lord, bringing goods gifts, and better blessings, given very early, and later gifts, leading to successes, and for a long time giving shelter. And so the greatest, and the best, and most beautiful benefits of sanctity fall likewise to our lot for the sacrifice, homage, propitiation, and the praise of the Bountiful Immortals, for the bringing prosperity to this abode, and for the prosperity of the entire creation of the holy, and the clean, and as for this, so for the opposition of the entire evil creation. And I pray for this as I praise through Righteousness, I who am beneficent, those who are likewise of a better mind.

TO THE FIRE

I offer my sacrifice and homage to thee, the Fire, as a good offering, and an offering with our hail of salvation, even as an offering of praise with benedictions, to thee, the Fire, O Ahura Mazda's son! Meet for sacrifice art thou, and worthy of our homage. And as meet for sacrifice, and thus worthy of our homage, mayest thou be in the houses of men who worship Mazda. Salvation be to this man who worships thee in verity and truth, with wood in hand, and Baresma ready, with flesh in hand, and holding too the mortar. And mayest thou be ever fed with wood as the prescription orders. Yea, mayest thou have thy perfume justly, and thy sacred butter without fail, and thine andirons regularly placed. Be of full-age as to thy nourishment, of the canon's age as to the measure of thy food, O Fire, Ahura Mazda's son! Be now aflame within this house; be ever without fail in flame; be all a-shine within this house; be on thy growth within this house; for long time be thou thus to the furtherance of the heroic renovation, to the completion of all progress, yea, even till the good heroic millennial time when that renovation shall have become complete. Give me, O Fire, Ahura Mazda's son! a speedy glory, speedy nourishment, and speedy booty, and abundant glory, abundant nourishment, abundant booty, an expanded mind, and nimbleness of tongue for soul and understanding, even an understanding continually growing in its largeness, and that never wanders, and long enduring virile power, an offspring sure of foot, that never sleeps on watch, and that rises quick from bed, and likewise a wakeful offspring, helpful to nurture, or reclaim, legitimate, keeping order in men's meetings, yea, drawing men to assemblies through their influence and word, grown to power, skilful, redeeming others from oppression, served by many followers, which may advance my line in prosperity and fame, and my Vîs, and my

Bantu, and my province, yea, an offering which may deliver orders to the Province as firm and righteous rulers. And mayest thou grant me, O Fire, Ahura Mazda's Son! that whereby instructors may be given me, now and for evermore, giving light to me of Heaven, the best life of the saints, brilliant, all glorious. And may I have experience of the good reward, and the good renown, and of the long forecasting preparation of the soul. The Fire of Ahura Mazda addresses this admonition to all for whom he cooks the night and morning meal. From all these, O Spitama! he wishes to secure good care, and healthful care as guarding for salvation, the care of a true praiser. At both the hands of all who come by me, I, the Fire, keenly look: What brings the mate to his mate, the one who walks at large, to him who sits at home? We worship the bounteous Fire, the swift-driving charioteer. And if this man who passes brings him wood brought with sacred care, or if he brings the Baresma spread with sanctity, or the Hadhâ-naêpata plant, then afterwards Ahura Mazda's Fire will bless him, contented, not offended, and in its satisfaction saying thus: May a herd of kine be with thee, and a multitude of men, may an active mind go with thee, and an active soul as well. As a blest soul mayest thou live through thy life, the nights which thou shall live. This is the blessing of the Fire for him who brings it wood well dried, sought out for flaming, purified with the earnest blessing of the sacred ritual truth. We strive after the flowing on of the good waters, and their ebb as well, and the sounding of their waves, desiring their propitiation; I desire to approach them with my praise.

TO THE BOUNTIFUL IMMORTALS

I would worship these with my sacrifice, those who rule aright, and who dispose of all aright, and this one especially I would approach with my praise (Ahura Mazda). He is thus hymned in our praise-songs. Yea, we worship in our sacrifice that deity and lord, who is Ahura Mazda, the Creator, the gracious helper, the maker of all good things; and we worship in our sacrifice Spitama Zarathustra, that chieftain of the rite. And we would declare those institutions established for us, exact and undeviating as they are. And I would declare forth those of Ahura Mazda, those of the Good Mind, and of Asha Vahista, and those of Khshatra-vairya, and those of the Bountiful Âramaiti, and those of Weal and Immortality, and those which appertain to the body of the Kine, and to the Kine's soul, and those which appertain to Ahura Mazda's Fire, and those of Sraosha the blessed, and of Rashnu the most just, and those of Mithra of the wide pastures, and of the good and holy Wind, and of the good Mazdayasnian Religion, and of the good and pious Prayer for blessings, and those of the good and pious Prayer which frees one from belying, and the good and pious Prayer for blessing against unbelieving words. And these we would declare in order that we may attain unto that speech which is uttered with true religious zeal, or that we may be as prophets of the provinces, that we may succor him who lifts his voice for Mazda, that we may be as prophets who smite with victory, the befriended of Ahura Mazda, and persons the most useful to him, holy men who think good thoughts, and speak good words, and do good deeds. That he may approach us with the Good Mind, and that our souls may advance in good, let it thus come; yea, "how may my soul advance in good? let it thus advance."

PRAISE OF THE HOLY BULL

Hail, bounteous bull! Hail to thee, beneficent bull! Hail to thee, who makest increase! Hail to thee, who makest growth! Hail to thee, who dost bestow his part upon the righteous faithful, and wilt bestow it on the faithful yet unborn! Hail to thee, whom the Gahi kills, and the ungodly Ashemaogha, and the wicked tyrant.

TO RAIN AS A HEALING POWER

"Come, come on, O clouds, from up above, down on the earth, by thousands of drops, by myriads of drops"—thus say, O holy Zarathustra! "to destroy sickness, to destroy death, to destroy the sickness that kills, to destroy death that kills, to destroy Gadha and Apagadha. If death come after noon, may healing come at eve! If death come at eve, may healing come at night! If death come at night, may healing come at dawn! And showers shower down new water, new earth, new plants, new healing powers, and new healing.

TO THE WATERS AND LIGHT OF THE SUN

"As the sea Vouru-kasha is the gathering place of the waters, rising up and going down, up the aërial way and down the earth, down the earth and up the aërial way: thus rise up and roll along! thou in whose rising and growing Ahura Mazda made the aërial way. Up! rise up and roll along! thou swift-horsed Sun, above Hara Berezaiti, and produce light for the world, and mayest thou, O man! rise up there, if thou art to abide in Garô-nmânem, along the path made by Mazda, along the way made by the gods, the watery way they opened. And the Holy Word shall keep away the evil. Of thee, O child! I will cleanse the birth and growth; of thee, O woman! I will make the body and the strength pure; I make thee rich in children and rich in milk; rich in seed, in milk, in fat, in marrow, and in offspring. I shall bring to thee a thousand pure springs, running towards the pastures that give food to the child."

TO THE WATERS AND LIGHT OF THE MOON

As the sea Vouru-kasha is the gathering place of the waters, rising up and going down, up the aërial way and down the earth, down the earth and up the aërial way: Thus rise up and roll along! thou in whose rising and growing Ahura Mazda made the earth. Up! rise up, thou Moon, that dost keep in thee the seed of the bull; rise up above Hara Berezaiti, and produce light for the world, and mayest thou, O man! rise up there, if thou art to abide in Garô-nmânem, along the path made by Mazda, along the way made by the gods, the watery way they opened. And the Holy Word shall keep away the evil: Of thee, O child! I will cleanse the birth and growth; of thee, O woman! I will make the body and the strength pure; I make thee rich in children and rich in milk; rich in seed, in milk, in fat, in marrow, and in offspring. I shall bring to thee a thousand pure springs, running towards the pastures that give food to the child.

TO THE WATERS AND LIGHT OF THE STARS

As the sea Vouru-kasha is the gathering place of the waters, rising up and going down, up the aërial way and down the earth, down the earth and up the aërial way: Thus rise up and roll along! thou in whose rising and growing Ahura Mazda made everything that grows. Up! rise up, ye deep Stars, that have in you the seed of waters; rise up above Hara Berezaiti, and produce light for the world, and mayest thou, O man! rise up there, if thou art to abide in Garô-nmânem, along the path made by Mazda, along the way made by the gods, the watery way they opened. Thus rise up and roll along! ye in whose rising and growing Ahura Mazda made everything that rises. In your rising, away will the Kahvuzi fly and cry; away will the Ayêhi fly and cry; away will the Gahi, who follows the Yâtu, fly and cry.

THE DHAMMAPADA

[*Translation by F. Max Müller*]

INTRODUCTION

THE "Dhammapada," or "Path to Virtue," is one of the most practical ethical hand-books of Buddhism. It is included in the canon of Buddhistic Scriptures, and is one of the Eastern books which can be read with delight to-day by those who are classed as general readers. It is divided into twenty-six chapters, and the keynote of it is struck by the sentence "The virtuous man is happy in this world, and he is happy in the next; he is happy in both. He is happy when he thinks of the good he has done; he is still more happy when going on the good path." The first step in the "good path" is earnestness, for as the writer says, "Earnestness is the path of immortality (Nirvâna), thoughtlessness the path of death; those who are in earnest do not die, those who are thoughtless are as if dead already." Earnestness, in this connection, evidently means the power of reflection, and of abstracting the mind from mundane things. There is something very inspiring in the sentence, "When the learned man drives away vanity by earnestness, he, the wise, climbing the terraced heights of wisdom, looks down upon the fools: free from sorrow he looks upon the sorrowing crowd, as one that stands on a mountain looks down upon them that stand upon the plain." This reminds us of Lucretius,

> "How sweet to stand, when tempests tear the main,
> On the firm cliff, and mark the seaman's toil!
> Not that another's danger soothes the soul,
> But from such toil how sweet to feel secure!
> How sweet, at distance from the strife, to view
> Contending hosts, and hear the clash of war!
> But sweeter far on Wisdom's height serene,
> Upheld by Truth, to fix our firm abode;
> To watch the giddy crowd that, deep below,
> Forever wander in pursuit of bliss;
> To mark the strife for honors, and renown,
> For wit and wealth, insatiate, ceaseless urged,
> Day after day, with labor unrestrained."

It is curious to see the atheistic Epicurean and the devout Buddhist meeting on a common ground. But the beauties of the "Dhammapada" can only be realized by a careful study of this charming work. We would point out, for instance, in the chapter on Flowers, what is a piece of golden advice to all readers of books: "The disciple will find out the plainly shown path of virtue, as a clever man finds the right flower."

Neither the date nor the authorship of the "Dhammapada" is known, but there is conclusive evidence that this canon existed before the Christian era. Many scholars agree in ascribing its utterances to Buddha himself, while others are of the opinion that it is a compilation made by Buddhist monks from various sources.

E. W.

THE DHAMMAPADA

CHAPTER I

THE TWIN-VERSES

ALL that we are is the result of what we have thought: it is founded on our thoughts, it is made up of our thoughts. If a man speaks or acts with an evil thought, pain follows him, as the wheel follows the foot of the ox that draws the carriage.

All that we are is the result of what we have thought: it is founded on our thoughts, it is made up of our thoughts. If a man speaks or acts with a pure thought, happiness follows him, like a shadow that never leaves him.

"He abused me, he beat me, he defeated me, he robbed me"—in those who harbor such thoughts hatred will never cease.

"He abused me, he beat me, he defeated me, he robbed me" —in those who do not harbor such thoughts hatred will cease.

For hatred does not cease by hatred at any time: hatred ceases by love—this is an old rule.

The world does not know that we must all come to an end here; but those who know it, their quarrels cease at once.

He who lives looking for pleasures only, his senses uncontrolled, immoderate in his food, idle, and weak, Mâra (the tempter) will certainly overthrow him, as the wind throws down a weak tree.

He who lives without looking for pleasures, his senses well controlled, moderate in his food, faithful and strong, him Mâra will certainly not overthrow, any more than the wind throws down a rocky mountain.

He who wishes to put on the yellow dress without having

cleansed himself from sin, who disregards also temperance and truth, is unworthy of the yellow dress.

But he who has cleansed himself from sin, is well grounded in all virtues, and endowed also with temperance and truth: he is indeed worthy of the yellow dress.

They who imagine truth in untruth, and see untruth in truth, never arrive at truth, but follow vain desires.

They who know truth in truth, and untruth in untruth, arrive at truth, and follow true desires.

As rain breaks through an ill-thatched house, passion will break through an unreflecting mind.

As rain does not break through a well-thatched house, passion will not break through a well-reflecting mind.

The evil-doer mourns in this world, and he mourns in the next; he mourns in both. He mourns and suffers when he sees the evil result of his own work.

The virtuous man delights in this world, and he delights in the next; he delights in both. He delights and rejoices, when he sees the purity of his own work.

The evil-doer suffers in this world, and he suffers in the next; he suffers in both. He suffers when he thinks of the evil he has done; he suffers more when going on the evil path.

The virtuous man is happy in this world, and he is happy in the next; he is happy in both. He is happy when he thinks of the good he has done; he is still more happy when going on the good path.

The thoughtless man, even if he can recite a large portion of the law, but is not a doer of it, has no share in the priesthood, but is like a cow-herd counting the cows of others.

The follower of the law, even if he can recite only a small portion of the law, but, having forsaken passion and hatred and foolishness, possesses true knowledge and serenity of mind, he, caring for nothing in this world or that to come, has indeed a share in the priesthood.

CHAPTER II

ON EARNESTNESS

EARNESTNESS is the path of immortality (Nirvâna), thoughtlessness the path of death. Those who are in earnest do not die, those who are thoughtless are as if dead already.

Having understood this clearly, those who are advanced in earnestness delight in earnestness, and rejoice in the knowledge of the elect.

These wise people, meditative, steady, always possessed of strong powers, attain to Nirvâna, the highest happiness.

If an earnest person has roused himself, if he is not forgetful, if his deeds are pure, if he acts with consideration, if he restrains himself, and lives according to law—then his glory will increase.

By rousing himself, by earnestness, by restraint and control, the wise man may make for himself an island which no flood can overwhelm.

Fools follow after vanity. The wise man keeps earnestness as his best jewel.

Follow not after vanity, nor after the enjoyment of love and lust! He who is earnest and meditative, obtains ample joy.

When the learned man drives away vanity by earnestness, he, the wise, climbing the terraced heights of wisdom, looks down upon the fools: free from sorrow he looks upon the sorrowing crowd, as one that stands on a mountain looks down upon them that stand upon the plain.

Earnest among the thoughtless, awake among the sleepers, the wise man advances like a racer, leaving behind the hack.

By earnestness did Maghavan (Indra) rise to the lordship of the gods. People praise earnestness; thoughtlessness is always blamed.

A Bhikshu (mendicant) who delights in earnestness, who looks with fear on thoughtlessness, moves about like fire, burning all his fetters, small or large.

A Bhikshu (mendicant) who delights in reflection, who looks with fear on thoughtlessness, cannot fall away from his perfect state—he is close upon Nirvâna.

CHAPTER III

THOUGHT

AS a fletcher makes straight his arrow, a wise man makes straight his trembling and unsteady thought, which is difficult to guard, difficult to hold back.

As a fish taken from his watery home and thrown on the dry ground, our thought trembles all over in order to escape the dominion of Mâra, the tempter.

It is good to tame the mind, which is difficult to hold in and flighty, rushing wherever it listeth; a tamed mind brings happiness.

Let the wise man guard his thoughts, for they are difficult to perceive, very artful, and they rush wherever they list: thoughts well guarded bring happiness.

Those who bridle their mind which travels far, moves about alone, is without a body, and hides in the chamber of the heart, will be free from the bonds of Mâra, the tempter.

If a man's faith is unsteady, if he does not know the true law, if his peace of mind is troubled, his knowledge will never be perfect.

If a man's thoughts are not dissipated, if his mind is not perplexed, if he has ceased to think of good or evil, then there is no fear for him while he is watchful.

Knowing that this body is fragile like a jar, and making his thought firm like a fortress, one should attack Mâra, the tempter, with the weapon of knowledge, one should watch him when conquered, and should never rest.

Before long, alas! this body will lie on the earth, despised, without understanding, like a useless log.

Whatever a hater may do to a hater, or an enemy to an enemy, a wrongly-directed mind will do him greater mischief.

Not a mother, not a father, will do so much, nor any other relatives; a well-directed mind will do us greater service.

CHAPTER IV

FLOWERS

WHO shall overcome this earth, and the world of Yama, the lord of the departed, and the world of the gods? Who shall find out the plainly shown path of virtue, as a clever man finds the right flower?

The disciple will overcome the earth, and the world of Yama, and the world of the gods. The disciple will find out the plainly shown path of virtue, as a clever man finds the right flower.

He who knows that this body is like froth, and has learnt that it is as unsubstantial as a mirage, will break the flower-pointed arrow of Mâra, and never see the king of death.

Death carries off a man who is gathering flowers, and whose mind is distracted, as a flood carries off a sleeping village.

Death subdues a man who is gathering flowers, and whose mind is distracted, before he is satiated in his pleasures.

As the bee collects nectar and departs without injuring the flower, or its color or scent, so let a sage dwell in his village.

Not the perversities of others, not their sins of commission or omission, but his own misdeeds and negligences should a sage take notice of.

Like a beautiful flower, full of color, but without scent, are the fine but fruitless words of him who does not act accordingly.

But, like a beautiful flower, full of color and full of scent, are the fine and fruitful words of him who acts accordingly.

As many kinds of wreaths can be made from a heap of flowers, so many good things may be achieved by a mortal when once he is born.

The scent of flowers does not travel against the wind, nor that of sandal-wood, or of Tagara and Mallikâ flowers; but the odor of good people travels even against the wind; a good man pervades every place.

Sandal-wood or Tagara, a lotus-flower, or a Vassikî, among these sorts of perfumes, the perfume of virtue is unsurpassed.

Mean is the scent that comes from Tagara and sandal-wood;

the perfume of those who possess virtue rises up to the gods as the highest.

Of the people who possess these virtues, who live without thoughtlessness, and who are emancipated through true knowledge, Mâra, the tempter, never finds the way.

As on a heap of rubbish cast upon the highway the lily will grow full of sweet perfume and delight, thus among those who are mere rubbish the disciple of the truly enlightened Buddha shines forth by his knowledge above the blinded worldling.

CHAPTER V

THE FOOL

LONG is the night to him who is awake; long is a mile to him who is tired; long is life to the foolish who do not know the true law.

If a traveller does not meet with one who is his better, or his equal, let him firmly keep to his solitary journey; there is no companionship with a fool.

"These sons belong to me, and this wealth belongs to me," with such thoughts a fool is tormented. He himself does not belong to himself; how much less sons and wealth?

The fool who knows his foolishness, is wise at least so far. But a fool who thinks himself wise, he is called a fool indeed.

If a fool be associated with a wise man even all his life, he will perceive the truth as little as a spoon perceives the taste of soup.

If an intelligent man be associated for one minute only with a wise man, he will soon perceive the truth, as the tongue perceives the taste of soup.

Fools of poor understanding have themselves for their greatest enemies, for they do evil deeds which bear bitter fruits.

That deed is not well done of which a man must repent, and the reward of which he receives crying and with a tearful face.

No, that deed is well done of which a man does not repent, and the reward of which he receives gladly and cheerfully.

As long as the evil deed done does not bear fruit, the fool

thinks it is like honey; but when it ripens, then the fool suffers grief.

Let a fool month after month eat his food (like an ascetic) with the tip of a blade of Kuśa-grass, yet is he not worth the sixteenth particle of those who have well weighed the law.

An evil deed, like newly-drawn milk, does not turn suddenly; smouldering, like fire covered by ashes, it follows the fool.

And when the evil deed, after it has become known, turns to sorrow for the fool, then it destroys his bright lot, nay, it cleaves his head.

Let the fool wish for a false reputation, for precedence among the Bhikshus, for lordship in the convents, for worship among other people!

"May both the layman and he who has left the world think that this is done by me; may they be subject to me in everything which is to be done or is not to be done," thus is the mind of the fool, and his desire and pride increase.

"One is the road that leads to wealth, another the road that leads to Nirvâna"—if the Bhikshu, the disciple of Buddha, has learnt this, he will not yearn for honor, he will strive after separation from the world.

CHAPTER VI

THE WISE MAN

IF you see a man who shows you what is to be avoided, who administers reproofs, and is intelligent, follow that wise man as you would one who tells of hidden treasures; it will be better, not worse, for him who follows him.

Let him admonish, let him teach, let him forbid what is improper!—he will be beloved of the good, by the bad he will be hated.

Do not have evil-doers for friends, do not have low people for friends: have virtuous people for friends, have for friends the best of men.

He who drinks in the law lives happily with a serene mind: the sage rejoices always in the law, as preached by the elect.

Well-makers lead the water wherever they like; fletchers bend the arrow; carpenters bend a log of wood; wise people fashion themselves.

As a solid rock is not shaken by the wind, wise people falter not amidst blame and praise.

Wise people, after they have listened to the laws, become serene, like a deep, smooth, and still lake.

Good men indeed walk warily under all circumstances; good men speak not out of a desire for sensual gratification; whether touched by happiness or sorrow wise people never appear elated or depressed.

If, whether for his own sake, or for the sake of others, a man wishes neither for a son, nor for wealth, nor for lordship, and if he does not wish for his own success by unfair means, then he is good, wise, and virtuous.

Few are there among men who arrive at the other shore (become Arhats); the other people here run up and down the shore.

But those who, when the law has been well preached to them, follow the law, will pass over the dominion of death, however difficult to cross.

A wise man should leave the dark state of ordinary life, and follow the bright state of the Bhikshu. After going from his home to a homeless state, he should in his retirement look for enjoyment where enjoyment seemed difficult. Leaving all pleasures behind, and calling nothing his own, the wise man should purge himself from all the troubles of the mind.

Those whose mind is well grounded in the seven elements of knowledge, who without clinging to anything, rejoice in freedom from attachment, whose appetites have been conquered, and who are full of light, they are free even in this world.

CHAPTER VII

THE VENERABLE

THERE is no suffering for him who has finished his journey, and abandoned grief, who has freed himself on all sides, and thrown off all fetters.

They exert themselves with their thoughts well-collected, they do not tarry in their abode; like swans who have left their lake, they leave their house and home.

Men who have no riches, who live on recognized food, who have perceived void and unconditioned freedom (Nirvâna), their path is difficult to understand, like that of birds in the air.

He whose appetites are stilled, who is not absorbed in enjoyment, who has perceived void and unconditioned freedom (Nirvâna), his path is difficult to understand, like that of birds in the air.

The gods even envy him whose senses, like horses well broken in by the driver, have been subdued, who is free from pride, and free from appetites; such a one who does his duty is tolerant like the earth, or like a threshold; he is like a lake without mud; no new births are in store for him.

His thought is quiet, quiet are his word and deed, when he has obtained freedom by true knowledge, when he has thus become a quiet man.

The man who is free from credulity, but knows the uncreated, who has cut all ties, removed all temptations, renounced all desires, he is the greatest of men.

In a hamlet or in a forest, on sea or on dry land, wherever venerable persons (Arahanta) dwell, that place is delightful.

Forests are delightful; where the world finds no delight, there the passionless will find delight, for they look not for pleasures.

CHAPTER VIII

THE THOUSANDS

EVEN though a speech be a thousand (of words), but made up of senseless words, one word of sense is better, which if a man hears, he becomes quiet.

Even though a Gâthâ (poem) be a thousand (of words), but made up of senseless words, one word of a Gâthâ is better, which if a man hears, be becomes quiet.

Though a man recite a hundred Gâthâs made up of senseless words, one word of the law is better, which if a man hears, he becomes quiet.

If one man conquer in battle a thousand times a thousand men, and if another conquer himself, he is the greatest of conquerors.

One's own self conquered is better than all other people; not even a god, a Gandharva, not Mâra (with Brâhman) could change into defeat the victory of a man who has vanquished himself, and always lives under restraint.

If a man for a hundred years sacrifice month by month with a thousand, and if he but for one moment pay homage to a man whose soul is grounded in true knowledge, better is that homage than a sacrifice for a hundred years.

If a man for a hundred years worship Agni (fire) in the forest, and if he but for one moment pay homage to a man whose soul is grounded in true knowledge, better is that homage than sacrifice for a hundred years.

Whatever a man sacrifice in this world as an offering or as an oblation for a whole year in order to gain merit, the whole of it is not worth a quarter a farthing; reverence shown to the righteous is better.

He who always greets and constantly reveres the aged, four things will increase to him: life, beauty, happiness, power.

But he who lives a hundred years, vicious and unrestrained, a life of one day is better if a man is virtuous and reflecting.

And he who lives a hundred years, ignorant and unrestrained, a life of one day is better if a man is wise and reflecting.

And he who lives a hundred years, idle and weak, a life of one day is better if a man has attained firm strength.

And he who lives a hundred years, not seeing beginning and end, a life of one day is better if a man sees beginning and end.

And he who lives a hundred years, not seeing the immortal place, a life of one day is better if a man sees the immortal place.

And he who lives a hundred years, not seeing the highest law, a life of one day is better if a man sees the highest law.

CHAPTER IX

EVIL

A MAN should hasten towards the good, and should keep his thought away from evil; if a man does what is good slothfully, his mind delights in evil.

If a man commits a sin, let him not do it again; let him not delight in sin: the accumulation of evil is painful.

If a man does what is good, let him do it again; let him delight in it: the accumulation of good is delightful.

Even an evil-doer sees happiness so long as his evil deed does not ripen; but when his evil deed ripens, then does the evil-doer see evil.

Even a good man sees evil days so long as his good deed does not ripen; but when his good deed ripens, then does the good man see good things.

Let no man think lightly of evil, saying in his heart, It will not come nigh unto me. Even by the falling of water-drops a water-pot is filled; the fool becomes full of evil, even if he gather it little by little.

Let no man think lightly of good, saying in his heart, It will not come nigh unto me. Even by the falling of water-drops a water-pot is filled; the wise man becomes full of good, even if he gather it little by little.

Let a man avoid evil deeds, as a merchant, if he has few companions and carries much wealth, avoids a dangerous road; as a man who loves life avoids poison.

He who has no wound on his hand, may touch poison with his hand; poison does not affect one who has no wound; nor is there evil for one who does not commit evil.

If a man offend a harmless, pure, and innocent person, the evil falls back upon that fool, like light dust thrown up against the wind.

Some people are born again; evil-doers go to hell; righteous people go to heaven; those who are free from all worldly desires attain Nirvâna.

Not in the sky, not in the midst of the sea, not if we enter into the clefts of the mountains, is there known a spot in the whole world where a man might be freed from an evil deed.

Not in the sky, not in the midst of the sea, not if we enter into the clefts of the mountains, is there known a spot in the whole world where death could not overcome the mortal.

CHAPTER X

PUNISHMENT

ALL men tremble at punishment, all men fear death; remember that you are like unto them, and do not kill, nor cause slaughter.

All men tremble at punishment, all men love life; remember that thou art like unto them, and do not kill, nor cause slaughter.

He who, seeking his own happiness, punishes or kills beings who also long for happiness, will not find happiness after death.

He who, seeking his own happiness, does not punish or kill beings who also long for happiness, will find happiness after death.

Do not speak harshly to anyone; those who are spoken to will answer thee in the same way. Angry speech is painful: blows for blows will touch thee.

If, like a shattered metal plate (gong), thou utter nothing, then thou hast reached Nirvâna; anger is not known to thee.

As a cow-herd with his staff drives his cows into the stable, so do Age and Death drive the life of men.

A fool does not know when he commits his evil deeds: but the wicked man burns by his own deeds, as if burnt by fire.

He who inflicts pain on innocent and harmless persons, will soon come to one of these ten states:—

He will have cruel suffering, loss, injury of the body, heavy affliction, or loss of mind.

A misfortune coming from the king, or a fearful accusation, or loss of relations, or destruction of treasures.

Lightning-fire will burn his houses; and when his body is destroyed, the fool will go to hell.

Not nakedness, not platted hair, not dirt, not fasting, or lying on the earth, not rubbing with dust, not sitting motionless, can purify a mortal who has not overcome desires.

He who, though dressed in fine apparel, exercises tranquillity, is quiet, subdued, restrained, chaste, and has ceased to find fault with all other beings, he indeed is a Brâhmana, an ascetic (Sramana), a friar (Bhikshu).

Is there in this world any man so restrained by shame that he does not provoke reproof, as a noble horse the whip?

Like a noble horse when touched by the whip, be ye strenuous and eager, and by faith, by virtue, by energy, by meditation, by discernment of the law, you will overcome this great pain, perfect in knowledge and in behavior, and never forgetful.

Well-makers lead the water wherever they like; fletchers bend the arrow; carpenters bend a log of wood; good people fashion themselves.

CHAPTER XI

OLD AGE

HOW is there laughter, how is there joy, as this world is always burning? Do you not seek a light, ye who are surrounded by darkness?

Look at this dressed-up lump, covered with wounds, joined together, sickly, full of many schemes, but which has no strength, no hold!

This body is wasted, full of sickness, and frail; this heap of corruption breaks to pieces, life indeed ends in death.

After one has looked at those gray bones, thrown away like gourds in the autumn, what pleasure is there left in life!

After a stronghold has been made of the bones, it is covered with flesh and blood, and there dwell in it old age and death, pride and deceit.

The brilliant chariots of kings are destroyed, the body also approaches destruction, but the virtue of good people never approaches destruction—thus do the good say to the good.

A man who has learnt little, grows old like an ox; his flesh grows, but his knowledge does not grow.

Looking for the maker of this tabernacle, I have run through a course of many births, not finding him; and painful is birth again and again. But now, maker of the tabernacle, thou hast been seen; thou shalt not make up this tabernacle again. All thy rafters are broken, thy ridge-pole is sundered; the mind, approaching the Eternal (Visankhâra, Nirvâna), has attained to the extinction of all desires.

Men who have not observed proper discipline, and have not gained wealth in their youth, perish like old herons in a lake without fish.

Men who have not observed proper discipline, and have not gained wealth in their youth, lie, like broken bows, sighing after the past.

CHAPTER XII

SELF

IF a man hold himself dear, let him watch himself carefully; during one at least out of the three watches a wise man should be watchful.

Let each man direct himself first to what is proper, then let him teach others; thus a wise man will not suffer.

If a man make himself as he teaches others to be, then, being himself well subdued, he may subdue others; for one's own self is difficult to subdue.

Self is the lord of self, who else could be the lord? With self well subdued, a man finds a lord such as few can find.

The evil done by one's self, self-forgotten, self-bred, crushes the foolish, as a diamond breaks even a precious stone.

He whose wickedness is very great brings himself down to that state where his enemy wishes him to be, as a creeper does with the tree which it surrounds.

Bad deeds, and deeds hurtful to ourselves, are easy to do; what is beneficial and good, that is very difficult to do.

The foolish man who scorns the rule of the venerable (Arhat), of the elect (Ariya), of the virtuous, and follows a false doctrine, he bears fruit to his own destruction, like the fruits of the Katthaka reed.

By one's self the evil is done, by one's self one suffers; by one's self evil is left undone, by one's self one is purified. The pure and the impure stand and fall by themselves, no one can purify another.

Let no one forget his own duty for the sake of another's, however great; let a man, after he has discerned his own duty, be always attentive to his duty.

CHAPTER XIII

THE WORLD

DO not follow the evil law! Do not live on in thoughtlessness! Do not follow false doctrine! Be not a friend of the world.

Rouse thyself! do not be idle! Follow the law of virtue! The virtuous rest in bliss in this world and in the next.

Follow the law of virtue; do not follow that of sin. The virtuous rest in bliss in this world and in the next.

Look upon the world as you would on a bubble, look upon it as you would on a mirage: the king of death does not see him who thus looks down upon the world.

Come, look at this world, glittering like a royal chariot; the foolish are immersed in it, but the wise do not touch it.

He who formerly was reckless and afterwards became sober brightens up this world, like the moon when freed from clouds.

He whose evil deeds are covered by good deeds, brightens up this world, like the moon when freed from clouds.

This world is dark, few only can see here; a few only go to heaven, like birds escaped from the net.

The swans go on the path of the sun, they go miraculously through the ether; the wise are led out of this world, when they have conquered Mâra and his train.

If a man has transgressed the one law, and speaks lies, and scoffs at another world, there is no evil he will not do.

The uncharitable do not go to the world of the gods; fools only do not praise liberality; a wise man rejoices in liberality, and through it becomes blessed in the other world.

Better than sovereignty over the earth, better than going to heaven, better than lordship over all worlds, is the reward of Sotâpatti, the first step in holiness.

CHAPTER XIV

THE BUDDHA—THE AWAKENED

HE whose conquest cannot be conquered again, into whose conquest no one in this world enters, by what track can you lead him, the Awakened, the Omniscient, the trackless?

He whom no desire with its snares and poisons can lead astray, by what track can you lead him, the Awakened, the Omniscient, the trackless?

Even the gods envy those who are awakened and not forgetful, who are given to meditation, who are wise, and who delight in the repose of retirement from the world.

Difficult to obtain is the conception of men, difficult is the life of mortals, difficult is the hearing of the True Law, difficult is the birth of the Awakened (the attainment of Buddhahood).

Not to commit any sin, to do good, and to purify one's mind, that is the teaching of all the Awakened.

The Awakened call patience the highest penance, long-suffering the highest Nirvâna; for he is not an anchorite (Pravragita) who strikes others, he is not an ascetic (Sramana) who insults others.

Not to blame, not to strike, to live restrained under the law, to be moderate in eating, to sleep and sit alone, and to dwell on the highest thoughts—this is the teaching of the Awakened.

There is no satisfying lusts, even by a shower of gold pieces; he who knows that lusts have a short taste and cause pain, he is wise; even in heavenly pleasures he finds no satisfaction, the disciple who is fully awakened delights only in the destruction of all desires.

Men, driven by fear, go to many a refuge, to mountains and forests, to groves and sacred trees.

But that is not a safe refuge, that is not the best refuge; a man is not delivered from all pains after having gone to that refuge.

He who takes refuge with Buddha, the Law, and the Church; he who, with clear understanding, sees the four holy truths: pain, the origin of pain, the destruction of pain, and the eightfold holy way that leads to the quieting of pain;—that is the safe refuge, that is the best refuge; having gone to that refuge, a man is delivered from all pain.

A supernatural person (a Buddha) is not easily found: he is not born everywhere. Wherever such a sage is born, that race prospers.

Happy is the arising of the Awakened, happy is the teaching of the True Law, happy is peace in the church, happy is the devotion of those who are at peace.

He who pays homage to those who deserve homage, whether the awakened (Buddha) or their disciples, those who have overcome the host of evils, and crossed the flood of sorrow, he who pays homage to such as have found deliverance and know no fear, his merit can never be measured by anyone.

CHAPTER XV

HAPPINESS

WE live happily indeed, not hating those who hate us! among men who hate us we dwell free from hatred!

We live happily indeed, free from ailments among the ailing! among men who are ailing let us dwell free from ailments!

We live happily indeed, free from greed among the greedy! among men who are greedy let us dwell free from greed!

We live happily indeed, though we call nothing our own! We shall be like the bright gods, feeding on happiness!

Victory breeds hatred, for the conquered is unhappy. He who has given up both victory and defeat, he, the contented, is happy.

There is no fire like passion; there is no losing throw like hatred; there is no pain like this body; there is no happiness higher than rest.

Hunger is the worst of diseases, the elements of the body the greatest evil; if one knows this truly, that is Nirvâna, the highest happiness.

Health is the greatest of gifts, contentedness the best riches; trust is the best of relationships, Nirvâna the highest happiness.

He who has tasted the sweetness of solitude and tranquillity, is free from fear and free from sin, while he tastes the sweetness of drinking in the law.

The sight of the elect (Ariya) is good, to live with them is always happiness; if a man does not see fools, he will be truly happy.

He who walks in the company of fools suffers a long way; company with fools, as with an enemy, is always painful; company with the wise is pleasure, like meeting with kinsfolk.

Therefore, one ought to follow the wise, the intelligent, the learned, the much enduring, the dutiful, the elect; one ought to follow such a good and wise man, as the moon follows the path of the stars.

CHAPTER XVI

PLEASURE

HE who gives himself to vanity, and does not give himself to meditation, forgetting the real aim of life and grasping at pleasure, will in time envy him who has exerted himself in meditation.

Let no man ever cling to what is pleasant, or to what is unpleasant. Not to see what is pleasant is pain, and it is pain to see what is unpleasant.

Let, therefore, no man love anything; loss of the beloved is evil. Those who love nothing, and hate nothing, have no fetters.

From pleasure comes grief, from pleasure comes fear; he who is free from pleasure knows neither grief nor fear.

From affection comes grief, from affection comes fear; he who is free from affection knows neither grief nor fear.

From lust comes grief, from lust comes fear; he who is free from lust knows neither grief nor fear.

From love comes grief, from love comes fear; he who is free from love knows neither grief nor fear.

From greed comes grief, from greed comes fear; he who is free from greed knows neither grief nor fear.

He who possesses virtue and intelligence, who is just, speaks the truth, and does what is his own business, him the world will hold dear.

He in whom a desire for the Ineffable (Nirvâna) has sprung up, who in his mind is satisfied, and whose thoughts are not bewildered by love, he is called ûrdhvamsrotas (carried upwards by the stream).

Kinsmen, friends, and lovers salute a man who has been long away, and returns safe from afar.

In like manner his good works receive him who has done good, and has gone from this world to the other;—as kinsmen receive a friend on his return.

CHAPTER XVII

ANGER

LET a man leave anger, let him forsake pride, let him overcome all bondage! No sufferings befall the man who is not attached to name and form, and who calls nothing his own.

He who holds back rising anger like a rolling chariot, him I call a real driver; other people are but holding the reins.

Let a man overcome anger by love, let him overcome evil by good; let him overcome the greedy by liberality, the liar by truth!

Speak the truth, do not yield to anger; give, if thou art asked for little; by these three steps thou wilt go near the gods.

The sages who injure nobody, and who always control their body, they will go to the unchangeable place (Nirvâna), where, if they have gone, they will suffer no more.

Those who are ever watchful, who study day and night, and who strive after Nirvâna, their passions will come to an end.

This is an old saying, O Atula, this is not as if of to-day: "They blame him who sits silent, they blame him who speaks much, they also blame him who says little; there is no one on earth who is not blamed."

There never was, there never will be, nor is there now, a man who is always blamed, or a man who is always praised.

But he whom those who discriminate praise continually day after day, as without blemish, wise, rich in knowledge and virtue, who would dare to blame him, like a coin made of gold from the Gambû river? Even the gods praise him, he is praised even by Brâhman.

Beware of bodily anger, and control thy body! Leave the sins of the body, and with thy body practise virtue!

Beware of the anger of the tongue, and control thy tongue! Leave the sins of the tongue, and practise virtue with thy tongue!

Beware of the anger of the mind, and control thy mind! Leave the sins of the mind, and practise virtue with thy mind!

The wise who control their body, who control their tongue, the wise who control their mind, are indeed well controlled.

CHAPTER XVIII

IMPURITY

THOU art now like a sear leaf, the messengers of death (Yama) have come near to thee; thou standest at the door of thy departure, and thou hast no provision for thy journey.

Make thyself an island, work hard, be wise! When thy impurities are blown away, and thou art free from guilt, thou wilt enter into the heavenly world of the elect (Ariya).

Thy life has come to an end, thou art come near to death (Yama), there is no resting-place for thee on the road, and thou hast no provision for thy journey.

Make thyself an island, work hard, be wise! When thy impurities are blown away, and thou art free from guilt, thou wilt not enter again into birth and decay.

Let a wise man blow off the impurities of himself, as a smith blows off the impurities of silver, one by one, little by little, and from time to time.

As the impurity which springs from the iron, when it springs from it, destroys it; thus do a transgressor's own works lead him to the evil path.

The taint of prayers is non-repetition; the taint of houses, non-repair; the taint of complexion is sloth; the taint of a watchman, thoughtlessness.

Bad conduct is the taint of woman, niggardliness the taint of a benefactor; tainted are all evil ways, in this world and in the next.

But there is a taint worse than all taints—ignorance is the greatest taint. O mendicants! throw off that taint, and become taintless!

Life is easy to live for a man who is without shame: a crow hero, a mischief-maker, an insulting, bold, and wretched fellow.

But life is hard to live for a modest man, who always looks for what is pure, who is disinterested, quiet, spotless, and intelligent.

He who destroys life, who speaks untruth, who in the world takes what is not given him, who goes to another man's wife; and the man who gives himself to drinking intoxicating liquors, he, even in this world, digs up his own root.

O man, know this, that the unrestrained are in a bad state; take care that greediness and vice do not bring thee to grief for a long time!

The world gives according to their faith or according to their pleasure: if a man frets about the food and the drink given to others, he will find no rest either by day or by night.

He in whom that feeling is destroyed, and taken out with the very root, finds rest by day and by night.

There is no fire like passion, there is no shark like hatred, there is no snare like folly, there is no torrent like greed.

The fault of others is easily perceived, but that of one's self is difficult to perceive; a man winnows his neighbor's faults like chaff, but his own fault he hides, as a cheat hides the bad die from the player.

If a man looks after the faults of others, and is always inclined to be offended, his own passions will grow, and he is far from the destruction of passions.

There is no path through the air, a man is not a Samana outwardly. The world delights in vanity, the Tathâgatas (the Buddhas) are free from vanity.

There is no path through the air, a man is not a Samana outwardly. No creatures are eternal; but the awakened (Buddha) are never shaken.

CHAPTER XIX

THE JUST

A MAN is not just if he carries a matter by violence; no, he who distinguishes both right and wrong, who is learned and guides others, not by violenee, but by the same law, being a guardian of the law and intelligent, he is called just.

A man is not learned because he talks much; he who is patient, free from hatred and fear, he is called learned.

A man is not a supporter of the law because he talks much; even if a man has learnt little, but sees the law bodily, he is a supporter of the law, a man who never neglects the law.

A man is not an elder because his head is gray; his age may be ripe, but he is called "Old-in-vain."

He in whom there is truth, virtue, pity, restraint, moderation, he who is free from impurity and is wise, he is called an elder.

An envious, stingy, dishonest man does not become respectable by means of much talking only, or by the beauty of his complexion.

He in whom all this is destroyed, and taken out with the very root, he, when freed from hatred, is called respectable.

Not by tonsure does an undisciplined man who speaks falsehood become a Samana; can a man be a Samana who is still held captive by desire and greediness?

He who always quiets the evil, whether small or large, he is called a Samana (a quiet man), because he has quieted all evil.

A man is not a mendicant (Bhikshu) simply because he asks others for alms; he who adopts the whole law is a Bhikshu, not he who only begs.

He who is above good and evil, who is chaste, who with care passes through the world, he indeed is called a Bhikshu.

A man is not a Muni because he observes silence if he is foolish and ignorant; but the wise who, as with the balance, chooses the good and avoids evil, he is a Muni, and is a Muni thereby; he who in this world weighs both sides is called a Muni.

A man is not an elect (Ariya) because he injures living creatures; because he has pity on all living creatures, therefore is a man called Ariya.

Not only by discipline and vows, not only by much learning, not by entering into a trance, not by sleeping alone, do I earn the happiness of release which no worldling can know. O Bhikshu, he who has obtained the extinction of desires has obtained confidence.

CHAPTER XX

THE WAY

THE best of ways is the eightfold; the best of truths the four words; the best of virtues passionlessness; the best of men he who has eyes to see.

This is the way, there is no other that leads to the purifying of intelligence. Go on this path! This is the confusion of Mâra, the tempter.

If you go on this way, you will make an end of pain! The way preached by me, when I had understood the removal of the thorns in the flesh.

You yourself must make an effort. The Tathâgatas (Buddhas) are only preachers. The thoughtful who enter the way are freed from the bondage of Mâra.

"All created things perish," he who knows and sees this becomes passive in pain; this is the way to purity.

"All created things are grief and pain," he who knows and sees this becomes passive in pain; this is the way that leads to purity.

"All forms are unreal," he who knows and sees this becomes passive in pain; this is the way that leads to purity.

He who does not rouse himself when it is time to rise, who, though young and strong, is full of sloth, whose will and thought are weak, that lazy and idle man never finds the way to knowledge.

Watching his speech, well restrained in mind, let a man never commit any wrong with his body! Let a man but keep these three roads of action clear, and he will achieve the way which is taught by the wise.

Through zeal knowledge is gained, through lack of zeal knowledge is lost; let a man who knows this double path of gain and loss thus place himself that knowledge may grow.

Cut down the whole forest of desires, not a tree only! Danger comes out of the forest of desires. When you have cut down both the forest of desires and its undergrowth, then, Bhikshus, you will be rid of the forest and of desires!

So long as the desire of man towards women, even the smallest, is not destroyed, so long is his mind in bondage, as the calf that drinks milk is to its mother.

Cut out the love of self, like an autumn lotus, with thy hand! Cherish the road of peace. Nirvâna has been shown by Sugata (Buddha).

" Here I shall dwell in the rain, here in winter and summer," thus the fool meditates, and does not think of death.

Death comes and carries off that man, honored for his children and flocks, his mind distracted, as a flood carries off a sleeping village.

Sons are no help, nor a father, nor relations; there is no help from kinsfolk for one whom death has seized.

A wise and well-behaved man who knows the meaning of this should quickly clear the way that leads to Nirvâna.

CHAPTER XXI

MISCELLANEOUS

IF by leaving a small pleasure one sees a great pleasure, let a wise man leave the small pleasure, and look to the great.

He who, by causing pain to others, wishes to obtain pleasure for himself, he, entangled in the bonds of hatred, will never be free from hatred.

What ought to be done is neglected, what ought not to be done is done; the desires of unruly, thoughtless people are always increasing.

But they whose whole watchfulness is always directed to their body, who do not follow what ought not to be done, and who steadfastly do what ought to be done, the desires of such watchful and wise people will come to an end.

A true Brâhmana goes scathless, though he have killed father and mother, and two valiant kings, though he has destroyed a kingdom with all its subjects.

A true Brâhmana goes scathless, though he have killed father and mother, and two holy kings, and an eminent man besides.

The disciples of Gotama (Buddha) are always well awake, and their thoughts day and night are always set on Buddha.

The disciples of Gotama are always well awake, and their thoughts day and night are always set on the law.

The disciples of Gotama are always well awake, and their thoughts day and night are always set on the church.

The disciples of Gotama are always well awake, and their thoughts day and night are always set on their body.

The disciples of Gotama are always well awake, and their mind day and night always delights in compassion.

The disciples of Gotama are always well awake, and their mind day and night always delights in meditation.

It is hard to leave the world to become a friar, it is hard to enjoy the world; hard is the monastery, painful are the houses; painful it is to dwell with equals to share everything in common, and the itinerant mendicant is beset with pain. Therefore let no man be an itinerant mendicant, and he will not be beset with pain.

A man full of faith, if endowed with virtue and glory, is respected, whatever place he may choose.

Good people shine from afar, like the snowy mountains; bad people are not seen, like arrows shot by night.

Sitting alone, lying down alone, walking alone without ceasing, and alone subduing himself, let a man be happy near the edge of a forest.

CHAPTER XXII

THE DOWNWARD COURSE

HE who says what is not goes to hell; he also who, having done a thing, says I have not done it. After death both are equal: they are men with evil deeds in the next world.

Many men whose shoulders are covered with the yellow gown are ill-conditioned and unrestrained; such evil-doers by their evil deeds go to hell.

Better it would be to swallow a heated iron ball, like flaring fire, than that a bad unrestrained fellow should live on the charity of the land.

Four things does a reckless man gain who covets his neighbor's wife—demerit, an uncomfortable bed, thirdly, punishment, and lastly, hell.

There is demerit, and the evil way to hell: there is the short pleasure of the frightened in the arms of the frightened, and the king imposes heavy punishment; therefore let no man think of his neighbor's wife.

As a grass-blade, if badly grasped, cuts the arm, badly-practised asceticism leads to hell.

An act carelessly performed, a broken vow, and hesitating obedience to discipline (Brâhma-kariyam), all these bring no great reward.

If anything is to be done, let a man do it, let him attack it vigorously! A careless pilgrim only scatters the dust of his passions more widely.

An evil deed is better left undone, for a man repents of it afterwards; a good deed is better done, for having done it, one does not repent.

Like a well-guarded frontier fort, with defences within and without, so let a man guard himself. Not a moment should escape, for they who allow the right moment to pass, suffer pain when they are in hell.

They who are ashamed of what they ought not to be ashamed of, and are not ashamed of what they ought to be ashamed of, such men, embracing false doctrines, enter the evil path.

They who fear when they ought not to fear, and fear not when they ought to fear, such men, embracing false doctrines, enter the evil path.

They who see sin where there is no sin, and see no sin where there is sin, such men, embracing false doctrines, enter the evil path.

They who see sin where there is sin, and no sin where there is no sin, such men, embracing the true doctrine, enter the good path.

CHAPTER XXIII

THE ELEPHANT

SILENTLY I endured abuse as the elephant in battle endures the arrow sent from the bow: for the world is ill-natured.

They lead a tamed elephant to battle, the king mounts a tamed elephant; the tamed is the best among men, he who silently endures abuse.

Mules are good, if tamed, and noble Sindhu horses, and elephants with large tusks; but he who tames himself is better still.

For with these animals does no man reach the untrodden country (Nirvâna), where a tamed man goes on a tamed animal—on his own well-tamed self.

The elephant called Dhanapâlaka, his temples running with pungent sap, and who is difficult to hold, does not eat a morsel when bound; the elephant longs for the elephant grove.

If a man becomes fat and a great eater, if he is sleepy and rolls himself about, that fool, like a hog fed on grains, is born again and again.

This mind of mine went formerly wandering about as it liked, as it listed, as it pleased; but I shall now hold it in thoroughly, as the rider who holds the hook holds in the furious elephant.

Be not thoughtless, watch your thoughts! Draw yourself out of the evil way, like an elephant sunk in mud.

If a man find a prudent companion who walks with him, is wise, and lives soberly, he may walk with him, overcoming all dangers, happy, but considerate.

If a man find no prudent companion who walks with him, is wise, and lives soberly, let him walk alone, like a king who has left his conquered country behind—like an elephant in the forest.

It is better to live alone: there is no companionship with a fool; let a man walk alone, let him commit no sin, with few wishes, like an elephant in the forest.

If the occasion arises, friends are pleasant; enjoyment is pleasant, whatever be the cause; a good work is pleasant in the hour of death; the giving up of all grief is pleasant.

Pleasant in the world is the state of a mother, pleasant the state of a father, pleasant the state of a Samana, pleasant the state of a Brâhmana.

Pleasant is virtue lasting to old age, pleasant is a faith firmly rooted; pleasant is attainment of intelligence, pleasant is avoiding of sins.

CHAPTER XXIV

THIRST

THE thirst of a thoughtless man grows like a creeper; he runs from life to life, like a monkey seeking fruit in the forest.

Whomsoever this fierce poisonous thirst overcomes, in this world, his sufferings increase like the abounding Birana grass.

But from him who overcomes this fierce thirst, difficult to be conquered in this world, sufferings fall off, like water-drops from a lotus leaf.

This salutary word I tell you, " Do ye, as many as are here assembled, dig up the root of thirst, as he who wants the sweet-scented Usîra root must dig up the Bîrana grass, that Mâra, the tempter, may not crush you again and again, as the stream crushes the reeds."

As a tree, even though it has been cut down, is firm so long as its root is safe, and grows again, thus, unless the feeders of thirst are destroyed, this pain of life will return again and again.

He whose thirty-six streams are strongly flowing in the channels of pleasure, the waves—his desires which are set on passion—will carry away that misguided man.

The channels run everywhere, the creeper of passion stands sprouting; if you see the creeper springing up, cut its root by means of knowledge.

A creature's pleasures are extravagant and luxurious; given up to pleasure and deriving happiness, men undergo again and again birth and decay.

Beset with lust, men run about like a snared hare; held in fetters and bonds, they undergo pain for a long time, again and again.

Beset with lust, men run about like a snared hare; let therefore the mendicant drive out thirst, by striving after passionlessness for himself.

He who, having got rid of the forest of lust (after having reached Nirvâna), gives himself over to forest-life (to lust), and who, when free from the forest (from lust), runs to the forest (to lust), look at that man! though free, he runs into bondage.

Wise people do not call that a strong fetter which is made of iron, wood, or hemp; passionately strong is the care for precious stones and rings, for sons and a wife.

That fetter wise people call strong which drags down, yields, but is difficult to undo; after having cut this at last, people leave the world, free from cares, and leaving the pleasures of love behind.

Those who are slaves to passions, run down the stream of desires, as a spider runs down the web which he has made himself; when they have cut this, at last, wise people go onwards, free from cares, leaving all pain behind.

Give up what is before, give up what is behind, give up what is between, when thou goest to the other shore of existence; if thy mind is altogether free, thou wilt not again enter into birth and decay.

If a man is tossed about by doubts, full of strong passions, and yearning only for what is delightful, his thirst will grow more and more, and he will indeed make his fetters strong.

If a man delights in quieting doubts, and, always reflecting, dwells on what is not delightful, he certainly will remove, nay, he will cut the fetter of Mâra.

He who has reached the consummation, who does not tremble, who is without thirst and without sin, he has broken all the thorns of life: this will be his last body.

He who is without thirst and without affection, who understands the words and their interpretation, who knows the order of letters (those which are before and which are after), he has received his last body, he is called the great sage, the great man.

"I have conquered all, I know all, in all conditions of life I am free from taint; I have left all, and through the destruction of thirst I am free; having learnt myself, whom should I indicate as my teacher?"

The gift of the law exceeds all gifts; the sweetness of the law exceeds all sweetness; the delight in the law exceeds all delights; the extinction of thirst overcomes all pain.

Riches destroy the foolish, if they look not for the other shore; the foolish by his thirst for riches destroys himself, as if he were destroying others.

The fields are damaged by weeds, mankind is damaged by passion: therefore a gift bestowed on the passionless brings great reward.

The fields are damaged by weeds, mankind is damaged by hatred: therefore a gift bestowed on those who do not hate brings great reward.

The fields are damaged by weeds, mankind is damaged by vanity: therefore a gift bestowed on those who are free from vanity brings great reward.

The fields are damaged by weeds, mankind is damaged by lust: therefore a gift bestowed on those who are free from lust brings great reward.

CHAPTER XXV

THE BHIKSHU

RESTRAINT in the eye is good, good is restraint in the ear, in the nose restraint is good, good is restraint in the tongue.

In the body restraint is good, good is restraint in speech, in thought restraint is good, good is restraint in all things. A Bhikshu, restrained in all things, is freed from all pain.

He who controls his hand, he who controls his feet, he who controls his speech, he who is well controlled, he who delights inwardly, who is collected, who is solitary and content, him they call Bhikshu.

The Bhikshu who controls his mouth, who speaks wisely and calmly, who teaches the meaning and the law, his word is sweet.

He who dwells in the law, delights in the law, meditates on the law, recollects the law: that Bhikshu will never fall away from the true law.

Let him not despise what he has received, nor ever envy others: a mendicant who envies others does not obtain peace of mind.

A Bhikshu who, though he receives little, does not despise what he has received, even the gods will praise him, if his life is pure, and if he is not slothful.

He who never identifies himself with name and form, and does not grieve over what is no more, he indeed is called a Bhikshu.

The Bhikshu who behaves with kindness, who is happy in the doctrine of Buddha, will reach the quiet place (Nirvâna), happiness arising from the cessation of natural inclinations.

O Bhikshu, empty this boat! if emptied, it will go quickly; having cut off passion and hatred, thou wilt go to Nirvâna.

Cut off the five fetters, leave the five, rise above the five. A Bhikshu, who has escaped from the five fetters, he is called Oghatinna—" saved from the flood."

Meditate, O Bhikshu, and be not heedless! Do not direct thy thought to what gives pleasure, that thou mayest not for thy heedlessness have to swallow the iron ball in hell, and that thou mayest not cry out when burning, " This is pain."

Without knowledge there is no meditation, without meditation there is no knowledge: he who has knowledge and meditation is near unto Nirvâna.

A Bhikshu who has entered his empty house, and whose mind is tranquil, feels a more than human delight when he sees the law clearly.

As soon as he has considered the origin and destruction of the elements of the body, he finds happiness and joy which belong to those who know the immortal (Nirvâna).

And this is the beginning here for a wise Bhikshu: watchfulness over the senses, contentedness, restraint under the law; keep noble friends whose life is pure, and who are not slothful.

Let him live in charity, let him be perfect in his duties; then in the fulness of delight he will make an end of suffering.

As the Vassikâ plant sheds its withered flowers, men should shed passion and hatred, O ye Bhikshus!

The Bhikshu whose body and tongue and mind are quieted, who is collected, and has rejected the baits of the world, he is called quiet.

Rouse thyself by thyself, examine thyself by thyself, thus self-protected and attentive wilt thou live happily, O Bhikshu!

For self is the lord of self, self is the refuge of self; therefore curb thyself as the merchant curbs a noble horse.'

The Bhikshu, full of delight, who is happy in the doctrine of Buddha will reach the quiet place (Nirvâna), happiness consisting in the cessation of natural inclinations.

He who, even as a young Bhikshu, applies himself to the doctrine of Buddha, brightens up this world, like the moon when free from clouds.

CHAPTER XXVI

THE BRAHMANA

STOP the stream valiantly, drive away the desires, O Brâhmana! When you have understood the destruction of all that was made, you will understand that which was not made.

If the Brâhmana has reached the other shore in both laws, in restraint and contemplation, all bonds vanish from him who has obtained knowledge.

He for whom there is neither the hither nor the further shore, nor both, him, the fearless and unshackled, I call indeed a Brâhmana.

He who is thoughtful, blameless, settled, dutiful, without passions, and who has attained the highest end, him I call indeed a Brâhmana.

The sun is bright by day, the moon shines by night, the warrior is bright in his armor, the Brâhmana is bright in his meditation; but Buddha, the Awakened, is bright with splendor day and night.

Because a man is rid of evil, therefore he is called Brâhmana; because he walks quietly, therefore he is called Samana; because he has sent away his own impurities, therefore he is called Pravragita (Pabbagita, a pilgrim).

No one should attack a Brâhmana, but no Brâhmana, if attacked, should let himself fly at his aggressor! Woe to him who strikes a Brâhmana, more woe to him who flies at his aggressor!

It advantages a Brâhmana not a little if he holds his mind back from the pleasures of life; the more all wish to injure has vanished, the more all pain will cease.

Him I call indeed a Brâhmana who does not offend by body, word, or thought, and is controlled on these three points.

He from whom he may learn the law, as taught by the Well-awakened (Buddha), him let him worship assiduously, as the Brâhmana worships the sacrificial fire.

A man does not become a Brâhmana by his plaited hair, by his family, or by birth; in whom there is truth and righteousness, he is blessed, he is a Brâhmana.

What is the use of plaited hair, O fool! what of the raiment of goat-skins? Within thee there is ravening, but the outside thou makest clean.

The man who wears dirty raiments, who is emaciated and covered with veins, who meditates alone in the forest, him I call indeed a Brâhmana.

I do not call a man a Brâhmana because of his origin or of his mother. He is indeed arrogant, and he is wealthy: but the poor, who is free from all attachments, him I call indeed a Brâhmana.

Him I call indeed a Brâhmana who, after cutting all fetters, never trembles, is free from bonds and unshackled.

Him I call indeed a Brâhmana who, after cutting the strap and the thong, the rope with all that pertains to it, has destroyed all obstacles, and is awakened.

Him I call indeed a Brâhmana who, though he has committed no offence, endures reproach, stripes, and bonds: who has endurance for his force, and strength for his army.

Him I call indeed a Brâhmana who is free from anger, dutiful, virtuous, without appetites, who is subdued, and has received his last body.

Him I call indeed a Brâhmana who does not cling to sensual pleasures, like water on a lotus leaf, like a mustard seed on the point of a needle.

Him I call indeed a Brâhmana who, even here, knows the end of his own suffering, has put down his burden, and is unshackled.

Him I call indeed a Brâhmana whose knowledge is deep, who possesses wisdom, who knows the right way and the wrong, and has attained the highest end.

Him I call indeed a Brâhmana who keeps aloof both from laymen and from mendicants, who frequents no houses, and has but few desires.

Him I call indeed a Brâhmana who without hurting any creatures, whether feeble or strong, does not kill nor cause slaughter.

Him I call indeed a Brâhmana who is tolerant with the intolerant, mild with the violent, and free from greed among the greedy.

Him I call indeed a Brâhmana from whom anger and hatred, pride and hypocrisy have dropped like a mustard seed from the point of a needle.

Him I call indeed a Brâhmana who utters true speech, instructive and free from harshness, so that he offend no one.

Him I call indeed a Brâhmana who takes nothing in the world that is not given him, be it long or short, small or large, good or bad.

Him I call indeed a Brâhmana who fosters no desires for this world or for the next, has no inclinations, and is unshackled.

Him I call indeed a Brâhmana who has no interests, and when he has understood the truth, does not say How, how? and who has reached the depth of the Immortal.

Him I call indeed a Brâhmana who in this world has risen above both ties, good and evil, who is free from grief, from sin, and from impurity.

Him I call indeed a Brâhmana who is bright like the moon, pure, serene, undisturbed, and in whom all gayety is extinct.

Him I call indeed a Brâhmana who has traversed this miry road, the impassable world, difficult to pass, and its vanity, who has gone through, and reached the other shore, is thoughtful, steadfast, free from doubts, free from attachment, and content.

Him I call indeed a Brâhmana who in this world, having abandoned all desires, travels about without a home, and in whom all concupiscence is extinct.

Him I call indeed a Brâhmana who, having abandoned all longings, travels about without a home, and in whom all covetousness is extinct.

Him I call indeed a Brâhmana who, after leaving all bondage to men, has risen above all bondage to the gods, and is free from all and every bondage.

Him I call indeed a Brâhmana who has left what gives pleasure and what gives pain, who is cold, and free from all germs of renewed life: the hero who has conquered all the worlds.

Him I call indeed a Brâhmana who knows the destruction and the return of beings everywhere, who is free from bondage, welfaring (Sugata), and awakened (Buddha).

Him I call indeed a Brâhmana whose path the gods do not know, nor spirits (Gandharvas), nor men, whose passions are extinct, and who is an Arhat.

Him I call indeed a Brâhmana who calls nothing his own, whether it be before, behind, or between; who is poor, and free from the love of the world.

Him I call indeed a Brâhmana, the manly, the noble, the hero, the great sage, the conqueror, the indifferent, the accomplished, the awakened.

Him I call indeed a Brâhmana who knows his former abodes, who sees heaven and hell, has reached the end of births, is perfect in knowledge, a sage, and whose perfections are all perfect.

THE UPANISHADS

[*Translation by F. Max Müller*]

INTRODUCTION

THE "Upanishads" are reckoned to be from a hundred and fifty to a hundred and seventy in number. The date of the earliest of them is about B.C. 600; that is an age anterior to the rise of Buddha. They consist of various disquisitions on the nature of man, the Supreme Being, the human soul, and immortality. They are part of Sanscrit Brahmanic literature, and have the authority of revealed, in contradistinction to traditional truth. We see in these books the struggle of the human mind to attain to a knowledge of God and the destiny of man. The result is the formulation of a definite theosophy, in which we find the Brahman in his meditation trusting to the intuitions of his own spirit, the promptings of his own reason, or the combinations of his own fancy, for a revelation of the truth. The result is given us in these wonderful books. We call them wonderful, because the unaided mind of man never attained, in any other literature, to a profounder insight into spiritual things. The Western reader may find in an "Upanishad" many things that seem to him trifling and absurd, many things obscure and apparently meaningless. It is very easy to ridicule this kind of literature. But as a matter of fact these ancient writings well repay study, as the most astounding productions of the human intellect. In them we see the human mind wrestling with the greatest thoughts that had ever yet dawned upon it, and trying to grasp and to measure the mighty vision before which it was humbled to the dust. The seer, in order to communicate to the world the result of his meditations, seems to catch at every symbol and every word hallowed by familiar usage, in order to set out in concrete shape the color and dimensions of mystic verities; he is employing an old language for the expression of new truths; he is putting new wine into old wine-skins, which burst and the wine is spilt; words fail, and the meaning is lost. It is not lost, however, to those who will try to study the "Upanishads" from within, and not from without: who will try to put himself in the attitude of those earnest and patient explorers who brought so much light into the human life of the East, and so much joy and tranquillity to the perturbed spirit of their fellow-men. Those who thus study these ancient writings will find in them the fundamental principles of a definite theology, and, more wonderful still, the beginnings of that which became afterwards known to the Greeks, and has been known ever since, as metaphysics: that is, scientific transcendentalism. This much will be apparent to anyone who will read and study the "Kaushitaki-Upanishad," which is one of the most wonderful of the religious books of the East. Laying aside the doctrine of metempsychosis and the idea of reincarnation, there is something sublime and inspiring in the imagery with which the destiny of the soul after death is described, while in the metaphysical subtlety of this book we find an argument against materialism which is just as fresh now as when it was first stated.

E. W.

THE UPANISHADS

KAUSHÎTAKI - UPANISHAD

THE COUCH OF BRAHMAN

KITRA GANGYÂYANI, wishing to perform a sacrifice, chose Âruni Uddâlaka, to be his chief priest. But Âruni sent his son, Svetaketu, and said: "Perform the sacrifice for him." When Svetaketu had arrived, Kitra asked him: "Son of Gautama, is there a hidden place in the world where you are able to place me, or is it the other way, and are you going to place me in the world to which that other way leads?"[1]

He answered and said: "I do not know this. But, let me ask the master." Having approached his father, he asked: "Thus has Kitra asked me; how shall I answer?"

Âruni said: "I also do not know this. Only after having learnt the proper portion of the Veda in Kitra's own dwelling, shall we obtain what others give us, i.e., knowledge. Come, we will both go."

[1] The question put by Kitra to Svetaketu is very obscure, and was probably from the first intended to be obscure in its very wording. Kitra wished to ask, doubtless, concerning the future life. That future life is reached by two roads; one leading to the world of Brahman (the conditioned), beyond which there lies one other stage only, represented by knowledge of, and identity with the unconditioned Brahman; the other leading to the world of the fathers, and from thence, after the reward of good works has been consumed, back to a new round of mundane existence. There is a third road for creatures which live and die, worms, insects, and creeping things, but they are of little consequence. Now it is quite clear that the knowledge which King Kitra possesses, and which Svetaketu does not possess, is that of the two roads after death, sometimes called the right and the left, or the southern and northern roads. The northern or left road, called also the path of the Devas, passes on from light and day to the bright half of the moon; the southern or right road, called also the path of the fathers, passes on from smoke and night to the dark half of the moon. Both roads therefore meet in the moon, but diverge afterwards. While the northern road passes by the six months when the sun moves towards the north, through the sun, moon, and the lightning to the world of Brahman, the southern passes by the six months when the sun moves towards the south, to the world of the fathers, the ether, and the moon. The great difference, however, between the two roads is, that while those who travel on the former do not return again to a new life on earth, but reach in the end a true knowledge of the unconditioned Brahman, those who pass on to the world of the fathers and the moon return to earth to be born again and again. The speculations on the fate of the soul after death seem to have been peculiar to the royal families of India, while the Brahmans dwelt more on what may be called the shorter cut, a knowledge of Brahman as the true Self. To know, with them, was to be, and, after the dissolution of the body, they looked forward to immediate emancipation, without any further wanderings.

Having said this he took fuel in his hand, like a pupil, and approached Kitra Gângyâyani, saying: "May I come near to you?" He replied: "You are worthy of Brahman, O Gautama, because you were not led away by pride. Come hither, I shall make you know clearly."

And Kitra said: "All who depart from this world go to the moon. In the former, the bright half, the moon delights in their spirits; in the other, the dark half, the moon sends them on to be born again. Verily, the moon is the door of the Svarga, i.e., the heavenly world. Now, if a man objects to the moon and is not satisfied with life there, the moon sets him free. But if a man does not object, then the moon sends him down as rain upon this earth. And according to his deeds and according to his knowledge he is born again here as a worm, or as an insect, or as a fish, or as a bird, or as a lion, or as a boar, or as a serpent, or as a tiger, or as a man, or as something else in different places. When he has thus returned to the earth, someone, a sage, asks: 'Who art thou?' And he should answer: 'From the wise moon, who orders the seasons, when it is born consisting of fifteen parts, from the moon who is the home of our ancestors, the seed was brought. This seed, even me, they, the gods, mentioned in the Pañkâgnividyâ, gathered up in an active man, and through an active man they brought me to a mother. Then I, growing up to be born, a being living by months, whether twelve or thirteen, was together with my father, who also lived by years of twelve or thirteen months, that I might either know the true Brahman or not know it. Therefore, O ye seasons, grant that I may attain immortality, i.e., knowledge of Brahman. By this my true saying, by this my toil, beginning with the dwelling in the moon and ending with my birth on earth, I am like a season, and the child of the seasons.' 'Who art thou?' the sage asks again. 'I am thou,' he replies. Then he sets him free to proceed onward.

"He, at the time of death, having reached the path of the gods, comes to the world of Agni, or fire, to the world of Vâyu, or air, to the world of Varuna, to the world of Indra, to the world of Pragâpati, to the world of Brahman. In that world there is the lake Âra, the moments called Yeshtiha, the river Vigarâ, i.e., age-less, the tree Ilyâ, the city Sâlagya, the palace Aparâgita, i.e., unconquerable, the door-keepers Indra and Pragâpati, the hall of Brahman, called Vibhu (built by vibhu, egoism), the throne Vikakshanâ, i.e., perception, the couch Amitaugas or endless splendor, and the beloved Mânasî, i.e., mind, and her image Kâkshushi, the eye, who, as if taking flowers, are weaving the worlds, and the Apsaras, the Ambâs, or sacred scriptures, and Ambâyavîs, or understanding, and the rivers Ambayâs leading to the knowledge of Brahman. To this world he who knows the Paryanka-vidyâ approaches. Brahman says to him: 'Run towards him, servants, with such worship as is due to myself. He has reached the river Vigarâ, the age-less, he will never age.'

"Then five hundred Apsaras go towards him, one hundred with garlands in their hands, one hundred with ointments in their hands, one hundred with perfumes in their hands, one hundred with garments in their hands, one hundred with fruit in their hands. They adorn him with an adornment worthy of Brahman, and when thus adorned with the adornment of Brahman, the knower of Brahman moves towards Brahman. He comes to the lake Âra, and he crosses it by the mind, while those who come to it without knowing the truth, are drowned. He comes to the moments called Yeshtiha, they flee from him. He comes to the river Vigarâ, and crosses it by the mind alone, and there shakes off his good and evil deeds. His beloved relatives obtain the good, his unbeloved relatives the evil he has done. And as a man, driving in a chariot, might look at the two wheels without being touched by them, thus he will look at day and night, thus at good and evil deeds, and at all pairs, all correlative things, such as light and darkness, heat and cold. Being freed from good and freed from evil, he, the knower of Brahman, moves towards Brahman.

"He approaches the tree Ilya, and the odor of Brahman reaches him. He approaches the city Sâlagya, and the flavor of Brahman reaches him. He approaches the palace Aparâgita, and the splendor of Brahman reaches him. He approaches the door-keepers Indra and Pragâpati, and they run away from him. He approaches the hall Vibhu, and the glory of Brahman reaches him and he thinks, 'I am Brahman.' He approaches the throne Vikakshanâ. The Sâman verses, Brihad and Rathantara, are the eastern feet of that throne; the Sâman verses, Syaita and Naudhasa, its western feet; the Sâman verses, Vairûpa and Vairâga, its sides lengthways, south and north; the Sâman verses, Sâkvara and Raivata, its sides crossways, east and west. That throne is Pragñâ, knowledge, for by knowledge, self-knowledge, he sees clearly. He approaches the couch Amitaugas. That is Prâna, i.e., speech. The past and the future are its eastern feet; prosperity and earth its western feet; the Sâman verses, Brihad and Rathantara, are the two sides lengthways of the couch, south and north; the Sâman verses, Bhadra and Yagñâyagñiya, are its cross-sides at the head and feet, east and west; the Rik and Sâman are the long sheets, east and west; the Yagus the cross-sheets, south and north; the moon-beam the cushion; the Udgîtha the white coverlet; prosperity the pillow. On this couch sits Brahman, and he who knows himself one with Brahman, sitting on the couch, mounts it first with one foot only. Then Brahman says to him: 'Who art thou?' and he shall answer: 'I am like a season, and the child of the seasons, sprung from the womb of endless space, from the light, from the luminous Brahman. The light, the origin of the year, which is the past, which is the present, which is all living things, and all elements, is the Self. Thou art the Self. What thou art, that am I.' Brahman says to him: 'Who am I?' He shall answer: 'That which is, the true.' Brahman asks: 'What is the true?' He says to him: 'What is different from the gods and from the senses that is Sat, but the gods and the senses are Tyam. Therefore, by that name Sattya, or true, is called all this whatever there is. All this thou art.' This is also declared by a verse: 'This great Rishi, whose belly is the Yagus, the head the Sâman, the form the Rik, is to be known as being imperishable, as being Brahman.'

"Brahman says to him: 'How dost thou obtain my male names?' He should answer: 'By breath.' Brahman asks: 'How my female names?' He should answer: 'By speech.' Brahman asks: 'How my neuter names?' He should answer: 'By mind.' 'How smells?' 'By the nose.' 'How forms?' 'By the eye.' 'How sounds?' 'By the ear.' 'How flavors of food?' 'By the tongue.' 'How actions?' 'By the hands.' 'How pleasures and pain?' 'By the body.' 'How joy, delight, and offspring?' 'By the organ.' 'How journeyings?' 'By the feet.' 'How thoughts, and what is to be known and desired?' 'By knowledge alone.'

"Brahman says to him: 'Water indeed is this my world, the whole Brahman world, and it is thine.'

"Whatever victory, whatever might belongs to Brahman, that victory and that might he obtains who knows this, yea, who knows this."[2]

KNOWLEDGE OF THE LIVING SPIRIT

"Prâna, or breath,[3] is Brahman," thus says Kaushîtaki. "Of this prâna, which is Brahman, the mind is the messenger, speech the housekeeper, the eye the guard, the ear the informant. He who knows mind as the messenger of prâna, which is Brahman, becomes possessed of the messenger. He who knows speech as the housekeeper, becomes possessed of the housekeeper. He who knows the eye as the guard, becomes possessed of the guard. He who knows the ear as the informant, becomes possessed of the informant.

"Now to that prâna, which is Brahman, all these deities, mind, speech, eye, ear, bring an offering, though he asks not for it, and thus to him who knows this all creatures bring an offering, though he asks not for it. For him who knows this, there is this Upanishad, or secret vow, 'Beg not!' As a man who has begged through a village and got nothing sits down and says, 'I shall never eat anything given by those people,' and as then those who formerly refused him press him to accept their alms, thus is the rule for him who begs not, but the charitable will press him and say, 'Let us give to thee.'

"Prâna, or breath, is Brahman," thus says Paingya. "And in that prâna, which is Brahman, the eye stands firm behind speech, the ear stands firm behind the eye, the mind stands firm behind the ear, and the spirit stands firm behind the mind.[4] To that prâna, which is Brahman, all these deities bring an offering, though he asks not for it, and thus to him who knows this, all creatures bring an offering, though he asks not for it. For him who knows this, there is this Upanishad, or secret vow,

[2] Who knows the conditioned and mythological form of Brahman as here described, sitting on the couch.

[3] In the first chapter it was said, "He approaches the couch Amitaugas, that is prâna" (breath, spirit, life). Therefore having explained in the first chapter the knowledge of the couch (of Brahman), the next subject to be explained is the knowledge of prâna, the living spirit, taken for a time as Brahman, or the last cause of everything.

[4] Speech is uncertain, and has to be checked by the eye. The eye is uncertain, taking mother of pearl for silver, and must be checked by the ear. The ear is uncertain, and must be checked by the mind, for unless the mind is attentive, the ear hears not. The mind, lastly, depends on the spirit, for without spirit there is no mind.

'Beg not!' As a man who has begged through a village and got nothing sits down and says, 'I shall never eat anything given by those people,' and as then those who formerly refused him press him to accept their alms, thus is the rule for him who begs not, but the charitable will press him and say, 'Let us give to thee.'

"Now follows the attainment of the highest treasure, i.e., spirit.[5] If a man meditates on that highest treasure, let him on a full moon or a new moon, or in the bright fortnight, under an auspicious Nakshatra, at one of these proper times, bending his right knee, offer oblations of ghee with a ladle, after having placed the fire, swept the ground, strewn the sacred grass, and sprinkled water. Let him say: 'The deity called Speech is the attainer, may it attain this for me from him who possesses and can bestow what I wish for. Svâhâ to it!' 'The deity called prâna, or breath, is the attainer, may it attain this for me from him. Svâhâ to it!' 'The deity called the eye is the attainer, may it attain this for me from him. Svâhâ to it!' 'The deity called the ear is the attainer, may it attain this for me from him. Svâhâ to it!' 'The deity called mind is the attainer of it, may it attain this for me from him. Svâhâ to it!' 'The deity called knowledge is the attainer of it, may it attain this for me from him. Svâhâ to it!'

"Then having inhaled the smell of the smoke, and having rubbed his limbs with the ointment of ghee, walking on in silence, let him declare his wish, or let him send a messenger. He will surely obtain his wish.

"Now follows the Daiva Smara, the desire to be accomplished by the gods. If a man desires to become dear to any man or woman, or to any men or women, then at one of the fore-mentioned proper times he offers, in exactly the same manner as before, oblations of ghee, saying: 'I offer thy speech in myself, I this one here, Svâhâ.' 'I offer thy ear in myself, I this one here, Svâhâ.' 'I offer thy mind in myself, I this one here, Svâhâ.' 'I offer thy knowledge in myself, I this one here, Svâhâ.' Then having inhaled the smell of the smoke, and having rubbed his limbs with the ointment of ghee, walking on in silence, let him try to come in contact or let him stand speaking in the wind, so that the wind may carry his

[5] The vital spirits are called the highest treasure, because a man surrenders everything to preserve his vital spirits or his life.

words to the person by whom he desires to be loved. Surely he becomes dear, and they think of him.

"Now follows the restraint instituted by Pratardana, the son of Divodâsa: they call it the inner Agni-hotri. So long as a man speaks, he cannot breathe, he offers all the while his breath in his speech. And so long as a man breathes, he cannot speak, he offers all the while his speech in his breath. These two endless and immortal oblations he offers always, whether waking or sleeping. Whatever other oblations there are (those, e.g., of the ordinary Agni-hotri, consisting of milk and other things), they have an end, for they consist of works which, like all works, have an end. The ancients, knowing this the best Agni-hotri, did not offer the ordinary Agni-hotri.

"Uktha is Brahman, thus said Sushkabhringâra. Let him meditate on the uktha as the same with the Rik, and all beings will praise him as the best. Let him meditate on it as the same with the Yagus, and all beings will join before him as the best. Let him meditate on it as the same with the Sâman, and all beings will bow before him as the best. Let him meditate on it as the same with might, let him meditate on it as the same with glory, let him meditate on it as the same with splendor. For as the bow is among weapons the mightiest, the most glorious, the most splendid, thus is he who knows this among all beings the mightiest, the most glorious, the most splendid. The Adhvaryu conceives the fire of the altar, which is used for the sacrifice, to be himself. In it he the Adhvaryu weaves the Yagus portion of the sacrifice. And in the Yagus portion the Hotri weaves the Rik portion of the sacrifice. And in the Rik portion the Udgâtri weaves the Sâman portion of the sacrifice. He, the Adhvaryu, or prâna, is the self of the threefold knowledge; he indeed is the self of prâna. He who knows this is the self of it, i.e., becomes prâna.

"Next follow the three kinds of meditation of the all-conquering Kaushitaki. The all-conquering Kaushîtaki adores the sun when rising, having put on the sacrificial cord,* having brought water, and having thrice sprinkled the water-cup, saying: 'Thou art the deliverer, deliver me from sin.' In the same manner he adores the sun when in the zenith, saying: 'Thou art the highest deliverer, deliver me highly from sin.'

* This is one of the earliest, if not the earliest mention of the yagñopavîta, the sacred cord as worn over the left shoulder for sacrificial purposes.

In the same manner he adores the sun when setting, saying: 'Thou art the full deliverer, deliver me fully from sin.' Thus he fully removes whatever sin he committed by day and by night. And in the same manner he who knows this, likewise adores the sun, and fully removes whatever sin he committed by day and by night.

"Then, secondly, let him worship every month in the year at the time of the new moon, the moon as it is seen in the west in the same manner as before described with regard to the sun, or let him send forth his speech towards the moon with two green blades of grass, saying: 'O thou who art mistress of immortal joy, through that gentle heart of mine which abides in the moon, may I never weep for misfortune concerning my children.'

"The children of him who thus adores the moon do not indeed die before him. Thus it is with a man to whom a son is already born.

"Now for one to whom no son is born as yet. He mutters the three Rik verses. 'Increase, O Soma! may vigor come to thee.' 'May milk, may food go to thee.' 'That ray which the Âdityas gladden.'

"Having muttered these three Rik verses, he says: 'Do not increase by our breath, by our offspring, by our cattle; he who hates us and whom we hate, increase by his breath, by his offspring, by his cattle. Thus I turn the turn of the god, I return the turn of Âditya.' After these words, having raised the right arm towards Soma, he lets it go again.

"Then, thirdly, let him worship on the day of the full moon the moon as it is seen in the east in the same manner, saying: 'Thou art Soma, the king, the wise, the five-mouthed, the lord of creatures. The Brahmana is one of thy mouths; with that mouth thou eatest the kings; make me an eater of food by that mouth! The king is one of thy mouths; with that mouth thou eatest the people; make me an eater of food by that mouth! The hawk is one of thy mouths; with that mouth thou eatest the birds; make me an eater of food by that mouth! Fire is one of thy mouths; with that mouth thou eatest this world; make me an eater of food by that mouth! In thee there is the fifth mouth; with that mouth thou eatest all beings; make me an eater of food by that mouth! Do not decrease by our life, by our offspring, by our cattle; he who hates us and whom we hate, decrease by his life, by his offspring, by his cattle. Thus I turn the turn of the god, I return the turn of Âditya.' After these words, having raised the right arm, he lets it go again.

"Next, having addressed these prayers to Soma, when being with his wife, let him stroke her heart, saying: 'O fair one, who hast obtained immortal joy by that which has entered thy heart through Pragâpati, mayest thou never fall into sorrow about thy children.' Her children then do not die before her.

"Next, if a man has been absent and returns home, let him kiss his son's head, saying: 'Thou springest from every limb, thou art born from the heart, thou, my son, art my self indeed: live thou a hundred harvests.' He gives him his name, saying: 'Be thou a stone, be thou an axe, be thou solid gold; thou, my son, art light indeed: live thou a hundred harvests.' He pronounces his name. Then he embraces him, saying: 'As Pragâpati the lord of creatures embraced his creatures for their welfare, thus I embrace thee,' (pronouncing his name). Then he mutters into his right ear, saying: 'O thou, quick Maghavan, give to him.' 'O Indra, bestow thy best wishes'—thus he whispers into his left ear. Let him then thrice kiss his head, saying: 'Do not cut off the line of our race, do not suffer. Live a hundred harvests of life; I kiss thy head, O son, with thy name.' He then thrice makes a lowing sound over his head, saying: 'I low over thee with the lowing sound of cows.'

"Next follows the Daiva Parimara, the dying around of the gods, the absorption of the two classes of gods, mentioned before, into prâna or Brahman. This Brahman shines forth indeed when the fire burns, and it dies when it burns not. Its splendor goes to the sun alone, the life prâna, the moving principle, to the air.

"This Brahman shines forth indeed when the sun is seen, and it dies when it is not seen. Its splendor goes to the moon alone, the life to the air.

"This Brahman shines forth indeed when the moon is seen, and it dies when it is not seen. Its splendor goes to the lightning alone, its life to the air.

"This Brahman shines forth indeed when the lightning flashes, and it dies when it flashes not. Its splendor goes to the air, and the life to the air.

"Thus all these deities (fire, sun, moon, lightning), having entered the air, though dead, do not vanish; and out of the very air they rise again. So much with reference to the deities. Now then, with reference to the body.

"This Brahman shines forth indeed when one speaks with speech, and it dies when one does not speak. His splendor goes to the eye alone, the life to breath.

"This Brahman shines forth indeed when one sees with the eye, and it dies when one does not see. Its splendor goes to the ear alone, the life to breath.

"This Brahman shines forth indeed when one hears with the ear, and it dies when one does not hear. Its splendor goes to the mind alone, the life to breath.

"This Brahman shines forth indeed when one thinks with the mind, and it dies when one does not think. Its splendor goes to the breath alone, and the life to breath.

"Thus all these deities (the senses, etc.), having entered breath or life alone, though dead, do not vanish; and out of very breath they rise again. And if two mountains, the southern and northern, were to move forward trying to crush him who knows this, they would not crush him. But those who hate him and those whom he hates, they die around him.

"Next follows the Nihsreyasâdâna, i.e., the accepting of the preëminence of breath or life by the other gods. The deities, speech, eye, ear, mind, contending with each for who was the best, went out of this body, and the body lay without breathing, withered, like a log of wood. Then speech went into it, but speaking by speech, it lay still. Then the eye went into it, but speaking by speech, and seeing by the eye, it lay still. Then the ear went into it, but speaking by speech, seeing by the eye, hearing by the ear, it lay still. Then mind went into it, but speaking by speech, seeing by the eye, hearing by the ear, thinking by the mind, it lay still. Then breath went into it, and thence it rose at once. All these deities, having recognized the preëminence in life, and having comprehended life alone as the conscious self, went out of this body with all these five different kinds of life, and resting in the air, knowing that life had entered the air and merged in the ether, they went to heaven. And in the same manner he who knows this, having recognized the preëminence in prâna, and having comprehended life alone as the conscious self, goes out of this body with all these, does no longer believe in this body, and resting in the air, and merged in the ether, he goes to heaven: he goes to where those gods are. And having reached this heaven, he, who knows this, becomes immortal with that immortality which those gods enjoy.

"Next follows the father's tradition to the son, and thus they explain it. The father, when going to depart, calls his son, after having strewn the house with fresh grass, and having laid the sacrificial fire, and having placed near it a pot of water with a jug, full of rice, himself covered with a new cloth, and dressed in white. He places himself above his son, touching his organs with his own organs, or he may deliver the tradition to him while he sits before him. Then he delivers it to him. The father says: 'Let me place my speech in thee.' The son says: 'I take thy speech in me.' The father says: 'Let me place my scent in thee.' The son says: 'I take thy scent in me.' The father says: 'Let me place my eye in thee.' The son says: 'I take thy eye in me.' The father says: 'Let me place my ear in thee.' The son says: 'I take thy ear in me.' The father says: 'Let me place my tastes of food in thee.' The son says: 'I take thy tastes of food in me.' The father says: 'Let me place my actions in thee.' The son says: 'I take thy actions in me.' The father says: 'Let me place my pleasure and pain in thee.' The son says: 'I take thy pleasure and pain in me.' The father says: 'Let me place happiness, joy, and offspring in thee.' The son says: 'I take thy happiness, joy, and offspring in me.' The father says: 'Let me place my walking in thee.' The son says: 'I take thy walking in me.' The father says: 'Let me place my mind in thee.' The son says: 'I take thy mind in me.' The father says: 'Let me place my knowledge in thee.' The son says: 'I take thy knowledge in me.' But if the father is very ill, he may say shortly: 'Let me place my spirits in thee,' and the son: 'I take thy spirits in me.'

"Then the son walks round his father, keeping his right side towards him, and goes away. The father calls after him: 'May fame, glory of countenance, and honor always follow thee.' Then the other looks back over his left shoulder, covering himself with his hand or the hem of his garment, saying: 'Obtain the heavenly worlds and all desires.'

"If the father recovers, let him be under the authority of his son, or let him wander about as an ascetic. But if he departs, then let them despatch him, as he ought to be despatched, yea, as he ought to be despatched."

LIFE AND CONSCIOUSNESS

Pratardana, the son of Divodâsa, King of Kâsi, came by means of fighting and strength to the beloved abode of Indra. Indra said to him: "Pratardana, let me give you a boon to choose." And Pratardana answered: "Do you yourself choose that boon for me which you deem most beneficial for a man." Indra said to him: "No one who chooses, chooses for another; choose thyself." Then Pratardana replied: "Then that boon to choose is no boon for me."

Then, however, Indra did not swerve from the truth, for Indra is truth. Indra said to him: "Know me only; that is what I deem most beneficial for man, that he should know me. I slew the three-headed son of Tvashtri; I delivered the Arunmukhas, the devotees, to the wolves; breaking many treaties, I killed the people of Prahlâda in heaven, the people of Puloma in the sky, the people of Kâlakañga on earth. And not one hair of me was harmed there. And he who knows me thus, by no deed of his is his life harmed: not by the murder of his mother, not by the murder of his father, not by theft, not by the killing of a Brahman. If he is going to commit a sin, the bloom does not depart from his face. I am prâna, meditate on me as the conscious self, as life, as immortality. Life is prâna, prâna is life. Immortality is prâna, prâna is immortality. As long as prâna dwells in this body, so long surely there is life. By prâna he obtains immortality in the other world, by knowledge true conception. He who meditates on me as life and immortality, gains his full life in this world, and obtains in the Svarga world immortality and indestructibility."

Pratardana said: "Some maintain here, that the prânas become one, for otherwise no one could at the same time make known a name by speech, see a form with the eye, hear a sound with the ear, think a thought with the mind. After having become one, the prânas perceive all these together, one by one. While speech speaks, all prânas speak after it. While the eye sees, all prânas see after it. While the ear hears, all prânas hear after it. While the mind thinks, all prânas think after it. While the prâna breathes, all prânas breathe after it."

"Thus it is indeed," said Indra, "but nevertheless there is a preëminence among the prânas. Man lives deprived of speech, for we see dumb people. Man lives deprived of sight, for we see blind people. Man lives deprived of hearing, for we see deaf people. Man lives deprived of mind, for we see infants. Man lives deprived of his arms, deprived of his legs, for we see it thus. But prâna alone is the conscious self, and having laid hold of this body, it makes it rise up. Therefore it is said, 'Let man worship it alone as uktha.' What is prâna, that is pragñâ, or self-consciousness; what is pragñâ (self-consciousness), that is prâna, for together they live in this body, and together they go out of it. Of that, this is the evidence, this is the understanding. When a man, being thus asleep, sees no dream whatever, he becomes one with that prâna alone. Then speech goes to him, when he is absorbed in prâna, with all names, the eye with all forms, the ear with all sounds, the mind with all thoughts. And when he awakes, then, as from a burning fire sparks proceed in all directions; thus from that self the prânas proceed, each towards its place: from the prânas the gods, from the gods the worlds.

"Of this, this is the proof, this is the understanding. When a man is thus sick, going to die, falling into weakness and faintness, they say: 'His thought has departed, he hears not, he sees not, he speaks not, he thinks not.' Then he becomes one with that prâna alone. Then speech goes to him who is absorbed in prâna, with all names, the eye with all forms, the ear with all sounds, the mind with all thoughts. And when he departs from this body, he departs together with all these.

"Speech gives up to him who is absorbed in prâna all names, so that by speech he obtains all names. The nose gives up to him all odors, so that by scent he obtains all odors. The eye gives up to him all forms, so that by the eye he obtains all forms. The ear gives up to him all sounds, so that by the ear he obtains all sounds. The mind gives up to him all thoughts, so that by the mind he obtains all thoughts. This is the complete absorption in prâna. And what is prâna is pragñâ, or self-consciousness; what it pragñâ, is prâna. For together do these two live in the body, and together do they depart.

"Now we shall explain how all things become one in that

self-consciousness. Speech is one portion taken out of pragñâ, or self-conscious knowledge: the word is its object, placed outside. The nose is one portion taken out of it, the odor is its object, placed outside. The eye is one portion taken out of it, the form is its object, placed outside. The ear is one portion taken out of it, the sound is its object, placed outside. The tongue is one portion taken out of it, the taste of food is its object, placed outside. The two hands are one portion taken out of it, their action is their object, placed outside. The body is one portion taken out of it, its pleasure and pain are its object, placed outside. The organ is one portion taken out of it, happiness, joy, and offspring are its object, placed outside. The two feet are one portion taken out of it, movements are their object, placed outside. Mind is one portion taken out of it, thoughts and desires are its object, placed outside.

"Having by self-conscious knowledge taken possession of speech, he obtains by speech all words. Having taken possession of the nose, he obtains all odors. Having taken possession of the eye, he obtains all forms. Having taken possession of the ear, he obtains all sounds. Having taken possession of the tongue, he obtains all tastes of food. Having taken possession of the two hands, he obtains all actions. Having taken possession of the body, he obtains pleasure and pain. Having taken possession of the organ, he obtains happiness, joy, and offspring. Having taken possession of the two feet, he obtains all movements. Having taken possession of mind, he obtains all thoughts.

"For without self-consciousness speech does not make known to the self any word.[7] 'My mind was absent,' he says, 'I did not perceive that word.' Without self-consciousness the nose does not make known any odor. 'My mind was absent,' he says, 'I did not perceive that odor.' Without self-consciousness the eye does not make known any form. 'My mind was absent,' he says, 'I did not perceive that form.'

[7] Professor Cowell has translated a passage from the commentary which is interesting as showing that its author and the author of the Upanishads too had a clear conception of the correlative nature of knowledge. "The organ of sense," he says, "cannot exist without pragñâ (self-consciousness), nor the objects of sense be obtained without the organ, therefore—on the principle, that when one thing cannot exist without another, that thing is said to be identical with the other—as the cloth, for instance, being never perceived without the threads, is identical with them, or the (false perception of) silver being never found without the mother of pearl is identical with it, so the objects of sense being never found without the organs are identical with them, and the organs being never found without pragñâ (self-consciousness) are identical with it.

Without self-consciousness the ear does not make known any sound. 'My mind was absent,' he says, 'I did not perceive that sound.' Without self-consciousness the tongue does not make known any taste. 'My mind was absent,' he says, 'I did not perceive that taste.' Without self-consciousness the two hands do not make known any act. 'Our mind was absent,' they say, 'we did not perceive any act.' Without self-consciousness the body does not make known pleasure or pain. 'My mind was absent,' he says, 'I did not perceive that pleasure or pain.' Without self-consciousness the organ does not make known happiness, joy, or offspring. 'My mind was absent,' he says, 'I did not perceive that happiness, joy, or offspring. Without self-consciousness the two feet do not make known any movement. 'Our mind was absent,' they say, 'we did not perceive that movement.' Without self-consciousness no thought succeeds, nothing can be known that is to be known.

"Let no man try to find out what speech is, let him know the speaker. Let no man try to find out what odor is, let him know him who smells. Let no man try to find out what form is, let him know the seer. Let no man try to find out what sound is, let him know the hearer. Let no man try to find out the tastes of food, let him know the knower of tastes. Let no man try to find out what action is, let him know the agent. Let no man try to find out what pleasure and pain are, let him know the knower of pleasure and pain. Let no man try to find out what happiness, joy, and offspring are, let him know the knower of happiness, joy, and offspring. Let no man try to find out what movement is, let him know the mover. Let no man try to find out what mind is, let him know the thinker. These ten objects (what is spoken, smelled, seen, felt) have reference to self-consciousness; the ten subjects (speech, the senses, mind) have reference to objects. If there were no objects, there would be no subjects; and if there were no subjects, there would be no objects. For on either side alone nothing could be achieved. But the self of pragñâ, consciousness, and prâna, life, is not many, but one. For as in a car the circumference of a wheel is placed on the spokes, and the spokes on the nave, thus are these objects, as a circumference, placed on the subjects as spokes, and the subjects on the prâna. And that prâna, the living and breathing power, indeed is the self of pragñâ, the self-conscious self: blessed, imperishable, immortal. He does not increase by a good action, nor decrease by a bad action. For the self of prâna and pragñâ makes him, whom he wishes to lead up from these worlds, do a good deed; and the same makes him, whom he wishes to lead down from these worlds, do a bad deed. And he is the guardian of the world, he is the king of the world, he is the lord of the universe—and he is my (Indra's) self: thus let it be known, yea, thus let it be known!

SELECTIONS FROM THE KORAN

[*Translation by George Sale*]

INTRODUCTION

THE importance of the "Koran" lies in the fact that it is a religious book of the East, read and stored in the memory of a hundred millions of people of different races and civilizations, inhabiting countries extending from the western borders of China to the pillars of Hercules. It is considered by the Mohammedan to contain all the knowledge and all the literature necessary for men. When it was demanded of Mohammed to confirm the authority of his mission by some work of wonder, he pointed to the "Koran," and exclaimed, "Behold the greatest miracle of all." The learned men of Alexandria asked the Caliph Omar to give to them the vast library at Alexandria. "If those books," he replied, "contain anything which is contrary to the 'Koran' they deserve to be destroyed. If they contain what is written in the 'Koran,' they are unnecessary." He ordered them to be distributed among the baths of the city, to serve as fuel for their furnaces.

The composition of the "Koran" is all the work of Mohammed. He himself claimed that he spoke merely as the oracle of God. The commands and injunctions are in the first person, as if spoken by the Divine Being. The passionate enthusiasm and religious earnestness of the prophet are plainly seen in these strange writings. Sometimes, however, he sinks into the mere Arabian story-teller, whose object is the amusement of his people. He is not a poet, but when he deals with the unity of God, with the beneficence of the Divine Being, with the wonders of Nature, with the beauty of resignation, he exhibits a glowing rhetoric, a power of gorgeous imagery, of pathos, and religious devotion, that make the "Koran" the first written work in the Arabian tongue.

If we take Mohammed's own account of the composition of the volume, we must believe that the completed "Koran" existed from all eternity, on a tablet preserved in the upper heavens. Once a year, during the period of the prophet's active work, fragments of this tablet were brought down by the angel

Gabriel to the lower heavens of the moon, and imparted to the prophet, who was periodically transported to that celestial sphere. The words were recited by the angel, and dictated by the prophet to his scribe. These detached scraps were written on the ribs of palm leaves, or the shoulder-blades of sheep, or parchment, and were stored in a chest, in which they were kept until the caliphat of Abu Bekr, in the seventh century, when they were collected in one volume. Such marvels of revelation were made at different periods to the prophet, and were called Surahs, and formed separate chapters in the Koran as we have it to-day. Some of these Surahs contradict what had previously been uttered by the prophet, but this discrepancy is obviated by the expedient of what is called "abrogation," and the more recent utterances were held to supersede and rescind those which were contradictory to it in the earlier revelation.

It may well be believed that these sibylline leaves of Mohammedanism make up a heterogeneous jumble of varied elements. Some of the chapters are long, others are short; now the prophet seems to be caught up by a whirlwind, and is brought face to face with ineffable mysteries, of which he speaks in the language of rhapsody. At other times he is dry and prosaic, indulging in wearisome iterations, and childish trivialities. Now he assumes the plain, clear voice of the law-giver, or raises his accents into the angry threatenings of the relentless and bloodthirsty fanatic. Yet throughout the whole volume there is a strain of religious resignation, of trust in God, of hopefulness under adversity, of kindliness towards men, which reveal a nobility of ideal, a simplicity and purity in the conception of the Divine Being, and the relations of human life, which make the work not without inspiration, even to the thoughtful man of the nineteenth century. The Koran must always be considered one of the most potent of religious books, one of the greatest documents which reveal the struggle of the human heart after a knowledge of God, and of faithful accomplishment of the Divine will. Perhaps the essence of the work as furnishing a philosophy of life, is contained in the axioms of Abu Bekr, one of the most exalted in character of Mohammed's successors. "Good actions," he says, "are a guard against the blows of adversity." And again, "Death is the easiest of all things after it, and the hardest of all things before it." To which we may add the sentence of Ali, "Riches without God are the greatest poverty and misery."

There are twenty-nine chapters of the "Koran," which begin with certain letters of the alphabet: some with a single one, others with more. These letters the Mohammedans believe to be the peculiar marks of the "Koran," and to conceal several profound mysteries, the certain understanding of which, the more intelligent confess, has not been communicated to any mortal, their prophet only excepted. Notwithstanding which, some will take the liberty of guessing at their meaning by that species of Cabbala called by the Jews, Notarikon, and suppose the letters to stand for as many words expressing the names and attributes of God, his works, ordinances, and decrees; and therefore these mysterious letters, as well as the verses themselves, seem in the "Koran" to be called signs. Others explain the intent of these letters from their nature or organ, or else from their value in numbers, according to another species of the Jewish Cabbala called Gemátria; the uncertainty of these conjectures sufficiently appears from their disagreement. Thus, for example, five chapters, one of which is the second, begin with the letters A.L.M., which some imagine to stand for *Allah latîf magîd*—"God is gracious and to be glorified"—or, *Ana li minni*—"to me and from me"—belongs all perfection, and proceeds all good; or else for *Ana Allah âlam*—"I am the most wise God"—taking the first letter to mark the beginning of the first word, the second the middle of the second word, and the third the last of the third word: or for "Allah, Gabriel, Mohammed," the author, revealer, and preacher of the "Koran." Others say that as the letter A belongs to the lower part of the throat, the first of the organs of speech; L to the palate, the middle organ; and M to the lips, which are the last organs; so these letters signify that God is the beginning, middle, and end, or ought to be praised in the beginning, middle, and end of all our words and actions; or, as the total value of those three letters in numbers is seventy-one, they signify that in the space of so many years, the religion preached in the "Koran" should be fully established. The conjecture of a learned Christian is, at least, as certain as any of the former, who supposes those letters were set there by the amanuensis, for *Amar li Mohammed*—"at the command of Mohammed"—as the five letters prefixed to the nineteenth chapter seem to be there written by a Jewish scribe, for *Cob yaas*—"thus he commanded."

The general contents of the "Koran" may be divided under three heads: First, precepts and laws in matters of religion, such as prayer, fasting, pilgrimage; there are laws also given in the affairs of the civil life, such as marriage, the possession and bequeathing of property, and the administration of justice. The second division would include histories, which consist in a great part of incidents from the Bible, as Christians know it. Mohammed probably picked up a good deal of hearsay knowledge in this department from Jews and Christians. Some of his historical incidents are purely fabulous, others are perversions or falsifications of the Scriptural narrative. This portion of the "Koran," interesting and anecdotic as it is, is the least satisfactory of the work, and shows the writer in his true ignorance, and disregard for historic verification. When, for instance, he confounds Miriam, the sister of Moses, with Mary the Mother of Christ, he shows himself lost in truly Oriental clouds of mystic error. The third element in the "Koran" is a large body of admonitions, many of them addressed to the outside world, and to unbelievers who are exhorted to accept the creed that there is one God and Mohammed is His prophet. War is put forth as a legitimate method of propagating the faith. The duties of life, such as justice, temperance, resignation and industry, are enforced. Hell is threatened to infidels and immoral people; and from whatever sources the writer derived his materials there can be no doubt that the moral scheme he promulgated was in every sense a revelation to the degraded idolaters and fire-worshippers, amongst whom he discharged the mission of his life. Mohammed preached what he called the truth, with the sword in one hand and the "Koran" in the other. But the empire established by the sword would long since have crumbled into dust like that of Alexander or Augustus, unless the "Koran" had fixed its teaching in the minds of the conquered, had regulated by its precepts their social and political life, had supported and exalted their faith with the doctrine of one Almighty and beneficent God; had cheered them with the hope of a Resurrection, and illuminated their minds with the vision of a Paradise, the grossest of whose delights were afterwards to be interpreted by Arabic commentators in accordance with the highest spiritual capabilities of the human race.

E. W.

MOHAMMED AND MOHAMMEDANISM

By Thomas Carlyle

FROM the first rude times of Paganism among the Scandinavians in the North, we advance to a very different epoch of religion, among a very different people: Mohammedanism among the Arabs. A great change; what a change and progress is indicated here, in the universal condition and thoughts of men!

The Hero is not now regarded as a God among his fellowmen; but as one God-inspired, as a Prophet. It is the second phasis of Hero-worship: the first or oldest, we may say, has passed away without return; in the history of the world there will not again be any man, never so great, whom his fellow-men will take for a god. Nay we might rationally ask, Did any set of human beings ever really think the man they *saw* there standing beside them a god, the maker of this world? Perhaps not: it was usually some man they remembered, or *had* seen. But neither can this any more be. The Great Man is not recognized henceforth as a god any more.

It was a rude gross error, that of counting the Great Man a god. Yet let us say that it is at all times difficult to know *what* he is, or how to account of him and receive him! The most significant feature in the history of an epoch is the manner it has of welcoming a Great Man. Ever, to the true instincts of men, there is something godlike in him. Whether they shall take him to be a god, to be a prophet, or what they shall take him to be? that is ever a grand question; by their way of answering that, we shall see, as through a little window, into the very heart of these men's spiritual condition. For at bottom the Great Man, as he comes from the hand of Nature, is ever the same kind of thing: Odin, Luther, Johnson, Burns; I hope to make it appear that these are all originally of one stuff; that only by the world's reception of them, and the shapes they assume, are they so immeasurably diverse. The worship of Odin astonishes us,—to fall prostrate before the Great Man, into *deliquium* of love and wonder over him, and feel in their hearts that he was a denizen of the skies, a god! This was imperfect enough: but to welcome, for example, a Burns as we did, was that what we can call perfect? The most precious gift that Heaven can give to the Earth; a man of "genius" as we call it; the Soul of a Man actually sent down from the skies with a God's-message to us,—this we waste away as an idle artificial firework, sent to amuse us a little, and sink it into ashes, wreck, and ineffectuality: *such* reception of a Great Man I do not call very perfect either! Looking into the heart of the thing, one may perhaps call that of Burns a still uglier phenomenon, betokening still sadder imperfections in mankind's ways, than the Scandinavian method itself! To fall into mere unreasoning *deliquium* of love and admiration, was not good; but such unreasoning, nay irrational supercilious no-love at all is perhaps still worse!—It is a thing forever changing, this of Hero-worship: different in each age, difficult to do well in any age. Indeed, the heart of the whole business of the age, one may say, is to do it well.

We have chosen Mohammed not as the most eminent Prophet; but as the one we are freest to speak of. He is by no means the truest of Prophets; but I do esteem him a true one. Further, as there is no danger of our becoming, any of us, Mohammedans, I mean to say all the good of him I justly can. It is the way to get at his secret: let us try to understand what *he* meant with the world; what the world meant and means with him, will then be a more answerable question. Our current hypothesis about Mohammed, that he was a scheming Impostor, a Falsehood incarnate, that his religion is a mere mass of quackery and fatuity, begins really to be now untenable to any one. The lies, which well-meaning zeal has heaped round this man, are disgraceful to ourselves only. When Pococke inquired of Grotius where the proof was of that story of the pigeon, trained to pick peas from Mohammed's ear, and pass for an angel dictating to him, Grotius answered that there was no proof! It is really time to dismiss all that. The word this man spoke has been the life-guidance now of a hundred-and-eighty millions of men these twelve-hundred years. These hundred-and-eighty millions were made by God as well as we.

A greater number of God's creatures believe in Mohammed's word at this hour than in any other word whatever. Are we to suppose that it was a miserable piece of spiritual legerdemain, this which so many creatures of the Almighty have lived by and died by? I, for my part, cannot form any such supposition. I will believe most things sooner than that. One would be entirely at a loss what to think of this world at all, if quackery so grew and were sanctioned here.

Alas, such theories are very lamentable. If we would attain to knowledge of anything in God's true Creation, let us disbelieve them wholly! They are the product of an Age of Scepticism; they indicate the saddest spiritual paralysis, and mere death-life of the souls of men: more godless theory, I think, was never promulgated in this Earth. A false man found a religion? Why, a false man cannot build a brick house! If he do not know and follow *truly* the properties of mortar, burnt clay and what else he works in, it is no house that he makes, but a rubbish-heap. It will not stand for twelve centuries, to lodge a hundred-and-eighty millions; it will fall straightway. A man must conform himself to Nature's laws, *be* verily in communion with Nature and the truth of things, or Nature will answer him, No, not at all! Specíosities are specious—ah me!—a Cagliostro, many Cagliostros, prominent world-leaders, do prosper by their quackery, for a day. It is like a forged bank-note; they get it passed out of *their* worthless hands: others, not they, have to smart for it. Nature bursts-up in fire-flames, French Revolutions and suchlike, proclaiming with terrible veracity that forged notes are forged.

But of a Great Man especially, of him I will venture to assert that it is incredible he should have been other than true. It seems to me the primary foundation of him, and of all that can lie in him, this. No Mirabeau, Napoleon, Burns, Cromwell, no man adequate to do anything, but is first of all in right earnest about it; what I call a sincere man. I should say *sincerity*, a deep, great, genuine sincerity, is the first characteristic of all men in any way heroic. Not the sincerity that calls itself sincere; ah no, that is a very poor matter indeed; —a shallow braggart conscious sincerity; oftenest self-conceit mainly. The Great Man's sincerity is of the kind he cannot speak of, is not conscious of: nay, I suppose, he is conscious rather of *in*sincerity; for what man can walk accurately by the law of truth for one day? No, the Great Man does not boast himself sincere, far from that; perhaps does not ask himself if he is so: I would say rather, his sincerity does not depend on himself; he cannot help being sincere! The great Fact of Existence is great to him. Fly as he will, he cannot get out of the awful presence of this Reality. His mind is so made; he is great by that, first of all. Fearful and wonderful, real as Life, real as Death, is this Universe to him. Though all men should forget its truth, and walk in a vain show, he cannot. At all moments the Flame-image glares-in upon him; undeniable, there, there!—I wish you to take this as my primary definition of a Great Man. A little man may have this, it is competent to all men that God has made: but a Great Man cannot be without it.

Such a man is what we call an *original* man; he comes to us at first-hand. A messenger he, sent from the Infinite Unknown with tidings to us. We may call him Poet, Prophet, God;—in one way or other, we all feel that the words he utters are as no other man's words. Direct from the Inner Fact of things:—he lives, and has to live, in daily communion with that. Hearsays cannot hide it from him; he is blind, homeless, miserable, following hearsays; *it* glares-in upon him. Really his utterances, are they not a kind of "revelation";—what we must call such for want of other name? It is from the heart of the world that he comes; he is portion of the primal reality of things. God has made many revelations: but this man too, has not God made him, the latest and newest of all? The "inspiration of the Almighty giveth *him* understanding": we must listen before all to him.

This Mohammed, then, we will in no wise consider as an Inanity and Theatricality, a poor conscious ambitious schemer; we cannot conceive him so. The rude message he delivered was a real one withal; an earnest confused voice from the unknown Deep. The man's words were not false, nor his workings here below; no Inanity and Simulacrum; a fiery mass of Life cast-up from the great bosom of Nature herself. To *kindle* the world; the world's Maker had ordered it so. Neither can the faults. imperfections, insincerities even, of Mohammed, if such were never so well proved against him, shake this primary fact about him.

On the whole, we make too much of faults; the details of the business hide the real centre of it. Faults? The greatest of faults, I should say, is to be conscious of none. Readers of the Bible above all, one would think, might know better. Who is called there " the man according to God's own heart "? David, the Hebrew King, had fallen into sins enough; blackest crimes; there was no want of sins. And thereupon the unbelievers sneer and ask, Is this your man according to God's heart? The sneer, I must say, seems to me but a shallow one. What are faults, what are the outward details of a life; if the inner secret of it, the remorse, temptations, true, often-baffled, never-ended struggle of it, be forgotten? " It is not in man that walketh to direct his steps." Of all acts, is not, for a man, *repentance* the most divine? The deadliest sin, I say, were that same supercilious consciousness of no sin;—that is death; the heart so conscious is divorced from sincerity, humility, and fact; is dead: it is " pure " as dead dry sand is pure. David's life and history, as written for us in those Psalms of his, I consider to be the truest emblem ever given of a man's moral progress and warfare here below. All earnest souls will ever discern in it the faithful struggle of an earnest human soul towards what is good and best. Struggle often baffled, sore baffled, down as into entire wreck; yet a struggle never ended; ever, with tears, repentance, true unconquerable purpose, begun anew. Poor human nature! Is not a man's walking, in truth, always that: " a succession of falls "? Man can do no other. In this wild element of a Life, he has to struggle onwards; now fallen, deep-abased; and ever, with tears, repentance, with bleeding heart, he has to rise again, struggle again still onwards. That his struggle *be* a faithful unconquerable one: that is the question of questions. We will put-up with many sad details, if the soul of it were true. Details by themselves will never teach us what it is. I believe we misestimate Mohammed's faults even as faults: but the secret of him will never be got by dwelling there. We will leave all this behind us; and assuring ourselves that he did mean some true thing, ask candidly what it was or might be.

These Arabs Mohammed was born among are certainly a notable people. Their country itself is notable; the fit habitation for such a race. Savage inaccessible rock-mountains, great grim deserts, alternating with beautiful strips of verdure: wherever water is, there is greenness, beauty; odoriferous balm-shrubs, date-trees, frankincense-trees. Consider that wide waste horizon of sand, empty, silent, like a sand-sea, dividing habitable place from habitable. You are all alone there, left alone with the Universe; by day a fierce sun blazing down on it with intolerable radiance; by night the great deep Heaven with its stars. Such a country is fit for a swift-handed, deep-hearted race of men. There is something most agile, active, and yet most meditative, enthusiastic in the Arab character. The Persians are called the French of the East; we will call the Arabs Oriental Italians. A gifted noble people; a people of wild strong feelings, and of iron restraint over these: the characteristic of noblemindedness, of genius. The wild Bedouin welcomes the stranger to his tent, as one having right to all that is there; were it his worst enemy, he will slay his foal to treat him, will serve him with sacred hospitality for three days, will set him fairly on his way;—and then, by another law as sacred, kill him if he can. In words too, as in action. They are not a loquacious people, taciturn rather; but eloquent, gifted when they do speak. An earnest, truthful kind of men. They are, as we know, of Jewish kindred: but with that deadly terrible earnestness of the Jews they seem to combine something graceful, brilliant, which is not Jewish. They had "poetic contests" among them before the time of Mohammed. Sale says, at Ocadh, in the South of Arabia, there were yearly fairs, and there, when the merchandising was done, Poets sang for prizes:—the wild people gathered to hear that.

One Jewish quality these Arabs manifest; the outcome of many or of all high qualities: what we may call religiosity. From of old they had been zealous worshippers, according to their light. They worshipped the stars, as Sabeans; worshipped many natural objects—recognized them as symbols, immediate manifestations, of the Maker of Nature. It was wrong; and yet not wholly wrong. All God's works are still in a sense symbols of God. Do we not, as I urged, still account it a merit to recognize a certain inexhaustible significance, "poetic beauty" as we name it, in all natural objects whatsoever? A man is a poet, and honored, for doing that, and speaking or singing it—a kind of diluted worship. They had many Prophets, these Arabs; Teachers each to his tribe, each according to the light he had. But indeed, have we not from of old the noblest of proofs, still palpable to every one of us, of what devoutness and noblemindedness had dwelt in these rustic thoughtful peoples? Biblical critics seem agreed that our own *Book of Job* was written in that region of the world. I call that, apart from all theories about it, one of the grandest things ever written with pen. One feels, indeed, as if it were not Hebrew; such a noble universality, different from noble patriotism or sectarianism, reigns in it. A noble Book; all men's Book! It is our first, oldest statement of the never-ending Problem,—man's destiny, and God's ways with him here in this earth. And all in such free flowing outlines; grand in its sincerity, in its simplicity; in its epic melody, and repose of reconcilement. There is the seeing eye, the mildly understanding heart. So *true* everyway; true eyesight and vision for all things; material things no less than spiritual: the Horse—"hast thou clothed his neck with *thunder?*"—he "*laughs* at the shaking of the spear!" Such living likenesses were never since drawn. Sublime sorrow, sublime reconciliation; oldest choral melody as of the heart of mankind;—so soft, and great; as the summer midnight, as the world with its seas and stars! There is nothing written, I think, in the Bible or out of it, of equal literary merit.—

To the idolatrous Arabs one of the most ancient universal objects of worship was that Black Stone, still kept in the building called Caabah at Mecca. Diodorus Siculus mentions this Caabah in a way not to be mistaken, as the oldest, most honored temple in his time; that is, some half-century before our Era. Silvestre de Sacy says there is some likelihood that the Black Stone is an aerolite. In that case, some man might *see* it fall out of Heaven! It stands now beside the Well Zemzem; the Caabah is built over both. A Well is in all places a beautiful affecting object, gushing out like life from the hard earth;—still more so in those hot dry countries, where it is the first condition of being. The Well Zemzem has its name from the bubbling sound of the waters, *zem-zem;* they think it is the Well which Hagar found with her little Ishmael in the wilderness: the aerolite and it have been sacred now, and had a Caabah over them, for thousands of years. A curious object, that Caabah! There it stands at this hour, in the black cloth-covering the Sultan sends it yearly; "twenty-seven cubits high;"; with circuit, with double circuit of pillars, with festoon rows of lamps and quaint ornaments: the lamps will be lighted again *this* night—to glitter again under the stars. An authentic fragment of the oldest Past. It is the *Keblah* of all Moslem: from Delhi all onwards to Morocco, the eyes of innumerable praying men are turned towards *it*, five times, this day and all days: one of the notablest centres in the Habitation of Men.

It had been from the sacredness attached to this Caabah Stone and Hagar's Well, from the pilgrimings of all tribes of Arabs thither, that Mecca took its rise as a Town. A great town once, though much decayed now. It has no natural advantage for a town; stands in a sandy hollow amid bare barren hills, at a distance from the sea; its provisions, its very bread, have to be imported. But so many pilgrims needed lodgings: and then all places of pilgrimage do, from the first, become places of trade. The first day pilgrims meet, merchants have also met: where men see themselves assembled for one object, they find that they can accomplish other objects which depend on meeting together. Mecca became the Fair of all Arabia. And thereby indeed the chief staple and warehouse of whatever Commerce there was between the Indian and the Western countries, Syria, Egypt, even Italy. It had at one time a population of 100,000; buyers, forwarders of those Eastern and Western products; importers for their own behoof of provisions and corn. The government was a kind of irregular aristocratic republic, not without a touch of theocracy. Ten Men of a chief tribe, chosen in some rough way, were Governors of Mecca, and Keepers of the Caabah. The Koreish were the chief tribe in Mohammed's time; his own family was of that tribe. The rest of the Nation, fractioned and cut-asunder by deserts, lived under similar rude patriarchal governments by one or several: herdsmen, carriers, traders, generally robbers too; being oftenest at war one with another, or with all: held together by no open bond, if it were not this meeting at the Caabah, where all forms of Arab Idolatry assembled in common adoration;—held mainly by the *inward* indissoluble bond of a common blood and language. In this way had the Arabs lived for long ages, unnoticed by the world; a people of great qualities, unconsciously waiting for the day when they should become notable to all the world. Their Idolatries appear to have been in a tottering state; much was getting into confusion and fermentation among them. Obscure tidings of the most important Event ever transacted in this world, the Life and Death of the Divine Man in Judea, at once the symptom and cause of immeasurable change to all people in the world, had in the course of centuries reached into Arabia too; and could not but, of itself, have produced fermentation there.

It was among this Arab people, so circumstanced, in the year 570 of our Era, that the man Mohammed was born. He was of the family of Hashem, of the Koreish tribe as we said; though poor, connected with the chief persons of his country. Almost at his birth he lost his Father; at the age of six years his Mother too, a woman noted for her beauty, her worth and sense: he fell to the charge of his Grandfather, an old man, a hundred years old. A good old man: Mohammed's Father, Abdallah, had been his youngest favorite son. He saw in Mohammed, with his old life-worn eyes, a century old, the lost Abdallah come back again, all that was left of Abdallah. He loved the little orphan Boy greatly; used to say they must take care of that beautiful little Boy, nothing in their kindred was more precious than he. At his death, while the boy was still but two years old, he left him in charge to Abu Thaleb the eldest of the Uncles, as to him that now was head of the house. By this Uncle, a just and rational man as everything betokens, Mohammed was brought-up in the best Arab way.

Mohammed, as he grew up, accompanied his Uncle on trading journeys and suchlike; in his eighteenth year one finds him a fighter following his Uncle in war. But perhaps the most significant of all his journeys is one we find noted as of some years' earlier date: a journey to the Fairs of Syria. The young man here first came in contact with a quite foreign world,—with one foreign element of endless moment to him: the Christian Religion. I know not what to make of that "Sergius, the Nestorian Monk," whom Abu Thaleb and he are said to have lodged with; or how much any monk could have taught one still so young. Probably enough it is greatly exaggerated, this of the Nestorian Monk. Mohammed was only fourteen; had no language but his own: much in Syria must have been a strange unintelligible whirlpool to him. But the eyes of the lad were open; glimpses of many things would doubtless be taken-in, and lie very enigmatic as yet, which were to ripen in a strange way into views, into beliefs and insights one day. These journeys to Syria were probably the beginning of much to Mohammed.

One other circumstance we must not forget: that he had no school-learning; of the thing we call school-learning none at all. The art of writing was but just introduced into Arabia; it seems to be the true opinion that Mohammed never could write! Life in the Desert, with its experiences, was all his education. What of this infinite Universe he, from his dim place, with his own eyes and thoughts, could take in, so much and no more of it was he to know. Curious, if we will reflect on it, this of having no books. Except by what he could see for himself, or hear of by uncertain rumor of speech in the obscure Arabian Desert, he could know nothing. The wisdom that had been before him or at a distance from him in the world, was in a manner as good as not there for him. Of the great brother souls, flame-beacons through so many lands and times, no one directly communicates with this great soul. He is alone there, deep down in the bosom of the Wilderness; has to grow up so,—alone with Nature and his own Thoughts.

But, from an early age, he had been remarked as a thoughtful man. His companions named him "*Al Amin*, the Faithful." A man of truth and fidelity; true in what he did, in what he spake and thought. They noted that *he* always meant something. A man rather taciturn in speech; silent when there was nothing to be said; but pertinent, wise, sincere, when he did speak; always throwing light on the matter. This is the only sort of speech *worth* speaking! Through life we find him to have been regarded as an altogether solid, brotherly, genuine man. A serious, sincere character; yet amiable, cordial, companionable, jocose even;—a good laugh in him withal: there are men whose laugh is as untrue as anything about them; who cannot laugh. One hears of Mohammed's beauty: his fine sagacious honest face, brown florid complexion, beaming black eyes;—I somehow like too that vein on the brow, which swelled-up black when he was in anger: like the "horse-shoe vein" in Scott's *Red-gauntlet*. It was a kind of feature in the Hashem family, this black swelling vein in the brow; Mahomet had it prominent, as would appear. A spontaneous, passionate, yet just, true-meaning man! Full of wild faculty, fire and light; of wild worth, all uncultured; working out his life-task in the depths of the Desert there.

How he was placed with Kadijah, a rich Widow, as her Steward, and travelled in her business, again to the Fairs of Syria; how he managed all, as one can well understand, with fidelity, adroitness; how her gratitude, her regard for him grew: the story of their marriage is altogether a graceful intelligible one, as told us by the Arab authors. He was twenty-five; she forty, though still beautiful. He seems to have lived in a most affectionate, peaceable, wholesome way with this wedded benefactress; loving her truly, and her alone. It goes greatly against the impostor theory, the fact that he lived in this entirely unexceptionable, entirely quiet and commonplace way, till the heat of his years was done. He was forty before he talked of any mission from Heaven. All his irregularities, real and supposed, date from after his fiftieth year, when the good Kadijah died. All his "ambition," seemingly, had been, hitherto, to live an honest life; his "fame," the mere good opinion of neighbors that knew him, had been sufficient hitherto. Not till he was already getting old, the prurient heat of his life all burnt out, and *peace* growing to be the chief thing this world could give him, did he start on the "career of ambition"; and, belying all his past character and existence, set-up as a wretched empty charlatan to acquire what he could now no longer enjoy! For my share, I have no faith whatever in that.

Ah no: this deep-hearted Son of the Wilderness, with his beaming black eyes and open social deep soul, had other thoughts in him than ambition. A silent great soul; he was one of those who cannot *but* be in earnest; whom Nature herself has appointed to be sincere. While others walk in formulas and hearsays, contented enough to dwell there, this man could not screen himself in formulas; he was alone with his own soul and the reality of things. The great Mystery of Existence, as I said, glared-in upon him, with its terrors, with its splendors; no hearsays could hide that unspeakable fact, "Here am I!" Such *sincerity*, as we named it, has in very truth something of divine. The word of such a man is a Voice direct from Nature's own Heart. Men do and must listen to that as to nothing else;—all else is wind in comparison. From of old, a thousand thoughts, in his pilgrimings and wanderings, had been in this man: What am I? What *is* this unfathomable Thing I live in, which men name Universe? What is Life; what is Death? What am I to believe? What am I to do? The grim rocks of Mount Hara, of Mount Sinai, the stern sandy solitudes answered not. The great Heaven rolling silent overhead, with its blue-glancing stars, answered not. There was no answer. The man's own soul, and what of God's inspiration dwelt there, had to answer!

It is the thing which all men have to ask themselves; which we too have to ask, and answer. This wild man felt it to be of *infinite* moment; all other things of no moment whatever in comparison. The jargon of argumentative Greek Sects, vague traditions of Jews, the stupid routine of Arab Idolatry: there was no answer in these. A Hero, as I repeat, has this first distinction, which indeed we may call first and last, the Alpha and Omega of his whole Heroism, That he looks through the shows of things into *things*. Use and wont, respectable hearsay, respectable formula: all these are good, or are not good. There is something behind and beyond all these, which all these must correspond with, be the image of, or they are—*Idolatries;* "bits of black wood pretending to be God"; to the earnest soul a mockery and abomination. Idolatries never so gilded waited on by heads of the Koreish, will do nothing for this man. Though all men walk by them, what good is it? The great Reality stands glaring there upon *him*. He there has to answer it, or perish miserably. Now, even now, or else through all Eternity never! Answer it; *thou* must find an answer.—Ambition? What could all Arabia do for this man; with the crown of Greek Heraclius, of Persian Chosroes, and all crowns in the Earth;—what could they all do for him? It was not of the Earth he wanted to hear tell; it was of the Heaven above and of the Hell beneath. All crowns and sovereignties whatsoever, where would *they* in a few brief years be? To be Sheik of Mecca or Arabia, and have a bit of gilt wood put into your hand,—will that be one's salvation? I decidedly think, not. We will leave it altogether, this impostor hypothesis, as not credible; not very tolerable even, worthy chiefly of dismissal by us.

Mohammed had been wont to retire yearly, during the

month Ramadhan, into solitude and silence; as indeed was the Arab custom; a praiseworthy custom, which such a man, above all, would find natural and useful. Communing with his own heart, in the silence of the mountains; himself silent; open to the "small still voices": it was a right natural custom! Mohammed was in his fortieth year, when having withdrawn to a cavern in Mount Hara, near Mecca, during this Ramadhan, to pass the month in prayer, and meditation on those great questions, he one day told his wife Kadijah, who with his household was with him or near him this year, that by the unspeakable special favor of Heaven he had now found it all out; was in doubt and darkness no longer, but saw it all. That all these Idols and Formulas were nothing, miserable bits of wood; that there was One God in and over all; and we must leave all idols, and look to Him. That God is great; and that there is nothing else great! He is the Reality. Wooden Idols are not real; He is real. He made us at first, sustains us yet; we and all things are but the shadow of Him; a transitory garment veiling the Eternal Splendor. "*Allah akbar,*" God is great;—and then also "*Islam,*" That we must *submit* to God. That our whole strength lies in resigned submission to Him, whatsoever He do to us. For this world, and for the other! The thing He sends to us, were it death and worse than death, shall be good, shall be best; we resign ourselves to God.—"If this be *Islam,*" says Goethe, "do we not all live in *Islam?*" Yes, all of us that have any moral life; we all live so. It has ever been held the highest wisdom for a man not merely to submit to Necessity,—Necessity will make him submit,—but to know and believe well that the stern thing which Necessity had ordered was the wisest, the best, the thing wanted there. To cease his frantic pretension of scanning this great God's-World in his small fraction of a brain; to know that it *had* verily, though deep beyond his soundings, a Just Law, that the soul of it was Good;—that his part in it was to conform to the Law of the Whole, and in devout silence follow that; not questioning it, obeying it as unquestionable.

I say, this is yet the only true morality known. A man is right and invincible, virtuous and on the road towards sure conquest, precisely while he joins himself to the great deep Law of the World, in spite of all superficial laws, temporary appearances, profit-and-loss calculations; he is victorious while he coöperates with that great central Law, not victorious otherwise:—and surely his first chance of coöperating with it, or getting into the course of it, is to know with his whole soul that it *is;* that it is good, and alone good! This is the soul of Islam; it is properly the soul of Christianity;—for Islam is definable as a confused form of Christianity; had Christianity not been, neither had it been. Christianity also commands us, before all, to be resigned to God. We are to take no counsel with flesh-and-blood; give ear to no vain cavils, vain sorrows and wishes: to know that we know nothing; that the worst and cruelest to our eyes is not what it seems; that we have to receive whatsoever befalls us as sent from God above, and say, It is good and wise, God is great! "Though He slay me, yet will I trust in Him." Islam means in its way Denial of Self, Annihilation of Self. This is yet the highest Wisdom that Heaven has revealed to our Earth.

Such light had come, as it could, to illuminate the darkness of this wild Arab soul. A confused dazzling splendor as of life and Heaven, in the great darkness which threatened to be death: he called it revelation and the angel Gabriel;—who of us yet can know what to call it? It is the "inspiration of the Almighty that giveth us understanding." To *know;* to get into the truth of anything, is ever a mystic act,—of which the best Logics can but babble on the surface. "Is not Belief the true god-announcing Miracle?" says Novalis.—That Mohammed's whole soul, set in flame with this grand Truth vouchsafed him, should feel as if it were important and the only important thing, was very natural. That Providence had unspeakably honored *him* by revealing it, saving him from death and darkness; that he therefore was bound to make known the same to all creatures: this is what was meant by "Mohammed is the Prophet of God"; this too is not without its true meaning.—

The good Kadijah, we can fancy, listened to him with wonder, with doubt: at length she answered: Yes, it was *true* this that he said. One can fancy too the boundless gratitude of Mohammed; and how of all the kindnesses she had done him, this of believing the earnest struggling word he now spoke was the greatest. "It is certain," says Novalis, "my Conviction gains infinitely, the moment another soul will believe in it." It is a boundless favor.—He never forgot this good Kadijah.

Long afterwards, Ayesha his young favorite wife, a woman who indeed distinguished herself among the Moslem, by all manner of qualities, through her whole long life; this young brilliant Ayesha was, one day, questioning him: "Now am not I better than Kadijah? She was a widow; old, and had lost her looks: you love me better than you did her?"—"No, by Allah!" answered Mohammed: "No, by Allah! She believed in me when none else would believe. In the whole world I had but one friend, and she was that!"—Seid, his Slave, also believed in him; these with his young Cousin Ali, Abu Thaleb's son, were his first converts.

He spoke of his Doctrine to this man and that; but the most treated it with ridicule, with indifference; in three years, I think, he had gained but thirteen followers. His progress was slow enough. His encouragement to go on, was altogether the usual encouragement that such a man in such a case meets. After some three years of small success, he invited forty of his chief kindred to an entertainment; and there stood-up and told them what his pretension was: that he had this thing to promulgate abroad to all men; that it was the highest thing, the one thing: which of them would second him in that? Amid the doubt and silence of all, young Ali, as yet a lad of sixteen, impatient of the silence, started-up, and exclaimed in passionate fierce language that he would! The assembly, among whom was Abu Thaleb, Ali's Father, could not be unfriendly to Mohammed; yet the sight there, of one unlettered elderly man, with a lad of sixteen, deciding on such an enterprise against all mankind, appeared ridiculous to them; the assembly broke-up in laughter. Nevertheless it proved not a laughable thing; it was a very serious thing! As for this young Ali, one cannot but like him. A noble-minded creature, as he shows himself, now and always afterwards; full of affection, of fiery daring. Something chivalrous in him; brave as a lion; yet with a grace, a truth and affection worthy of Christian knighthood. He died by assassination in the Mosque at Bagdad; a death occasioned by his own generous fairness, confidence in the fairness of others: he said if the wound proved not unto death, they must pardon the Assassin; but if it did, then they must slay him straightway, that so they two in the same hour might appear before God, and see which side of that quarrel was the just one!

Mohammed naturally gave offence to the Koreish, Keepers of the Caabah, superintendents of the Idols. One or two men of influence had joined him: the thing spread slowly, but it was spreading. Naturally he gave offence to everybody: Who is this that pretends to be wiser than we all; that rebukes us all, as mere fools and worshippers of wood! Abu Thaleb the good Uncle spoke with him: Could he not be silent about all that; believe it all for himself, and not trouble others, anger the chief men, endanger himself and them all, talking of it? Mohammed answered: If the Sun stood on his right hand and the Moon on his left, ordering him to hold his peace, he could not obey! No: there was something in this Truth he had got which was of Nature herself; equal in rank to Sun, or Moon, or whatsoever thing Nature had made. It would speak itself there, so long as the Almighty allowed it, in spite of Sun and Moon, and all Koreish and all men and things. It must do that, and could do no other. Mohammed answered so; and, they say, "burst into tears." Burst into tears: he felt that Abu Thaleb was good to him; that the task he had got was no soft, but a stern and great one.

He went on speaking to who would listen to him; publishing his Doctrine among the pilgrims as they came to Mecca; gaining adherents in this place and that. Continual contradiction, hatred, open or secret danger attended him. His powerful relations protected Mohammed himself; but by and by, on his own advice, all his adherents had to quit Mecca, and seek refuge in Abyssinia over the sea. The Koreish grew ever angrier; laid plots, and swore oaths among them, to put Mohammed to death with their own hands. Abu Thaleb was dead, the good Kadijah was dead. Mohammed is not solicitous of sympathy from us; but his outlook at this time was one of the dismallest. He had to hide in caverns, escape in disguise; fly hither and thither; homeless, in continual peril of his life. More than once it seemed all-over with him; more than once it turned on a straw, some rider's horse taking fright or the like, whether Mohammed and his Doctrine had not ended there, and not been heard of at all. But it was not to end so.

In the thirteenth year of his mission, finding his enemies all banded against him, forty sworn men, one out of every tribe, waiting to take his life, and no continuance possible at Mecca for him any longer, Mohammed fled to the place then called Yathreb, where he had gained some adherents; the place they now call Medina, or "*Medinat al Nabi*, the City of the Prophet," from that circumstance. It lay some 200 miles off, through rocks and deserts; not without great difficulty, in such mood as we may fancy, he escaped thither, and found welcome. The whole East dates its era from this Flight, *Hegira* as they name it: the Year 1 of this Hegira is 622 of our Era, the fifty-third of Mohammed's life. He was now becoming an old man; his friends sinking round him one by one; his path desolate, encompassed with danger: unless he could find hope in his own heart, the outward face of things was but hopeless for him. It is so with all men in the like case. Hitherto Mohammed had professed to publish his Religion by the way of preaching and persuasion alone. But now, driven foully out of his native country, since unjust men had not only given no ear to his earnest Heaven's-message, the deep cry of his heart, but would not even let him live if he kept speaking it,—the wild Son of the Desert resolved to defend himself, like a man and Arab. If the Koreish will have it so, they shall have it. Tidings, felt to be of infinite moment to them and all men, they would not listen to these; would trample them down by sheer violence, steel and murder: well, let steel try it then! Ten years more this Mohammed had; all of fighting, of breathless impetuous toil and struggle; with what result we know.

Much has been said of Mohammed's propagating his Religion by the sword. It is no doubt far nobler what we have to boast of the Christian Religion, that it propagated itself peaceably in the way of preaching and conviction. Yet withal, if we take this for an argument of the truth or falsehood of a religion, there is a radical mistake in it. The sword indeed: but where will you get your sword! Every new opinion, at its starting, is precisely in a *minority of one*. In one man's head alone, there it dwells as yet. One man alone of the whole world believes it; there is one man against all men. That *he* take a sword, and try to propagate with that, will do little for him. You must first get your sword! On the whole, a thing will propagate itself as it can. We do not find, of the Christian Religion either, that it always disdained the sword, when once it had got one. Charlemagne's conversion of the Saxons was not by preaching. I care little about the sword:

I will allow a thing to struggle for itself in this world, with any sword or tongue or implement it has, or can lay hold of. We will let it preach, and pamphleteer, and fight, and to the uttermost bestir itself, and do, beak and claws, whatsoever is in it; very sure that it will, in the long-run, conquer nothing which does not deserve to be conquered. What is better than itself, it cannot put away, but only what is worse. In this great Duel, Nature herself is umpire, and can do no wrong: the thing which is deepest-rooted in Nature, what we call *truest*, that thing and not the other will be found growing at last.

Here however, in reference to much that there is in Mohammed and his success, we are to remember what an umpire Nature is; what a greatness, composure of depth and tolerance there is in her. You take wheat to cast into the Earth's bosom: your wheat may be mixed with chaff, chopped straw, barn-sweepings, dust and all imaginable rubbish; no matter: you cast it into the kind just Earth; she grows the wheat,—the whole rubbish she silently absorbs, shrouds *it* in, says nothing of the rubbish. The yellow wheat is growing there; the good Earth is silent about all the rest,—has silently turned all the rest to some benefit too, and makes no complaint about it! So everywhere in Nature! She is true and not a lie; and yet so great, and just, and motherly in her truth. She requires of a thing only that it *be* genuine of heart; she will protect it if so; will not, if not so. There is a soul of truth in all the things she ever gave harbor to. Alas, is not this the history of all highest Truth that comes or ever came into the world? The *body* of them all is imperfection, an element of light *in* darkness: to us they have to come embodied in mere Logic, in some merely *scientific* Theorem of the Universe; which *cannot* be complete; which cannot but be found, one day, *in*complete, erroneous, and so die and disappear. The body of all Truth dies; and yet in all, I say, there is a soul which never dies; which in new and ever-nobler embodiment lives immortal as man himself! It is the way with Nature. The genuine essence of Truth never dies. That it be genuine, a voice from the great Deep of Nature, there is the point at Nature's judgment-seat. What *we* call pure or impure, is not with her the final question. Not how much chaff is in you; but whether you have any wheat. Pure? I might say to many a man: Yes, you are pure; pure enough; but you are chaff,—insincere hypothesis, hearsay, formality; you never were in contact with the great heart of the Universe at all; you are properly neither pure nor impure; you *are* nothing, Nature has no business with you.

Mohammed's Creed we called a kind of Christianity; and really, if we look at the wild rapt earnestness with which it was believed and laid to heart, I should say a better kind than that of those miserable Syrian Sects, with their vain janglings about *Homoiousion* and *Homoousion*, the head full of worthless noise, the heart empty and dead! The truth of it is imbedded in portentous error and falsehood; but the truth of it makes it be believed, not the falsehood: it succeeded by its truth. A bastard kind of Christianity, but a living kind; with a heart-life in it; not dead, chopping barren logic merely! Out of all that rubbish of Arab idolatries, argumentative theologies, traditions, subtleties, rumors and hypotheses of Greeks and Jews, with their idle wiredrawings, this wild man of the Desert, with his wild sincere heart, earnest as death and life, with his great flashing natural eyesight, had seen into the kernel of the matter. Idolatry is nothing: these Wooden Idols of yours, "ye rub them with oil and wax, and the flies stick on them,"—these are wood, I tell you! They can do nothing for you; they are an impotent blasphemous pretence; a horror and abomination, if ye knew them. God alone is; God alone has power; He made us, He can kill us and keep us alive: "*Allah akbar*, God is great." Understand that His will is the best for you; that howsoever sore to flesh-and-blood, you will find it the wisest, best: you are bound to take it so; in this world and in the next, you have no other thing that you can do!

And now if the wild idolatrous men did believe this, and with their fiery hearts lay hold of it to do it, in what form soever it came to them, I say it was well worthy of being believed. In one form or the other, I say it is still the one thing worthy of being believed by all men. Man does hereby become the high-priest of this Temple of a World. He is in harmony with the Decrees of the Author of this World; coöperating with them, not vainly withstanding them: I know, to this day, no better definition of Duty than that same. All that is *right* includes itself in this of coöperating with the real Tendency of the World: you succeed by this (the World's Tendency will succeed), you are good, and in the right course there.

Homoiousion, *Homoousion*, vain logical jangle, then or before or at any time, may jangle itself out, and go whither and how it likes: this is the *thing* it all struggles to mean, if it would mean anything. If it do not succeed in meaning this, it means nothing. Not that Abstractions, logical Propositions, be correctly worded or incorrectly; but that living concrete Sons of Adam do lay this to heart: that is the important point. Islam devoured all these vain jangling Sects; and I think had right to do so. It was a Reality, direct from the great Heart of Nature once more. Arab idolatries, Syrian formulas, whatsoever was not equally real, had to go up in flame,—mere dead *fuel*, in various senses, for this which was *fire*.

It was during these wild warfarings and strugglings, especially after the Flight to Mecca, that Mohammed dictated at intervals his Sacred Book, which they name *Koran*, or *Reading*, "Thing to be read." This is the Work he and his disciples made so much of, asking all the world, Is not that a miracle? The Mohammedans regard their Koran with a reverence which few Christians pay even to their Bible. It is admitted everywhere as the standard of all law and all practice; the thing to be gone-upon in speculation and life: the message sent direct out of Heaven, which this earth has to conform to, and walk by; the thing to be read. Their Judges decide by it; all Moslem are bound to study it, seek in it for the light of their life. They have mosques where it is all read daily; thirty relays of priests take it up in succession, get through the whole each day. There, for twelve-hundred years, has the voice of this Book, at all moments, kept sounding through the ears and the hearts of so many men. We hear of Mohammedan Doctors that had read it seventy-thousand times!

Very curious: if one sought for "discrepancies of national taste," here surely were the most eminent instance of that! We also can read the Koran; our Translation of it, by Sale, is known to be a very fair one. I must say, it is as toilsome reading as I ever undertook. A wearisome confused jumble, crude, incondite; endless iterations, long-windedness, entanglement; most crude, incondite;—insupportable stupidity, in short! Nothing but a sense of duty could carry any European through the Koran. We read in it, as we might in the State-Paper Office, unreadable masses of lumber, that perhaps we may get some glimpses of a remarkable man. It is true we have it under disadvantages: the Arabs see more method in it than we. Mohammed's followers found the Koran lying all in fractions, as it had been written-down at first promulgation; much of it, they say, on shoulder-blades of mutton flung pell-mell into a chest; and they published it, without any discoverable order as to time or otherwise;—merely trying, as would seem, and this not very strictly, to put the longest chapters first. The real beginning of it, in that way, lies almost at the end: for the earliest portions were the shortest. Read in its historical sequence it perhaps would not be so bad. Much of it, too, they say, is rhythmic; a kind of wild chanting song, in the original. This may be a great point; much perhaps has been lost in the Translation here. Yet with every allowance, one feels it difficult to see how any mortal ever could consider this Koran as a Book written in Heaven, too good for the Earth; as a well-written book, or indeed as a *book* at all; and not a bewildered rhapsody; *written*, so far as writing goes, as badly as almost any book ever was! So much for national discrepancies, and the standard of taste.

Yet I should say, it was not unintelligible how the Arabs might so love it. When once you get this confused coil of a Koran fairly off your hands, and have it behind you at a distance, the essential type of it begins to disclose itself; and in this there is a merit quite other than the literary one. If a book come from the heart, it will contrive to reach other hearts; all art and authorcraft are of small amount to that. One would say the primary character of the Koran is this of its *genuineness*, of its being a *bona-fide* book. Prideaux, I know, and others, have represented it as a mere bundle of juggleries; chapter after chapter got-up to excuse and varnish the author's successive sins, forward his ambitions and quackeries: but really it is time to dismiss all that. I do not assert Mohammed's continual sincerity: who is continually sincere? But I confess I can make nothing of the critic, in these times, who would accuse him of deceit *prepense;* of conscious deceit generally, or perhaps at all;—still more, of living in a mere element of conscious deceit, and writing this Koran as a forger and juggler would have done! Every candid eye, I think, will read the Koran far otherwise than so. It is the confused ferment of a great rude human soul; rude, untutored, that cannot even read; but fervent, earnest, struggling vehemently to utter itself in words. With a kind of breathless intensity he strives to utter himself; the thoughts crowd on him pell-mell: for very multitude of things to say, he can get nothing said. The meaning that is in him shapes itself into no form of composition, is stated in no sequence, method, or coherence;—they are not *shaped* at all, these thoughts of his; flung-out unshaped, as they struggle and tumble there, in their chaotic inarticulate state. We said "stupid": yet natural stupidity is by no means the character of Mohammed's Book; it is natural uncultivation rather. The man has not studied speaking; in the haste and pressure of continual fighting, has not time to mature himself into fit speech. The panting breathless haste and vehemence of a man struggling in the thick of battle for life and salvation; this is the mood he is in! A headlong haste; for very magnitude of meaning, he cannot get himself articulated into words. The successive utterances of a soul in that mood, colored by the various vicissitudes of three-and-twenty years; now well uttered, now worse: this is the Koran.

For we are to consider Mohammed, through these three-and-twenty years, as the centre of a world wholly in conflict, Battles with the Koreish and Heathen, quarrels among his own people, backslidings of his own wild heart; all this kept him in a perpetual whirl, his soul knowing rest no more. In wakeful nights, as one may fancy, the wild soul of the man, tossing amid these vortices, would hail any light of a decision for them as a veritable light from Heaven; *any* making-up of his mind, so blessed, indispensable for him there, would seem the inspiration of a Gabriel. Forger and juggler? No, no! This great fiery heart, seething, simmering like a great furnace of thoughts, was not a juggler's. His life was a Fact to him; this God's Universe an awful Fact and Reality. He has faults enough. The man was an uncultured semi-barbarous Son of Nature, much of the Bedouin still clinging to him: we must take him for that. But for a wretched Simulacrum, a hungry Impostor without eyes or heart, practising for a mess of pottage such blasphemous swindlery, forgery of celestial documents, continual high-treason against his Maker and Self, we will not and cannot take him.

Sincerity, in all senses, seems to me the merit of the Koran; what had rendered it precious to the wild Arab men. It is, after all, the first and last merit in a book; gives rise to merits of all kinds,—nay, at bottom, it alone can give rise to merit of any kind. Curiously, through these incondite masses of tradition, vituperation, complaint, ejaculation in the Koran, a vein of true direct insight, of what we might almost call poetry, is found straggling. The body of the Book is made up of mere tradition, and as it were vehement enthusiastic extempore preaching. He returns forever to the old stories of the Prophets as they went current in the Arab memory: how Prophet after Prophet, the Prophet Abraham, the Prophet Hud, the Prophet Moses, Christian and other real and fabulous Prophets, had come to this Tribe and to that, warning men of their sin; and been received by them even as he Mohammed was,—which is a great solace to him. These things he repeats ten, perhaps twenty times; again and ever again, with wearisome iteration; has never done repeating them. A brave Samuel Johnson, in his forlorn garret, might con-over the Biographies of Authors in that way! This is the great staple of the Koran. But curiously, through all this, comes ever and anon some glance as of the real thinker and seer. He has actually an eye for the world, this Mohammed: with a certain directness and rugged vigour, he brings home still, to our heart, the thing his own heart has been opened to. I make but little of his praises of Allah, which many praise; they are borrowed I suppose mainly from the Hebrew, at least they are far surpassed there. But the eye that flashes direct into the heart of things, and *sees* the truth of them; this is to me a highly interesting object. Great Nature's own gift; which she bestows on all; but which only one in the thousand does not cast sorrowfully away: it is what I call sincerity of vision; the test of a sincere heart.

Mohammed can work no miracles; he often answers impatiently: I can work no miracles. I? "I am a Public Preacher"; appointed to preach this doctrine to all creatures. Yet the world, as we can see, had really from of old been all one great miracle to him. Look over the world, says he; is it not wonderful, the work of Allah; wholly "a sign to you," if your eyes were open! This Earth, God made it for you; "appointed paths in it"; you can live in it, go to and fro on it.—The clouds in the dry country of Arabia, to Mohammed they are very wonderful: Great clouds, he says, born in the deep bosom of the Upper Immensity, where do they come from? They hang there, the great black monsters; pour-down their rain-deluges "to revive a dead earth," and grass springs, and "tall leafy palm-trees with their date-clusters hanging round. Is not that a sign?" Your cattle too,—Allah made them; serviceable dumb creatures; they change the grass into milk; you have your clothing from them, very strange creatures; they come ranking home at evening-time, "and," adds he, "and are a credit to you"! Ships also,—he talks often about ships: Huge moving mountains, they spread-out their cloth wings, go bounding through the water there, Heaven's wind driving them; anon they lie motionless, God has withdrawn the wind, they lie dead, and cannot stir! Miracles? cries he; What miracle would you have? Are not you yourselves there? God made *you*, "shaped you out of a little clay." Ye were small once; a few years ago ye were not at all. Ye have beauty, strength, thoughts, "ye have compassion on one another." Old age comes-on you, and gray hairs; your strength fades into feebleness; ye sink down, and again are not. "Ye have compassion on one another": this struck me much: Allah might have made you having no compassion on one another,—how had it been then! This is a great direct thought, a glance at first-hand into the very fact of things. Rude vestiges of poetic genius, of whatsoever is best and truest, are visible in this man. A strong untutored intellect; eyesight, heart: a strong wild man,—might have shaped himself into Poet, King, Priest, any kind of Hero.

To his eyes it is forever clear that this world wholly is miraculous. He sees what, as we said once before, all great thinkers, the rude Scandinavians themselves, in one way or other, have contrived to see: That this so solid-looking material world is, at bottom, in very deed, Nothing; is a visual and tactual Manifestation of God's-power and presence,—a shadow hung-out by Him on the bosom of the void Infinite; nothing more. The mountains, he says, these great rock-mountains, they shall dissipate themselves "like clouds"; melt into the Blue as clouds do, and not be! He figures the Earth, in the Arab fashion, Sale tells us, as an immense Plain or flat Plate of ground, the mountains are set on that to *steady* it. At the Last Day they shall disappear "like clouds"; the whole Earth shall go spinning, whirl itself off into wreck, and as dust and vapor vanish in the Inane. Allah withdraws his hand from it, and it ceases to be. The universal empire of Allah, presence everywhere of an unspeakable Power, a Splendor, and a Terror not to be named, as the true force, essence and reality, in all things whatsoever, was continually clear to this man. What a modern talks-of by the name, Forces of Nature, Laws of Nature; and does not figure as a divine thing; not even as one thing at all, but as a set of things, undivine enough,—saleable, curious, good for propelling steamships! With our Sciences and Cyclopædias, we are apt to forget the *divineness*, in those laboratories of ours. We ought not to forget it! That once well forgotten, I know not what else were worth remembering. Most sciences, I think, were then a very dead thing; withered, contentious, empty;—a thistle in late autumn. The best science, without this, is but as the dead *timber;* it is not the growing tree and forest,—which gives ever-new timber, among other things! Man cannot *know* either, unless he can *worship* in some way. His knowledge is a pedantry, and dead thistle, otherwise.

Much has been said and written about the sensuality of Mohammed's Religion; more than was just. The indulgences, criminal to us, which he permitted, were not of his appointment; he found them practised, unquestioned from immemorial time in Arabia; what he did was to curtail them, restrict them, not on one but on many sides. His Religion is not an easy one: with rigorous fasts, lavations, strict complex formulas, prayers five times a day, and abstinence from wine, it did not "succeed by being an easy religion." As if indeed any religion, or cause holding of religion, could succeed by that! It is a calumny on men to say that they are roused to heroic action by ease, hope of pleasure, recompense,—sugar-plums of any kind, in this world or the next! In the meanest mortal there lies something nobler. The poor swearing soldier, hired to be shot, has his "honor of a soldier," different from drill-regulations and the shilling a day. It is not to taste sweet things, but to do noble and true things, and vindicate himself under God's Heaven as a god-made Man, that the poorest son of Adam dimly longs. Show him the way of doing that, the dullest daydrudge kindles into a hero. They wrong man greatly who say he is to be seduced by ease. Difficulty, abnegation, martyrdom, death are the *allurements* that act on the heart of man. Kindle the inner genial life of him, you have a flame that burns-up all lower considerations. Not happiness, but something higher: one sees this even in the frivolous classes, with their "point of honor" and the like. Not by flattering our appetites; no, by awakening the Heroic that slumbers in every heart, can any Religion gain followers.

Mohammed himself, after all that can be said about him, was not a sensual man. We shall err widely if we consider this man as a common voluptuary, intent mainly on base enjoyments,—nay on enjoyments of any kind. His household was of the frugalest; his common diet barley-bread and water: sometimes for months there was not a fire once lighted on his hearth. They record with just pride that he would mend his own shoes, patch his own cloak. A poor, hard-toiling, ill-provided man; careless of what vulgar men toil for. Not a bad man, I should say; something better in him than *hunger* of any sort,—or these wild Arab men, fighting and jostling three-and-twenty years at his hand, in close contact with him always, would not have reverenced him so! They were wild men, bursting ever and anon into quarrel, into all kinds of fierce sincerity; without right worth and manhood, no man could have commanded them. They called him Prophet, you say? Why, he stood there face to face with them; bare, not enshrined in any mystery; visibly clouting his own cloak, cobbling his own shoes; fighting, counselling, ordering in the midst of them: they must have seen what kind of a man he *was*, let him be *called* what you like! No emperor with his tiara was obeyed as this man in a cloak of his own clouting during three-and-twenty years of rough actual trial. I find something of a veritable Hero necessary for that, of itself.

His last words are a prayer; broken ejaculations of a heart struggling up, in trembling hope, towards its Maker. We cannot say that his religion made him *worse;* it made him better; good, not bad. Generous things are recorded of him: when he lost his Daughter, the thing he answers is, in his own dialect, everyway sincere, and yet equivalent to that of Christians, "The Lord giveth, and the Lord taketh away; blessed be the name of the Lord." He answered in like manner of Seid, his emancipated well-beloved Slave, the second of the believers. Seid had fallen in the War of Tabûc, the first of Mohammed's fightings with the Greeks. Mohammed said,

It was well; Seid had done his Master's work, Seid had now gone to his Master: it was all well with Seid. Yet Seid's daughter found him weeping over the body;—the old gray-haired man melting in tears! "What do I see?" said she.—"You see a friend weeping over his friend."—He went out for the last time into the mosque, two days before his death; asked, If he had injured any man? Let his own back bear the stripes. If he owed any man? A voice answered, "Yes, me three drachms," borrowed on such an occasion. Mohammed ordered them to be paid: "Better be in shame now," said he, "than at the Day of Judgment."—You remember Kadijah, and the "No, by Allah!" Traits of that kind show us the genuine man, the brother of us all, brought visible through twelve centuries,—the veritable Son of our common Mother.

Withal I like Mohammed for his total freedom from cant. He is a rough self-helping son of the wilderness; does not pretend to be what he is not. There is no ostentatious pride in him; but neither does he go much upon humility: he is there as he can be, in cloak and shoes of his own clouting; speaks plainly to all manner of Persian Kings, Greek Emperors, what it is they are bound to do; knows well enough, about himself, "the respect due unto thee." In a life-and-death war with Bedouins, cruel things could not fail; but neither are acts of mercy, of noble natural pity and generosity, wanting. Mohammed makes no apology for the one, no boast of the other. They were each the free dictate of his heart; each called-for, there and then. Not a mealy-mouthed man! A candid ferocity, if the case call for it, is in him; he does not mince matters! The War of Tabûc is a thing he often speaks of: his men refused, many of them, to march on that occasion; pleaded the heat of the weather, the harvest, and so forth; he can never forget that. Your harvest? It lasts for a day. What will become of your harvest through all Eternity? Hot weather? Yes, it was hot; "but Hell will be hotter!" Sometimes a rough sarcasm turns-up: He says to the unbelievers, Ye shall have the just measure of your deeds at that Great Day. They will be weighed-out to you; ye shall not have short weight!—Everywhere he fixes the matter in his eye; he *sees* it: his heart, now and then, is as if struck dumb by the greatness of it. "Assuredly," he says: that word, in the Koran, is written-down sometimes as a sentence by itself: "Assuredly."

No *Dilettanteism* in this Mohammed; it is a business of Reprobation and Salvation with him, of Time and Eternity: he is in deadly earnest about it! Dilettanteism, hypothesis, speculation, a kind of amateur-search for Truth, toying and coquetting with Truth: this is the sorest sin. The root of all other imaginable sins. It consists in the heart and soul of the man never having been *open* to Truth;—"living in a vain show." Such a man not only utters and produces falsehoods, but *is* himself a falsehood. The rational moral principle, spark of the Divinity, is sunk deep in him, in quiet paralysis of life-death. The very falsehoods of Mohammed are truer than the truths of such a man. He is the insincere man: smooth-polished, respectable in some times and places; inoffensive, says nothing harsh to anybody; most *cleanly,*—just as carbonic acid is, which is death and poison.

We will not praise Mohammed's moral precepts as always of the superfinest sort; yet it can be said that there is always a tendency to good in them; that they are the true dictates of a heart aiming towards what is just and true. The sublime forgiveness of Christianity, turning of the other cheek when the one has been smitten, is not here: you *are* to revenge yourself, but it is to be in measure, not overmuch, or beyond justice. On the other hand, Islam, like any great Faith, and insight into the essence of man, is a perfect equalizer of men: the soul of one believer outweighs all earthly kingships; all men, according to Islam too, are equal. Mohammed insists not on the propriety of giving alms, but on the necessity of it: he marks-down by law how much you are to give, and it is at your peril if you neglect. The tenth part of a man's annual income, whatever that may be, is the *property* of the poor, of those that are afflicted and need help. Good all this: the natural voice of humanity, of pity and equity dwelling in the heart of this wild Son of Nature speaks *so.*

Mohammed's Paradise is sensual, his Hell sensual: true; in the one and the other there is enough that shocks all spiritual feeling in us. But we are to recollect that the Arabs already had it so; that Mohammed, in whatever he changed of it, softened and diminished all this. The worst sensualities, too, are the work of doctors, followers of his, not his work. In the

Koran there is really very little said about the joys of Paradise; they are intimated rather than insisted on. Nor is it forgotten that the highest joys even there shall be spiritual; the pure Presence of the Highest, this shall infinitely transcend all other joys. He says, "Your salutation shall be, Peace." *Salam,* Have Peace!—the thing that all rational souls long for, and seek, vainly here below, as the one blessing. "Ye shall sit on seats, facing one another: all grudges shall be taken away out of your hearts." All grudges! Ye shall love one another freely; for each of you, in the eyes of his brothers, there will be Heaven enough!

In reference to this of the sensual Paradise and Mohammed's sensuality, the sorest chapter of all for us, there were many things to be said; which it is not convenient to enter upon here. Two remarks only I shall make, and therewith leave it to your candor. The first is furnished me by Goethe; it is a casual hint of his which seems well worth taking note of. In one of his Delineations, in *Meister's Travels* it is, the hero comes-upon a Society of men with very strange ways, one of which was this: "We require," says the Master, "that each of our people shall restrict himself in one direction," shall go right against his desire in one matter, and *make* himself do the thing he does not wish, "should we allow him the greater latitude on all other sides." There seems to me a great justness in this. Enjoying things which are pleasant; that is not the evil: it is the reducing of our moral self to slavery by them that is. Let a man assert withal that he is king over his habitudes; that he could and would shake them off, on cause shown: this is an excellent law. The Month Ramadhan for the Moslem, much in Mohammed's Religion, much in his own Life, bears in that direction; if not by forethought, or clear purpose of moral improvement on his part, then by a certain healthy manful instinct, which is as good.

But there is another thing to be said about the Mohammedan Heaven and Hell. This namely, that, however gross and material they may be, they are an emblem of an everlasting truth, not always so well remembered elsewhere. That gross sensual Paradise of his; that horrible flaming Hell; the great enormous Day of Judgment he perpetually insists on: what is all this but a rude shadow, in the rude Bedouin imagination, of that grand spiritual Fact, and Beginning of Facts, which it is ill for us too if we do not all know and feel: the Infinite Nature of Duty? That man's actions here are of *infinite* moment to him, and never die or end at all; that man, with his little life, reaches upwards high as Heaven, downwards low as Hell, and in his threescore years of Time holds an Eternity fearfully and wonderfully hidden: all this had burnt itself, as in flame-characters, into the wild Arab soul. As in flame and lightning, it stands written there; awful, unspeakable, ever present to him. With bursting earnestness, with a fierce savage sincerity, halt, articulating, not able to articulate, he strives to speak it, bodies it forth in that Heaven and that Hell. Bodied forth in what way you will, it is the first of all truths. It is venerable under all embodiments. What is the chief end of man here below? Mohammed has answered this question, in a way that might put some of *us* to shame! He does not, like a Bentham, a Paley, take Right and Wrong, and calculate the profit and loss, ultimate pleasure of the one and of the other; and summing all up by addition and subtraction into a net result, ask you, Whether on the whole the Right does not preponderate considerably? No; it is not *better* to do the one than the other; the one is to the other as life is to death,—as Heaven is to Hell. The one must in nowise be done, the other in nowise left undone. You shall not measure them; they are incommensurable: the one is death eternal to a man, the other is life eternal. Benthamee Utility, virtue by Profit and Loss; reducing this God's-world to a dead brute Steam-engine, the infinite celestial Soul of Man to a kind of Hay-balance for weighing hay and thistles on, pleasures and pains on:—if you ask me which gives, Mohammed or they, the beggarlier and falser view of Man and his Destinies in this Universe, I will answer, It is not Mohammed!——

On the whole, we will repeat that this Religion of Mohammed's is a kind of Christianity; has a genuine element of what is spiritually highest looking through it, not to be hidden by all its imperfections. The Scandinavian God *Wish*, the god of all rude men,—this has been enlarged into a Heaven by Mohammed; but a Heaven symbolical of sacred Duty, and to be earned by faith and well-doing, by valiant action, and a divine patience which is still more valiant. It is Scandinavian Paganism, and a truly celestial element super-added to that. Call it not false; look not at the falsehood of it, look at the truth of it. For these twelve centuries, it has been the religion and life-guidance of the fifth part of the whole kindred of Mankind. Above all things, it has been a religion heartily *believed.* These Arabs believe their religion, and try to live by it! No Christians, since the early ages, or only perhaps the English Puritans in modern times, have ever stood by their Faith as the Moslem do by theirs,—believing it wholly, fronting Time with it, and Eternity with it. This night the watchman on the streets of Cairo when he cries, "Who goes?" will hear from the passenger, along with his answer, "There is no God but God." *Allah akbar, Islam,* sounds through the souls, and whole daily existence, of these dusky millions. Zealous missionaries preach it abroad among Malays, black Papuans, brutal Idolaters;—displacing what is worse, nothing that is better or good.

To the Arab Nation it was as a birth from darkness into light; Arabia first became alive by means of it. A poor shepherd people, roaming unnoticed in its deserts since the creation of the world: a Hero-Prophet was sent down to them with a word they could believe: see, the unnoticed becomes world-notable, the small has grown world-great; within one century afterwards, Arabia is at Grenada on this hand, at Delhi on that;—glancing in valor and splendor and the light of genius, Arabia shines through long ages over a great section of the world. Belief is great, life-giving. The history of a Nation becomes fruitful, soul-elevating, great, so soon as it believes. These Arabs, the man Mohammed, and that one century,—is it not as if a spark had fallen, one spark, on a world of what seemed black unnoticeable sand; but lo, the sand proves explosive powder, blazes heaven-high from Delhi to Grenada! I said, the Great Man was always as lightning out of Heaven; the rest of men waited for him like fuel, and then they too would flame.

THE KORAN

CHAPTER I

Entitled, the Preface, or Introduction—Revealed at Mecca

In the Name of the Most Merciful God.

PRAISE be to God, the Lord of all creatures, the most merciful, the king of the day of judgment. Thee do we worship, and of thee do we beg assistance. Direct us in the right way, in the way of those to whom thou hast been gracious; not of those against whom thou art incensed, nor of those who go astray.*

CHAPTER II

Entitled, the Cow[1]—Revealed Partly at Mecca, and Partly at Medina

In the Name of the Most Merciful God.

A. L. M. There is no doubt in this book; it is a direction to the pious, who believe in the mysteries of faith, who observe the appointed times of prayer, and distribute alms out of what we have bestowed on them; and who believe in that revelation, which hath been sent down unto thee, and that which hath been sent down unto the prophets before thee, and have firm assurance in the life to come: these are directed by their Lord, and they shall prosper. As for the un-

*This chapter is a prayer, and held in great veneration by the Mohammedans, who give it several other honorable titles; as the chapter of prayer, of praise, of thanksgiving, of treasure. They esteem it as the quintessence of the whole Koran, and often repeat it in their devotions both public and private, as the Christians do the Lord's Prayer.

[1] This title was occasioned by the story of the red heifer, mentioned p. 217.

believers, it will be equal to them whether thou admonish them, or do not admonish them; they will not believe. God hath sealed up their hearts and their hearing; a dimness covereth their sight, and they shall suffer a grievous punishment. There are some who say, We believe in God and the last day, but are not really believers; they seek to deceive God, and those who do believe, but they deceive themselves only, and are not sensible thereof. There is an infirmity in their hearts, and God hath increased that infirmity; and they shall suffer a most painful punishment because they have disbelieved. When one saith unto them, Act not corruptly in the earth, they reply, Verily, we are men of integrity. Are not they themselves corrupt doers? but they are not sensible thereof. And when one saith unto them, Believe ye as others believe; they answer, Shall we believe as fools believe? Are not they themselves fools? but they know it not. When they meet those who believe, they say, We do believe: but when they retire privately to their devils, they say, We really hold with you, and only mock at those people: God shall mock at them, and continue them in their impiety; they shall wander in confusion. These are the men who have purchased error at the price of true direction: but their traffic hath not been gainful, neither have they been rightly directed. They are like unto one who kindleth a fire, and when it hath enlightened all around him, God taketh away their light and leaveth them in darkness, they shall not see; they are deaf, dumb, and blind, therefore will they not repent. Or like a stormy cloud from heaven, fraught with darkness, thunder, and lightning, they put their fingers in their ears, because of the noise of the thunder, for fear of death; God encompasseth the infidels: the lightning wanteth but little of taking away their sight; so often as it enlighteneth them, they walk therein, but when darkness cometh on them, they stand still; and if God so pleased, He would certainly deprive them of their hearing and their sight, for God is almighty. O men of Mecca! serve your Lord who hath created you, and those who have been before you: peradventure ye will fear him; who hath spread the earth as a bed for you, and the heaven as a covering, and hath caused water to descend from heaven, and thereby produced fruits for your sustenance. Set not up therefore any equals unto God, against your own knowledge. If ye be in doubt concerning that revelation which we have sent down unto our servant, produce a chapter like unto it, and call upon your witnesses, besides God, if ye say truth. But if ye do it not, nor shall ever be able to do it, justly fear the fire whose fuel is men and stones, prepared for the unbelievers. But bear good tidings unto those who believe, and do good works, that they shall have gardens watered by rivers; so often as they eat of the fruit thereof for sustenance, they shall say, This is what we have formerly eaten of; and they shall be supplied with several sorts of fruit having a mutual resemblance to one another. There shall they enjoy wives subject to no impurity, and there shall they continue forever. Moreover God will not be ashamed to propound in a parable a gnat, or even a more despicable thing: for they who believe will know it to be the truth from their Lord; but the unbelievers will say, What meaneth God by this parable? he will thereby mislead many, and will direct many thereby: but he will not mislead any thereby, except the transgressors, who make void the covenant of God after the establishing thereof, and cut in sunder that which God hath commanded to be joined, and act corruptly in the earth; they shall perish. How is it that ye believe not in God? Since ye were dead, and he gave you life; he will hereafter cause you to die, and will again restore you to life; then shall ye return unto him. It is he who hath created for you whatsoever is on earth, and then set his mind to the creation of heaven, and formed it into seven heavens; he knoweth all things. When thy Lord said unto the angels, I am going to place a substitute on earth,[2] they said, Wilt thou place there one who will do evil therein, and shed blood? but we celebrate thy praise, and sanctify thee. God answered, Verily I know that which ye know not; and he

[2] Concerning the creation of Adam, here intimated, the Mohammedans have several peculiar traditions. They say the angels, Gabriel, Michael, and Israfil, were sent by God, one after another, to fetch for that purpose seven handfuls of earth from different depths, and of different colors (whence some account for the various complexion of mankind); but the earth being apprehensive of the consequence, and desiring them to represent her fear to God that the creature he designed to form would rebel against him, and draw down his curse upon her, they returned without performing God's command; whereupon he sent Azrail on the same errand, who executed his commission without remorse, for which reason God appointed that angel to separate the souls from the bodies, being therefore called the angel of death. The earth he had taken was carried into Arabia, to a place between Mecca and Tayef, where, being first kneaded by the angels, it was afterwards fashioned by God himself into a human form, and left to dry for the space of forty days, or, as others say, as many years, the angels in the meantime often visiting it, and Eblis (then one of the angels who are nearest to God's presence, afterwards the devil) among the rest; but he, not contented with looking on it, kicked it with his foot, and knowing God designed that creature to be his superior, took a secret resolution never to acknowledge him as such. After this, God animated the figure of clay and endued it with an intelligent soul, and when he had placed him in paradise, formed Eve out of his left side.

taught Adam the names of all things, and then proposed them to the angels, and said, Declare unto me the names of these things if ye say truth. They answered, Praise be unto thee, we have no knowledge but what thou teachest us, for thou art knowing and wise. God said, O Adam, tell them their names. And when he had told them their names, God said, Did I not tell you that I know the secrets of heaven and earth, and know that which ye discover, and that which ye conceal? And when we said unto the angels, Worship Adam, they all worshipped him, except Eblis, who refused, and was puffed up with pride, and became of the number of unbelievers.[3] And we said, O Adam, dwell thou and thy wife in the garden, and eat of the fruit thereof plentifully wherever ye will; but approach not this tree, lest ye become of the number of the transgressors. But Satan caused them to forfeit paradise, and turned them out of the state of happiness wherein they had been; whereupon we said, Get ye down, the one of you an enemy unto the other; and there shall be a dwelling-place for you on earth, and a provision for a season. And Adam learned words of prayer from his Lord, and God turned unto him, for he is easy to be reconciled and merciful. We said, Get ye all down from hence; hereafter shall there come unto you a direction from me, and whoever shall follow my direction, on them shall no fear come, neither shall they be grieved; but they who shall be unbelievers, and accuse our signs of falsehood, they shall be the companions of hell fire, therein shall they remain forever. O children of Israel,[4] remember my favor wherewith I have favored you; and perform your covenant with me and I will perform my covenant with you; and revere me; and believe in the revelation which I have sent down, confirming that which is with you, and be not the first who believe not therein, neither exchange my signs for a small price; and fear me. Clothe not the truth with vanity, neither conceal the truth against your own knowledge; observe the stated times of prayer, and pay your legal alms, and bow down yourselves with those who bow down. Will ye com-

[3] This occasion of the devil's fall has some affinity with an opinion which has been pretty much entertained among Christians, viz., that the angels being informed of God's intention to create man after his own image, and to dignify human nature by Christ's assuming it, some of them, thinking their glory to be eclipsed thereby, envied man's happiness, and so revolted.

[4] The Jews are here called upon to receive the Koran, as verifying and confirming the Pentateuch, particularly with respect to the unity of God, and the mission of Mohammed. And they are exhorted not to conceal the passages of their law which bear witness to those truths, nor to corrupt them by publishing false copies of the Pentateuch, for which the writers were but poorly paid.

mand men to do justice, and forget your own souls? yet ye read the book of the law: do ye not therefore understand? Ask help with perseverance and prayer; this indeed is grievous, unless to the humble, who seriously think they shall meet their Lord, and that to him they shall return. O children of Israel, remember my favor wherewith I have favored you, and that I have preferred you above all nations: dread the day wherein one soul shall not make satisfaction for another soul, neither shall any intercession be accepted from them, nor shall any compensation be received, neither shall they be helped. Remember when we delivered you from the people of Pharaoh, who grievously oppressed you, they slew your male children, and let your females live: therein was a great trial from your Lord. And when we divided the sea for you and delivered you, and drowned Pharaoh's people while ye looked on. And when we treated with Moses forty nights; then ye took the calf[5] for your God, and did evil; yet afterwards we forgave you, that peradventure ye might give thanks. And when we gave Moses the book of the law, and the distinction between good and evil, that peradventure ye might be directed. And when Moses said unto his people, O my people, verily ye have injured your own souls, by your taking the calf for your God; therefore be turned unto your Creator, and slay those among you who have been guilty of that crime; this will be better for you in the sight of your Creator; and thereupon he turned unto you, for he is easy to be reconciled, and merciful. And when ye said, O Moses, we will not believe thee, until we see God manifestly; therefore a punishment came upon you, while ye looked on; then we raised you to life after ye had been dead, that peradventure ye might give thanks. And we caused clouds to overshadow you, and manna and quails[6] to descend upon you, saying, Eat of the good things which we have given you for food:

[5] The person who cast this calf, the Mohammedans say, was (not Aaron but) al Sâmeri, one of the principal men among the children of Israel, some of whose descendants it is pretended still inhabit an island of that name in the Arabian Gulf. It was made of the rings and bracelets of gold, silver, and other materials, which the Israelites had borrowed of the Egyptians; for Aaron, who commanded in his brother's absence, having ordered al Sâmeri to collect those ornaments from the people, who carried on a wicked commerce with them, and to keep them together till the return of Moses; al Sâmeri, understanding the founder's art, put them into a furnace to melt them down into one mass, which came out in the form of a calf.

[6] The eastern writers say these quails were of a peculiar kind, to be found nowhere but in Yaman, from whence they were brought by a south wind in great numbers to the Israelites' camp in the desert. The Arabs call these birds Salwâ, which is plainly the same with the Hebrew Salwim, and say they have no bones, but are eaten whole.

and they injured not us, but injured their own souls. And when we said, Enter into this city, and eat of the provisions thereof plentifully as ye will; and enter the gate worshipping, and say, Forgiveness! we will pardon you your sins, and give increase unto the well-doers. But the ungodly changed the expression into another, different from what had been spoken unto them; and we sent down upon the ungodly indignation from heaven, because they had transgressed. And when Moses asked drink for his people, we said, Strike the rock with thy rod; and there gushed thereout twelve fountains according to the number of the tribes, and all men knew their respective drinking-place. Eat and drink of the bounty of God, and commit not evil in the earth, acting unjustly. And when ye said, O Moses, we will by no means be satisfied with one kind of food; pray unto thy Lord therefore for us, that he would produce for us of that which the earth bringeth forth, herbs, and cucumbers, and garlic, and lentils, and onions; Moses answered, Will ye exchange that which is better, for that which is worse? Get ye down into Egypt, for there shall ye find what ye desire; and they were smitten with vileness and misery, and drew on themselves indignation from God. This they suffered, because they believed not in the signs of God, and killed the prophets unjustly; this, because they rebelled and transgressed. Surely those who believe, and those who Judaize, and Christians, and Sabeans, whoever believeth in God, and the last day, and doth that which is right, they shall have their reward with their Lord; there shall come no fear on them, neither shall they be grieved. Call to mind also when we accepted your covenant, and lifted up the mountain of Sinai over you, saying, Receive the law which we have given you, with a resolution to keep it, and remember that which is contained therein, that ye may beware. After this ye again turned back, so that if it had not been for God's indulgence and mercy towards you, ye had certainly been destroyed. Moreover, ye know what befell those of your nation who transgressed on the Sabbath day: We said unto them, Be ye changed into apes, driven away from the society of men. And we made them an example unto those who were contemporary with them, and unto those who came after them, and a warning to the pious. And when Moses said unto his people, Verily God commandeth you to sacrifice a cow;[7]

[7] The occasion of this sacrifice is thus related: A certain man at his death left his son, then a child, a cow-calf, which wandered in the desert till he

they answered, Dost thou make a jest of us? Moses said, God forbid that I should be one of the foolish. They said, Pray for us unto thy Lord, that he would show us what cow it is. Moses answered, He saith, She is neither an old cow, nor a young heifer, but of a middle-age between both: do ye therefore that which ye are commanded. They said, Pray for us unto the Lord, that he would show us what color she is of. Moses answered, He saith, She is a red cow, intensely red, her color rejoiceth the beholders. They said, Pray for us unto thy Lord, that he would further show us what cow it is, for several cows with us are like one another, and we, if God please, will be directed. Moses answered, He saith, She is a cow not broken to plough the earth, or water the field: a sound one, there is no blemish in her. They said, Now hast thou brought the truth. Then they sacrificed her; yet they wanted little of leaving it undone. And when ye slew a man, and contended among yourselves concerning him, God brought forth to light that which ye concealed. For we said, Strike the dead body with part of the sacrificed cow; so God raiseth the dead to life, and showeth you his signs, that peradventure ye may understand. Then were your hearts hardened after this, even as stones, or exceeding them in hardness: for from some stones have rivers burst forth, others have been rent in sunder, and water hath issued from them, and others have fallen down for fear of God. But God is not regardless of that which ye do. Do ye therefore desire that the Jews should believe you? yet a part of them

came to age; at which time his mother told him the heifer was his, and bid him fetch her, and sell her for three pieces of gold. When the young man came to the market with his heifer, an angel in the shape of a man accosted him, and bid him six pieces of gold for her; but he would not take the money till he had asked his mother's consent; which when he had obtained, he returned to the market-place, and met the angel, who now offered him twice as much for the heifer, provided he would say nothing of it to his mother; but the young man refusing, went and acquainted her with the additional offer. The woman perceiving it was an angel, bid her son go back and ask him what must be done with the heifer; whereupon the angel told the young man that in a little time the children of Israel would buy that heifer of him at any price. And soon after it happened that an Israelite, named Hammiel, was killed by a relation of his, who, to prevent discovery, conveyed the body to a place considerably distant from that where the act was committed. The friends of the slain man accused some other persons of the murder before Moses; but they denying the fact, and there being no evidence to convict them, God commanded a cow, of such and such particular marks, to be killed; but there being no other which answered the description except the orphan's heifer, they were obliged to buy her for as much gold as her hide would hold; according to some, for her full weight in gold, and as others say, for ten times as much. This heifer they sacrificed, and the dead body being, by divine direction, struck with a part of it, revived, and standing up, named the person who had killed him; after which it immediately fell down dead again. The whole story seems to be borrowed from the red heifer which was ordered by the Jewish law to be burnt, and the ashes kept for purifying those who happened to touch a dead corpse; and from the heifer directed to be slain for the expiation of an uncertain murder. See Deut. xxi. 1-9.

heard the word of God, and then perverted it, after they had understood it, against their own conscience. And when they meet the true believers, they say, We believe: but when they are privately assembled together, they say, Will ye acquaint them with what God hath revealed unto you, that they may dispute with you concerning it in the presence of your Lord? Do ye not therefore understand? Do not they know that God knoweth that which they conceal as well as that which they publish? But there are illiterate men among them, who know not the book of the law, but only lying stories, although they think otherwise. And woe unto them who transcribe corruptly the book of the law with their hands, and then say, This is from God: that they may sell it for a small price. Therefore woe unto them because of that which their hands have written; and woe unto them for that which they have gained. They say, The fire of hell shall not touch us but for a certain number of days. Answer, Have ye received any promise from God to that purpose? for God will not act contrary to his promise: or do ye speak concerning God that which ye know not? Verily whoso doth evil, and is encompassed by his iniquity, they shall be the companions of hell fire, they shall remain therein forever: but they who believe and do good works, they shall be the companions of paradise, they shall continue therein forever. Remember also, when we accepted the covenant of the children of Israel, saying, Ye shall not worship any other except God, and ye shall show kindness to your parents and kindred, and to orphans, and to the poor, and speak that which is good unto men, and be constant at prayer, and give alms. Afterwards ye turned back, except a few of you, and retired afar-off. And when we accepted your covenant, saying, Ye shall not shed your brother's blood, nor dispossess one another of your habitations, then ye confirmed it, and were witnesses thereto. Afterwards ye were they who slew one another, and turned several of your brethren out of their houses, mutually assisting each other against them with injustice and enmity; but if they come captives unto you, ye redeem them: yet it is equally unlawful for you to dispossss them. Do ye therefore believe in part of the book of the law, and reject other parts thereof? But whoso among you doth this, shall have no other reward than shame in this life, and on the day of resurrection they shall be sent to a most grievous punishment; for God is not regardless of that which ye do. These are they who have purchased this present life, at the price of that which is to come; wherefore their punishment shall not be mitigated, neither shall they be helped. We formerly delivered the book of the law unto Moses, and caused apostles to succeed him, and gave evident miracles to Jesus the son of Mary, and strengthened him with the holy spirit. Do ye therefore, whenever an apostle cometh unto you with that which your souls desire not, proudly reject him, and accuse some of imposture, and slay others? The Jews say, Our hearts are uncircumcised: but God hath cursed them with their infidelity, therefore few shall believe. And when a book came unto them from God, confirming the scriptures which were with them, although they had before prayed for assistance against those who believed not, yet when that came unto them which they knew to be from God, they would not believe therein: therefore the curse of God shall be on the infidels. For a vile price have they sold their souls, that they should not believe in that which God hath sent down; out of envy, because God sendeth down his favors to such of his servants as he pleaseth: therefore they brought on themselves indignation on indignation; and the unbelievers shall suffer an ignominious punishment. When one saith unto them, Believe in that which God hath sent down; they answer, We believe in that which hath been sent down unto us: and they reject what hath been revealed since, although it be the truth, confirming that which is with them. Say, Why therefore have ye slain the prophets of God in times past, if ye be true believers? Moses formerly came unto you with evident signs, but ye afterwards took the calf for your god and did wickedly. And when we accepted your covenant, and lifted the mountain of Sinai over you, saying, Receive the law which we have given you, with a resolution to perform it, and hear; they said, We have heard, and have rebelled: and they were made to drink down the calf into their hearts for their unbelief. Say, A grievous thing hath your faith commanded you, if ye be true believers. Say, If the future mansion with God be prepared peculiarly for you, exclusive of the rest of mankind, wish for death, if ye say truth: but they will never wish for it, because of that which their hands have sent before them; God knoweth the wicked doers; and thou shalt surely find them of all men the most covetous of life, even more than the idolaters: one of them would desire his life to be prolonged a thousand years, but none shall reprieve himself from punishment, that his life may be prolonged: God seeth that which they do. Say, Whoever is an enemy to Gabriel (for he hath caused the Koran to descend on thy heart, by the permission of God, confirming that which was before revealed, a direction, and good tidings to the faithful); whosoever is an enemy to God, or his angels, or his apostles, or to Gabriel, or Michael, verily God is an enemy to the unbelievers. And now we have sent down unto thee evident signs, and none will disbelieve them but the evil-doers. Whenever they make a covenant, will some of them reject it? yea, the greater part of them do not believe. And when there came unto them an apostle from God, confirming that scripture which was with them, some of those to whom the scriptures were given, cast the book of God behind their backs, as if they knew it not: and they followed the device which the devils devised against the kingdom of Solomon; and Solomon was not an unbeliever; but the devils believed not, they taught men sorcery, and that which was sent down to the two angels at Babel, Harût, and Marût: yet those who taught no man until they had said, Verily we are a temptation, therefore be not an unbeliever. So men learned from those two a charm by which they might cause division between a man and his wife; but they hurt none thereby, unless by God's permission; and they learned that which would hurt them, and not profit them; and yet they knew that he who bought that art should have no part in the life to come, and woful is the price for which they have sold their souls, if they knew it. But if they had believed and feared God, verily the reward they would have had from God would have been better, if they had known it. O true believers, say not to our apostle, Raina; but say, Ondhorna;[8] and hearken: the infidels shall suffer a grievous punishment. It is not the desire of the unbelievers, either among those unto whom the scriptures have been given, or among the idolaters, that any good should be sent down unto you from your Lord: but God will appropriate his mercy unto whom he pleaseth; for God is exceeding beneficent. Whatever verse we shall abrogate, or cause thee to forget, we will bring a better than it, or one like

[8] Those two Arabic words have both the same signification, viz., Look on us; and are a kind of salutation. Mohammed had a great aversion to the first, because the Jews frequently used it in derision, it being a word of reproach in their tongue. They alluded, it seems, to the Hebrew verb *ruá*, which signifies to be bad or mischievous.

unto it. Dost thou not know that God is almighty? Dost thou not know that unto God belongeth the kingdom of heaven and earth? neither have ye any protector or helper except God. Will ye require of your apostle according to that which was formerly required of Moses? but he that hath exchanged faith for infidelity, hath already erred from the straight way. Many of those unto whom the scriptures have been given, desire to render you again unbelievers, after ye have believed; out of envy from their souls, even after the truth is become manifest unto them; but forgive them, and avoid them, till God shall send his command; for God is omnipotent. Be constant in prayer, and give alms; and what good ye have sent before for your souls, ye shall find it with God; surely God seeth that which ye do. They say, Verily none shall enter paradise, except they who are Jews or Christians: this is their wish. Say, Produce your proof of this, if ye speak truth. Nay, but he who resigneth himself to God, and doth that which is right, he shall have his reward with his Lord; there shall come no fear on them, neither shall they be grieved. The Jews say, The Christians are grounded on nothing; and the Christians say, The Jews are grounded on nothing; yet they both read the scriptures. So likewise say they who know not the scripture, according to their saying. But God shall judge between them on the day of the resurrection, concerning that about which they now disagree. Who is more unjust than he who prohibiteth the temples of God, that his name should be remembered therein, and who hasteth to destroy them? Those men cannot enter therein, but with fear: they shall have shame in this world, and in the next a grievous punishment. To God belongeth the east and the west; therefore, whithersoever ye turn yourselves to pray, there is the face of God; for God is omnipresent and omniscient. They say God hath begotten children. God forbid! To him belongeth whatever is in heaven, and on earth; all is possessed by him, the Creator of heaven and earth; and when he decreeth a thing, he only saith unto it, Be, and it is. And they who know not the scriptures say, Unless God speak unto us, or thou show us a sign, we will not believe. So said those before them, according to their saying: their hearts resemble each other. We have already shown manifest signs unto people who firmly believe; we have sent thee in truth, a bearer of good tidings, and a preacher; and thou shalt not be questioned concerning the companions of hell. But the Jews will not be pleased with thee, neither the Christians, until thou follow their religion; say, The direction of God is the true direction. And verily if thou follow their desires, after the knowledge which hath been given thee, thou shalt find no patron or protector against God. They to whom we have given the book of the Koran, and who read it with its true reading, they believe therein; and whoever believeth not therein, they shall perish. O children of Israel, remember my favor wherewith I have favored you, and that I have preferred you before all nations; and dread the day wherein one soul shall not make satisfaction for another soul, neither shall any compensation be accepted from them, nor shall any intercession avail, neither shall they be helped. Remember when the Lord tried Abraham by certain words, which he fulfilled: God said, Verily I will constitute thee a model of religion unto mankind; he answered, And also of my posterity; God said, My covenant doth not comprehend the ungodly. And when we appointed the holy house of Mecca to be the place of resort for mankind, and a place of security; and said, Take the station of Abraham for a place of prayer; and we covenanted with Abraham and Ismael, that they should cleanse my house for those who should compass it, and those who should be devoutly assiduous there, and those who should bow down and worship. And when Abraham said, Lord, make this a territory of security, and bounteously bestow fruits on its inhabitants, such of them as believe in God and the last day; God answered, And whoever believeth not, I will bestow on him little: afterwards I will drive him to the punishment of hell fire; an ill journey shall it be! And when Abraham and Ismael raised the foundations of the house, saying, Lord, accept it from us, for thou art he who heareth and knoweth: Lord, make us also resigned unto thee, and of our posterity a people resigned unto thee, and show us our holy ceremonies, and be turned unto us, for thou art easy to be reconciled, and merciful; Lord, send them likewise an apostle from among them, who may declare thy signs unto them, and teach them the book of the Koran and wisdom, and may purify them; for thou art mighty and wise. Who will be averse to the religion of Abraham, but he whose mind is infatuated? Surely we have chosen him in this world, and in that which is to come he shall be one of the righteous. When his Lord said unto him, Resign thyself unto me, he answered, I have resigned myself unto the Lord of all creatures. And Abraham bequeathed this religion to his children, and Jacob did the same, saying, My children, verily, God hath chosen this religion for you, therefore die not, unless ye also be resigned. Were ye present when Jacob was at the point of death? when he said to his sons, Whom will ye worship after me? They answered, We will worship thy God, and the God of thy fathers, Abraham and Ismael, and Isaac, one God, and to him will we be resigned. That people are now passed away, they have what they have gained, and ye shall have what ye gain; and ye shall not be questioned concerning that which they have done. They say, Become Jews or Christians that ye may be directed. Say, Nay, we follow the religion of Abraham the orthodox, who was no idolater. Say, We believe in God, and that which hath been sent down unto us, and that which hath been sent down unto Abraham, and Ismael, and Isaac, and Jacob, and the tribes, and that which was delivered unto Moses, and Jesus, and that which was delivered unto the prophets from their Lord: We make no distinction between any of them, and to God are we resigned. Now if they believe according to what ye believe, they are surely directed, but if they turn back, they are in schism. God shall support thee against them, for he is the hearer, the wise. The baptism of God [9] have we received, and who is better than God to baptize? him do we worship. Say, Will ye dispute with us concerning God, who is our Lord, and your Lord? we have our works, and ye have your works, and unto him are we sincerely devoted. Will ye say, Truly Abraham, and Ismael, and Isaac, and Jacob, and the tribes were Jews or Christians? Say, Are ye wiser, or God? And who is more unjust than he who hideth the testimony which he hath received from God? But God is not regardless of that which ye do. That people are passed away, they have what they have gained, and ye shall have what ye gain, nor shall ye be questioned concerning that which they have done. The foolish men will say, What hath turned them from their Keblah, towards which they formerly prayed? [10] Say, Unto God belongeth the east

[9] By baptism is to be understood the religion which God instituted in the beginning; because the signs of it appear in the person who professes it, as the signs of water appear in the clothes of him that is baptized.

[10] At first, Mohammed and his followers observed no particular rite in turning their faces towards any certain place, or quarter, of the world, when they prayed; it being declared to be perfectly indifferent.

and the west: he directeth whom he pleaseth into the right way. Thus have we placed you, O Arabians, an intermediate nation, that ye may be witnesses against the rest of mankind, and that the apostle may be a witness against you. We appointed the Keblah towards which thou didst formerly pray, only that we might know him who followeth the apostle, from him who turneth back on his heels; though this change seem a great matter, unless unto those whom God hath directed. But God will not render your faith of no effect; for God is gracious and merciful unto man. We have seen thee turn about thy face towards heaven with uncertainty, but we will cause thee to turn thyself towards a Keblah that will please thee. Turn, therefore, thy face towards the holy temple of Mecca; and wherever ye be, turn your faces towards that place. They to whom the scripture hath been given, know this to be truth from their Lord. God is not regardless of that which ye do. Verily although thou shouldst show unto those to whom the scripture hath been given all kinds of signs, yet they will not follow thy Keblah, neither shalt thou follow their Keblah; nor will one part of them follow the Keblah of the other. And if thou follow their desires, after the knowledge which hath been given thee, verily thou wilt become one of the ungodly. They to whom we have given the scripture know our apostle, even as they know their own children; but some of them hide the truth, against their own knowledge. Truth is from thy Lord, therefore thou shalt not doubt. Every sect hath a certain tract of heaven to which they turn themselves in prayer; but do ye strive to run after good things: wherever ye be, God will bring you all back at the resurrection, for God is almighty. And from what place soever thou comest forth, turn thy face towards the holy temple; for this is truth from thy Lord; neither is God regardless of that which ye do. From what place soever thou comest forth, turn thy face towards the holy temple; and wherever ye be, thitherward turn your faces, lest men have matter of dispute against you; but as for those among them who are unjust doers, fear them not, but fear me, that I may accomplish my grace upon you, and that ye may be directed. As we have sent unto you an apostle from among you, to rehearse our signs unto you, and to purify you, and to teach you the book of the Koran and wisdom, and to teach you that which ye knew not: therefore remember me, and I will remember you, and give thanks unto me, and be not unbelievers. O true believers, beg assistance with patience and prayer, for God is with the patient. And say not of those who are slain in fight for the religion of God, that they are dead; yea, they are living: but ye do not understand. We will surely prove you by afflicting you in some measure with fear, and hunger, and decrease of wealth, and loss of lives, and scarcity of fruits; but bear good tidings unto the patient, who when a misfortune befalleth them, say, We are God's, and unto him shall we surely return. Upon them shall be blessings from their Lord and mercy, and they are the rightly directed. Moreover Safa and Merwah are two of the monuments of God: whoever therefore goeth on pilgrimage to the temple of Mecca or visiteth it, it shall be no crime in him if he compass them both. And as for him who voluntarily performeth a good work; verily God is grateful and knowing. They who conceal any of the evident signs, or the direction which we have sent down, after what we have manifested unto men in the scripture, God shall curse them; and they who curse shall curse them. But as for those who repent and amend, and make known what they concealed, I will be turned unto them, for I am easy to be reconciled and merciful. Surely they who believe not, and die in their unbelief, upon them shall be the curse of God, and of the angels, and of all men; they shall remain under it forever, their punishment shall not be alleviated, neither shall they be regarded. Your God is one God, there is no God but He, the most merciful. Now in the creation of heaven and earth, and the vicissitude of night and day, and in the ship which saileth in the sea, laden with what is profitable for mankind, and in the rain-water which God sendeth from heaven, quickening thereby the dead earth, and replenishing the same with all sorts of cattle, and in the change of winds, and the clouds that are compelled to do service between heaven and earth, are signs to people of understanding: yet some men take idols beside God, and love them as with the love due to God; but the true believers are more fervent in love towards God. Oh that they who act unjustly did perceive, when they behold their punishment, that all power belongeth unto God, and that he is severe in punishing! When those who have been followed, shall separate themselves from their followers, and shall see the punishment, and the cords of relation between them shall be cut asunder; the followers shall say, If we could return to life, we would separate ourselves from them, as they have now separated themselves from us. So God will show them their works; they shall sigh grievously, and shall not come forth from the fire of hell. O men, eat of that which is lawful and good on the earth; and tread not in the steps of the devil, for he is your open enemy. Verily he commandeth you evil and wickedness, and that ye should say that of God which ye know not. And when it is said unto them who believe not, Follow that which God hath sent down; they answer, Nay, but we will follow that which we found our fathers practised. What? though their fathers knew nothing, and were not rightly directed? The unbelievers are like unto one who crieth aloud to that which heareth not so much as his calling, or the sound of his voice. They are deaf, dumb, and blind, therefore they do not understand. O true believers, eat of the good things which we have bestowed on you for food, and return thanks unto God, if ye serve him. Verily he hath forbidden you to eat that which dieth of itself, and blood, and swine's flesh, and that on which any other name but God's hath been invocated.[11] But he who is forced by necessity, not lusting, nor returning to transgress, it shall be no crime in him if he eat of those things, for God is gracious and merciful. Moreover they who conceal any part of the scripture which God hath sent down unto them, and sell it for a small price, they shall swallow into their bellies nothing but fire; God shall not speak unto them on the day of resurrection, neither shall he purify them, and they shall suffer a grievous punishment. These are they who have sold direction for error, and pardon for punishment: but how great will their suffering be in the fire! This they shall endure, because God sent down the book of the Koran with truth, and they who disagree concerning that book, are certainly in a wide mistake. It is not righteousness that ye turn your faces in prayer towards the east and the west, but righteousness is of him who believeth in God and the last day, and the angels, and the scriptures, and the prophets; who giveth money for God's sake unto his kindred, and unto orphans, and the needy, and the stranger, and those who ask, and for redemption of captives; who is constant at prayer, and giveth alms; and of those who perform their covenant, when they have covenanted, and who

[11] For this reason, whenever the Mohammedans kill any animal for food, they always say, *Bismi allah*, or "In the name of God"; which, if it be neglected, they think it not lawful to eat of it.

behave themselves patiently in adversity, and hardships, and in time of violence: these are they who are true, and these are they who fear God. O true believers, the law of retaliation is ordained you for the slain: the free shall die for the free, and the servant for the servant, and a woman for a woman; but he whom his brother shall forgive, may be prosecuted, and obliged to make satisfaction according to what is just, and a fine shall be set on him[12] with humanity. This is indulgence from your Lord, and mercy. And he who shall transgress after this, by killing the murderer, shall suffer a grievous punishment. And in this law of retaliation ye have life, O ye of understanding, that peradventure ye may fear. It is ordained you, when any of you is at the point of death, if he leave any goods, that he bequeath a legacy to his parents and kindred, according to what shall be reasonable.[13] This is a duty incumbent on those who fear God. But he who shall change the legacy, after he hath heard it bequeathed by the dying person, surely the sin thereof shall be on those who change it, for God is he who heareth and knoweth. Howbeit he who apprehendeth from the testator any mistake or injustice, and shall compose the matter between them, that shall be no crime in him, for God is gracious and merciful. O true believers, a fast is ordained you, as it was ordained unto those before you, that ye may fear God. A certain number of days shall ye fast: but he among you who shall be sick, or on a journey, shall fast an equal number of other days. And those who can keep it, and do not, must redeem their neglect by maintaining of a poor man. And he who voluntarily dealeth better with the poor man than he is obliged, this shall be better for him. But if ye fast it will be better for you, if ye knew it. The month of Ramadhan shall ye fast, in which the Koran was sent down from heaven, a direction unto men, and declarations of direction, and the distinction between good and evil. Therefore let him among you who shall be present in this month, fast the same month; but he who shall be sick, or on a journey, shall fast the like number of other days. God would make this an ease unto you, and would not make it a difficulty unto you; that ye may fulfil the number of days, and

[12] This is the common practice in Mohammedan countries, particularly in Persia, where the relations of the deceased may take their choice, either to have the murderer put into their hands to be put to death, or else to accept of a pecuniary satisfaction.

[13] That is, the legacy was not to exceed a third part of the testator's substance, nor to be given where there was no necessity. But this injunction is abrogated by the law concerning inheritances.

glorify God, for that he hath directed you, and that ye may give thanks. When my servants ask thee concerning me, Verily I am near; I will hear the prayer of him that prayeth, when he prayeth unto me: but let them hearken unto me, and believe in me, that they may be rightly directed. It is lawful for you on the night of the fast to go in unto your wives: they are a garment unto you, and ye are a garment unto them. God knoweth that ye defraud yourselves therein, wherefore he turneth unto you and forgiveth you. Now therefore go in unto them; and earnestly desire that which God ordaineth you, and eat and drink, until ye can plainly distinguish a white thread from a black thread by the daybreak: then keep the fast until night, and go not in unto them, but be constantly present in the places of worship. These are the prescribed bounds of God, therefore draw not near them to transgress them. Thus God declareth his signs unto men, that ye may fear him. Consume not your wealth among yourselves in vain; nor present it unto judges, that ye may devour part of men's substance unjustly, against your own consciences. They will ask thee concerning the phases of the moon. Answer, They are times appointed unto men, and to show the season of the pilgrimage to Mecca. It is not righteousness that ye enter your houses by the back part thereof, but righteousness is of him who feareth God. Therefore enter your houses by their doors; and fear God, that ye may be happy. And fight for the religion of God against those who fight against you, but transgress not by attacking them first, for God loveth not the transgressors. And kill them wherever ye find them, and turn them out of that whereof they have dispossessed you; for temptation to idolatry is more grievous than slaughter: yet fight not against them in the holy temple, until they attack you therein; but if they attack you, slay them there. This shall be the reward of the infidels. But if they desist, God is gracious and merciful. Fight therefore against them, until there be no temptation to idolatry, and the religion be God's: but if they desist, then let there be no hostility, except against the ungodly. A sacred month for a sacred month, and the holy limits of Mecca, if they attack you therein, do ye also attack them therein in retaliation; and whoever transgresseth against you by so doing, do ye transgress against him in like manner as he hath transgressed against you, and fear God, and know that God is with those who fear him. Contribute out of your substance towards the defence of the religion of God, and throw not yourselves with your own hands into perdition; and do good, for God loveth those who do good. Perform the pilgrimage of Mecca, and the visitation of God; if ye be besieged, send that offering which shall be the easiest; and shave not your heads, until your offering reacheth the place of sacrifice. But whoever among you is sick, or is troubled with any distemper of the head, must redeem the shaving his head by fasting, or alms, or some offering. When ye are secure from enemies, he who tarrieth in the visitation of the temple of Mecca until the pilgrimage, shall bring that offering which shall be the easiest. But he who findeth not anything to offer, shall fast three days in the pilgrimage, and seven when ye are returned: they shall be ten days complete. This is incumbent on him whose family shall not be present at the holy temple. And fear God, and know that God is severe in punishing. The pilgrimage must be performed in the known months; whosoever therefore purposeth to go on pilgrimage therein, let him not know a woman, nor transgress, nor quarrel in the pilgrimage. The good which ye do, God knoweth it. Make provision for your journey; but the best provision is piety: and fear me, O ye of understanding. It shall be no crime in you, if ye seek an increase from your Lord, by trading during the pilgrimage. And when ye go in procession from Arafat, remember God near the holy monument; and remember him for that he hath directed you, although ye were before this of the number of those who go astray. Therefore go in procession from whence the people go in procession, and ask pardon of God, for God is gracious and merciful. And when ye have finished your holy ceremonies, remember God, according as ye remember your fathers, or with a more reverent commemoration. There are some men who say, O Lord, give us our portion in this world; but such shall have no portion in the next life: and there are others who say, O Lord, give us good in this world, and also good in the next world, and deliver us from the torment of hell fire. They shall have a portion of that which they have gained: God is swift in taking an account. Remember God the appointed number of days; but if any haste to depart from the valley of Mina in two days, it shall be no crime in him. And if any tarry longer, it shall be no crime in him, in him who feareth God. Therefore fear God, and know that unto him ye shall be gathered. There is a man who causeth thee to marvel [14] by his speech concerning this present life, and calleth God to witness that which is in his heart, yet he is most intent in opposing thee; and when he turneth away from thee, he hasteth to act corruptly in the earth, and to destroy that which is sown, and springeth up; [15] but God loveth not corrupt doing. And if one say unto him, Fear God; pride seizeth him, together with wickedness; but hell shall be his reward, and an unhappy couch shall it be. There is also a man who selleth his soul for the sake of those things which are pleasing unto God; [16] and God is gracious unto his servants. O true believers, enter into the true religion wholly, and follow not the steps of Satan, for he is your open enemy. If ye have slipped after the declarations of our will have come unto you, know that God is mighty and wise. Do the infidels expect less than that God should come down to them overshadowed with clouds, and the angels also? but the thing is decreed, and to God shall all things return. Ask the children of Israel how many evident signs we have showed them; and whoever shall change the grace of God, after it shall have come unto him, verily God will be severe in punishing him. The present life was ordained for those who believe not, and they laugh the faithful to scorn; but they who fear God shall be above them, on the day of the resurrection: for God is bountiful unto whom he pleaseth without measure. Mankind was of one faith, and God sent prophets bearing good tidings, and denouncing threats; and sent down with them the scripture in truth, that it might judge between men of that concerning which they disagreed: and none disagreed concerning it, except those to whom the same scriptures were delivered, after the declarations of God's will had come unto them, out of envy among themselves. And God directed those who believed, to that truth concerning which they disagreed, by his will: for God directeth whom he pleaseth into the right way. Did ye think ye should enter paradise, when as yet no such thing had happened unto you, as hath happened unto those who have been before you? They suffered calamity and tribulation, and were afflicted; so that the apostle, and they who believed

[14] This person was al Akhnas Ebn Shoraik, a fair-spoken dissembler, who swore that he believed in Mohammed, and pretended to be one of his friends, and to contemn this world. But God here reveals to the prophet his hypocrisy and wickedness.

[15] Setting fire to his neighbor's corn, and killing his asses by night.

[16] The person here meant was one Soheib, who being persecuted by the idolaters of Mecca forsook all he had, and fled to Medina.

with him, said, When will the help of God come? Is not the help of God nigh? They will ask thee what they shall bestow in alms: Answer, The good which ye bestow, let it be given to parents, and kindred, and orphans, and the poor, and the stranger. Whatsoever good ye do, God knoweth it. War is enjoined you against the Infidels; but this is hateful unto you: yet perchance ye hate a thing which is better for you, and perchance ye love a thing which is worse for you: but God knoweth and ye know not. They will ask thee concerning the sacred month, whether they may war therein: Answer, To war therein is grievous; but to obstruct the way of God, and infidelity towards him, and to keep men from the holy temple, and to drive out his people from thence, is more grievous in the sight of God, and the temptation to idolatry is more grievous than to kill in the sacred months. They will not cease to war against you, until they turn you from your religion, if they be able: but whoever among you shall turn back from his religion, and die an infidel, their works shall be vain in this world and the next; they shall be the companions of hell fire, they shall remain therein forever. But they who believe, and who fly for the sake of religion, and fight in God's cause, they shall hope for the mercy of God; for God is gracious and merciful. They will ask thee concerning wine[17] and lots:[18] Answer, In both there is great sin, and also some things of use unto men, but their sinfulness is greater than their use. They will ask thee also what they shall bestow in alms: Answer, What ye have to spare. Thus God showeth his signs unto you, that peradventure ye might seriously think of this present world, and of the next. They will also ask thee concerning orphans: Answer, To deal righteously with them is best; and if ye intermeddle with the management of what belongs to them, do them no wrong; they are your brethren: God knoweth the corrupt dealer from the righteous; and if God please, he will surely distress you, for God is mighty and wise. Marry not women who are idolaters, until they believe: verily a maid-servant who believeth is better than an idolatress, although she please you more. And give not women who believe in marriage to the idolaters, until they believe; for verily a servant who is a true believer, is better than

[17] Under the name of wine all sorts of strong and inebriating liquors are comprehended.

[18] The original word, *al Meiser*, properly signifies a particular game performed with arrows, and much in use with the pagan Arabs. But by lots we are here to understand all games whatsoever, which are subject to chance or hazard, as dice and cards.

an idolater, though he please you more. They invite into hell fire, but God inviteth unto paradise and pardon through his will, and declareth his signs unto men, that they may remember. They will ask thee also concerning the courses of women: Answer, They are a pollution: therefore separate yourselves from women in their courses, and go not near them until they be cleansed. But when they are cleansed, go in unto them as God hath commanded you, for God loveth those who repent, and loveth those who are clean. Your wives are your tillage; go in therefore unto your tillage in what manner soever ye will: and do first some act that may be profitable unto your souls; and fear God, and know that ye must meet him; and bear good tidings unto the faithful. Make not God the object of your oaths, that ye may deal justly, and be devout, and make peace among men;[19] for God is he who heareth and knoweth. God will not punish you for an inconsiderate word in your oaths; but he will punish you for that which your hearts have assented unto: God is merciful and gracious. They who vow to abstain from their wives, are allowed to wait four months: but if they go back from their vow, verily God is gracious and merciful; and if they resolve on a divorce, God is he who heareth and knoweth. The women who are divorced shall wait concerning themselves until they have their courses thrice, and it shall not be lawful for them to conceal that which God hath created in their wombs, if they believe in God and the last day; and their husbands will act more justly to bring them back at this time, if they desire a reconciliation. The women ought also to behave towards their husbands in like manner as their husbands should behave towards them, according to what is just: but the men ought to have a superiority over them. God is mighty and wise. Ye may divorce your wives twice; and then either retain them with humanity, or dismiss them with kindness. But it is not lawful for you to take away anything of what ye have given them, unless both fear that they cannot observe the ordinances of God. And if ye fear that they cannot observe the ordinances of God, it shall be no crime in either of them on account of that for which the wife shall redeem herself. These

[19] Some commentators expound this negatively, "That ye will not deal justly, nor be devout . . ." For such wicked oaths, they say, were customary among the idolatrous inhabitants of Mecca; which gave occasion to the following saying of Mohammed: "When you swear to do a thing, and afterwards find it better to do otherwise, do that which is better, and make void your oath."

are the ordinances of God; therefore transgress them not; for whoever transgresseth the ordinances of God, they are unjust doers. But if the husband divorce her a third time, she shall not be lawful for him again, until she marry another husband. But if he also divorce her, it shall be no crime in them, if they return to each other, if they think they can observe the ordinances of God; and these are the ordinances of God: he declareth them to people of understanding. But when ye divorce women, and they have fulfilled their prescribed time, either retain them with humanity, or dismiss them with kindness; and retain them not by violence, so that ye transgress; for he who doth this, surely injureth his own soul. And make not the signs of God a jest: but remember God's favor towards you, and that he hath sent down unto you the book of the Koran, and wisdom, admonishing you thereby; and fear God, and know that God is omniscient. But when ye have divorced your wives, and they have fulfilled their prescribed time, hinder them not from marrying their husbands, when they have agreed among themselves according to what is honorable. This is given in admonition unto him among you who believeth in God, and the last day. This is most righteous for you, and most pure. God knoweth, but ye know not. Mothers, after they are divorced, shall give suck unto their children two full years, to him who desireth the time of giving suck to be completed; and the father shall be obliged to maintain them and clothe them in the meantime, according to that which shall be reasonable. No person shall be obliged beyond his ability. A mother shall not be compelled to what is unreasonable on account of her child, nor a father on account of his child. And the heir of the father shall be obliged to do in like manner. But if they choose to wean the child before the end of two years, by common consent and on mutual consideration, it shall be no crime in them. And if ye have a mind to provide a nurse for your children, it shall be no crime in you, in case ye fully pay what ye offer her, according to that which is just. And fear God, and know that God seeth whatever ye do. Such of you as die, and leave wives, their wives must wait concerning themselves four months and ten days, and when they shall have fulfilled their term, it shall be no crime in you, for that which they shall do with themselves, according to what is reasonable. God well knoweth that which ye do. And it shall be no crime in you, whether ye make public overtures of marriage unto such women, within the said four months and ten days, or whether ye conceal such your designs in your minds: God knoweth that ye will remember them. But make no promise unto them privately, unless ye speak honorable words; and resolve not on the knot of marriage, until the prescribed time be accomplished; and know that God knoweth that which is in your minds, therefore beware of him, and know that God is gracious and merciful. It shall be no crime in you, if ye divorce your wives, so long as ye have not touched them, nor settled any dowry on them. And provide for them (he who is at his ease must provide according to his circumstances, and he who is straitened according to his circumstances) necessaries, according to what shall be reasonable. This is a duty incumbent on the righteous. But if ye divorce them before ye have touched them, and have already settled a dowry on them, ye shall give them half of what ye have settled, unless they release any part, or he release part in whose hand the knot of marriage is; and if ye release the whole, it will approach nearer unto piety. And forget not liberality among you, for God seeth that which ye do. Carefully observe the appointed prayers, and the middle prayer,[20] and be assiduous therein, with devotion towards God. But if ye fear any danger, pray on foot or on horseback; and when ye are safe, remember God, how he hath taught you what as yet ye knew not. And such of you as shall die and leave wives, ought to bequeath their wives a year's maintenance, without putting them out of their houses: but if they go out voluntarily, it shall be no crime in you, for that which they shall do with themselves, according to what shall be reasonable; God is mighty and wise. And unto those who are divorced, a reasonable provision is also due; this is a duty incumbent on those who fear God. Thus God declareth his signs unto you, that ye may understand. Hast thou not considered those who left their habitations (and they were thousands) for fear of death? And God said unto them, Die; then he restored them to life, for God is gracious towards mankind; but the greater part of men do not give thanks. Fight for the religion of God, and know that God is he who heareth and knoweth. Who is he that will lend unto God on good usury? verily he will double it unto him manifold;

[20] Yahya interprets this from a tradition of Mohammed, who, being asked which was the middle prayer, answered, The evening prayer, which was instituted by the prophet Solomon.

for God contracteth and extendeth his hand as he pleaseth, and to him shall ye return. Hast thou not considered the assembly of the children of Israel, after the time of Moses; when they said unto their prophet Samuel, Set a king over us, that we may fight for the religion of God? The prophet answered, If ye are enjoined to go to war, will ye be near refusing to fight? They answered, And what should ail us that we should not fight for the religion of God, seeing we are dispossessed of our habitations, and deprived of our children? But when they were enjoined to go to war, they turned back, except a few of them: and God knew the ungodly. And their prophet said unto them, Verily God hath set Talût king over you: they answered, How shall he reign over us, seeing we are more worthy of the kingdom than he, neither is he possessed of great riches? Samuel said, Verily God hath chosen him before you, and hath caused him to increase in knowledge and stature, for God giveth his kingdom unto whom he pleaseth; God is bounteous and wise. And their prophet said unto them, Verily the sign of his kingdom shall be, that the ark shall come unto you: therein shall be tranquillity from your Lord, and the relics which have been left by the family of Moses, and the family of Aaron; the angels shall bring it. Verily this shall be a sign unto you, if ye believe. And when Talût departed with his soldiers, he said, Verily God will prove you by the river: for he who drinketh thereof, shall not be on my side (but he who shall not taste thereof he shall be on my side) except he who drinketh a draught out of his hand. And they drank thereof, except a few of them. And when they had passed the river, he and those who believed with him, they said, We have no strength to-day against Jalut and his forces. But they who considered that they should meet God at the resurrection, said, How often hath a small army discomfited a great army, by the will of God? and God is with those who patiently persevere. And when they went forth to battle against Jalut and his forces, they said, O Lord, pour on us patience, and confirm our feet, and help us against the unbelieving people. Therefore they discomfited them, by the will of God, and David slew Jalut. And God gave him the kingdom and wisdom, and taught him his will; and if God had not prevented men, the one by the other, verily the earth had been corrupted: but God is beneficent towards his creatures. These are the signs of God: we rehearse them unto thee with truth, and thou art surely one of those who have been sent by God. These are the apostles; we have preferred some of them before others: some of them hath God spoken unto, and hath exalted the degree of others of them. And we gave unto Jesus the son of Mary manifest signs, and strengthened him with the holy spirit. And if God had pleased, they who came after those apostles would not have contended among themselves, after manifest signs had been shown unto them. But they fell to variance; therefore some of them believed, and some of them believed not; and if God had so pleased, they would not have contended among themselves, but God doeth what he will. O true believers, give alms of that which we have bestowed on you, before the day cometh wherein there shall be no merchandising, nor friendship, nor intercession. The infidels are unjust doers. God! there is no God but he;[21] the living, the self-subsisting: neither slumber nor sleep seizeth him; to him belongeth whatsoever is in heaven, and on earth. Who is he that can intercede with him, but through his good pleasure! He knoweth that which is past, and that which is to come unto them, and they shall not comprehend anything of his knowledge, but so far as he pleaseth. His throne is extended over heaven and earth,[22] and the preservation of both is no burden unto him. He is the high, the mighty. Let there be no violence in religion. Now is right direction manifestly distinguished from deceit: whoever therefore shall deny Tagut, and believe in God, he shall surely take hold on a strong handle, which shall not be broken; God is he who heareth and seeth. God is the patron of those who believe; he shall lead them out of darkness into light: but as to those who believe not, their patrons are Tagut; they shall lead them from the light into darkness; they shall be the companions of hell fire, they shall remain therein forever. Hast thou not considered him who disputed with Abraham concerning his Lord, because God had given him the kingdom? When Abraham said, My Lord is he who giveth life, and killeth: he answered, I give life, and I kill. Abraham said, Verily God bringeth the sun from the east, now do thou bring

[21] The following seven lines contain a magnificent description of the divine majesty and providence; but it must not be supposed the translation comes up to the dignity of the original. This passage is justly admired by the Mohammedans, who recite it in their prayers; and some of them wear it about them, engraved on an agate or other precious stone.

[22] This throne, in Arabic called Corsi, is by the Mohammedans supposed to be God's tribunal, or seat of justice.

it from the west. Whereupon the infidel was confounded; for God directeth not the ungodly people. Or hast thou not considered how he behaved who passed by a city which had been destroyed, even to her foundations? He said, How shall God quicken this city, after she hath been dead? And God caused him to die for a hundred years, and afterwards raised him to life. And God said, How long hast thou tarried here? He answered, A day, or part of a day. God said, Nay, thou hast tarried here a hundred years. Now look on thy food and the drink, they are not yet corrupted; and look on thine ass: and this have we done that we might make thee a sign unto men. And look on the bones of thine ass, how we raise them, and afterwards clothe them with flesh. And when this was shown unto him, he said, I know that God is able to do all things. And when Abraham said, O Lord, show me how thou wilt raise the dead; God said, Dost thou not yet believe? He answered, Yea; but I ask this that my heart may rest at ease. God said, take therefore four birds, and divide them; then lay a part of them on every mountain; then call them, and they shall come swiftly unto thee: and know that God is mighty and wise. The similitude of those who lay out their substance for advancing the religion of God, is as a grain of corn which produceth seven ears, and in every ear a hundred grains; for God giveth twofold unto whom he pleaseth: God is bounteous and wise. They who lay out their substance for the religion of God, and afterwards follow not what they have so laid out by reproaches or mischief, they shall have their reward with their Lord; upon them shall no fear come, neither shall they be grieved. A fair speech, and to forgive, is better than alms followed by mischief. God is rich and merciful. O true believers, make not your alms of no effect by reproaching, or mischief, as he who layeth out what he hath to appear unto men to give alms, and believeth not in God and the last day. The likeness of such a one is as a flint covered with earth, on which a violent rain falleth, and leaveth it hard. They cannot prosper in anything which they have gained, for God directeth not the unbelieving people. And the likeness of those who lay out their substance from a desire to please God, and for an establishment for their souls, is as a garden on a hill, on which a violent rain falleth, and it bringeth forth its fruits twofold; and if a violent rain falleth not on it, yet the dew falleth thereon: and God seeth that which ye do. Doth any of you desire to have a garden of palm-trees and vines, through which rivers flow, wherein he may have all kinds of fruits, and that he may attain to old age, and have a weak offspring? then a violent fiery wind shall strike it, so that it shall be burned. Thus God declareth his signs unto you, that ye may consider. O true believers, bestow alms of the good things which ye have gained, and of that which we have produced for you out of the earth, and choose not the bad thereof, to give it in alms, such as ye would not accept yourselves, otherwise than by connivance: and know that God is rich and worthy to be praised. The devil threateneth you with poverty, and commandeth you filthy covetousness; but God promiseth you pardon from himself and abundance: God is bounteous and wise. He giveth wisdom unto whom he pleaseth; and he unto whom wisdom is given, hath received much good: but none will consider, except the wise of heart. And whatever alms ye shall give, or whatever vow ye shall vow, verily God knoweth it; but the ungodly shall have none to help them. If ye make your alms to appear, it is well; but if ye conceal them, and give them unto the poor, this will be better for you, and will atone for your sins: and God is well informed of that which ye do. The direction of them belongeth not unto thee; but God directeth whom he pleaseth. The good that ye shall give in alms shall redound unto yourselves; and ye shall not give unless out of desire of seeing the face of God. And what good thing ye shall give in alms, it shall be repaid you, and ye shall not be treated unjustly; unto the poor who are wholly employed in fighting for the religion of God, and cannot go to and fro in the earth; whom the ignorant man thinketh rich, because of their modesty: thou shalt know them by this mark, they ask not men with importunity; and what good ye shall give in alms, verily God knoweth it. They who distribute alms of their substance night and day, in private and in public, shall have their reward with the Lord; on them shall no fear come, neither shall they be grieved. They who devour usury shall not arise from the dead, but as he ariseth whom Satan hath infected by a touch: this shall happen to them because they say, Truly selling is but as usury: and yet God hath permitted selling and forbidden usury. He therefore who, when there cometh unto him an admonition from his Lord, abstaineth from usury for the future, shall have what is past forgiven him, and his affair belongeth unto God. But whoever returneth to usury, they shall be the companions of hell fire, they shall continue therein forever. God shall take his blessing from usury, and shall increase alms: for God loveth no infidel, or ungodly person. But they who believe and do that which is right, and observe the stated times of prayer, and pay their legal alms, they shall have their reward with their Lord: there shall come no fear on them, neither shall they be grieved. O true believers, fear God, and remit that which remaineth of usury, if ye really believe; but if ye do it not, hearken unto war, which is declared against you from God and his apostle: yet if ye repent, ye shall have the capital of your money. Deal not unjustly with others, and ye shall not be dealt with unjustly. If there be any debtor under a difficulty of paying his debt, let his creditor wait till it be easy for him to do it; but if ye remit it as alms, it will be better for you, if ye knew it. And fear the day wherein ye shall return unto God; then shall every soul be paid what it hath gained, and they shall not be treated unjustly. O true believers, when ye bind yourselves one to the other in a debt for a certain time, write it down; and let a writer write between you according to justice, and let not the writer refuse writing according to what God hath taught him; but let him write, and let him who oweth the debt dictate, and let him fear God his Lord, and not diminish aught thereof. But if he who oweth the debt be foolish, or weak, or be not able to dictate himself, let his agent dictate according to equity; and call to witness two witnesses of your neighboring men; but if there be not two men, let there be a man and two women of those whom ye shall choose for witnesses: if one of those women should mistake, the other of them will cause her to recollect. And the witnesses shall not refuse, whensoever they shall be called. And disdain not to write it down, be it a large debt, or be it a small one, until its time of payment: this will be more just in the sight of God, and more right for bearing witness, and more easy, that ye may not doubt. But if it be a present bargain which ye transact between yourselves, it shall be no crime in you, if ye write it not down. And take witnesses when ye sell one to the other, and let no harm be done to the writer, nor to the witness; which if ye do, it will surely be injustice in you: and fear God, and God will instruct you, for God knoweth all things. And if ye be on a journey, and find no writer, let pledges be taken: but if one of you trust the other, let him who is trusted return what he is trusted with, and fear God his Lord. And conceal not the testimony, for he who concealeth it hath surely a wicked heart: God knoweth that which ye do. Whatever is in heaven and on earth is God's; and whether ye manifest that which is in your minds, or conceal it, God will call you to account for it, and will forgive whom he pleaseth, and will punish whom he pleaseth; for God is almighty. The apostle believeth in that which hath been sent down unto him from his Lord, and the faithful also. Every one of them believeth in God, and his angels, and his scriptures, and his apostles: we make no distinction at all between his apostles.[23] And they say, We have heard, and do obey: we implore thy mercy, O Lord, for unto thee must we return. God will not force any soul beyond its capacity: it shall have the good which it gaineth, and it shall suffer the evil which it gaineth. O Lord, punish us not, if we forget, or act sinfully: O Lord, lay not on us a burden like that which thou hast laid on those who have been before us;[24] neither make us, O Lord, to bear what we have not strength to bear, but be favorable unto us, and spare us, and be merciful unto us. Thou art our patron, help us therefore against the unbelieving nations.

[23] But this, say the Mohammedans, the Jews do, who receive Moses but reject Jesus; and the Christians, who receive both those prophets, but reject Mohammed.

[24] That is, on the Jews, who, as the commentators tell us, were ordered to kill a man by way of atonement, to give one-fourth of their substance in alms, and to cut off an unclean ulcerous part, and were forbidden to eat fat, or animals that divided the hoof, and were obliged to observe the Sabbath, and other particulars wherein the Mohammedans are at liberty.

CHAPTER III

Entitled, the Family of Imran[1]—Revealed at Medina

In the Name of the Most Merciful God.

A. L. M.[2] There is no God but God, the living, self-subsisting: He hath sent down unto thee the book of the Koran with truth, confirming that which was revealed before it; for he had formerly sent down the law and the gospel, a direction unto men; and he had also sent down the distinction between good and evil. Verily those who believe not the signs of God, shall suffer a grievous punishment; for God is mighty, able to revenge. Surely nothing is hidden from God, of that which is on earth, or in heaven: it is he who formeth you in the wombs, as he pleaseth; there is no God but he, the mighty, the wise. It is he who hath sent down unto thee the book, wherein are some verses clear to be understood, they are the foundation of the book; and others are parabolical. But they whose hearts are perverse will follow that which is parabolical therein, out of love of schism, and a desire of the interpretation thereof; yet none knoweth the interpretation thereof, except God. But they who are well grounded in knowledge say, We believe therein, the whole is from our Lord; and none will consider except the prudent. O Lord, cause not our hearts to swerve from truth, after thou hast directed us: and give us from thee mercy, for thou art he who giveth. O Lord, thou shalt surely gather mankind together, unto a day of resurrection: there is no doubt of it, for God will not be contrary to the promise. As for the infidels, their wealth shall not profit them anything, nor their children, against God: they shall be the fuel of hell fire. According to the wont of the people of Pharaoh, and of those who went before them, they charged our signs with a lie; but God caught them in their wickedness, and God is severe in punishing. Say unto those who believe not, Ye shall be overcome, and thrown together

[1] This name is given in the Koran to the father of the Virgin Mary.

[2] The word Koran, derived from the verb *Karaa*, i.e., to read, signifies in Arabic "the reading," or rather "that which is to be read." The syllable *Al*, in the words Al* Koran, is only the Arabic article signifying "the," and ought to be omitted when the English article is prefixed.

into hell; an unhappy couch shall it be. Ye have already had a miracle shown you in two armies, which attacked each other:[3] one army fought for God's true religion, but the other were infidels; they saw the faithful twice as many as themselves in their eyesight; for God strengtheneth with his help whom he pleaseth. Surely herein was an example unto men of understanding. The love and eager desire of wives, and children, and sums heaped up of gold and silver, and excellent horses, and cattle, and land, is prepared for men: this is the provision of the present life; but unto God shall be the most excellent return. Say, Shall I declare unto you better things than this? For those who are devout are prepared with their Lord, gardens through which rivers flow; therein shall they continue forever: and they shall enjoy wives free from impurity, and the favor of God; for God regardeth his servants; who say, O Lord, we do sincerely believe; forgive us therefore our sins, and deliver us from the pain of hell fire: the patient, and the lovers of truth, and the devout, and the alms-givers, and those who ask pardon early in the morning. God hath borne witness that there is no God but he; and the angels, and those who are endowed with wisdom, profess the same; who executed righteousness; there is no God but he; the mighty, the wise. Verily the true religion in the sight of God, is Islam;[4] and they who had received the scriptures dissented not therefrom, until after the knowledge of God's unity had come unto them, out of envy among themselves; but whosoever believeth not in the signs of God, verily God will be swift in bringing him to account. If they dispute with thee, say, I have resigned myself unto God, and he who followeth me doth the same: and say unto them who have received the scriptures, and to the ignorant, Do ye profess the religion of Islam? Now if they embrace Islam, they are surely directed; but if they turn their

[3] The miracle, it is said, consisted in three things: (1.) Mohammed, by the direction of the angel Gabriel, took a handful of gravel and threw it towards the enemy in the attack, saying, "May their faces be confounded"; whereupon they immediately turned their backs and fled. But, though the prophet seemingly threw the gravel himself, yet it is told in the Koran that it was not he, but God, who threw it, that is to say, by the ministry of his angel. (2.) The Mohammedan troops seemed to the infidels to be twice as many in number as themselves, which greatly discouraged them. (3.) God sent down to their assistance first a thousand, and afterwards three thousand angels, led by Gabriel, mounted on his horse Haizum; and, according to the Koran, these celestial auxiliaries really did all the execution, though Mohammed's men imagined themselves did it, and fought stoutly at the same time.

[4] The proper name of the Mohammedan religion, which signifies the resigning or devoting one's self entirely to God and his service. This they say is the religion which all the prophets were sent to teach, being founded on the unity of God.

backs, verily unto thee belongeth preaching only; for God regardeth his servants. And unto those who believe not in the signs of God, and slay the prophets without a cause, and put those men to death who teach justice; denounce unto them a painful punishment. These are they whose works perish in this world, and in that which is to come; and they shall have none to help them. Hast thou not observed those unto whom part of the scripture was given? They were called unto the book of God, that it might judge between them; then some of them turned their backs, and retired afar-off. This they did because they said, The fire of hell shall by no means touch us, but for a certain number of days: and that which they had falsely devised, hath deceived them in their religion. How then will it be with them, when we shall gather them together at the day of judgment,[6] of which there is no doubt; and every soul shall be paid that which it hath gained, neither shall they be treated unjustly? Say, O God, who possessest the kingdom; thou givest the kingdom unto whom thou wilt, and thou takest away the kingdom from whom thou wilt: thou exaltest whom thou wilt, and thou humblest whom thou wilt: in thy hand is good, for thou art almighty. Thou makest the night to succeed the day: thou bringest forth the living out of the dead, and thou bringest forth the dead out of the living; and providest food for whom thou wilt without measure. Let not the faithful take the infidels for their protectors, rather than the faithful: he who doth this shall not be protected of God at all; unless ye fear any danger from them: but God warneth you to beware of himself; for unto God must ye return. Say, Whether ye conceal that which is in your breasts, or whether ye declare it, God knoweth it: for he knoweth whatever is in heaven, and whatever is on earth: God is almighty. On the last day every soul shall find the good which it hath wrought, present; and the evil which it hath wrought, it shall wish that between itself and that were a wide distance: but God warneth you to beware of himself; for God is gracious unto his servants. Say, If ye love God, follow me: then God shall love you, and forgive you your sins; for God is gracious and merciful. Say, Obey God, and his apostle: but if ye go back, verily God loveth not the unbelievers.

[6] The Mohammedans have a tradition that the first banner of the infidels that shall be set up, on the day of judgment, will be that of the Jews; and that God will first reproach them with their wickedness, over the heads of those who are present, and then order them to hell.

God hath surely chosen Adam, and Noah, and the family of Abraham, and the family of Imran above the rest of the world; a race descending the one from the other: God is he who heareth and knoweth. Remember when the wife of Imran said, Lord, verily I have vowed unto thee that which is in my womb, to be dedicated to thy service: accept it therefore of me; for thou art he who heareth and knoweth. And when she was delivered of it, she said, Lord, verily I have brought forth a female (and God well knew what she had brought forth), and a male is not as a female: I have called her Mary; and I commend her to thy protection, and also her issue, against Satan driven away with stones. Therefore the Lord accepted her with a gracious acceptance, and caused her to bear an excellent offspring. And Zacharias took care of the child; whenever Zacharias went into the chamber to her, he found provisions with her; and he said, O Mary, whence hadst thou this? she answered, This is from God: for God provideth for whom he pleaseth without measure. There Zacharias called on his Lord, and said, Lord, give me from thee a good offspring, for thou art the hearer of prayer. And the angels called to him, while he stood praying in the chamber, saying, Verily God promiseth thee a son named John, who shall bear witness to the Word which cometh from God; an honorable person, chaste, and one of the righteous prophets. He answered, Lord, how shall I have a son, when old age hath overtaken me, and my wife is barren? The angel said, So God doth that which he pleaseth. Zacharias answered, Lord, give me a sign. The angel said, Thy sign shall be, that thou shalt speak unto no man for three days, otherwise than by gesture: remember thy Lord often, and praise him evening and morning. And when the angels said, O Mary, verily God hath chosen thee, and hath purified thee, and hath chosen thee above all the women of the world: O Mary, be devout towards thy Lord, and worship, and bow down with those who bow down. This is a secret history: we reveal it unto thee, although thou wast not present with them when they threw in their rods to cast lots which of them should have the education of Mary: neither wast thou with them, when they strove among themselves. When the angels said, O Mary, verily God sendeth thee good tidings, that thou shalt bear the Word, proceeding from himself; his name shall be Christ Jesus the son of Mary, honorable in this world and in the world to come, and one of those who approach near to the presence of God; and he shall speak unto men in the cradle, and when he is grown up;[6] and he shall be one of the righteous: she answered, Lord, how shall I have a son, since a man hath not touched me? the angel said, So God createth that which he pleaseth: when he decreeth a thing, he only saith unto it, Be, and it is: God shall teach him the scripture, and wisdom, and the law, and the gospel; and shall appoint him his apostle to the children of Israel; and he shall say, Verily I come unto you with a sign from your Lord; for I will make before you, of clay, as it were the figure of a bird; then I will breathe thereon, and it shall become a bird, by the permission of God: and I will heal him that hath been blind from his birth, and the leper: and I will raise the dead by the permission of God: and I will prophesy unto you what ye eat, and what ye lay up for store in your houses. Verily herein will be a sign unto you, if ye believe. And I come to confirm the Law which was revealed before me, and to allow unto you as lawful, part of that which hath been forbidden you:[7] and I come unto you with a sign from your Lord; therefore fear God, and obey me. Verily God is my Lord, and your Lord: therefore serve him. This is the right way. But when Jesus perceived their unbelief, he said, Who will be my helpers towards God? The apostles[8] answered, We will be the helpers of God; we believe in God, and do thou bear witness that we are true believers. O Lord, we believe in that which thou has sent down, and we have followed thy apostle; write us down therefore with those who bear witness of him. And the Jews devised a stratagem against him; but God devised a stratagem against them; and God is the best deviser of stratagems. When God said, O Jesus, verily I will cause thee to die, and I will take thee up unto me,[9] and I will deliver thee from the unbelievers; and I will place those who follow thee above the unbelievers, until the day of resurrection: then unto me shall ye return, and I will judge between you of that concerning which ye disagree. Moreover, as for the infidels, I will punish them with a grievous punishment in this

[6] This phrase signifies a man in full age, that is, between thirty and thirty-four.

[7] Such as the eating of fish that have neither fins nor scales, the caul and fat of animals, and camel's flesh, and to work on the Sabbath.

[8] In Arabic, *al Hawâriyûn:* which word they derive from *Hâra*, "to be white," and suppose the apostles were so-called either from the candor and sincerity of their minds, or because they were princes and wore white garments, or else because they were by trade fullers.

[9] Some Mohammedans say this was done by the ministry of Gabriel; but others that a strong whirlwind took him up from Mount Olivet.

world, and in that which is to come; and there shall be none to help them. But they who believe, and do that which is right, he shall give them their reward; for God loveth not the wicked doers. These signs and this prudent admonition do we rehearse unto thee. Verily the likeness of Jesus in the sight of God is as the likeness of Adam: he created him out of the dust, and then said unto him, Be; and he was. This is the truth from thy Lord; be not therefore one of those who doubt: and whoever shall dispute with thee concerning him, after the knowledge which hath been given thee, say unto them, Come, let us call together our sons, and your sons, and our wives, and your wives, and ourselves, and yourselves; then let us make imprecations, and lay the curse of God on those who lie. Verily this is a true history: and there is no God but God; and God is most mighty, and wise. If they turn back, God well knoweth the evil-doers. Say, O ye who have received the scripture, come to a just determination between us and you; that we worship not any except God, and associate no creature with him; and that the one of us take not the other for lords, beside God. But if they turn back, say, Bear witness that we are true believers. O ye to whom the scriptures have been given, why do ye dispute concerning Abraham, since the Law and the Gospel were not sent down until after him? Do ye not therefore understand? Behold ye are they who dispute concerning that which ye have some knowledge in; why therefore do ye dispute concerning that which ye have no knowledge of? God knoweth, but ye know not. Abraham was neither a Jew, nor a Christian; but he was of the true religion, one resigned unto God, and was not of the number of the idolaters. Verily the men who are the nearest of kin unto Abraham, are they who follow him; and this prophet, and they who believe on him: God is the patron of the faithful. Some of those who have received the scriptures desire to seduce you; but they seduce themselves only, and they perceive it not. O ye who have received the scriptures, why do ye not believe in the signs of God, since ye are witnesses of them? O ye who have received the scriptures, why do ye clothe truth with vanity, and knowingly hide the truth? And some of those to whom the scriptures were given, say, Believe in that which hath been sent down unto those who believe, in the beginning of the day, and deny it in the end thereof; that they may go back from their faith: and believe him only who followeth your religion. Say, Verily the true direction is the direction of God, that there may be given unto some other a revelation like unto what hath been given unto you. Will they dispute with you before your Lord? Say, Surely excellence is in the hand of God, he giveth it unto whom he pleaseth; God is bounteous and wise: he will confer peculiar mercy on whom he pleaseth; for God is endued with great beneficence. There is of those who have received the scriptures, unto whom if thou trust a talent, he will restore it unto thee; and there is also of them, unto whom if thou trust a dinâr,[10] he will not restore it unto thee, unless thou stand over him continually with great urgency. This they do because they say, We are not obliged to observe justice with the heathen: but they utter a lie against God, knowingly. Yea; whoso keepeth his covenant, and feareth God, God surely loveth those who fear him. But they who make merchandise of God's covenant, and of their oaths, for a small price, shall have no portion in the next life, neither shall God speak to them or regard them on the day of resurrection, nor shall he cleanse them; but they shall suffer a grievous punishment. And there are certainly some of them, who read the scriptures perversely, that ye may think what they read to be really in the scriptures, yet it is not in the scripture; and they say, This is from God; but it is not from God: and they speak that which is false concerning God, against their own knowledge. It is not fit for a man, that God should give him a book of revelations, and wisdom, and prophecy; and then he should say unto men, Be ye worshippers of me, besides God; but he ought to say, Be ye perfect in knowledge and in works, since ye know the scriptures, and exercise yourselves therein. God hath not commanded you to take the angels and the prophets for your Lords: Will he command you to become infidels, after ye have been true believers? And remember when God accepted the covenant of the prophets, saying, This verily is the scripture and the wisdom which I have given you: hereafter shall an apostle come unto you, confirming the truth of that scripture which is with you; ye shall surely believe on him, and ye shall assist him. God said, Are ye firmly resolved, and do ye accept my covenant on this condition? They answered, We are firmly resolved: God

[10] A gold coin worth about $2.50.

said, Be ye therefore witnesses; and I also bear witness with you: and whosoever turneth back after this, they are surely the transgressors. Do they therefore seek any other religion but God's? since to him is resigned whosoever is in heaven or on earth, voluntarily, or of force: and to him shall they return. Say, We believe in God, and that which hath been sent down unto us, and that which was sent down unto Abraham, and Ismael, and Isaac, and Jacob, and the tribes, and that which was delivered to Moses, and Jesus, and the prophets from their Lord; we make no distinction between any of them; and to him are we resigned. Whoever followeth any other religion than Islam, it shall not be accepted of him: and in the next life he shall be of those who perish. How shall God direct men who have become infidels after they had believed, and borne witness that the apostle was true, and manifest declarations of the divine will had come unto them? for God directeth not the ungodly people. Their reward shall be, that on them shall fall the curse of God, and of angels, and of all mankind: they shall remain under the same forever; their torment shall not be mitigated, neither shall they be regarded; except those who repent after this, and amend; for God is gracious and merciful. Moreover they who become infidels after they have believed, and yet increase in infidelity, their repentance shall in no wise be accepted, and they are those who go astray. Verily they who believe not, and die in their unbelief, the world full of gold shall in no wise be accepted from any of them, even though he should give it for his ransom; they shall suffer a grievous punishment, and they shall have none to help them. Ye will never attain unto righteousness, until ye give in alms of that which ye love: and whatever ye give, God knoweth it. All food was permitted unto the children of Israel, except what Israel forbade unto himself before the Pentateuch was sent down. Say unto the Jews, Bring hither the Pentateuch and read it, if ye speak truth. Whoever therefore contriveth a lie against God after this, they will be evil-doers. Say, God is true: follow ye therefore the religion of Abraham the orthodox; for he was no idolater. Verily the first house appointed unto men to worship in was that which is in Becca;[11] blessed, and a direction to all creatures. Therein are manifest signs:

[11] Becca is another name of Mecca. Al Beidâwi observes that the Arabs used the "M" and "B" promiscuously in several words.

the place where Abraham stood; and whoever entereth therein, shall be safe. And it is a duty towards God, incumbent on those who are able to go thither, to visit this house; but whosoever disbelieveth, verily God needeth not the service of any creature. Say, O ye who have received the scriptures, why do ye not believe in the signs of God? Say, O ye who have received the scriptures, why do ye keep back from the way of God him who believeth? Ye seek to make it crooked, and yet are witnesses that it is the right: but God will not be unmindful of what ye do. O true believers, if ye obey some of those who have received the scripture, they will render you infidels, after ye have believed: and how can ye be infidels, when the signs of God are read unto you, and his apostle is among you? But he who cleaveth firmly unto God, is already directed into the right way. O believers, fear God with his true fear; and die not unless ye also be true believers. And cleave all of you unto the covenant of God, and depart not from it, and remember the favor of God towards you: since ye were enemies, and he reconciled your hearts, and ye became companions and brethren by his favor: and ye were on the brink of a pit of fire, and he delivered you thence. Thus God declareth unto you his signs, that ye may be directed. Let there be people among you, who invite to the best religion; and command that which is just, and forbid that which is evil; and they shall be happy. And be not as they who are divided, and disagree in matters of religion, after manifest proofs have been brought unto them: they shall suffer a great torment. On the day of resurrection some faces shall become white, and other faces shall become black. And unto them whose faces shall become black, God will say, Have ye returned unto your unbelief, after ye had believed? therefore taste the punishment, for that ye have been unbelievers: but they whose faces shall become white shall be in the mercy of God, therein shall they remain forever. These are the signs of God: we recite them unto thee with truth. God will not deal unjustly with his creatures. And to God belongeth whatever is in heaven and on earth; and to God shall all things return. Ye are the best nation that hath been raised up unto mankind: ye command that which is just, and ye forbid that which is unjust, and ye believe in God. And if they who have received the scriptures had believed, it had surely been the better for them: there are believers among them, but the greater part of them are transgressors. They shall not hurt you, unless with a slight hurt; and if they fight against you, they shall turn their backs to you, and they shall not be helped. They are smitten with vileness wheresoever they are found; unless they obtain security by entering into a treaty with God, and a treaty with men: and they draw on themselves indignation from God, and they are afflicted with poverty. This they suffer, because they disbelieved the signs of God, and slew the prophets unjustly; this, because they were rebellious, and transgressed. Yet they are not all alike: there are of those who have received the scriptures, upright people; they meditate on the signs of God in the night season, and worship; they believe in God and the last day; and command that which is just, and forbid that which is unjust, and zealously strive to excel in good works: these are of the righteous. And ye shall not be denied the reward of the good which ye do; for God knoweth the pious. As for the unbelievers, their wealth shall not profit them at all, neither their children, against God: they shall be the companions of hell fire; they shall continue therein forever. The likeness of that which they lay out in this present life, is as a wind wherein there is a scorching cold: it falleth on the standing corn of those men who have injured their own souls, and destroyeth it. And God dealeth not unjustly with them; but they injure their own souls. O true believers, contract not an intimate friendship with any besides yourselves: they will not fail to corrupt you. They wish for that which may cause you to perish: their hatred hath already appeared from out of their mouths; but what their breasts conceal is yet more inveterate. We have already shown you signs of their ill-will towards you, if ye understand. Behold, ye love them, and they do not love you: ye believe in all the scriptures, and when they meet you, they say, We believe; but when they assemble privately together, they bite their fingers' ends out of wrath against you. Say unto them, Die in your wrath: verily God knoweth the innermost part of your breasts. If good happen unto you, it grieveth them; and if evil befall you, they rejoice at it. But if ye be patient, and fear God, their subtlety shall not hurt you at all; for God comprehendeth whatever they do. Call to mind when thou wentest forth early from thy family, that thou mightest prepare the faithful a camp for war; and God heard and knew it; when two companies of you were anxiously thoughtful, so that ye became faint-hearted; but God was the supporter of them both; and in God let the faithful trust. And God had already given you the victory at Bedr, when ye were inferior in number; therefore fear God, that ye may be thankful. When thou saidst unto the faithful, Is it not enough for you, that your Lord should assist you with three thousand angels, sent down from heaven? Verily if ye persevere, and fear God, and your enemies come upon you suddenly, your Lord will assist you with five thousand angels, distinguished by their horses and attire. And this God designed only as good tidings for you that your hearts might rest secure: for victory is from God alone, the mighty, the wise. That he should cut off the uttermost part of the unbelievers, or cast them down, or that they should be overthrown and unsuccessful, is nothing to thee. It is no business of thine; whether God be turned unto them, or whether he punish them; they are surely unjust doers. To God belongeth whatsoever is in heaven and on earth: he spareth whom he pleaseth, and he punisheth whom he pleaseth; for God is merciful. O true believers, devour not usury, doubling it twofold; but fear God, that ye may prosper: and fear the fire which is prepared for the unbelievers; and obey God, and his apostle, that ye may obtain mercy. And run with emulation to obtain remission from your Lord, and paradise, whose breath equalleth the heavens and the earth, which is prepared for the godly; who give alms in prosperity and adversity; who bridle their anger and forgive men: for God loveth the beneficent.[12] And who, after they have committed a crime, or dealt unjustly with their own souls, remember God, and ask pardon for their sins (for who forgiveth sins except God?) and persevere not in what they have done knowingly: their reward shall be pardon from their Lord, and gardens wherein rivers flow, they shall remain therein forever: and how excellent is the reward of those who labor! There have already been before you examples of punishment of infidels, therefore go through the earth, and behold what hath been the end of those who accuse God's apostles of imposture.

[12] It is related of Hasan the son of Ali, that a slave having once thrown a dish on him boiling hot, as he sat at table, and fearing his master's resentment, fell immediately on his knees, and repeated these words, "Paradise is for those who bridle their anger." Hasan answered, "I am not angry." The slave proceeded, "and for those who forgive men." "I forgive you," said Hasan. The slave, however, finished the verse, adding, "for God loveth the beneficent." "Since it is so," replied Hasan, "I give you your liberty, and four hundred pieces of silver." A noble instance of moderation and generosity.

This book is a declaration unto men, and a direction and an admonition to the pious. And be not dismayed, neither be ye grieved; for ye shall be superior to the unbelievers if ye believe. If a wound hath happened unto you in war, a like wound hath already happened unto the unbelieving people: and we cause these days of different success interchangeably to succeed each other among men; that God may know those who believe, and may have martyrs from among you (God loveth not the workers of iniquity); and that God might prove those who believe, and destroy the infidels. Did ye imagine that ye should enter paradise, when as yet God knew not those among you who fought strenuously in his cause; nor knew those who persevered with patience? Moreover ye did some time wish for death before that ye met it; but ye have now seen it, and ye looked on, but retreated from it. Mohammed is no more than an apostle; the other apostles have already deceased before him: if he die therefore, or be slain, will ye turn back on your heels? but he who turneth back on his heels, will not hurt God at all; and God will surely reward the thankful. No soul can die unless by the permission of God, according to what is written in the book containing the determinations of things. And whoso chooseth the reward of this world, we will give him thereof: but whoso chooseth the reward of the world to come, we will give him thereof; and we will surely reward the thankful. How many prophets have encountered those who had many myriads of troops: and yet they desponded not in their mind for what had befallen them in fighting for the religion of God, and were not weakened, neither behaved themselves in an abject manner? God loveth those who persevere patiently. And their speech was no other than that they said, Our Lord forgive us our offences, and our transgressions in our business; and confirm our feet, and help us against the unbelieving people. And God gave them the reward of this world, and a glorious reward in the life to come; for God loveth the well-doers. O ye who believe, if ye obey the infidels, they will cause you to turn back on your heels, and ye will be turned back and perish: but God is your Lord; and he is the best helper. We will surely cast a dread into the hearts of the unbelievers, because they have associated with God that concerning which he sent them down no power: their dwelling shall be the fire of hell; and the receptacle of the wicked shall be miserable. God had already made good unto you his promise, when ye destroyed them by his permission, until ye became faint-hearted, and disputed concerning the command of the apostle, and were rebellious; after God had shown you what ye desired. Some of you chose this present world, and others of you chose the world to come. Then he turned you to flight from before them, that he might make trial of you (but he hath now pardoned you; for God is endued with beneficence towards the faithful); when ye went up as ye fled, and looked not back on any; while the apostle called you, in the uttermost part of you. Therefore God rewarded you with affliction on affliction, that ye be not grieved hereafter for the spoils which ye fail of, nor for that which befalleth you; for God is well acquainted with whatever ye do. Then he sent down upon you after affliction security; soft sleep which fell on some part of you; but other parts were troubled by their own souls; falsely thinking of God a foolish imagination, saying, Will anything of the matter happen unto us? Say, Verily the matter belongeth wholly unto God. They concealed in their minds what they declared not unto thee; saying, If anything of the matter had happend unto us, we had not been slain here. Answer, If ye had been in your houses, verily they would have gone forth to fight, whose slaughter was decreed, to the places where they died, and this came to pass that God might try what was in your breasts, and might discern what was in your hearts; for God knoweth the innermost parts of the breasts of men. Verily they among you who turned their backs on the day whereon the two armies met each other at Ohod, Satan caused them to slip, for some crime which they had committed: but now hath God forgiven them; for God is gracious and merciful. O true believers, be not as they who believe not, and said of their brethren, when they had journeyed in the land or had been at war, If they had been with us, those had not died, nor had these been slain: whereas what befell them was so ordained that God might make it matter of sighing in their hearts. God giveth life, and causeth to die: and God seeth that which ye do. Moreover, if ye be slain, or die in defence of the religion of God; verily pardon from God, and mercy, is better than what they heap together of worldly riches. And if ye die, or be slain, verily unto God shall ye be gathered. And as to the mercy granted unto the disobedient from God, thou, O Mohammed, hast been mild towards them; but if thou hadst been severe and hard-hearted, they had surely separated themselves from about thee. Therefore forgive them, and ask pardon for them: and consult them in the affair of war; and after thou hast deliberated, trust in God; for God loveth those who trust in him. If God help you, none shall conquer you; but if he desert you, who is it that will help you after him? Therefore in God let the faithful trust. It is not the part of a prophet to defraud, for he who defraudeth, shall bring with him what he hath defrauded anyone of, on the day of the resurrection.[13] Then shall every soul be paid what he hath gained; and they shall not be treated unjustly. Shall he therefore who followeth that which is well pleasing unto God, be as he who bringeth on himself wrath from God, and whose receptacle is hell? an evil journey shall it be thither. There shall be degrees of rewards and punishments with God, for God seeth what they do. Now hath God been gracious unto the believers when he raised up among them an apostle of their own nation,[14] who should recite his signs unto them, and purify them, and teach them the book of the Koran and wisdom; whereas they were before in manifest error. After a misfortune hath befallen you at Ohod (ye had already obtained two equal advantages), do ye say, Whence cometh this? Answer, This is from yourselves: for God is almighty. And what happened unto you, on the day whereon the two armies met, was certainly by the permission of God; and that he might know the faithful, and that he might know the ungodly. It was said unto them, Come, fight for the religion of God, or drive back the enemy: they answered, If we had known ye went out to fight, we had certainly followed you. They were on that day nearer unto unbelief than they were to faith; they spake with their mouths what was not in their hearts; but God perfectly knew what they concealed; who said of their brethren, while themselves stayed at home, if they had obeyed us, they had not been slain. Say, Then keep back death from yourselves, if ye say truth. Thou shalt in no wise reckon those who have been slain at Ohod in the cause of God, dead; nay, they are sustained alive with their Lord, rejoicing for what God of his favor hath granted them; and being glad for those who, coming after them, have not as

[13] According to a tradition of Mohammed, whoever cheateth another will on the day of judgment carry his fraudulent purchase publicly on his neck.

[14] Some copies, instead of *min anfosihim*, i.e., of themselves, read *min anfasihim*, i.e., of the noblest among them; for such was the tribe of Koreish, of which Mohammed was descended.

yet overtaken them, because there shall no fear come on them, neither shall they be grieved. They are filled with joy for the favor which they have received from God, and his bounty; and for that God suffereth not the reward of the faithful to perish. They who hearkened unto God and his apostle, after a wound had befallen them at Ohod, such of them as do good works, and fear God, shall have a great reward; unto whom certain men said, Verily the men of Mecca have already gathered forces against you, be ye therefore afraid of them: but this increaseth their faith, and they said, God is our support, and the most excellent patron. Wherefore they returned with favor from God, and advantage; no evil befell them: and they followed what was well pleasing unto God; for God is endowed with great liberality. Verily that devil would cause you to fear his friends: but be ye not afraid of them; but fear me, if ye be true believers. They shall not grieve thee, who emulously hasten unto infidelity; for they shall never hurt God at all. God will not give them a part in the next life, and they shall suffer a great punishment. Surely those who purchase infidelity with faith, shall by no means hurt God at all, but they shall suffer a grievous punishment. And let not the unbelievers think, because we grant them lives long and prosperous, that it is better for their souls: we grant them long and prosperous lives only that their iniquity may be increased; and they shall suffer an ignominious punishment. God is not disposed to leave the faithful in the condition which ye are now in, until he sever the wicked from the good; nor is God disposed to make you acquainted with what is a hidden secret, but God chooseth such of his apostles as he pleaseth, to reveal his mind unto: believe, therefore, in God, and his apostles; and if ye believe, and fear God, ye shall receive a great reward. And let not those who are covetous of what God of his bounty hath granted them, imagine that their avarice is better for them: nay, rather it is worse for them. That which they have covetously reserved shall be bound as a collar about their neck,[15] on the day of the resurrection; unto God belongeth the inheritance of heaven and earth; and God is well acquainted with what ye do. God hath already heard the saying of those who said, Verily God is poor, and we are

[15] Mohammed is said to have declared, that whoever pays not his legal contribution of alms duly shall have a serpent twisted about his neck at the resurrection.

rich: we will surely write down what they have said, and the slaughter which they have made of the prophets without a cause; and we will say unto them, Taste ye the pain of burning. This shall they suffer for the evil which their hands have sent before them, and because God is not unjust towards mankind; who also say, Surely God hath commanded us, that we should not give credit to any apostle, until one should come unto us with a sacrifice, which should be consumed by fire. Say, Apostles have already come unto you before me, with plain proofs, and with the miracle which ye mention: why therefore have ye slain them, if ye speak truth? If they accuse thee of imposture, the apostles before thee have also been accounted impostors, who brought evident demonstrations, and the scriptures, and the book which enlightened the understanding. Every soul shall taste of death, and ye shall have your rewards on the day of resurrection; and he who shall be far removed from hell fire, and shall be admitted into paradise, shall be happy: but the present life is only a deceitful provision. Ye shall surely be proved in your possessions, and in your persons; and ye shall bear from those unto whom the scripture was delivered before you, and from the idolaters, much hurt: but if ye be patient, and fear God, this is a matter that is absolutely determined. And when God accepted the covenant of those to whom the book of the law was given, saying, Ye shall surely publish it unto mankind, ye shall not hide it; yet they threw it behind their backs, and sold it for a small price; but woful is the price for which they have sold it.[16] Think not that they who rejoice at what they have done, and expect to be praised for what they have not done; think not, O prophet, that they shall escape from punishment, for they shall suffer a painful punishment; and unto God belongeth the kingdom of heaven and earth; God is almighty. Now in the creation of heaven and earth, and the vicissitude of night and day, are signs unto those who are endued with understanding; who remember God standing, and sitting, and lying on their sides; and meditate on the creation of heaven and earth, saying, O Lord, thou hast not created this in vain; far be it from thee: therefore deliver us from the torment of hell fire. O Lord, surely whom thou shalt throw into the fire, thou wilt also cover with shame; nor shall the ungodly have any to help

[16] That is, dearly shall they pay hereafter for taking bribes to stifle the truth. "Whoever concealeth the knowledge which God has given him," says Mohammed, "God shall put on him a bridle of fire on the day of resurrection."

them. O Lord, we have heard of a preacher [17] inviting us to the faith, and saying, Believe in your Lord: and we believed. O Lord, forgive us therefore our sins, and expiate our evil deeds from us, and make us to die with the righteous. O Lord, give us also the reward which thou hast promised by thy apostles; and cover us not with shame on the day of resurrection; for thou art not contrary to the promise. Their Lord therefore answereth them, saying, I will not suffer the work of him among you who worketh to be lost, whether he be male or female: the one of you is from the other. They therefore who have left their country, and have been turned out of their houses, and have suffered for my sake, and have been slain in battle; verily I will expiate their evil deeds from them, and I will surely bring them into gardens watered by rivers; a reward from God: and with God is the most excellent reward. Let not the prosperous dealing of the unbelievers in the land deceive thee: it is but a slender provision; and then their receptacle shall be hell; an unhappy couch shall it be. But they who fear their Lord shall have gardens through which rivers flow, they shall continue therein forever: this is the gift of God; for what is with God shall be better for the righteous than short-lived worldly prosperity. There are some of those who have received the scriptures, who believe in God, and that which hath been sent down unto you, and that which hath been sent down to them, submitting themselves unto God; they tell not the signs of God for a small price: these shall have their reward with their Lord; for God is swift in taking an account. O true believers, be patient, and strive to excel in patience, and be constant-minded, and fear God, that ye may be happy.

[17] Namely, Mohammed, with the Koran.

CHAPTER IV

Entitled, Women[1]—Revealed at Medina

In the Name of the Most Merciful God.

O MEN, fear your Lord, who hath created you out of one man, and out of him created his wife, and from them two hath multiplied many men and women: and fear God by whom ye beseech one another; and respect women who have borne you, for God is watching over you. And give the orphans when they come to age their substance; and render them not in exchange bad for good: and devour not their substance, by adding it to your substance; for this is a great sin. And if ye fear that ye shall not act with equity towards orphans of the female sex, take in marriage of such other women as please you, two, or three, or four, and not more. But if ye fear that ye cannot act equitably towards so many, marry one only, or the slaves which ye shall have acquired. This will be easier, that ye swerve not from righteousness. And give women their dowry freely; but if they voluntarily remit unto you any part of it, enjoy it with satisfaction and advantage. And give not unto those who are weak of understanding, the substance which God hath appointed you to preserve for them; but maintain them thereout, and clothe them, and speak kindly unto them. And examine the orphans until they attain the age of marriage: but if ye perceive they are able to manage their affairs well, deliver their substance unto them; and waste it not extravagantly, or hastily, because they grow up. Let him who is rich abstain entirely from the orphan's estates; and let him who is poor take thereof according to what shall be reasonable. And when ye deliver their substance unto them, call witnesses thereof in their presence: God taketh sufficient account of your actions. Men ought to have a part of what their parents and kindred leave behind them when they die: and women also ought to have a part of what their parents and kindred leave, whether it be little, or whether it be much; a determinate part is due to them. And when they who are of kin are present at

[1] This title was given to this chapter because it chiefly treats of matters relating to women: as marriages, divorces, dower, prohibited degrees.

the dividing of what is left, and also the orphans, and the poor; distribute unto them some part thereof; and if the estate be too small, at least speak comfortably unto them. And let those fear to abuse orphans, who if they leave behind them a weak offspring, are solicitous for them: let them therefore fear God, and speak that which is convenient. Surely they who devour the possessions of orphans unjustly, shall swallow down nothing but fire into their bellies, and shall broil in raging flames. God hath thus commanded you concerning your children. A male shall have as much as the share of two females: but if they be females only, and above two in number, they shall have two third-parts of what the deceased shall leave; and if there be but one, she shall have the half. And the parents of the deceased shall have each of them a sixth part of what he shall leave, if he have a child: but if he have no child, and his parents be his heirs, then his mother shall have the third part. And if he have brethren, his mother shall have a sixth part, after the legacies [1] which he shall bequeath, and his debts be paid. Ye know not whether your parents or your children be of greater use unto you. This is an ordinance from God, and God is knowing and wise. Moreover, ye may claim half of what your wives shall leave, if they have no issue; but if they have issue, then ye shall have the fourth part of what they shall leave, after the legacies which they shall bequeath, and the debts be paid. They also shall have the fourth part of what ye shall leave, in case ye have no issue; but if ye have issue, then they shall have the eighth part of what ye shall leave, after the legacies which ye shall bequeath and your debts be paid. And if a man or woman's substance be inherited by a distant relation, and he or she have a brother or sister; each of them two shall have a sixth part of the estate. But if there be more than this number, they shall be equal sharers in a third part, after payment of the legacies which shall be bequeathed, and the debts, without prejudice to the heirs. This is an ordinance from God: and God is knowing and gracious. These are the statutes of God. And whoso obeyeth God and his apostle, God shall lead him into gardens wherein rivers flow, they shall continue therein forever; and this shall be great happiness. But whoso disobeyeth God, and his apostle, and transgresseth his statutes, God shall cast him

[1] By legacies in this and the following passages, are chiefly meant those bequeathed to pious uses; for the Mohammedans approve not of a person's giving away his substance from his family and near relations on any other account.

into hell fire; he shall remain therein forever, and he shall suffer a shameful punishment. If any of your women be guilty of whoredom, produce four witnesses from among you against them, and if they bear witness against them, imprison them in separate apartments until death release them, or God affordeth them a way to escape.[3] And if two of you commit the like wickedness, punish them both: but if they repent and amend, let them both alone; for God is easy to be reconciled and merciful. Verily repentance will be accepted with God, from those who do evil ignorantly, and then repent speedily; unto them will God be turned: for God is knowing and wise. But no repentance shall be accepted from those who do evil until the time when death presenteth itself unto one of them, and he saith, Verily, I repent now; nor unto those who die unbelievers: for them have we prepared a grievous punishment. O true believers, it is not lawful for you to be heirs of women against their will, nor to hinder them from marrying others, that ye may take away part of what ye have given them in dowry; unless they have been guilty of a manifest crime: but converse kindly with them. And if ye hate them, it may happen that ye may hate a thing wherein God hath placed much good. If ye be desirous to exchange a wife for another wife, and ye have already given one of them a talent; take not away anything therefrom: will ye take it by slandering her, and doing her manifest injustice? And how can ye take it, since the one of you hath gone in unto the other, and they have received from you a firm covenant? Marry not women whom your fathers have had to wife (except what is already past): for this is uncleanness, and an abomination, and an evil way. Ye are forbidden to marry your mothers, and your daughters, and your sisters, and your aunts both on the father's and on the mother's side, and your brother's daughters, and your sister's daughters, and your mothers who have given you suck, and your foster-sisters, and your wives' mothers, and your daughters-in-law which are under your tuition, born of your wives unto whom ye have gone in (but if ye have not gone in unto them, it shall be no sin in you to marry them), and the wives of your sons who proceed out of your loins; and ye are also forbidden to take to wife two sis-

[3] Their punishment, in the beginning of Mohammedanism, was to be immured till they died, but afterwards this cruel doom was mitigated, and they might avoid it by undergoing the punishment ordained in its stead by the Sonna, according to which the maidens are to be scourged with a hundred stripes, and to be banished for a full year; and the married women to be stoned.

ters; except what is already past: for God is gracious and merciful. Ye are also forbidden to take to wife free women who are married, except those women whom your right hands shall possess as slaves.[4] This is ordained you from God. Whatever is beside this, is allowed you; that ye may with your substance provide wives for yourselves, acting that which is right, and avoiding whoredom. And for the advantage which ye receive from them, give them their reward, according to what is ordained: but it shall be no crime in you to make any other agreement among yourselves, after the ordinance shall be complied with; for God is knowing and wise. Whoso among you hath not means sufficient that he may marry free women, who are believers, let him marry with such of your maid-servants whom your right hands possess, as are true believers; for God well knoweth your faith. Ye are the one from the other; therefore marry them with the consent of their masters; and give them their dower according to justice; such as are modest, not guilty of whoredom, nor entertaining lovers. And when they are married, if they be guilty of adultery, they shall suffer half the punishment which is appointed for the free women.[5] This is allowed unto him among you, who feareth to sin by marrying free women; but if ye abstain from marrying slaves, it will be better for you; God is gracious and merciful. God is willing to declare these things unto you, and to direct you according to the ordinances of those who have gone before you, and to be merciful unto you. God is knowing and wise. God desireth to be gracious unto you; but they who follow their lusts, desire that ye should turn aside from the truth with great deviation. God is minded to make his religion light unto you: for man was created weak. O true believers, consume not your wealth among yourselves in vanity; unless there be merchandising among you by mutual consent: neither slay yourselves; for God is merciful towards you: and whoever doth this maliciously and wickedly, he will surely cast him to be broiled in hell

[4] According to this passage it is not lawful to marry a free woman that is already married, be she a Mohammedan or not, unless she be legally parted from her husband by divorce; but it is lawful to marry those who are slaves, or taken in war, after they shall have gone through the proper purifications, though their husbands be living. Yet, according to the decision of Abu Hanifah, it is not lawful to marry such whose husbands shall be taken, or in actual slavery with them.

[5] The reason of this is because they are not presumed to have had so good education. A slave, therefore, in such a case, is to have fifty stripes, and to be banished for half a year; but she shall not be stoned, because it is a punishment which cannot be inflicted by halves.

fire; and this is easy with God. If ye turn aside from the grievous sins,[6] of those which ye are forbidden to commit, we will cleanse you from your smaller faults; and will introduce you into paradise with an honorable entry. Covet not that which God hath bestowed on some of you preferably to others.[7] Unto the men shall be given a portion of what they shall have gained, and unto the women shall be given a portion of what they shall have gained: therefore ask God of his bounty; for God is omniscient. We have appointed unto everyone kindred, to inherit part of what their parents and relations shall leave at their deaths. And unto those with whom your right hands have made an alliance, give their part of the inheritance; for God is witness of all things. Men shall have the preëminence above women, because of those advantages wherein God hath caused the one of them to excel the other, and for that which they expend of their substance in maintaining their wives. The honest women are obedient, careful in the absence of their husbands, for that God preserveth them, by committing them to the care and protection of the men. But those, whose perverseness ye shall be apprehensive of, rebuke; and remove them into separate apartments, and chastise them.[8] But if they shall be obedient unto you, seek not an occasion of quarrel against them; for God is high and great. And if ye fear a breach between the husband and wife, send a judge out of his family, and a judge out of her family: if they shall desire a reconciliation, God will cause them to agree; for God is knowing and wise. Serve God, and associate no creature with him; and show kindness unto parents, and relations, and orphans, and the poor, and your neighbor who is of kin to you, and also your neighbor who is a stranger, and to your familiar companion, and the traveller, and the captives whom your right hands shall possess; for God loveth not the proud or vain-glorious, who are covetous, and recommend covetousness unto men, and conceal that which God of his bounty hath given them (we have prepared a shameful punishment for the unbelievers); and

[6] These sins al Beidâwi, from a tradition of Mohammed, reckons to be seven (equalling in number the sins called deadly by Christians), that is to say, idolatry, murder, falsely accusing modest women of adultery, wasting the substance of orphans, taking of usury, desertion in a religious expedition, and disobedience to parents.

[7] Such as honor, power, riches, and other worldly advantages.

[8] By this passage the Mohammedans are in plain terms allowed to beat their wives, in case of stubborn disobedience; but not in a violent or dangerous manner.

who bestow their wealth in charity to be observed of men, and believe not in God, nor in the last day; and whoever hath Satan for a companion, an evil companion hath he! And what harm would befall them if they should believe in God and the last day, and give alms out of that which God hath bestowed on them? since God knoweth them who do this. Verily God will not wrong anyone even the weight of an ant: and if it be a good action, he will double it, and will recompense it in his sight with a great reward. How will it be with the unbelievers when we shall bring a witness out of each nation against itself, and shall bring thee, O Mohammed, a witness against these people? In that day they who have not believed, and have rebelled against the apostle of God, shall wish the earth was levelled with them; and they shall not be able to hide any matter from God. O true believers, come not to prayers when ye are drunk, until ye understand what ye say; nor when ye are polluted by emission of seed, unless ye be travelling on the road, until ye wash yourselves. But if ye be sick, or on a journey, or any of you come from easing nature, or have touched women, and find no water; take fine clean sand and rub your faces and your hands therewith; for God is merciful and inclined to forgive. Hast thou not observed those unto whom part of the scriptures was delivered? they sell error, and desire that ye may wander from the right way; but God well knoweth your enemies. God is a sufficient patron, and God is a sufficient helper. Of the Jews there are some who pervert words from their places; and say, We have heard, and have disobeyed; and do thou hear without understanding our meaning, and look upon us: perplexing with their tongues, and reviling the true religion. But if they had said, We have heard, and do obey; and do thou hear, and regard us: certainly it were better for them, and more right. But God hath cursed them by reason of their infidelity; therefore a few of them only shall believe. O ye to whom the scriptures have been given, believe in the revelation which we have sent down, confirming that which is with you; before we deface your countenances, and render them as the back parts thereof; or curse them, as we cursed those who transgressed on the Sabbath day; and the command of God was fulfilled. Surely God will not pardon the giving him an equal; but will pardon any other sin, except that, to whom he pleaseth; and whoso giveth a companion unto God, hath devised a great wickedness.

Hast thou not observed those who justify themselves? But God justifieth whomsoever he pleaseth, nor shall they be wronged a hair. Behold, how they imagine a lie against God; and therein is iniquity sufficiently manifest. Hast thou not considered those to whom part of the scripture hath been given? They believe in false gods and idols,[9] and say of those who believe not, These are more rightly directed in the way of truth than they who believe on Mohammed. Those are the men whom God hath cursed; and unto him whom God shall curse, thou shalt surely find no helper. Shall they have a part of the kingdom, since even then they would not bestow the smallest matter on men? Do they envy other men that which God of his bounty hath given them? We formerly gave unto the family of Abraham a book of revelations and wisdom; and we gave them a great kingdom. There is of them who believeth on him; and there is of them who turneth aside from him: but the raging fire of hell is a sufficient punishment. Verily, those who disbelieve our signs, we will surely cast to be broiled in hell fire; so often as their skins shall be well burned, we will give them other skins in exchange, that they may taste the sharper torment; for God is mighty and wise. But those who believe and do that which is right, we will bring into gardens watered by rivers: therein shall they remain forever, and there shall they enjoy wives free from all impurity; and we will lead them into perpetual shades. Moreover, God commandeth you to restore what ye are trusted with, to the owners; and when ye judge between men, that ye judge according to equity: and surely an excellent virtue it is to which God exhorteth you; for God both heareth and seeth. O true believers, obey God, and obey the apostle, and those who are in authority among you: and if ye differ in anything, refer it unto God[10] and the apostle, if ye believe in God and the last day: this is better, and a fairer method of determination. Hast thou not observed those who pretend they believe in what hath been revealed unto thee, and what hath been revealed before thee? They desire to go to judgment before Taghût, although they have been commanded not to believe in him; and Satan desireth to seduce them into a wide error. And when it is said unto them, Come unto the book

[9] The Arabic is, in Jibt and Taghût. The former is supposed to have been the proper name of some idol; but it seems rather to signify any false deity in general. The latter we have explained already.

[10] That is, to the decision of the Koran.

which God hath sent down, and to the apostle; thou seest the ungodly turn aside from thee, with great aversion. But how will they behave when a misfortune shall befall them, for that which their hands have sent before them? Then will they come unto thee, and swear by God, saying, We intended no other than to do good, and to reconcile the parties. God knoweth what is in the hearts of these men; therefore let them alone, and admonish them, and speak unto them a word which may affect their souls. We have not sent any apostle, but that he might be obeyed by the permission of God: but if they, after they have injured their own souls, come unto thee, and ask pardon of God, and the apostle ask pardon for them, they shall surely find God easy to be reconciled and merciful. And by thy Lord they will not perfectly believe, until they make thee judge of their controversies; and shall not afterwards find in their own minds any hardship in what thou shalt determine, but shall acquiesce therein with entire submission. And if we had commanded them, saying, Slay yourselves, or depart from your houses, they would not have done it, except a few of them. And if they had done what they were admonished, it would certainly have been better for them, and more efficacious for confirming their faith; and we should then have surely given them in our sight an exceeding great reward, and we should have directed them in the right way. Whoever obeyeth God and the apostle, they shall be with those unto whom God hath been gracious, of the prophets, and the sincere, and the martyrs, and the righteous; and these are the most excellent company. This is bounty from God; and God is sufficiently knowing. O true believers, take your necessary precaution against your enemies, and either go forth to war in separate parties, or go forth all together in a body. There is of you who tarrieth behind; and if a misfortune befall you, he saith, Verily God hath been gracious unto me, that I was not present with them: but if success attend you from God, he will say (as if there was no friendship between you and him), Would to God I had been with them, for I should have acquired great merit. Let them therefore fight for the religion of God, who part with the present life in exchange for that which is to come; for whosoever fighteth for the religion of God, whether he be slain, or be victorious, we will surely give him a great reward. And what ails you, that ye fight not for God's true religion, and in defence of the weak among men, women, and children, who say, O Lord, bring us forth from this city, whose inhabitants are wicked; grant us from before thee a protector, and grant us from thee a defender. They who believe fight for the religion of God; but they who believe not fight for the religion of Taghût. Fight therefore against the friends of Satan, for the stratagem of Satan is weak. Hast thou not observed those unto whom it was said, Withhold your hands from war, and be constant at prayers, and pay the legal alms? But when war is commanded them, behold, a part of them fear men as they should fear God, or with a greater fear, and say, O Lord, wherefore hast thou commanded us to go to war, and hast not suffered us to wait our approaching end? Say unto them, The provision of this life is but small; but the future shall be better for him who feareth God; and ye shall not be in the least injured at the day of judgment. Wheresoever ye be, death will overtake you, although ye be in lofty towers. If good befall them, they say, This is from God; but if evil befall them, they say, This is from thee, O Mohammed: say, All is from God; and what aileth these people, that they are so far from understanding what is said unto them? Whatever good befalleth thee, O man, it is from God; and whatever evil befalleth thee, it is from thyself.[11] We have sent thee an apostle unto men, and God is a sufficient witness thereof. Whoever obeyeth the apostle, obeyeth God; and whoever turneth back, we have not sent thee to be a keeper over them. They say, Obedience: yet when they go forth from thee, part of them meditate by night a matter different from what thou speakest; but God shall write down what they meditate by night: therefore let them alone, and trust in God, for God is a sufficient protector. Do they not attentively consider the Koran? If it had been from any besides God, they would certainly have found therein many contradictions. When any news cometh unto them, either of security or fear, they immediately divulge it; but if they told it to the apostle and to those who are in authority among them, such of them would understand the truth of the matter, as inform themselves thereof from the apostle and his chiefs. And if the favor of God and his mercy had not been upon you, ye had followed the devil, except a few of you. Fight therefore for the religion of

[11] These words are not to be understood as contradictory to the preceding, "That all proceeds from God," since the evil which befalls mankind, though ordered by God, is yet the consequence of their own wicked actions.

God, and oblige not any to what is difficult, except thyself; however, excite the faithful to war, perhaps God will restrain the courage of the unbelievers; for God is stronger than they, and more able to punish. He who intercedeth between men with a good intercession shall have a portion thereof; and he who intercedeth with an evil intercession shall have a portion thereof; for God overlooketh all things. When ye are saluted with a salutation, salute the person with a better salutation, or at least return the same; for God taketh an account of all things. God! there is no God but he; he will surely gather you together on the day of resurrection; there is no doubt of it: and who is more true than God in what he saith? Why are ye divided concerning the ungodly into two parties; since God hath overturned them for what they have committed? Will ye direct him whom God hath led astray; since for him whom God shall lead astray, thou shalt find no true path? They desire that ye should become infidels, as they are infidels, and that ye should be equally wicked with themselves. Therefore take not friends from among them, until they fly their country for the religion of God; and if they turn back from the faith, take them, and kill them wherever ye find them; and take no friend from among them, nor any helper, except those who go unto a people who are in alliance with you, for those who come unto you, their hearts forbidding them either to fight against you, or to fight against their own people. And if God pleased he would have permitted them to have prevailed against you, and they would have fought against you. But if they depart from you, and fight not against you and offer you peace, God doth not allow you to take or kill them. Ye shall find others who are desirous to enter into a confidence with you, and at the same time to preserve a confidence with their own people: so often as they return to sedition, they shall be subverted therein; and if they depart not from you, and offer you peace, and restrain their hands from warring against you, take them and kill them wheresoever ye find them; over these have we granted you a manifest power. It is not lawful for a believer to kill a believer, unless it happen by mistake; and whoso killeth a believer by mistake, the penalty shall be the freeing of a believer from slavery, and a fine to be paid to the family of the deceased,[12] unless they remit it as alms: and if the slain person be

[12] Which fine is to be distributed according to the laws of inheritance given in the beginning of this chapter.

of a people at enmity with you, and be a true believer, the penalty shall be the freeing of a believer; but if he be of a people in confederacy with you, a fine to be paid to his family, and the freeing of a believer. And he who findeth not wherewith to do this, shall fast two months consecutively, as a penance enjoined from God; and God is knowing and wise. But whoso killeth a believer designedly, his reward shall be hell; he shall remain therein forever; and God shall be angry with him, and shall curse him, and shall prepare for him a great punishment. O true believers, when ye are on a march in defence of the true religion, justly discern such as ye shall happen to meet, and say not unto him who saluteth you, Thou art not a true believer; seeking the accidental goods of the present life; for with God is much spoil. Such have ye formerly been, but God hath been gracious unto you; therefore make a just discernment, for God is well acquainted with that which ye do. Those believers who sit still at home, not having any hurt, and those who employ their fortunes and their persons for the religion of God, shall not be held equal. God hath preferred those who employ their fortunes and their persons in that cause, to a degree of honor above those who sit at home: God hath indeed promised everyone paradise, but God hath preferred those who fight for the faith before those who sit still, by adding unto them a great reward, by degrees of honor conferred on them from him, and by granting them forgiveness and mercy; for God is indulgent and merciful. Moreover, unto those whom the angels put to death, having injured their own souls,[18] the angels said, Of what religion were ye? they answered, We were weak in the earth. The angels replied, Was not God's earth wide enough, that ye might fly therein to a place of refuge? Therefore their habitation shall be hell; and an evil journey shall it be thither: except the weak among men, and women, and children, who were not able to find means, and were not directed in the way; these peradventure God will pardon, for God is ready to forgive and gracious. Whosoever flieth from his country for the sake of God's true religion, shall find in the earth many forced to do the same, and plenty of provisions. And whoever departeth from his house, and flieth unto God

[18] These were certain inhabitants of Mecca, who held with the hare and ran with the hounds, for though they embraced Mohammedanism, yet they would not leave that city to join the prophet, as the rest of the Moslems did, but on the contrary went out with the idolaters, and were therefore slain with them at the battle of Bedr.

and his apostle, if death overtake him in the way, God will be obliged to reward him, for God is gracious and merciful. When ye march to war in the earth, it shall be no crime in you if ye shorten your prayers, in case ye fear the infidels may attack you; for the infidels are your open enemy. But when thou, O prophet, shalt be among them, and shalt pray with them, let a party of them arise to prayer with thee, and let them take their arms; and when they shall have worshipped, let them stand behind you, and let another party come that hath not prayed, and let them pray with thee, and let them be cautious and take their arms. The unbelievers would that ye should neglect your arms and your baggage while ye pray, that they might turn upon you at once. It shall be no crime in you, if ye be incommoded by rain, or be sick, that ye lay down your arms; but take your necessary precaution. God hath prepared for the unbelievers an ignominious punishment. And when ye shall have ended your prayer, remember God, standing, and sitting, and lying on your sides. But when ye are secure from danger, complete your prayers; for prayer is commanded the faithful, and appointed to be said at the stated times. Be not negligent in seeking out the unbelieving people, though ye suffer some inconvenience; for they also shall suffer, as ye suffer, and ye hope for a reward from God which they cannot hope for; and God is knowing and wise. We have sent down unto thee the book of the Koran with truth, that thou mayest judge between men through that wisdom which God showeth thee therein; and be not an advocate for the fraudulent; but ask pardon of God for thy wrong intention, since God is indulgent and merciful. Dispute not for those who deceive one another, for God loveth not him who is a deceiver or unjust. Such conceal themselves from men, but they conceal not themselves from God; for he is with them when they imagine by night a saying which pleaseth him not, and God comprehendeth what they do. Behold, ye are they who have disputed for them in this present life; but who shall dispute with God for them on the day of resurrection, or who will become their patron? yet he who doth evil, or injureth his own soul, and afterwards asketh pardon of God, shall find God gracious and merciful. Whoso committeth wickedness, committeth it against his own soul: God is knowing and wise. And whoso committeth a sin or iniquity, and afterwards layeth it on the innocent, he shall surely bear the guilt of calumny and manifest injustice. If the indulgence and mercy of God had not been upon thee, surely a part of them had studied to seduce thee; but they shall seduce themselves only, and shall not hurt thee at all. God hath sent down unto thee the book of the Koran and wisdom, and hath taught thee that which thou knewest not; for the favor of God hath been great towards thee. There is no good in the multitude of their private discourses, unless in the discourse of him who recommendeth alms, or that which is right, or agreement amongst men; whoever doth this out of a desire to please God we will surely give him a great reward. But whoso separateth himself from the apostle, after true direction hath been manifested unto him, and followeth any other way than that of the true believers, we will cause him to obtain that to which he is inclined, and will cast him to be burned in hell; and an unhappy journey shall it be thither. Verily God will not pardon the giving him a companion, but he will pardon any crime besides that, unto whom he pleaseth: and he who giveth a companion unto God, is surely led aside into a wide mistake: the infidels invoke beside him only female deities, and only invoke rebellious Satan. God cursed him; and he said, Verily I will take of thy servants a part cut off from the rest, and I will seduce them, and will insinuate vain desires into them, and I will command them, and they shall cut off the ears of cattle; and I will command them, and they shall change God's creature. But whoever taketh Satan for his patron, besides God, shall surely perish with a manifest destruction. He maketh them promises, and insinuateth into them vain desires; yet Satan maketh them only deceitful promises. The receptacle of these shall be hell, they shall find no refuge from it. But they who believe, and do good works, we will surely lead them into gardens, through which rivers flow; they shall continue therein forever, according to the true promise of God; and who is more true than God in what he saith? It shall not be according to your desires, nor according to the desires of those who have received the scriptures. Whoso doeth evil, shall be rewarded for it; and shall not find any patron or helper, beside God; but whoso doeth good works, whether he be male or female, and is a true believer, they shall be admitted into paradise, and shall not in the least be unjustly dealt with. Who is better in point of religion than he who resigneth himself unto God, and is a worker of righteousness, and followeth the law of Abraham the orthodox? since God took Abraham for his friend: and to God belongeth whatsoever is in heaven and on earth; God comprehendeth all things. They will consult thee concerning women; Answer, God instructeth you concerning them, and that which is read unto you in the book of the Koran concerning female orphans, to whom ye give not that which is ordained them, neither will ye marry them, and concerning weak infants, and that ye observe justice towards orphans: whatever good ye do, God knoweth it. If a woman fear ill usage, or aversion, from her husband, it shall be no crime in them if they agree the matter amicably between themselves; for a reconciliation is better than a separation. Men's souls are naturally inclined to covetousness: but if ye be kind towards women, and fear to wrong them, God is well acquainted with what ye do. Ye can by no means carry yourselves equally between women in all respects, although ye study to do it; therefore turn not from a wife with all manner of aversion, nor leave her like one in suspense: if ye agree, and fear to abuse your wives, God is gracious and merciful; but if they separate, God will satisfy them both of his abundance; for God is extensive and wise, and unto God belongeth whatsoever is in heaven and on earth. We have already commanded those unto whom the scriptures were given before you, and we command you also, saying, Fear God; but if ye disbelieve, unto God belongeth whatsoever is in heaven and on earth; and God is self-sufficient, and to be praised; for unto God belongeth whatsoever is in heaven and on earth, and God is a sufficient protector. If he pleaseth he will take you away, O men, and will produce others in your stead; for God is able to do this. Whoso desireth the reward of this world, verily with God is the reward of this world, and also of that which is to come; God both heareth and seeth. O true believers, observe justice when ye bear witness before God, although it be against yourselves, or your parents, or relations; whether the party be rich, or whether he be poor; for God is more worthy than them both: therefore follow not your own lust in bearing testimony, so that ye swerve from justice. And whether ye wrest your evidence, or decline giving it, God is well acquainted with that which ye do. O true believers, believe in God and his apostle, and the book which he hath caused to descend unto his apostle, and the book which he hath formerly sent down. And whosoever believeth not in God, and his angels, and his scriptures, and his apostles, and the last day, he surely erreth in a wide mistake. Moreover, they who believed, and afterwards became infidels, and then believed again, and after that disbelieved, and increased in infidelity, God will by no means forgive them, nor direct them into the right way. Declare unto the ungodly that they shall suffer a painful punishment. They who take the unbelievers for their protectors, besides the faithful, do they seek for power with them? since all power belongeth unto God. And he hath already revealed unto you, in the book of the Koran, the following passage: When ye shall hear the signs of God, they shall not be believed, but they shall be laughed to scorn. Therefore sit not with them who believe not, until they engage in different discourse; for if ye do, ye will certainly become like unto them. God will surely gather the ungodly and the unbelievers together in hell. They who wait to observe what befalleth you, if victory be granted you from God, say, Were we not with you? But if any advantage happen to the infidels, they say unto them, Were we not superior to you, and have we not defended you against the believers? God shall judge between you on the day of resurrection; and God will not grant the unbelievers means to prevail over the faithful. The hypocrites act deceitfully with God, but he will deceive them; and when they stand up to pray, they stand carelessly, affecting to be seen of men, and remember not God, unless a little, wavering between faith and infidelity, and adhering neither unto these nor unto those: and for him whom God shall lead astray, thou shalt find no true path. O true believers, take not the unbelievers for your protectors, besides the faithful. Will ye furnish God with an evident argument of impiety against you? Moreover, the hypocrites shall be in the lowest bottom of hell fire, and thou shalt not find any to help them thence. But they who repent and amend, and adhere firmly unto God, and approve the sincerity of their religion to God, they shall be numbered with the faithful; and God will surely give the faithful a great reward. And how should God go about to punish you, if ye be thankful and believe? for God is grateful and wise. God loveth not the speaking ill of anyone in public, unless he who is injured call for assistance; and God heareth and knoweth: whether ye publish a good action, or conceal it, or forgive evil, verily God is gracious and powerful. They who believe not in God and his apostles, and would make a distinction between God and his apostles, and say, We believe in some of the prophets, and reject others of them, and seek to take a middle way in this matter; these are really unbelievers, and we have prepared for the unbelievers an ignominious punishment. But they who believe in God and his apostles, and make no distinction between any of them, unto those will we surely give their reward; and God is gracious and merciful. They who have received the scriptures will demand of thee, that thou cause a book to descend unto them from heaven: they formerly asked of Moses a greater thing than this; for they said, Show us God visibly. Wherefore a storm of fire from heaven destroyed them, because of their iniquity. Then they took the calf for their God: after that evident proofs of the divine unity had come unto them; but we forgave them that, and gave Moses a manifest power to punish them. And we lifted the mountain of Sinai over them, when we exacted from them their covenant; and said unto them, Enter the gate of the city worshipping. We also said unto them, Transgress not on the Sabbath day. And we received from them a firm covenant, that they would observe these things. Therefore for that [14] they have made void their covenant, and have not believed in the signs of God, and have slain the prophets unjustly, and have said, Our hearts are uncircumcised (but God hath sealed them up, because of their unbelief; therefore they shall not believe, except a few of them): and for that they have not believed on Jesus, and have spoken against Mary a grievous calumny; and have said, Verily we have slain Christ Jesus the son of Mary, the apostle of God; yet they slew him not, neither crucified him, but he was represented by one in his likeness; and verily they who disagreed concerning him,[15] were in a doubt as to this matter, and had no sure knowledge thereof, but followed only an uncertain opinion. They did not really kill him; but God took him up unto himself: and God is mighty and wise. And there shall not be one of those who have received the scriptures,

[14] There being nothing in the following words of this sentence, to answer to the causal "for that," Jallalo'ddin supposes something to be understood to complete the sense, as "therefore we have cursed them," or the like.

[15] For some maintained that he was justly and really crucified; some insisted that it was not Jesus who suffered, but another who resembled him in the face, pretending the other parts of his body, and by their unlikeness plainly discovered the imposition; some said he was taken up into heaven; and others, that his manhood only suffered, and that his godhead ascended into heaven.

who shall not believe in him, before his death;[16] and on the day of resurrection he shall be a witness against them. Because of the iniquity of those who Judaize, we have forbidden them good things, which had been formerly allowed them; and because they shut out many from the way of God, and have taken usury, which was forbidden them by the law, and devoured men's substance vainly: we have prepared for such of them as are unbelievers a painful punishment. But those among them who are well grounded in knowledge, and the faithful, who believe in that which hath been sent down unto thee, and that which hath been sent down unto the prophets before thee, and who observe the stated times of prayer, and give alms, and believe in God and the last day; unto these will we give a great reward. Verily we have revealed our will unto thee, as we have revealed it unto Noah and the prophets who succeeded him; and as we revealed it unto Abraham, and Ismael, and Isaac, and Jacob, and the tribes, and unto Jesus, and Job, and Jonas, and Aaron, and Solomon; and we have given thee the Koran, as we gave the Psalms unto David: some apostles have we sent, whom we have formerly mentioned unto thee; and other apostles have we sent, whom we have not mentioned unto thee; and God spake unto Moses, discoursing with him; apostles declaring good tidings, and denouncing threats, lest men should have an argument of excuse against God, after the apostles had been sent unto them; God is mighty and wise. God is witness of that revelation which he hath sent down unto thee; he sent it down with his special knowledge: the angels also are witnesses thereof; but God is a sufficient witness. They who believe not, and turn aside others from the way of God, have erred in a wide mistake. Verily those who believe not, and act unjustly, God will by no means forgive, neither will he direct them into any other way than the way of hell; they shall

[16] This passage is expounded two ways. Some, referring the relative his to the first antecedent, take the meaning to be that no Jew or Christian shall die before he believes in Jesus: for they say, that when one of either of those religions is ready to breathe his last, and sees the angel of death before him, he shall then believe in that prophet as he ought, though his faith will not then be of any avail. According to a tradition of Hejâj, when a Jew is expiring, the angels will strike him on the back and face, and say to him, "O thou enemy of God, Jesus was sent as a prophet unto thee, and thou didst not believe on him;" to which he will answer, "I now believe him to be the servant of God"; and to a dying Christian they will say, "Jesus was sent as a prophet unto thee, and thou hast imagined him to be God, or the son of God," whereupon he will believe him to be the servant of God only, and his apostle. Others, taking the above-mentioned relative to refer to Jesus, suppose the intent of the passage to be, that all Jews and Christians in general shall have a right faith in that prophet before his death, that is, when he descends from heaven and returns into the world, where he is to kill Antichrist, and to establish the Mohammedan religion, and a most perfect tranquillity and security on earth.

remain therein forever: and this is easy with God. O men, now is the apostle come unto you, with truth from your Lord; believe therefore, it will be better for you. But if ye disbelieve, verily unto God belongeth whatsoever is in heaven and on earth; and God is knowing and wise. O ye who have received the scriptures, exceed not the just bounds in your religion, neither say of God any other than the truth. Verily Christ Jesus the son of Mary is the apostle of God, and his Word, which he conveyed into Mary, and a spirit proceeding from him. Believe, therefore, in God, and his apostles, and say not, There are three Gods; [17] forbear this; it will be better for you. God is but one God. Far be it from him that he should have a son! unto him belongeth whatsoever is in heaven and on earth; and God is a sufficient protector. Christ doth not proudly disdain to be a servant unto God; neither the angels who approach near to his presence: and whoso disdaineth his service, and is puffed up with pride, God will gather them all to himself, on the last day. Unto those who believe, and do that which is right, he shall give their rewards, and shall superabundantly add unto them of his liberality: but those who are disdainful and proud, he will punish with a grievous punishment; and they shall not find any to protect or to help them, besides God. O men, now is an evident proof come unto you from your Lord, and we have sent down unto you manifest light. They who believe in God and firmly adhere to him, he will lead them into mercy from him, and abundance; and he will direct them in the right way to himself. They will consult thee for thy decision in certain cases; say unto them, God giveth you these determinations, concerning the more remote degrees of kindred. If a man die without issue, and have a sister, she shall have the half of what he shall leave: [18] and he shall be heir to her,[19] in case she have no issue. But if there be two sisters, they shall have between them two third-parts of what he shall leave; and if there be several, both brothers and sisters, a male shall have as much as the portion of two females. God declareth unto you these precepts, lest ye err: and God knoweth all things.

[17] Namely, God, Jesus, and Mary—as the eastern writers mention a sect of Christians which held the Trinity to be composed of those three; but it is allowed that this heresy has been long since extinct. The passage, however, is equally levelled against the Holy Trinity, according to the doctrine of the orthodox Christians, who, as al Beidâwi acknowledges, believe the divine nature to consist of three persons, the Father, the Son, and the Holy Ghost; by the Father understanding God's essence, by the Son his knowledge, and by the Holy Ghost his life.

[18] And the other half will go to the public treasury.

[19] That is, he shall inherit her whole substance.

CHAPTER V

Entitled, the Table[1]—Revealed at Medina

In the Name of the Most Merciful God.

O TRUE believers, perform your contracts. Ye are allowed to eat the brute cattle,[2] other than what ye are commanded to abstain from; except the game which ye are allowed at other times, but not while ye are on pilgrimage to Mecca; God ordaineth that which he pleaseth. O true believers, violate not the holy rites of God, nor the sacred month,[3] nor the offering, nor the ornaments hung thereon, nor those who are travelling to the holy house, seeking favor from their Lord, and to please him. But when ye shall have finished your pilgrimage, then hunt. And let not the malice of some, in that they hindered you from entering the sacred temple, provoke you to transgress, by taking revenge on them in the sacred months. Assist one another according to justice and piety, but assist not one another in injustice and malice: therefore fear God; for God is severe in punishing. Ye are forbidden to eat that which dieth of itself, and blood, and swine's flesh, and that on which the name of any besides God hath been invocated, and that which hath been strangled, or killed by a blow, or by a fall, or by the horns of another beast, and that which hath been eaten by a wild beast, except what ye shall kill yourselves; and that which hath been sacrificed unto idols. It is likewise unlawful for you to make division by casting lots with arrows.[4] This is an impiety. On this day, woe be unto those who have apostatized from their religion; therefore fear not them, but fear me. This day have I perfected your religion for you, and

[1] This title is taken from the Table, which, towards the end of the chapter, is fabled to have been let down from heaven to Jesus. It is sometimes also called the chapter of Contracts, which word occurs in the first verse.

[2] As camels, oxen, and sheep; and also wild cows, antelopes, but not swine, nor what is taken in hunting during the pilgrimage.

[3] The sacred months in the Mohammedan calendar were the first, the seventh, the eleventh, and the twelfth.

[4] A game similar to raffling, arrowheads being used as counters.

have completed my mercy upon you; and I have chosen for you Islam, to be your religion. But whosoever shall be driven by necessity through hunger to eat of what we have forbidden, not designing to sin, surely God will be indulgent and merciful unto him. They will ask thee what is allowed them as lawful to eat? Answer, Such things as are good are allowed you; and what ye shall teach animals of prey to catch, training them up for hunting after the manner of dogs, and teaching them according to the skill which God hath taught you. Eat therefore of that which they shall catch for you; and commemorate the name of God thereon; and fear God, for God is swift in taking an account. This day are ye allowed to eat such things as are good, and the food of those to whom the scriptures were given is also allowed as lawful unto you; and your food is allowed as lawful unto them. And ye are also allowed to marry free women that are believers, and also free women of those who have received the scriptures before you, when ye shall have assigned them their dower; living chastely with them, neither committing fornication, nor taking them for concubines. Whoever shall renounce the faith, his work shall be vain, and in the next life he shall be of those who perish. O true believers, when ye prepare yourselves to pray, wash your faces, and your hands unto the elbows; and rub your heads, and your feet unto the ankles; and if ye be polluted and ye find no water, take fine clean sand, and rub your faces and your hands therewith; God will not put a difficulty upon you; but he desireth to purify you, and to complete his favor upon you, that ye may give thanks. Remember the favor of God towards you, and his covenant which he hath made with you, when ye said, We have heard, and will obey. Therefore fear God, for God knoweth the innermost parts of the breasts of men. O true believers, observe justice when ye appear as witnesses before God, and let not hatred towards any induce you to do wrong: but act justly; this will approach nearer unto piety; and fear God, for God is fully acquainted with what ye do. God hath promised unto those who believe, and do that which is right, that they shall receive pardon and a great reward. But they who believe not, and accuse our signs of falsehood, they shall be the companions of hell. O true believers, remember God's favor towards you, when certain men designed to stretch forth their hands against you, but he restrained their hands from hurting you; therefore fear God, and in God let the faithful trust. God formerly accepted the covenant of the children of Israel, and we appointed out of them twelve leaders: and God said, Verily, I am with you: if ye observe prayer, and give alms, and believe in my apostles, and assist them, and lend unto God on good usury, I will surely expiate your evil deeds from you, and I will lead you into gardens, wherein rivers flow: but he among you who disbelieveth after this, erreth from the straight path. Wherefore because they have broken their covenant, we have cursed them, and hardened their hearts; they dislocate the words of the Pentateuch from their places, and have forgotten part of what they were admonished; and thou wilt not cease to discover deceitful practices among them, except a few of them. But forgive them and pardon them, for God loveth the beneficent. And from those who say, We are Christians, we have received their covenant; but they have forgotten part of what they were admonished; wherefore we have raised up enmity and hatred among them, till the day of resurrection; and God will then surely declare unto them what they have been doing. O ye who have received the scriptures, now is our apostle come unto you, to make manifest unto you many things which ye concealed in the scriptures; and to pass over many things. Now is light and a perspicuous book of revelations come unto you from God. Thereby will God direct him who shall follow his good pleasure, into the paths of peace; and shall lead them out of darkness into light, by his will, and shall direct them in the right way. They are infidels, who say, Verily God is Christ the son of Mary. Say unto them, And who could obtain anything from God to the contrary, if he pleased to destroy Christ the son of Mary, and his mother, and all those who are on the earth? For unto God belongeth the kingdom of heaven and earth, and whatsoever is contained between them; he createth what he pleaseth, and God is almighty. The Jews and the Christians say, We are the children of God, and his beloved. Answer, Why therefore doth he punish you for your sins? Nay, but ye are men, of those whom he hath created. He forgiveth whom he pleaseth, and punisheth whom he pleaseth; and unto God belongeth the kingdom of heaven and earth, and of what is contained between them both; and unto him shall all things return. O ye who have received the scriptures, now is our apostle come unto you, declaring unto you the true religion, during the cessation of apostles,[5] lest ye should say, There came unto us no bearer of good tidings, nor any warner: but now is a bearer of good tidings and a warner come unto you; and God is almighty. Call to mind when Moses said unto his people, O my people, remember the favor of God towards you, since he hath appointed prophets among you, and constituted you kings, and bestowed on you what he hath given to no other nation in the world. O my people, enter the holy land, which God hath decreed you, and turn not your backs, lest ye be subverted and perish. They answered, O Moses, verily there are a gigantic people in the land; and we will by no means enter it, until they depart thence; but if they depart thence, then will we enter therein. And two men of those who feared God, unto whom God had been gracious, said, Enter ye upon them suddenly by the gate of the city; and when ye shall have entered the same, ye shall surely be victorious: therefore trust in God, if ye are true believers. They replied, O Moses, we will never enter the land, while they remain therein: go therefore thou, and thy Lord, and fight; for we will sit here. Moses said, O Lord, surely I am not master of any except myself, and my brother; therefore make a distinction between us and the ungodly people. God answered, Verily the land shall be forbidden them forty years; during which time they shall wander like men astonished in the earth; therefore be not thou solicitous for the ungodly people. Relate also unto them the history of the two sons of Adam, with truth. When they offered their offering, and it was accepted from one of them, and was not accepted from the other, Cain said to his brother, I will certainly kill thee. Abel answered, God only accepteth the offering of the pious; if thou stretchest forth thy hand against me, to slay me, I will not stretch forth my hand against thee, to slay thee; for I fear God the Lord of all creatures. I choose that thou shouldst bear my iniquity and thine own iniquity; and that thou become a companion of hell fire; for that is the reward of the unjust. But his soul suffered him to slay his brother, and he slew him; wherefore he became of the number of those who perish. And God sent a raven, which scratched the earth, to show him how he should hide the shame of his

[5] The Arabic word *al Fatra* signifies the intermediate space of time between two prophets, during which no new revelation or dispensation was given; as the interval between Moses and Jesus, and between Jesus and Mohammed, at the expiration of which last, Mohammed pretended to be sent.

brother, and he said, Woe is me! am I unable to be like this raven, that I may hide my brother's shame? and he became one of those who repent. Wherefore we commanded the children of Israel, that he who slayeth a soul, without having slain a body, or committed wickedness in the earth, shall be as if he had slain all mankind: but he who saveth a soul alive, shall be as if he had saved the lives of all mankind. Our apostles formerly came unto them, with evident miracles; then were many of them, after this, transgressors on the earth. But the recompense of those who fight against God and his apostles, and study to act corruptly in the earth, shall be, that they shall be slain, or crucified, or have their hands and their feet cut off on the opposite sides, or be banished the land. This shall be their disgrace in this world, and in the next world they shall suffer a grievous punishment; except those who shall repent, before ye prevail against them; for know that God is inclined to forgive, and be merciful. O true believers, fear God, and earnestly desire a near conjunction with him, and fight for his religion, that ye may be happy. Moreover, they who believe not, although they had whatever is in the earth, and as much more withal, that they might therewith redeem themselves from punishment on the day of resurrection: it shall not be accepted from them, but they shall suffer a painful punishment. They shall desire to go forth from the fire, but they shall not go forth from it, and their punishment shall be permanent. If a man or a woman steal, cut off their hands,* in retribution for that which they have committed; this is an exemplary punishment appointed by God; and God is mighty and wise. But whoever shall repent after his iniquity, and amend, verily God will be turned unto him, for God is inclined to forgive and be merciful. Dost thou not know that the kingdom of heaven and earth is God's? He punisheth whom he pleaseth, and he pardoneth whom he pleaseth; for God is almighty. O apostle, let them not grieve thee, who hasten to infidelity, either of those who say, We believe, with their mouths, but whose hearts believe not; or of the Jews, who hearken to a lie, and hearken to other people; who come not unto thee: they pervert the words of the law from their true

* But this punishment, according to the Sonna, is not to be inflicted, unless the value of the thing stolen amount to four dinârs, or about $10. For the first offence, the criminal is to lose his right hand, which is to be cut off at the wrist; for the second offence, his left foot, at the ankle; for the third, his left hand; for the fourth, his right foot; and if he continue to offend, he shall be scourged at the discretion of the judge.

places, and say, If this be brought unto you, receive it; but if it be not brought unto you, beware of receiving aught else; and in behalf of him whom God shall resolve to reduce, thou shalt not prevail with God at all. They whose hearts God shall not please to cleanse, shall suffer shame in this world, and a grievous punishment in the next: who hearken to a lie, and eat that which is forbidden. But if they come unto thee for judgment, either judge between them, or leave them; and if thou leave them, they shall not hurt thee at all. But if thou undertake to judge, judge between them with equity; for God loveth those who observe justice. And how will they submit to thy decision, since they have the law, containing the judgment of God? Then will they turn their backs, after this; but those are not true believers. We have surely sent down the law, containing direction, and light: thereby did the prophets, who professed the true religion, judge those who Judaized; and the doctors and priests also judged by the book of God, which had been committed to their custody; and they were witnesses thereof. Therefore fear not men, but fear me; neither sell my signs for a small price. And whoso judgeth not according to what God hath revealed, they are infidels. We have therein commanded them, that they should give life for life, and eye for eye, and nose for nose, and ear for ear, and tooth for tooth; and that wounds should also be punished by retaliation: but whoever should remit it as alms, it should be accepted as an atonement for him. And whoso judgeth not according to what God hath revealed, they are unjust. We also caused Jesus, the son of Mary, to follow the footsteps of the prophets, confirming the law which was sent down before him; and we gave him the gospel, containing direction and light; confirming also the law which was given before it, and a direction and admonition unto those who fear God: that they who have received the gospel might judge according to what God hath revealed therein: and whoso judgeth not according to what God hath revealed, they are transgressors. We have also sent down unto thee the book of the Koran with truth, confirming that scripture which was revealed before it; and preserving the same safe from corruption. Judge, therefore, between them according to that which God hath revealed; and follow not their desires, by swerving from the truth which hath come unto thee. Unto every one of you have we given a law, and an open path; and if God had pleased, he had surely made you one people; but he hath thought fit to give you different laws, that he might try you in that which he hath given you respectively. Therefore strive to excel each other in good works: unto God shall ye all return, and then will he declare unto you that concerning which ye have disagreed. Wherefore do thou, O prophet, judge between them according to that which God hath revealed, and follow not their desires; but beware of them, lest they cause thee to err from part of those precepts which God hath sent down unto thee; and if they turn back, know that God is pleased to punish them for some of their crimes; for a great number of men are transgressors. Do they therefore desire the judgment of the time of ignorance? but who is better than God, to judge between people who reason aright? O true believers, take not the Jews or Christians for your friends; they are friends the one to the other; but whoso among you taketh them for his friends, he is surely one of them: verily God directeth not unjust people. Thou shalt see those in whose hearts there is an infirmity, to hasten unto them, saying, We fear lest some adversity befall us; but it is easy for God to give victory, or a command from him, that they may repent of that which they concealed in their minds. And they who believe will say, Are these the men who have sworn by God, with a most firm oath, that they surely held with you? their works are become vain, and they are of those who perish. O true believers, whoever of you apostatizeth from his religion, God will certainly bring other people to supply his place, whom he will love, and who will love him; who shall be humble towards the believers, but severe to the unbelievers; they shall fight for the religion of God, and shall not fear the obloquy of the detractor. This is the bounty of God, he bestoweth it on whom he pleaseth: God is extensive and wise. Verily your protector is God, and his apostle, and those who believe, who observe the stated times of prayer, and give alms, and who bow down to worship. And whoso taketh God, and his apostle, and the believers for his friends, they are the party of God, and they shall be victorious. O true believers, take not such of those to whom the scriptures were delivered before you, or of the infidels, for your friends, who make a laughing-stock and a jest of your religion; but fear God, if ye be true believers; nor those who, when ye call to prayer, make a laughing-stock and a jest of it; this they do because they are people who do not understand. Say, O ye who have received the scriptures, do ye reject us for any other reason than because we believe in God, and that revelation which hath been sent down unto us, and that which was formerly sent down, and for that the greater part of you are transgressors? Say, Shall I denounce unto you a worse thing than this, as to the reward which ye are to expect with God? He whom God hath cursed, and with whom he hath been angry, having changed some of them into apes and swine, and who worship Taghût, they are in the worse condition, and err more widely from the straightness of the path. When they came unto you, they said, We believe: yet they entered into your company with infidelity, and went forth from you with the same; but God well knew what they concealed. Thou shalt see many of them hastening unto iniquity and malice, and to eat things forbidden; and woe unto them for what they have done. Unless their doctors and priests forbid them uttering wickedness, and eating things forbidden; woe unto them for what they shall have committed. The Jews say, the hand of God is tied up. Their hands shall be tied up, and they shall be cursed for that which they have said. Nay, his hands are both stretched forth; he bestoweth as he pleaseth: that which had been sent down unto thee from thy Lord, shall increase the transgression and infidelity of many of them; and we have put enmity and hatred between them, until the day of resurrection. So often as they shall kindle a fire for war, God shall extinguish it; and they shall set their minds to act corruptly in the earth, but God loveth not the corrupt doers. Moreover, if they who have received the scriptures believe, and fear God, we will surely expiate their sins from them, and we will lead them into gardens of pleasure; and if they observe the law, and the gospel, and the other scriptures which have been sent down unto them from their Lord, they shall surely eat of good things both from above them and from under their feet. Among them there are people who act uprightly; but how evil is that which many of them do work! O apostle, publish the whole of that which hath been sent down unto thee from thy Lord: for if thou do not, thou dost not in effect publish any part thereof; and God will defend thee against wicked men; for God directeth not the unbelieving people. Say, O ye who have received the scriptures, ye are not grounded on anything, until ye observe the law and the gospel, and that which hath been sent down unto you from your Lord. That which hath been sent down unto thee from thy Lord shall surely increase the transgression and infidelity of many of them: but be not thou solicitous for the unbelieving people. Verily they who believe, and those who Judaize, and the Sabeans, and the Christians, whoever of them believeth in God and the last day, and doth that which is right, there shall come no fear on them, neither shall they be grieved. We formerly accepted the covenant of the children of Israel, and sent apostles unto them. So often as an apostle came unto them with that which their souls desired not, they accused some of them of imposture, and some of them they killed: and they imagined that there should be no punishment for those crimes, and they became blind and deaf. Then was God turned unto them; afterwards many of them again became blind and deaf; but God saw what they did. They are surely infidels, who say, Verily God is Christ the son of Mary; since Christ said, O children of Israel, serve God, my Lord and your Lord; whoever shall give a companion unto God, God shall exclude him from paradise, and his habitation shall be hell fire; and the ungodly shall have none to help them. They are certainly infidels, who say, God is the third of three: for there is no God besides one God; and if they refrain not from what they say, a painful torment shall surely be inflicted on such of them as are unbelievers. Will they not therefore be turned unto God, and ask pardon of him? since God is gracious and merciful. Christ, the son of Mary, is no more than an apostle; other apostles have preceded him; and his mother was a woman of veracity: they both ate food. Behold, how we declare unto them the signs of God's unity; and then behold, how they turn aside from the truth. Say unto them, Will ye worship, besides God, that which can cause you neither harm nor profit? God is he who heareth and seeth. Say, O ye who have received the scriptures, exceed not the just bounds in your religion, by speaking beside the truth; neither follow the desires of people who have heretofore erred, and who have seduced many, and have gone astray from the straight path. Those among the children of Israel who believed not, were cursed by the tongue of David, and of Jesus the son of Mary. This befell them because they were rebellious and transgressed: they forbade not one another the wickedness which they committed; and woe unto them for what they committed. Thou shalt see many of them take for their friends those who believe not. Woe unto them for what their souls have sent before them, for that God is incensed against them, and they shall remain in torment forever. But, if they had believed in God, and the prophet, and that which hath been revealed unto him, they had not taken them for their friends; but many of them are evil-doers. Thou shalt surely find the most violent of all men in enmity against the true believers, to be the Jews and the idolaters: and thou shalt surely find those among them to be the most inclinable to entertain friendship for the true believers, who say, We are Christians. This cometh to pass, because there are priests and monks among them; and because they are not elated with pride. And when they hear that which hath been sent down to the apostle read unto them, thou shalt see their eyes overflow with tears, because of the truth which they perceive therein, saying, O Lord, we believe; write us down, therefore, with those who bear witness to the truth: and what should hinder us from believing in God, and the truth which hath come unto us, and from earnestly desiring that our Lord would introduce us into paradise with the righteous people. Therefore hath God rewarded them, for what they have said, with gardens through which rivers flow; they shall continue therein forever; and this is the reward of the righteous. But they who believe not, and accuse our signs of falsehood, they shall be the companions of hell. O true believers, forbid not the good things which God hath allowed you; but transgress not, for God loveth not the transgressors. And eat of what God hath given you for food that which is lawful and good: and fear God, in whom ye believe. God will not punish you for an inconsiderate word in your oaths; but he will punish you for what ye solemnly swear with deliberation. And the expiation of such an oath shall be the feeding of ten poor men with such moderate food as ye feed your own families withal; or to clothe them; or to free the neck of a true believer from captivity: but he who shall not find wherewith to perform one of these three things, shall fast three days. This is the expiation of your oaths, when ye swear inadvertently. Therefore keep your oaths. Thus God declareth unto you his signs, that ye may give thanks. O true believers, surely wine, and lots, and images, and divining arrows, are an abomination of the work of Satan; therefore avoid them, that ye may prosper. Satan seeketh to sow dissension and hatred among you, by means of wine and lots, and to divert you from remembering God, and from prayer; will ye not therefore abstain from them? Obey God, and obey the apostle, and take heed to yourselves: but if ye turn back, know that the duty of our apostle is only to preach publicly. In those who believe and do good works, it is no sin that they have tasted wine or gaming before they were forbidden; if they fear God, and believe, and do good works, and shall for the future fear God, and believe, and shall persevere to fear him, and to do good; for God loveth those who do good. O true believers, God will surely prove you in offering you plenty of game, which ye may take with your hands or your lances, that God may know who feareth him in secret; but whoever transgresseth after this, shall suffer a grievous punishment. O true believers, kill no game while ye are on pilgrimages; whosoever among you shall kill any designedly, shall restore the like of what ye shall have killed, in domestic animals, according to the determination of two just persons among you, to be brought as an offering to the Caabah; or in atonement thereof shall feed the poor; or instead thereof shall fast, that he may taste the heinousness of his deed. God hath forgiven what is past, but whoever returneth to transgress, God will take vengeance on him; for God is mighty and able to avenge. It is lawful for you to fish in the sea,[7] and to eat what ye shall catch, as a provision for you and for those who travel; but it is unlawful for you to hunt by land, while ye are performing the rites of pilgrimage; therefore fear God, before whom ye shall be assembled at the last day. God hath appointed the Caabah, the holy house, an establishment for mankind; and hath ordained the sacred month, and the offering, and the ornaments hung thereon. This hath he done that ye might know that God knoweth whatsoever is in heaven and on earth, and that God is omniscient. Know that God is severe in punishing, and that God is ready to forgive and be merciful. The duty of our apostle is to preach only; and God knoweth that which ye discover, and that which ye conceal. Say, Evil and Good shall not be equally esteemed of, though the abundance of evil pleaseth thee; therefore fear God, O ye of understanding, that ye may be happy. O true believers, inquire not

[7] This is to be understood of fish that live altogether in the sea, and not of those that live in the sea and on land both, as crabs. The Turks, who are Hanifites, never eat this sort of fish; but the sect of Malec Ebn Ans, and perhaps some others, make no scruple of it.

concerning things which, if they be declared unto you, may give you pain; but if ye ask concerning them when the Koran is sent down, they will be declared unto you: God pardoneth you as to these matters; for God is ready to forgive and gracious. People who have been before you formerly inquired concerning them; and afterwards disbelieved therein. God hath not ordained anything concerning Bahira, nor Sâïba, nor Wasîla, nor Hâmi;[8] but the unbelievers have invented a lie against God: and the greater part of them do not understand. And when it was said unto them, Come unto that which God hath revealed, and to the apostles; they answered, That religion which we found our fathers to follow is sufficient for us. What though their fathers knew nothing, and were not rightly directed? O true believers, take care of your souls. He who erreth shall not hurt you, while ye are rightly directed: unto God shall ye all return, and he will tell you that which ye have done. O true believers, let witnesses be taken between you, when death approaches any of you, at the time of making the testament; let there be two witnesses, just men, from among you; or two others of a different tribe or faith from yourselves, if ye be journeying in the earth, and the accident of death befall you. Ye shall shut them both up, after the afternoon prayer, and they shall swear by God, if ye doubt them, and they shall say, We will not sell our evidence for a bribe, although the person concerned be one who is related to us, neither will we conceal the testimony of God, for then should we certainly be of the number of the wicked. But if it appear that both have been guilty of iniquity, two others shall stand up in their place, of those who have convicted them of falsehood, the two nearest in blood, and they shall swear by God, saying, Verily our testimony is more true than the testimony of these two, neither have we prevaricated; for then should we become of the number of the unjust. This will be easier, that men may give testimony according to the plain intention thereof, or fear lest a different oath be given, after their oath. Therefore fear God, and hearken; for God directeth not the unjust people. On a certain day shall God assemble the apostles, and shall say unto them, What answer was returned you, when ye preached unto the people to whom

[8] These were the names given by the pagan Arabs to certain camels or sheep which were turned loose to feed, and exempted from common services, in some particular cases; having their ears slit, or some other mark, that they might be known; and this they did in honor of their gods. Which superstitions are here declared to be no ordinances of God, but the inventions of foolish men.

ye were sent? They shall answer, We have no knowledge but thou art the knower of secrets. When God shall say, O Jesus, son of Mary, remember my favor towards thee, and towards thy mother; when I strengthened thee with the holy spirit, that thou shouldst speak unto men in the cradle, and when thou wast grown up; and when I taught thee the scripture, and wisdom, and the law and the gospel; and when thou didst create of clay as it were the figure of a bird, by my permission, and didst breathe thereon, and it became a bird by my permission; and thou didst heal one blind from his birth and the leper, by my permission; and when thou didst bring forth the dead from their graves, by my permission; and when I withheld the children of Israel from killing thee, when thou hadst come unto them with evident miracles, and such of them as believed not, said, This is nothing but manifest sorcery. And when I commanded the apostles of Jesus, saying, Believe in me and in my messenger; they answered, We do believe; and do thou bear witness that we are resigned unto thee. Remember when the apostles said, O Jesus, son of Mary, is thy Lord able to cause a table to descend unto us from heaven?* He answered, hear God, if ye be true believers. They said, We desire to eat thereof, and that our hearts may rest at ease, and that we may know that thou hast told us the truth, and that we may be witnesses thereof. Jesus, the son of Mary, said, O God our Lord, cause a table to descend unto us from heaven, that the day of its descent may become a festival day unto us, unto the first of us, and unto the last of us, and a sign from thee; and do thou provide food for us, for thou art the best provider. God said, Verily I will cause it to descend unto you; but whoever among you shall disbelieve hereafter, I will surely punish him with a punishment wherewith I will not punish any other creature. And when God shall say unto Jesus, at the last day, O Jesus, son of Mary, hast thou said unto men, Take me and my mother for two gods, beside God? He shall answer, Praise be unto thee! it is not for me to say that which I ought not; if I had said so, thou wouldst surely have known it: thou knowest what is in me, but I know not what is in thee; for thou art the knower of secrets. I have

* This miracle is thus related by the commentators: Jesus having, at the request of his followers, asked it of God, a red table immediately descended, in their sight, between two clouds, and was set before them; whereupon he rose up, and having made the ablution, prayed, and then took off the cloth which covered the table, saying, "In the name of God, the best provider of food."

not spoken to them any other than what thou didst command me; namely, Worship God, my Lord and your Lord: and I was a witness of their actions while I stayed among them; but since thou hast taken me to thyself, thou hast been the watcher over them; for thou art witness of all things. If thou punish them, they are surely thy servants; and if thou forgive them, thou art mighty and wise. God will say, This day shall their veracity be of advantage unto those who speak truth; they shall have gardens wherein rivers flow, they shall remain therein forever: God hath been well pleased in them, and they have been well pleased in him. This shall be great felicity. Unto God belongeth the kingdom of heaven and of earth, and of whatever therein is; and he is almighty.

LIFE OF BUDDHA

—

BY

ASVAGHOSHA BODHISATTVA

[*Translated from Sanscrit into Chinese by Dharmaraksha, A.D. 420; from Chinese into English by Samuel Beal*]

INTRODUCTION

BUDDHA is undoubtedly the most potent name as a religious teacher, in the whole of Asia. The propaganda of the Buddhistic faith passed from the valley of the Indus to the valley of the Ganges, and from Ceylon to the Himalayas; thence it traversed China, and its conquests seem to have been permanent. The religion of Buddha is so far different from that of Confucius, and so far resembles Christianity, that it combines mysticism with asceticism—a practical rule of personal conduct with a consistent transcendentalism. It has, moreover, the great advantage of possessing a highly fascinating and romantic gospel, or biography, of its founder. Gautama, as the hero of Arnold's "Light of Asia," is very well known to English readers, and, although Sir Edwin Arnold is not by any means a poet of the first order, he has done a great deal to familiarize the Anglo-Saxon mind with Oriental life and thought. A far more faithful life of Buddha is that written some time in the first century of our era by the twelfth Buddhist patriarch Asvaghosha. This learned ecclesiastic appears to have travelled about through different districts of India, patiently collecting the stories and traditions which related to the life of his master. These he wove into a Sanscrit poem, which three hundred years later was translated into Chinese, from which version our present translation is made. There can be no doubt that the author of the Sanscrit poem was a famous preacher and musician. Originally living in central India, he seems to have wandered far and wide exercising his office, and reciting or singing his poem—a sacred epic, more thrilling to the ears of India than the wrath of Achilles, or the voyages of Ulysses. We are told that Asvaghosha took a choir of musicians with him, and many were converted to Buddhism through the combined persuasiveness of poetry and preaching. The present life of Buddha, although it labors under the disadvantage of transfusion from Sanscrit into Chinese, and from Chinese into English, is by no means destitute of poetic color and aroma. When, for instance, we read of the grief-stricken Yasodhara that "her breath failed her, and sinking thus she fell upon the dusty ground," we come upon a stately pathos, worthy of Homer or Lucretius. And what can be more beautiful than the account of Buddha's conversion and sudden conviction, that all earthly things were vanity. The verses once heard linger in the memory so as almost to ring in the ears: "Thus did he complete the end of self, as fire goes out for want of grass. Thus he had done what he would have men do: he first had found the way of perfect knowledge. He finished thus the first great lesson; entering the great Rishi's house, the darkness disappeared, light burst upon him; perfectly silent and at rest, he reached the last exhaustless source of truth; lustrous with all wisdom the great Rishi sat, perfect in gifts, whilst one convulsive throe shook the wide earth."

E. W.

LIFE OF BUDDHA

CHAPTER I

The Birth

THERE was a descendant of the Ikshvâku family, an invincible Sâkya monarch, pure in mind and of unspotted virtue, called therefore Pure-rice, or Suddhodana. Joyously reverenced by all men, as the new moon is welcomed by the world, the king indeed was like the heaven-ruler Sakra, his queen like the divine Saki. Strong and calm of purpose as the earth, pure in mind as the water-lily, her name, figuratively assumed, Mâyâ, she was in truth incapable of class-comparison. On her in likeness as the heavenly queen descended the spirit and entered her womb. A mother, but free from grief or pain, she was without any false or illusory mind. Disliking the clamorous ways of the world, she remembered the excellent garden of Lumbinî, a pleasant spot, a quiet forest retreat, with its trickling fountains, and blooming flowers and fruits. Quiet and peaceful, delighting in meditation, respectfully she asked the king for liberty to roam therein; the king, understanding her earnest desire, was seized with a seldom-felt anxiety to grant her request. He commanded his kinsfolk, within and without the palace, to repair with her to that garden shade; and now the queen Mâyâ knew that her time for child-bearing was come. She rested calmly on a beautiful couch, surrounded by a hundred thousand female attendants; it was the eighth day of the fourth moon, a season of serene and agreeable character.

Whilst she thus religiously observed the rules of a pure discipline, Bodhisattva was born from her right side, come to deliver the world, constrained by great pity, without causing his mother pain or anguish. As king Yu-liu was born from the thigh, as King Pi-t'au was born from the hand, as King Man-to was born from the top of the head, as King Kia-k'ha was born from the arm-pit, so also was Bodhisattva on the day of his birth produced from the right side; gradually emerging from the womb, he shed in every direction the rays of his glory. As one born from recumbent space, and not through the gates of life, through countless kalpas, practising virtue, self-conscious he came forth to life, without confusion. Calm and collected, not falling headlong was he born, gloriously manifested, perfectly adorned, sparkling with light he came from the womb, as when the sun first rises from the East.

Men indeed regarded his exceeding great glory, yet their sight remained uninjured: he allowed them to gaze, the brightness of his person concealed for the time, as when we look upon the moon in the heavens. His body, nevertheless, was effulgent with light, and like the sun which eclipses the shining of the lamp, so the true gold-like beauty of Bodhisattva shone forth, and was diffused everywhere. Upright and firm and unconfused in mind, he deliberately took seven steps, the soles of his feet resting evenly upon the ground as he went, his footmarks remained bright as seven stars.

Moving like the lion, king of beasts, and looking earnestly towards the four quarters, penetrating to the centre the principles of truth, he spake thus with the fullest assurance: This birth is in the condition of a Buddha; after this I have done with renewed birth; now only am I born this once, for the purpose of saving all the world.

And now from the midst of heaven there descended two streams of pure water, one warm, the other cold, and baptized his head, causing refreshment to his body. And now he is placed in the precious palace hall, a jewelled couch for him to sleep upon, and the heavenly kings with their golden flowery hands hold fast the four feet of the bed. Meanwhile the Devas in space, seizing their jewelled canopies, attending, raise in responsive harmony their heavenly songs, to encourage him to accomplish his perfect purpose.

Then the Nâga-râgas filled with joy, earnestly desiring to show their reverence for the most excellent law, as they had paid honor to the former Buddhas, now went to meet Bodhisattva; they scattered before him Mandâra flowers, rejoicing with heartfelt joy to pay such religious homage; and so, again, Tathâgata having appeared in the world, the Suddha angels rejoiced with gladness; with no selfish or partial joy, but for the sake of religion they rejoiced, because creation, engulfed in the ocean of pain, was now to obtain perfect release.

Then the precious Mountain-râga, Sumeru, firmly holding this great earth when Bodhisattva appeared in the world, was swayed by the wind of his perfected merit. On every hand the world was greatly shaken, as the wind drives the tossing boat; so also the minutest atoms of sandal perfume, and the hidden sweetness of precious lilies floated on the air, and rose through space, and then commingling, came back to earth; so again the garments of Devas descending from heaven touching the body, caused delightful thrills of joy; the sun and moon with constant course redoubled the brilliancy of their light, whilst in the world the fire's gleam of itself prevailed without the use of fuel. Pure water, cool and refreshing from the springs, flowed here and there, self-caused; in the palace all the waiting women were filled with joy at such an unprecedented event. Proceeding all in company, they drink and bathe themselves; in all arose calm and delightful thoughts; countless inferior Devas, delighting in religion, like clouds assembled.

In the garden of Lumbinî, filling the spaces between the trees, rare and special flowers, in great abundance, bloomed out of season. All cruel and malevolent kinds of beings, together conceived a loving heart; all diseases and afflictions among men without a cure applied, of themselves were healed. The various cries and confused sounds of beasts were hushed and silence reigned; the stagnant water of the river-courses flowed apace, whilst the polluted streams became clear and pure. No clouds gathered throughout the heavens, whilst angelic music, self-caused, was heard around; the whole world of sentient creatures enjoyed peace and universal tranquillity.

Just as when a country visited by desolation, suddenly obtains an enlightened ruler, so when Bodhisattva was born, he came to remove the sorrows of all living things.

Mâra,[1] the heavenly monarch, alone was grieved and rejoiced not. The Royal Father (Suddhodana), beholding his son, strange and miraculous, as to his birth, though self-possessed and assured in his soul, was yet moved with astonishment and

[1] Mâra, the king of the world of desire. According to the Buddhist theogony he is the god of sensual love. He holds the world in sin. He was the enemy of Buddha, and endeavored in every way to defeat him. He is also described as the king of death.

his countenance changed, whilst he alternately weighed with himself the meaning of such an event, now rejoiced and now distressed.

The queen-mother beholding her child, born thus contrary to laws of nature, her timorous woman's heart was doubtful; her mind, through fear, swayed between extremes: Not distinguishing the happy from the sad portents, again and again she gave way to grief; and now the aged women of the world, in a confused way supplicating heavenly guidance, implored the gods to whom their rites were paid, to bless the child; to cause peace to rest upon the royal child. Now there was at this time in the grove, a certain soothsayer, a Brahman, of dignified mien and wide-spread renown, famed for his skill and scholarship: beholding the signs, his heart rejoiced, and he exulted at the miraculous event. Knowing the king's mind to be somewhat perplexed, he addressed him with truth and earnestness: "Men born in the world, chiefly desire to have a son the most renowned; but now the king, like the moon when full, should feel in himself a perfect joy, having begotten an unequalled son, (for by this the king) will become illustrious among his race; let then his heart be joyful and glad, banish all anxiety and doubt, the spiritual omens that are everywhere manifested indicate for your house and dominion a course of continued prosperity. The most excellently endowed child now born will bring deliverance to the entire world: none but a heavenly teacher has a body such as this, golden-colored, gloriously resplendent. One endowed with such transcendent marks must reach the state of Samyak-Sambodhi, or, if he be induced to engage in worldly delights, then he must become a universal monarch; everywhere recognized as the ruler of the great earth, mighty in his righteous government, as a monarch ruling the four empires, uniting under his sway all other rulers; as among all lesser lights, the sun's brightness is by far the most excellent. But if he seek a dwelling among the mountain forests, with single heart searching for deliverance, having arrived at the perfection of true wisdom, he will become illustrious throughout the world; for as Mount Sumeru is monarch among all mountains, or, as gold is chief among all precious things; or, as the ocean is supreme among all streams; or, as the moon is first among the stars; or, as the sun is brightest of all luminaries, so Tathâgata, born in the world, is the most eminent of men; his eyes clear and expanding, the lashes both above and below moving with the lid, the iris of the eye of a clear blue color, in shape like the moon when half full, such characteristics as these, without contradiction, foreshadow the most excellent condition of perfect wisdom."

At this time the king addressed the twice-born,[a] "If it be as you say, with respect to these miraculous signs, that they indicate such consequences, then no such case has happened with former kings, nor down to our time has such a thing occurred." The Brahman addressed the king thus, "Say not so; for it is not right; for with regard to renown and wisdom, personal celebrity, and worldly substance, these four things indeed are not to be considered according to precedent or subsequence; but whatever is produced according to nature, such things are liable to the law of cause and effect: but now whilst I recount some parallels let the king attentively listen:—Bhrigu, Angira, these two of Rishi family, having passed many years apart from men, each begat an excellently endowed son; Brihaspati with Sukra, skilful in making royal treatises, not derived from former families (or tribes); Sârasvata, the Rishi, whose works have long disappeared, begat a son, Po-lo-sa, who compiled illustrious Sûtras and Shâstras; that which now we know and see, is not therefore dependent on previous connection; Vyâsa, the Rishi, the author of numerous treatises, after his death had among his descendants Poh-mi (Vâlmîki), who extensively collected Gâthâ sections; Atri, the Rishi, not understanding the sectional treatise on medicine, afterwards begat Âtreya, who was able to control diseases; the twice-born Rishi Kusi (Kusika), not occupied with heretical treatises, afterwards begat Kia-ti-na-râga, who thoroughly understood heretical systems; the sugar-cane monarch, who began his line, could not restrain the tide of the sea, but Sagara-râga, his descendant, who begat a thousand royal sons, he could control the tide of the great sea so that it should come no further. Ganaka, the Rishi, without a teacher acquired power of abstraction. All these, who obtained such renown, acquired powers of themselves; those distinguished before, were afterwards forgotten; those before forgotten, became afterwards distinguished; kings like these and god-like Rishis have no need of family inheritance, and therefore the world need not regard those going before or fol-

[a] That is, the Brahman wearing the twice-born thread.

lowing. So, mighty king! is it with you: you should experience true joy of heart, and because of this joy should banish forever doubt or anxiety." The king, hearing the words of the seer, was glad, and offered him increased gifts.

"Now have I begotten a valiant son," he said, "who will establish a wheel authority, whilst I, when old and gray-headed, will go forth to lead a hermit's life, so that my holy, king-like son may not give up the wqrld and wander through mountain forests."

And now near the spot within the garden, there was a Rishi, leading the life of an ascetic; his name was Asita, wonderfully skilful in the interpretation of signs; he approached the gate of the palace; the king beholding him exclaimed, "This is none other but Brahmadeva, himself enduring penance from love of true religion, these two characteristics so plainly visible as marks of his austerities." Then the king was much rejoiced; and forthwith he invited him within the palace, and with reverence set before him entertainment, whilst he, entering the inner palace, rejoiced only in prospect of seeing the royal child.

Although surrounded by the crowd of court ladies, yet still he was as if in desert solitude; and now they place a preaching throne and pay him increased honor and religious reverence, as Antideva râga reverenced the priest Vasishtha. Then the king, addressing the Rishi, said: "Most fortunate am I, great Rishi! that you have condescended to come here to receive from me becoming gifts and reverence; I pray you therefore enter on your exhortation."

Thus requested and invited, the Rishi felt unutterable joy, and said, "All hail, ever victorious monarch! possessed of all noble, virtuous qualities, loving to meet the desires of those who seek, nobly generous in honoring the true law, conspicuous as a race for wisdom and humanity, with humble mind you pay me homage, as you are bound. Because of your righteous deeds in former lives, now are manifested these excellent fruits; listen to me, then, whilst I declare the reason of the present meeting. As I was coming on the sun's way, I heard the Devas in space declare that the king had born to him a royal son, who would arrive at perfect intelligence; moreover I beheld such other portents, as have constrained me now to seek your presence; desiring to see the Sâkya monarch who will erect the standard of the true law."

The king, hearing the Rishi's words, was fully assured; escaping from the net of doubt, he ordered an attendant to bring the prince, to exhibit him to the Rishi. The Rishi, beholding the prince, the thousand-rayed wheel on the soles of his feet, the web-like filament between his fingers, between his eyebrows the white wool-like prominence, his complexion bright and lustrous; seeing these wonderful birth-portents, the seer wept and sighed deeply.

The king beholding the tears of the Rishi, thinking of his son, his soul was overcome, and his breath fast held his swelling heart. Thus alarmed and ill at ease, unconsciously he arose from his seat, and bowing his head at the Rishi's feet, he addressed him in these words: "This son of mine, born thus wonderfully, beautiful in face, and surpassingly graceful, little different from the gods in form, giving promise of superiority in the world, ah! why has he caused thee grief and pain? Forbid it, that my son should die! or should be short-lived!—the thought creates in me grief and anxiety; that one athirst, within reach of the eternal draught,[8] should after all reject and lose it! sad indeed! Forbid it, he should lose his wealth and treasure! dead to his house! lost to his country! for he who has a prosperous son in life, gives pledge that his country's weal is well secured; and then, coming to die, my heart will rest content, rejoicing in the thought of offspring surviving me; even as a man possessed of two eyes, one of which keeps watch, while the other sleeps; not like the frost-flower of autumn, which, though it seems to bloom, is not a reality. A man who, midst his tribe and kindred, deeply loves a spotless son, at every proper time in recollection of it has joy; O! that you would cause me to revive!"

The Rishi, knowing the king-sire to be thus greatly afflicted at heart, immediately addressed the Mahârâga: "Let not the king be for a moment anxious! the words I have spoken to the king, let him ponder these, and not permit himself to doubt; the portents now are as they were before, cherish then no other thoughts! But recollecting I myself am old, on that account I could not hold my tears; for now my end is coming on. But this son of thine will rule the world, born for the sake of all that lives! this is indeed one difficult to meet with; he shall give up his royal estate, escape from the domain of the five desires,

[8] The "eternal draught" or "sweet dew" of Ambrosia. This expression is constantly used in Buddhist writings. It corresponds with the Pâli amatam, which Childers explains as the "drink of the gods."

with resolution and with diligence practise austerities, and then awakening, grasp the truth. Then constantly, for the world's sake (all living things), destroying the impediments of ignorance and darkness, he shall give to all enduring light, the brightness of the sun of perfect wisdom. All flesh submerged in the sea of sorrow; all diseases collected as the bubbling froth; decay and age like the wild billows; death like the engulfing ocean; embarking lightly in the boat of wisdom he will save the world from all these perils, by wisdom stemming back the flood. His pure teaching like to the neighboring shore, the power of meditation, like a cool lake, will be enough for all the unexpected birds; thus deep and full and wide is the great river of the true law; all creatures parched by the drought of lust may freely drink thereof, without stint; those enchained in the domain of the five desires, those driven along by many sorrows, and deceived amid the wilderness of birth and death, in ignorance of the way of escape, for these Bodhisattva has been born in the world, to open out a way of salvation. The fire of lust and covetousness, burning with the fuel of the objects of sense, he has caused the cloud of his mercy to rise, so that the rain of the law may extinguish them. The heavy gates of gloomy unbelief, fast kept by covetousness and lust, within which are confined all living things, he opens and gives free deliverance. With the tweezers of his diamond wisdom he plucks out the opposing principles of lustful desire. In the self-twined meshes of folly and ignorance all flesh poor and in misery, helplessly lying, the king of the law has come forth, to rescue these from bondage. Let not the king in respect of this his son encourage in himself one thought of doubt or pain; but rather let him grieve on account of the world, led captive by desire, opposed to truth; but I, indeed, amid the ruins of old age and death, am far removed from the meritorious condition of the holy one, possessed indeed of powers of abstraction, yet not within reach of the gain he will give, to be derived from his teaching as the Bodhisattva; not permitted to hear his righteous law, my body worn out, after death, alas! destined to be born as a Deva [4] still liable to the three calamities, old age, decay, and death, therefore I weep."

The king and all his household attendants, hearing the words

[4] The condition of the highest Deva, according to Buddhism, does not exempt him from re-birth; subject to the calamities incident on such a renewal of life.

of the Rishi, knowing the cause of his regretful sorrow, banished from their minds all further anxiety: "And now," the king said, "to have begotten this excellent son, gives me rést at heart; but that he should leave his kingdom and home, and practise the life of an ascetic, not anxious to ensure the stability of the kingdom, the thought of this still brings with it pain."

At this time the Rishi, turning to the king with true words, said, "It must be even as the king anticipates, he will surely arrive at perfect enlightenment." Thus having appeased every anxious heart among the king's household, the Rishi by his own inherent spiritual power ascended into space and disappeared.

At this time Suddhodana râga, seeing the excellent marks (predictive signs) of his son, and, moreover, hearing the words of Asita, certifying that which would surely happen, was greatly affected with reverence to the child: he redoubled measures for its protection, and was filled with constant thought; moreover, he issued decrees through the empire, to liberate all captives in prison, according to the custom when a royal son was born, giving the usual largess, in agreement with the directions of the Sacred Books, and extending his gifts to all; or, all these things he did completely. When the child was ten days old, his father's mind being now quite tranquil, he announced a sacrifice to all the gods, and prepared to give liberal offerings to all the religious bodies; Srâmanas and Brahmanas invoked by their prayers a blessing from the gods, whilst he bestowed gifts on the royal kinspeople and the ministers and the poor within the country; the women who dwelt in the city or the villages, all those who needed cattle or horses or elephants or money, each, according to his necessities, was liberally supplied. Then, selecting by divination a lucky time, they took the child back to his own palace, with a double-feeding white-pure-tooth, carried in a richly-adorned chariot (cradle), with ornaments of every kind and color round his neck; shining with beauty, exceedingly resplendent with unguents. The queen embracing him in her arms, going around, worshipped the heavenly spirits. Afterwards she remounted her precious chariot, surrounded by her waiting women; the king, with his ministers and people, and all the crowd of attendants, leading the way and following, even as the ruler of heaven, Sakra, is surrounded by crowds of Devas; as Mahesvara, when suddenly his six-faced child was born; arranging every kind of present, gave gifts, and asked for blessings; so now the king, when his royal son was born, made all his arrangements in like manner. So Vaisravana, the heavenly king, when Nalakûvara was born, surrounded by a concourse of Devas, was filled with joy and much gladness; so the king, now the royal prince was born, in the kingdom of Kapila, his people and all his subjects were likewise filled with joy.

Living in the Palace

And now in the household of Suddhodana râga, because of the birth of the royal prince, his clansmen and younger brethren, with his ministers, were all generously disposed, whilst elephants, horses and chariots, and the wealth of the country, and precious vessels, daily increased and abounded, being produced wherever requisite; so, too, countless hidden treasures came of themselves from the earth. From the midst of the pure snowy mountains, a wild herd of white elephants, without noise, of themselves, came; not curbed by any, self-subdued, every kind of colored horse, in shape and quality surpassingly excellent, with sparkling jewelled manes and flowing tails, came prancing round, as if with wings; these too, born in the desert, came at the right time, of themselves. A herd of pure-colored, well-proportioned cows, fat and fleshy, and remarkable for beauty, giving fragrant and pure milk with equal flow, came together in great number at this propitious time. Enmity and envy gave way to peace; content and rest prevailed on every side; whilst there was closer union amongst the true of heart, discord and variance were entirely appeased; the gentle air distilled a seasonable rain, no crash of storm or tempest was heard, the springing seeds, not waiting for their time, grew up apace and yielded abundant increase; the five cereals grew ripe with scented grain, soft and glutinous, easy of digestion; all creatures big with young, possessed their bodies in ease and their frames well gathered. All men, even those who had not received the seeds of instruction derived from the four holy ones;[5] all these, throughout the world, born under the control of selfish appetite, without any thought for others' goods, had no proud, envious longings;

[5] This seems to mean that those who had not received benefit from the teaching of the four previous Buddhas, that even these were placable and well-disposed.

no angry, hateful thoughts. All the temples of the gods and sacred shrines, the gardens, wells, and fountains, all these like things in heaven, produced of themselves, at the proper time, their several adornments. There was no famishing hunger, the soldiers' weapons were at rest, all diseases disappeared; throughout the kingdom all the people were bound close in family love and friendship; piously affectioned they indulged in mutual pleasures, there were no impure or polluting desires; they sought their daily gain righteously, no covetous money-loving spirit prevailed, but with religious purpose they gave liberally; there was no thought of any reward or return, but all practised the four rules of purity; and every hateful thought was suppressed and destroyed. Even as in days gone by, Manu râga begat a child called "Brilliancy of the Sun," on which there prevailed through the country great prosperity, and all wickedness came to an end; so now the king having begotten a royal prince, these marks of prosperity were seen; and because of such a concourse of propitious signs, the child was named Siddhârtha.* And now his royal mother, the queen Mâyâ, beholding her son born under such circumstances, beautiful as a child of heaven, adorned with every excellent distinction, from excessive joy which could not be controlled died, and was born in heaven. Then Pragâpatî Gautamî, beholding the prince, like an angel, with beauty seldom seen on earth, seeing him thus born and now his mother dead, loved and nourished him as her own child; and the child regarded her as his mother.

So as the light of the sun or the moon, little by little increases, the royal child also increased each day in every mental excellency and beauty of person; his body exhaled the perfume of priceless sandal-wood, decorated with the famed Gambunada gold gems; divine medicines there were to preserve him in health, glittering necklaces upon his person; the members of tributary states, hearing that the king had an heir born to him, sent their presents and gifts of various kinds: oxen, sheep, deer, horses, and chariots, precious vessels and elegant ornaments, fit to delight the heart of the prince; but though presented with such pleasing trifles, the necklaces and other pretty ornaments, the mind of the prince was unmoved, his bodily frame small in-

* The description here given of the peace and content prevailing in the world on the birth of Bodhisattva (and his name given to him in consequence) resembles the account of the golden age in classic authors.

deed, but his heart established; his mind at rest within its own high purposes, was not to be disturbed by glittering baubles.

And now he was brought to learn the useful arts, when lo! once instructed he surpassed his teachers. His father, the king, seeing his exceeding talent, and his deep purpose to have done with the world and its allurements, began to inquire as to the names of those in his tribe who were renowned for elegance and refinement. Elegant and graceful, and a lovely maiden, was she whom they called Yasodhârâ; in every way fitting to become a consort for the prince, and to allure by pleasant wiles his heart. The prince with a mind so far removed from the world, with qualities so distinguished, and with so charming an appearance, like the elder son of Brahmadeva, Sanatkumâra (She-na Kiu-ma-lo); the virtuous damsel, lovely and refined, gentle and subdued in manner; majestic like the queen of heaven, constant ever, cheerful night and day, establishing the palace in purity and quiet, full of dignity and exceeding grace, like a lofty hill rising up in space; or as a white autumn cloud; warm or cool according to the season; choosing a proper dwelling according to the year, surrounded by a return of singing women, who join their voices in harmonious heavenly concord, without any jarring or unpleasant sound, exciting in the hearers forgetfulness of worldly cares. As the heavenly Gandharvas of themselves, in their beauteous palaces, cause the singing women to raise heavenly strains, the sounds of which and their beauty ravish both eyes and heart—so Bodhisattva dwelt in his lofty palace, with music such as this. The king, his father, for the prince's sake, dwelt purely in his palace, practising every virtue; delighting in the teaching of the true law, he put away from him every evil companion, that his heart might not be polluted by lust; regarding inordinate desire as poison, keeping his passion and his body in due control, destroying and repressing all trivial thoughts; desiring to enjoy virtuous conversation, loving instruction fit to subdue the hearts of men, aiming to accomplish the conversion of unbelievers; removing all schemes of opposition from whatever source they came by the enlightening power of his doctrine, aiming to save the entire world; thus he desired that the body of people should obtain rest; even as we desire to give peace to our children, so did he long to give rest to the world. He also attended to his religious duties, sacrificing by fire to all the spirits, with clasped hands adoring the moon, bathing his body in the waters of the Ganges; cleansing his heart in the waters of religion, performing his duties with no private aim, but regarding his child and the people at large; loving righteous conversation, righteous words with loving aim; loving words with no mixture of falsehood, true words imbued by love, and yet withal so modest and self-distrustful, unable on that account to speak as confident of truth; loving to all, and yet not loving the world; with no thought of selfishness or covetous desire; aiming to restrain the tongue and in quietness to find rest from wordy contentions, not seeking in the multitude of religious duties to condone for a worldly principle in action, but aiming to benefit the world by a liberal and unostentatious charity; the heart without any contentious thought, but resolved by goodness to subdue the contentious; desiring to mortify the passions, and to destroy every enemy of virtue; not multiplying coarse or unseemly words, but exhorting to virtue in the use of courteous language; full of sympathy and ready charity, pointing out and practising the way of mutual dependence; receiving and understanding the wisdom of spirits and Rishis; crushing and destroying every cruel and hateful thought. Thus his fame and virtue were widely renowned, and yet himself finally (or, forever) separate from the ties of the world, showing the ability of a master builder, laying a good foundation of virtue, an example for all the earth; so a man's heart composed and at rest, his limbs and all his members will also be at ease. And now the son of Suddhodana, and his virtuous wife Yasodharâ, as time went on, growing to full estate, their child Râhula was born; and then Suddhodana râga considered thus: "My son, the prince, having a son born to him, the affairs of the empire will be handed down in succession, and there will be no end to its righteous government; the prince having begotten a son, will love his son as I love him, and no longer think about leaving his home as an ascetic, but devote himself to the practice of virtue; I now have found complete rest of heart, like one just born to heavenly joys."

Like as in the first days of the kalpa, Rishi-kings by the way in which they walked, practising pure and spotless deeds, offered up religious offerings, without harm to living thing, and illustriously prepared an excellent karma, so the king excelling in the excellence of purity in family and excellence of wealth, excelling in strength and every exhibition of prowess, reflected the glory of his name through the world, as the sun sheds abroad his thousand rays. But now, being the king of men, or a king among men, he deemed it right to exhibit his son's prowess, for the sake of his family and kin, to exhibit him; to increase his family's renown, his glory spread so high as even to obtain the name of "God begotten"; and having partaken of these heavenly joys, enjoying the happiness of increased wisdom; understanding the truth by his own righteousness, derived from previous hearing of the truth. Would that this might lead my son, he prayed, to love his child and not forsake his home; the kings of all countries, whose sons have not yet grown up, have prevented them exercising authority in the empire, in order to give their minds relaxation, and for this purpose have provided them with worldly indulgences, so that they may perpetuate the royal seed; so now the king, having begotten a royal son, indulged him in every sort of pleasure; desiring that he might enjoy these worldly delights, and not wish to wander from his home in search of wisdom. In former times the Bodhisattva kings, although their way (life) has been restrained, have yet enjoyed the pleasures of the world, and when they have begotten a son, then separating themselves from family ties, have afterwards entered the solitude of the mountains, to prepare themselves in the way of a silent recluse.

Disgust at Sorrow

Without are pleasant garden glades, flowing fountains, pure refreshing lakes, with every kind of flower, and trees with fruit, arranged in rows, deep shade beneath. There, too, are various kinds of wondrous birds, flying and sporting in the midst, and on the surface of the water the four kinds of flowers, bright colored, giving out their floating scent; minstrel maidens cause their songs and chorded music, to invite the prince. He, hearing the sounds of singing, sighs for the pleasures of the garden shades, and cherishing within these happy thoughts, he dwelt upon the joys of an outside excursion; even as the chained elephant ever longs for the free desert wilds.

The royal father, hearing that the prince would enjoy to wander through the gardens, first ordered all his attendant officers to adorn and arrange them, after their several offices:—To make level and smooth the king's highway, to remove from the path all offensive matter, all old persons, diseased or deformed, all those suffering through poverty or great grief, so that his son in his present humor might see nothing likely to afflict his heart. The adornments being duly made, the prince was invited to an audience; the king seeing his son approach, patted his head, and looking at the color of his face, feelings of sorrow and joy intermingled, bound him. His mouth willing to speak, his heart restrained.

Now see the jewel-fronted gaudy chariot; the four equally pacing, stately horses; good-tempered and well trained; young and of graceful appearance; perfectly pure and white, and draped with flowery coverings. In the same chariot stands the stately driver; the streets were scattered over with flowers; precious drapery fixed on either side of the way, with dwarfed trees lining the road, costly vessels employed for decoration, hanging canopies and variegated banners, silken curtains, moved by the rustling breeze; spectators arranged on either side of the path. With bodies bent and glistening eyes, eagerly gazing, but not rudely staring, as the blue lotus flower they bent drooping in the air, ministers and attendants flocking round him, as stars following the chief of the constellation; all uttering the same suppressed whisper of admiration, at a sight so seldom seen in the world; rich and poor, humble and exalted, old and young and middle-aged, all paid the greatest respect, and invoked blessings on the occasion.

So the country-folk and the town-folk, hearing that the prince was coming forth, the well-to-do not waiting for their servants, those asleep and awake not mutually calling to one another, the six kinds of creatures not gathered together and penned, the money not collected and locked up, the doors and gates not fastened, all went pouring along the way on foot; the towers were filled, the mounds by the trees, the windows and the terraces along the streets; with bent body fearing to lift their eyes, carefully seeing that there was nothing about them to offend, those seated on high addressing those seated on the ground, those going on the road addressing those passing on high, the mind intent on one object alone; so that if a heavenly form had flown past, or a form entitled to highest respect, there would have been no distraction visible, so intent was the body and so immovable the limbs. And now beautiful as the opening lily, he advances towards the garden glades, wishing to accomplish the words of the holy prophet (Rishi). The prince, seeing the ways prepared and watered and the joyous holiday appearance of the people; seeing too the drapery and chariot, pure, bright, shining, his heart exulted greatly and rejoiced. The people (on their part) gazed at the prince, so beautifully adorned, with all his retinue, like an assembled company of kings gathered to see a heaven-born prince. And now a Deva-râga of the Pure abode, suddenly appears by the side of the road; his form changed into that of an old man, struggling for life, his heart weak and oppressed. The prince seeing the old man, filled with apprehension, asked his charioteer, "What kind of man is this? his head white and his shoulders bent, his eyes bleared and his body withered, holding a stick to support him along the way. Is his body suddenly dried up by the heat, or has he been born in this way?" The charioteer, his heart much embarrassed, scarcely dared to answer truly, till the pure-born (Deva) added his spiritual power, and caused him to frame a reply in true words: "His appearance changed, his vital powers decayed, filled with sorrow, with little pleasure, his spirits gone, his members nerveless, these are the indications of what is called 'old age.' This man was once a sucking child, brought up and nourished at his mother's breast, and as a youth full of sportive life, handsome, and in enjoyment of the five pleasures; as years passed on, his frame decaying, he is brought now to the waste of age."

The prince, greatly agitated and moved, asked his charioteer another question and said, "Is yonder man the only one afflicted with age, or shall I, and others also, be such as he?" The charioteer again replied and said, "Your highness also inherits this lot: as time goes on, the form itself is changed, and this must doubtless come, beyond all hindrance. The youthful form must wear the garb of age, throughout the world, this is the common lot."

Bodhisattva, who had long prepared the foundation of pure and spotless wisdom, broadly setting the root of every high quality, with a view to gather large fruit in his present life, hearing these words respecting the sorrow of age, was afflicted in mind, and his hair stood upright. Just as the roll of the thunder and the storm alarm and put to flight the cattle, so was Bodhisattva affected by the words; shaking with apprehension, he deeply sighed; constrained at heart because of the pain of age; with shaking head and constant gaze, he thought upon this misery of decay; what joy or pleasure can men take, he thought, in that which soon must wither, stricken by the marks of age; affecting all without exception; though gifted now with youth and strength, yet not one but soon must change and pine away. The eye beholding such signs as these before it, how can it not be oppressed by a desire to escape? Bodhisattva then addressed his charioteer: "Quickly turn your chariot and go back. Ever thinking on this subject of old age approaching, what pleasures now can these gardens afford, the years of my life like the fast-flying wind; turn your chariot, and with speedy wheels take me to my palace." And so his heart keeping in the same sad tone, he was as one who returns to a place of entombment; unaffected by any engagement or employment, so he found no rest in anything within his home.

The king hearing of his son's sadness urged his companions to induce him again to go abroad, and forthwith incited his ministers and attendants to decorate the gardens even more than before. The Deva then caused himself to appear as a sick man; struggling for life, he stood by the wayside, his body swollen and disfigured, sighing with deep-drawn groans; his hands and knees contracted and sore with disease, his tears flowing as he piteously muttered his petition. The prince asked his charioteer, "What sort of man, again, is this?"

Replying, he said, "This is a sick man. The four elements all confused and disordered, worn and feeble, with no remaining strength, bent down with weakness, looking to his fellow-men for help." The prince hearing the words thus spoken, immediately became sad and depressed in heart, and asked, "Is this the only man afflicted thus, or are others liable to the same calamity?" In reply he said, "Through all the world, men are subject to the same condition; those who have bodies must endure affliction, the poor and ignorant, as well as the rich and great." The prince, when these words met his ears, was oppressed with anxious thought and grief; his body and his mind were moved throughout, just as the moon upon the ruffled tide. "Placed thus in the great furnace of affliction, say! what rest or quiet can there be! Alas! that worldly men, blinded by ignorance and oppressed with dark delusion, though the robber sickness may appear at any time, yet live with blithe and joyous hearts!" On this, turning his chariot back again, he grieved to think upon the pain of sickness. As a man beaten and wounded sore, with body weakened, leans upon his staff, so dwelt he in the seclusion of his palace, lone-seeking, hating worldly pleasures.

The king, hearing once more of his son's return,-asked anxiously the reason why, and in reply was told—" he saw the pain of sickness." The king, in fear, like one beside himself, roundly blamed the keepers of the way; his heart constrained, his lips spoke not; again he increased the crowd of music-women, the sounds of merriment twice louder than aforetime, if by these sounds and sights the prince might be gratified; and indulging worldly feelings, might not hate his home. Night and day the charm of melody increased, but his heart was still unmoved by it. The king himself then went forth to observe everything successively, and to make the gardens even yet more attractive, selecting with care the attendant women, that they might excel in every point of personal beauty; quick in wit and able to arrange matters well, fit to ensnare men by their winning looks; he placed additional keepers along the king's way, he strictly ordered every offensive sight to be removed, and earnestly exhorted the illustrious coachman, to look well and pick out the road as he went. And now that Deva of the Pure abode, again caused the appearance of a dead man; four persons carrying the corpse lifted it on high, and appeared (to be going on) in front of Bodhisattva; the surrounding people saw it not, but only Bodhisattva and the charioteer. Once more he asked, " What is this they carry? with streamers and flowers of every choice description, whilst the followers are overwhelmed with grief, tearing their hair and wailing piteously." And now the gods instructing the coachman, he replied and said, " This is a dead man: all his powers of body destroyed, life departed; his heart without thought, his intellect dispersed; his spirit gone, his form withered and decayed; stretched out as a dead log; family ties broken —all his friends who once loved him, clad in white cerements, now no longer delighting to behold him, remove him to lie in some hollow ditch tomb." The prince hearing the name of Death, his heart constrained by painful thoughts, he asked, " Is this the only dead man, or does the world contain like instances?" Replying thus he said, " All, everywhere, the same; he who begins his life must end it likewise; the strong and lusty and the middle-aged, having a body, cannot but decay and die." The prince was now harassed and perplexed in mind; his body bent upon the chariot leaning-board, with bated breath and struggling accents, stammered thus, "Oh worldly men! how fatally deluded! beholding everywhere the body brought to dust, yet everywhere the more carelessly living; the heart is neither lifeless wood nor stone, and yet it thinks not 'all is vanishing!'" Then turning, he directed his chariot to go back, and no longer waste his time in wandering. How could he, whilst in fear of instant death, go wandering here and there with lightened heart! The charioteer remembering the king's exhortation feared much nor dared go back; straightforward then he pressed his panting steeds, passed onward to the gardens, came to the groves and babbling streams of crystal water, the pleasant trees, spread out with gaudy verdure, the noble living things and varied beasts so wonderful, the flying creatures and their notes melodious; all charming and delightful to the eye and ear, even as the heavenly Nandavana.

Putting Away Desire

On the prince entering the garden the women came around to pay him court; and to arouse in him thoughts frivolous; with ogling ways and deep design, each one setting herself off to best advantage; or joining together in harmonious concert, clapping their hands, or moving their feet in unison, or joining close, body to body, limb to limb; or indulging in smart repartees, and mutual smiles; or assuming a thoughtful saddened countenance, and so by sympathy to please the prince, and provoke in him a heart affected by love. But all the women beheld the prince, clouded in brow, and his god-like body not exhibiting its wonted signs of beauty; fair in bodily appearance, surpassingly lovely, all looked upwards as they gazed, as when we call upon the moon Deva to come; but all their subtle devices were ineffectual to move Bodhisattva's heart.

At last commingling together they join and look astonished and in fear, silent without a word. Then there was a Brahmaputra, whose name was called Udâyi (Yau-to-i). He, addressing the women, said, "Now all of you, so graceful and fair, see if you cannot by your combined power hit on some device; for beauty's power is not forever. Still it holds the world in bondage, by secret ways and lustful arts; but no such loveliness in all the world as yours, equal to that of heavenly nymphs; the gods beholding it would leave their queens, spirits and Rishis would be misled by it; why not then the prince, the son of an earthly king? why should not his feelings be aroused? This prince indeed, though he restrains his heart and holds it fixed, pure-minded, with virtue uncontaminated, not to be overcome by power of women; yet of old there was Sundarî (Su-to-li) able to destroy the great Rishi, and to lead him to indulge in love, and so degrade his boasted eminence; undergoing long penance, Gautama fell likewise by the arts of a heavenly queen; Shing-kü, a Rishi putra, practising lustful indulgences according to fancy, was lost. The Brahman Rishi Visvâmitra (Pi-she-po), living religiously for ten thousand years, deeply ensnared by a heavenly queen, in one day was completely shipwrecked in faith; thus those enticing women, by their power, overcame the Brahman ascetics; how much more may ye, by your arts, overpower the resolves of the king's son; strive therefore after new devices, let not the king fail in a successor to the throne; women, though naturally weak, are high and potent in the way of ruling men. What may not their arts accomplish in promoting in men a lustful desire?" At this time all the attendant women, hearing throughout the words of Udâyi, increasing their powers of pleasing, as the quiet horse when touched by the whip, went into the presence of the royal prince, and each one strove in the practice of every kind of art. They joined in music and in smiling conversation, raising their eyebrows, showing their white teeth, with ogling looks, glancing one at the other, their light drapery exhibiting their white bodies, daintily moving with mincing gait, acting the part of a bride as if coming gradually nearer, desiring to promote in him a feeling of love, remembering the words of the great king, "With dissolute form and slightly clad, forgetful of modesty and womanly reserve." The prince with resolute heart was silent and still, with unmoved face he sat; even as the great elephant-dragon, whilst the entire herd moves round him; so nothing could disturb or move his heart, dwelling in their midst as in a confined room. Like the divine Sakra, around whom all the Devîs assemble, so was the prince as he dwelt in the gardens; the maidens encircling him thus; some arranging their dress, others washing their hands or feet, others perfuming their bodies with scent, others twining flowers for decoration, others making strings for jewelled necklets, others rubbing or striking their bodies, others resting, or lying, one beside the other; others, with head inclined, whispering secret words, others engaged in common sports, others talking of amorous things, others assuming lustful attitudes, striving thus to move his heart. But Bodhisattva, peaceful and collected, firm as a rock, difficult to move, hearing all these women's talk, unaffected either to joy or sorrow, was driven still more to serious thought, sighing to witness such strange conduct, and beginning to understand the women's design, by these means to disconcert his mind, not knowing that youthful beauty soon falls, destroyed by old age and death, fading and perishing! This is the great distress! What ignorance and delusion (he reflected) overshadow their minds: "Surely they ought to consider old age, disease, and death, and day and night stir themselves up to exertion, whilst this sharp double-edged sword hangs over the neck. What room for sport or laughter, beholding those monsters, old age, disease, and death? A man who is unable to resort to this inward knowledge, what is he but a wooden or a plaster man, what heart-consideration in such a case! Like the double tree that appears in the desert, with leaves and fruit all perfect and ripe, the first cut down and destroyed, the other unmoved by apprehension, so it is in the case of the mass of men: they have no understanding either!"

At this time Udâyi came to the place where the prince was, and observing his silent and thoughtful mien, unmoved by any desire for indulgence, he forthwith addressed the prince, and said, "The Mahâraga, by his former appointment, has selected me to act as friend to his son; may I therefore speak some friendly words? an enlightened friendship is of three sorts: that which removes things unprofitable, promotes that which is real gain, and stands by a friend in adversity. I claim the name of 'enlightened friend,' and would renounce all that is magisterial, but yet not speak lightly or with indifference. What then are the three sources of advantage? listen, and I will now utter true words, and prove myself a true and sincere adviser. When the years are fresh and ripening, beauty and pleasing qualities in bloom, not to give proper weight to woman's influence, this is a weak man's policy. It is right sometimes to be of a crafty mind, submitting to those little subterfuges which find a place in the heart's undercurrents, and obeying what those thoughts suggest in way of pleasures to be got from dalliance: this is no wrong in woman's eye! even if now the heart has no desire, yet it is fair to follow such devices; agreement is the joy of woman's heart, acquiescence is the substance (the full) of true adornment; but if a man reject these overtures, he's like a tree deprived of leaves and fruits; why then ought you to yield and acquiesce? that you may share in all these things. Because in taking, there's an end of trouble—no light and changeful thoughts then worry us—for pleasure is the first and foremost thought of all, the gods themselves cannot dispense with it. Lord Sakra was drawn by it to love the wife of Gautama the Rishi; so likewise the Rishi Agastya, through a long period of discipline, practising austerities, from hankering after a heavenly queen (Devî), lost all reward of his religious endeavors, the Rishi Brihaspati, and Kandradeva putra; the Rishi Parâsara, and Kavañgara (Kia-pin-ke-lo). All these, out of many others, were overcome by woman's love. How much more then, in your case, should you partake in such pleasant joys; nor refuse, with wilful heart, to participate in the worldly delights, which your present station, possessed of such advantages, offers you, in the presence of these attendants."

At this time the royal prince, hearing the words of his friend Udâyi, so skilfully put, with such fine distinction, cleverly citing worldly instances, answered thus to Udâyi: "Thank you for having spoken sincerely to me; let me likewise answer you in the same way, and let your heart suspend its judgment whilst you listen:—It is not that I am careless about beauty, or am ignorant of the power of human joys, but only that I see on all the impress of change; therefore my heart is sad and heavy; if these things were sure of lasting, without the ills of age, disease, and death, then would I too take my fill of love; and to the end find no disgust or sadness. If you will undertake to cause these women's beauty not to change or wither in the future, then, though the joy of love may have its evil, still it might hold the mind in thraldom. To know that other men grow old, sicken, and die, would be enough to rob such joys of satisfaction; yet how much more in their own case (knowing this) would discontentment fill the mind; to know such pleasures hasten to decay, and their bodies likewise; if, notwithstanding this, men yield to the power of love, their case indeed is like the very beasts. And now you cite the names of many Rishis, who practised lustful ways in life; their cases likewise cause me sorrow, for in that they did these things, they perished. Again, you cite the name of that illustrious king, who freely gratified his passions, but he, in like way, perished in the act; know, then, that he was not a conqueror; with smooth words to conceal an intrigue, and to persuade one's neighbor to consent, and by consenting to defile his mind; how can this be called a just device? It is but to seduce one with a hollow lie—such ways are not for me to practise; or, for those who love the truth and honesty; for they are, forsooth, unrighteous ways, and such a disposition is hard to reverence; shaping one's conduct after one's likings, liking this or that, and seeing no harm in it, what method of experience is this! A hollow compliance, and a protesting heart, such method is not for me to follow; but this I know, old age, disease, and death, these are the great afflictions which accumulate, and overwhelm me with their presence; on these I find no friend to speak, alas! alas! Udâyi! these, after all, are the great concerns; the pain of birth, old age, disease, and death; this grief is that we have to fear; the eyes see all things falling to decay, and yet the heart finds joy in following them; but I have little strength of purpose, or command; this heart of mine is feeble and distraught, reflecting thus on age, disease, and death. Distracted, as I never was before; sleepless by night and day, how can I then indulge in pleasure? Old age, disease, and death consuming me, their certainty beyond a doubt, and still to have no heavy thoughts, in truth my heart would be a log or stone." Thus the prince, for Uda's sake, used every kind of skilful argument, describing all the pains of pleasure; and not perceiving that the day declined. And now the waiting women all, with music and their various attractions, seeing that all were useless for the end, with shame began to flock back to the city; the prince beholding all the gardens, bereft of their gaudy ornaments, the women all returning home, the place becoming silent and deserted, felt with twofold strength the thought of impermanence. With saddened mien going back, he entered his palace.

The king, his father, hearing of the prince, his heart estranged from thoughts of pleasure, was greatly overcome with sorrow, and like a sword it pierced his heart. Forthwith assembling all his council, he sought of them some means to gain his end; they all replied, "These sources of desire are not enough to hold and captivate his heart."

Leaving the City

And so the king increased the means for gratifying the appetite for pleasure; both night and day the joys of music wore out the prince, opposed to pleasure; disgusted with them, he desired their absence, his mind was weaned from all such thoughts, he only thought of age, disease, and death; as the lion wounded by an arrow.

The king then sent his chief ministers, and the most distinguished of his family, young in years and eminent for beauty, as well as for wisdom and dignity of manners, to accompany and rest with him, both night and day, in order to influence the prince's mind. And now within a little interval, the prince again requested the king that he might go abroad.

Once more the chariot and the well-paced horses were prepared, adorned with precious substances and every gem; and then with all the nobles, his associates, surrounding him, he left the city gates. Just as the four kinds of flower, when the sun shines, open out their leaves, so was the prince in all his spiritual splendor; effulgent in the beauty of his youth-time. As he proceeded to the gardens from the city, the road was well prepared, smooth, and wide, the trees were bright with flowers and fruit, his heart was joyous, and forgetful of its care.

Now by the roadside, as he beheld the ploughmen, plodding along the furrows, and the writhing worms, his heart again was moved with piteous feeling, and anguish pierced his soul afresh; to see those laborers at their toil, struggling with painful work, their bodies bent, their hair dishevelled, the dripping sweat upon their faces, their persons fouled with mud and dust; the ploughing oxen, too, bent by the yokes, their lolling tongues and gaping mouths. The nature of the prince, loving, compassionate, his mind conceived most poignant sorrow, and nobly moved to sympathy, he groaned with pain; then stooping down he sat upon the ground, and watched this painful scene of suffering; reflecting on the ways of birth and death! "Alas! he cried, for all the world! how dark and ignorant, void of understanding!" And then to give his followers chance of rest, he bade them each repose where'er they list, whilst he beneath the shadow of a Gambu tree, gracefully seated, gave himself to thought. He pondered on the fact of life and death, inconstancy, and endless progress to decay. His heart thus fixed without confusion, the five senses covered and clouded over, lost in possession of enlightenment and insight, he entered on the first pure state of ecstasy. All low desire removed, most perfect peace ensued; and fully now in Samâdhi he saw the misery and utter sorrow of the world; the ruin wrought by age, disease, and death; the great misery following on the body's death; and yet men not awakened to the truth! oppressed with others' suffering (age, disease, and death), this load of sorrow weighed his mind. "I now will seek," he said, "a noble law, unlike the worldly methods known to men. I will oppose disease and age and death, and strive against the mischief wrought by these on men."

Thus lost in tranquil contemplation, he considered that youth, vigor, and strength of life, constantly renewing themselves, without long stay, in the end fulfil the rule of ultimate destruction. Thus he pondered, without excessive joy or grief, without hesitation or confusion of thought, without dreaminess or extreme longing, without aversion or discontent, but perfectly at peace, with no hindrance, radiant with the beams of increased illumination. At this time a Deva of the Pure abode, transforming himself into the shape of a Bhikshu, came to the place where the prince was seated; the prince with due consideration rose to meet him, and asked him who he was. In reply he said, "I am a Shâman, depressed and sad at thought of age, disease, and death; I have left my home to seek some way of rescue, but everywhere I find old age, disease, and death; all things hasten to decay and there is no permanency. Therefore I search for the happiness of something that decays not, that never perishes, that never knows beginning, that looks with equal mind on enemy and friend, that heeds not wealth nor beauty; the happiness of one who finds repose alone in solitude, in some unfrequented dell, free from molestation, all thoughts about the world destroyed; dwelling in some lonely hermitage, untouched by any worldly source of pollution, begging for food sufficient for the body." And forthwith as he stood before the prince, gradually rising up he disappeared in space.

The prince, with joyful mind, considering, recollected former Buddhas, established thus in perfect dignity of manner; with noble mien and presence, as this visitor. Thus calling things to mind with perfect self-possession, he reached the thought of righteousness, and by what means it can be gained Indulging thus for some time in thoughts of religious solitude, he now suppressed his feelings and controlled his members, and rising turned again towards the city. His followers all flocked after him, calling him to stop and not go far from them, but in his mind these secret thoughts so held him, devising means by which to escape from the world, that though his body moved along the road, his heart was far away among the mountains; even as the bound and captive elephant ever thinks about his desert wilds. The prince now entering the city, there met him men and women, earnest for their several ends; the old besought him for their children, the young sought something for the wife, others sought something for their brethren; all those allied by kinship or by family, aimed to obtain their several suits, all of them joined in relationship dreading the pain of separation. And now the prince's heart was filled with joy, as he suddenly heard those words " separation and association." " These are joyful sounds to me," he said, " they assure me that my vow shall be accomplished." Then deeply pondering the joy of " snapped relationship," the idea of Nirvâna, deepened and widened in him, his body as a peak of the Golden Mount, his shoulder like the elephant's, his voice like the spring-thunder, his deep-blue eye like that of the king of oxen; his mind full of religious thoughts, his face bright as the full moon, his step like that of the lion king, thus he entered his palace; even as the son of Lord Sakra, or Sakra-putra, his mind reverential, his person dignified, he went straight to his father's presence, and with head inclined, inquired, " Is the king well? " Then he explained his dread of age, disease, and death, and sought respectfully permission to become a hermit. " For all things in the world," he said, " though now united, tend to separation." Therefore he prayed to leave the world; desiring to find " true deliverance."

His royal father hearing the words " leave the world," was forthwith seized with great heart-trembling, even as the strong wild elephant shakes with his weight the boughs of some young sapling; going forward, seizing the prince's hands, with falling tears, he spake as follows: " Stop! nor speak such words, the time is not yet come for ' a religious life; ' you are young and strong, your heart beats full, to lead a religious life frequently involves trouble; it is rarely possible to hold the desires in check, the heart not yet estranged from their enjoyment; to leave your home and lead a painful ascetic life, your heart can hardly yet resolve on such a course. To dwell amidst the desert wilds or lonely dells, this heart of yours would not be perfectly at rest, for though you love religious matters, you are not yet like me in years; you should undertake the kingdom's government, and let me first adopt ascetic life; but to give up your father and your sacred duties, this is not to act religiously; you should suppress this thought of 'leaving home,' and undertake your worldly duties, find your delight in getting an illustrious name, and after this give up your home and family."

The prince, with proper reverence and respectful feelings, again besought his royal father; but promised if he could be saved from four calamities, that he would give up the thought of "leaving home." If he would grant him life without end, no disease, nor undesirable old age, and no decay of earthly possessions, then he would obey and give up the thought of "leaving home."

The royal father then addressed the prince, "Speak not such words as these, for with respect to these four things, who is there able to prevent them, or say nay to their approach; asking such things as these, you would provoke men's laughter! But put away this thought of 'leaving home,' and once more take yourself to pleasure."

The prince again besought his father, "If you may not grant me these four prayers, then let me go I pray, and leave my home. O! place no difficulties in my path; your son is dwelling in a burning house, would you indeed prevent his leaving it! To solve a doubt is only reasonable, who could forbid a man to seek its explanation? Or if he were forbidden, then by self-destruction he might solve the difficulty, in an unrighteous way: and if he were to do so, who could restrain him after death?"

The royal father, seeing his son's mind so firmly fixed that it could not be turned, and that it would be waste of strength to bandy further words or arguments, forthwith commanded more attendant women, to provoke still more his mind to pleasure; day and night he ordered them to keep the roads and ways, to the end that he might not leave his palace. He moreover ordered all the ministers of the country to come to the place where dwelt the prince, to quote and illustrate the rules of filial piety, hoping to cause him to obey the wishes of the king.

The prince, beholding his royal father bathed with tears and o'erwhelmed with grief, forthwith returned to his abode, and sat himself in silence to consider; all the women of the palace, coming towards him, waited as they circled him, and gazed in silence on his beauteous form. They gazed upon him not with furtive glance, but like the deer in autumn brake looks wistfully at the hunter; around the prince's straight and handsome form, bright as the mountain of true gold (Sumeru). The dancing women gathered doubtingly, waiting to hear him bid them sound their music; repressing every feeling of the heart through fear, even as the deer within the brake; now gradually the day began to wane, the prince still sitting in the evening light, his glory streaming forth in splendor, as the sun lights up Mount Sumeru; thus seated on his jewelled couch, surrounded by the fumes of sandal-wood, the dancing women took their places round; then sounded forth their heavenly music, even as Vaisaman produces every kind of rare and heavenly sounds. The thoughts which dwelt within the prince's mind entirely drove from him desire for music, and though the sounds filled all the place, they fell upon his ear unnoticed. At this time the Deva of the Pure abode, knowing the prince's time was come, the destined time for quitting home, suddenly assumed a form and came to earth, to make the shapes of all the women unattractive, so that they might create disgust, and no desire arise from thought of beauty. Their half-clad forms bent in ungainly attitudes, forgetful in their sleep, their bodies crooked or supine, the instruments of music lying scattered in disorder; leaning and facing one another, or with back to back, or like those beings thrown into the abyss, their jewelled necklets bound about like chains, their clothes and undergarments swathed around their persons; grasping their instruments, stretched along the earth, even as those undergoing punishment at the hands of keepers, their garments in confusion, or like the broken kani flower; or some with bodies leaning in sleep against the wall, in fashion like a hanging bow or horn, or with their hands holding to the window-frames, and looking like an outstretched corpse. Their mouths half opened or else gaping wide, the loathsome dribble trickling forth, their heads uncovered and in wild disorder, like some unreasoning madman's; the flower wreaths torn and hanging across their face, or slipping off the face upon the ground; others with body raised as if in fearful dread, just like the lonely desert bird; or others pillowed on their neighbor's lap, their hands and feet entwined together, whilst others smiled or knit their brows in turn; some with eyes closed and open mouth, their bodies lying in wild disorder, stretched here and there, like corpses thrown together. And now the prince seated, in his beauty, looked with thought on all the waiting women; before, they had appeared exceeding lovely, their laughing words, their hearts so light and gay, their forms so plump and young, their looks so bright; but now, how changed! so uninviting and repulsive. And such is woman's disposition! how can they, then, be ever dear, or closely trusted; such false appearances! and unreal pretences; they only madden and delude the minds of men.

"And now," he said, "I have awakened to the truth! Resolved am I to leave such false society." At this time the Deva of the Pure abode descended and approached, unfastening the doors. The prince, too, at this time rose and walked along, amid the prostrate forms of all the women; with difficulty reaching the inner hall, he called to Kandaka, in these words, "My mind is now athirst and longing for the draught of the fountain of sweet dew; saddle then my horse, and quickly bring it here. I wish to reach the deathless city; my heart is fixed beyond all change, resolved I am and bound by sacred oath; these women, once so charming and enticing, now behold I altogether loathsome; the gates, which were before fast-barred and locked, now stand free and open! these evidences of something supernatural, point to a climax of my life."

Then Kandaka stood reflecting inwardly, whether to obey or not the prince's order, without informing his royal father of it, and so incur the heaviest punishment.

The Devas then gave spiritual strength; and unperceived the horse equipped came round, with even pace; a gallant steed, with all his jewelled trappings for a rider; high-maned, with flowing tail, broad-backed, short-haired and eared, with belly like the deer's, head like the king of parrots, wide forehead, round and claw-shaped nostrils, breath like the dragon's, with breast and shoulders square, true and sufficient marks of his high breed. The royal prince, stroking the horse's neck, and rubbing down his body, said, "My royal father ever rode on thee, and found thee brave in fight and fearless of the foe; now I desire to rely on thee alike! to carry me far off to the stream (ford) of endless life, to fight against and overcome the opposing force of men, the men who associate in search of pleasure, the men who engage in the search after wealth, the crowds who follow and flatter such persons; in opposing sorrow, friendly help is difficult to find, in seeking religious truth there must be rare enlightenment, let us then be knit together thus as friends; then, at last, there will be rest from sorrow. But now I wish to go abroad, to give deliverance from pain; now then, for your own sake it is, and for the sake of all your kind, that you should exert your strength, with noble pace, without lagging or weariness." Having thus exhorted him, he bestrode his horse, and grasping the reins proceeded forth; the man like the sun shining forth from his tabernacle, the horse like the white floating cloud, exerting himself but without exciting haste, his breath concealed and without snorting; four spirits (Devas) accompanying him, held up his feet, heedfully concealing his advance, silently and without noise; the heavy gates fastened and barred, the heavenly spirits of themselves caused to open. Reverencing deeply the virtuous father, loving deeply the unequalled son, equally affected with love towards all the members of his family these Devas took their place.

Suppressing his feelings, but not extinguishing his memory, lightly he advanced and proceeded beyond the city, pure and spotless as the lily flowers which spring from the mud; looking up with earnestness at his father's palace, he announced his purpose—unwitnessed and unwritten—"If I escape not birth, old age, and death, for evermore I pass not thus along." All the concourse of Devas, the space-filling Nâgas and spirits followed joyfully and exclaimed, "Well! well!" in confirmation of the true words he spoke. The Nâgas and the company of Devas acquired a condition of heart difficult to obtain, and each with his own inherent light led on the way shedding forth their brightness. Thus man and horse, both strong of heart, went onwards, lost to sight like streaming stars, but ere the eastern quarter flashed with light, they had advanced three yoganas.

CHAPTER II

The Return of Kandaka

AND now the night was in a moment gone, and sight restored to all created things, when the royal prince looked through the wood, and saw the abode of Po-ka, the Rishi. The purling streams so exquisitely pure and sparkling, and the wild beasts all unalarmed at man, caused the royal prince's heart to exult. Tired, the horse stopped of his own will, to breathe. "This, then," he thought, "is a good sign and fortunate, and doubtless indicates divine approval." And now he saw belonging to the Rishi, the various vessels used for asking charity, and other things arranged by him in order, without the slightest trace of negligence. Dismounting then he stroked his horse's head, and cried, "You now have borne me well!"

With loving eyes he looked at Kandaka: eyes like the pure cool surface of a placid lake and said, "Swift-footed! like a horse in pace, yea! swift as any light-winged bird, ever have you followed after me when riding, and deeply have I felt my debt of thanks, but not yet had you been tried in other ways; I only knew you as a man true-hearted, my mind now wonders at your active powers of body; these two I now begin to see are yours; a man may have a heart most true and faithful, but strength of body may not too be his; bodily strength and perfect honesty of heart, I now have proof enough are yours. To be content to leave the tinselled world, and with swift foot to follow me, who would do this but for some profit; if without profit to his kin, who would not shun it? But you, with no private aim, have followed me, not seeking any present recompense; as we nourish and bring up a child, to bind together and bring honor to a family, so we also reverence and obey a father, to gain obedience and attention from a begotten son; in this way all think of their own advantage; but you have come with me disdaining profit; with many words I cannot hold you here, so let me say in brief to you, we have now ended our relationship; take, then, my horse and ride back again; for me, during the long night past, that place I sought to reach now I have obtained."

Then taking off his precious neck-chain, he handed it to Kandaka. "Take this," he said, "I give it you, let it console you in your sorrow." The precious jewel in the tire that bound his head, bright-shining, lighting up his person, taking off and placing in his extended palm, like the sun which lights up Sumeru, he said, "O Kandaka! take this gem, and going back to where my father is, take the jewel and lay it reverently before him, to signify my heart's relation to him; and then, for me, request the king to stifle every fickle feeling of affection, and say that I, to escape from birth and age and death, have entered on the wild forest of painful discipline; not that I may get a heavenly birth, much less because I have no tenderness of heart, or that I cherish any cause of bitterness, but only that I may escape this weight of sorrow. The accumulated long-night weight of covetous desire (love), I now desire to ease the load so that it may be overthrown forever; therefore I seek the way of ultimate escape; if I should obtain emancipation, then shall I never need to put away my kindred, to leave my home, to sever ties of love. O! grieve not for your son! The five desires of sense beget the sorrow; those held by lust themselves induce the sorrow. My very ancestors, victorious kings, thinking their throne established and immovable, have handed down to me their kingly wealth; I, thinking only on religion, put it all away; the royal mothers at the end of life their cherished treasures leave for their sons, those sons who covet much such worldly profit; but I rejoice to have acquired religious wealth; if you say that I am young and tender, and that the time for seeking wisdom is not come, you ought to know that to seek true religion, there never is a time not fit; impermanence and fickleness, the hate of death, these ever follow us, and therefore I embrace the present day, convinced that now is time to seek religion. With such entreaties as the above, you must make matters plain on my behalf; but, pray you, cause my father not to think longingly after me; let him destroy all recollection of me, and cut out from his soul the ties of love; and you, grieve not because of what I say, but recollect to give the king my message."

Kandaka hearing respectfully the words of exhortation, blinded and confused through choking sorrow, with hands outstretched did worship; and answering the prince, he spoke, "The orders that you give me will, I fear, add grief to grief, and sorrow thus increased will deepen, as the elephant who struggles into deeper mire. When the ties of love are rudely snapped, who, that has any heart, would not grieve! The golden ore may still by stamping be broken up, how much more the feelings choked with sorrow! the prince has grown up in a palace, with every care bestowed upon his tender person, and now he gives his body to the rough and thorny forest; how will he be able to bear a life of privation? When first you ordered me to equip your steed, my mind was indeed sorely troubled, but the heavenly powers urged me on, causing me to hasten the preparation of the horse, but what is the intention that urges the prince, to resolve thus to leave his secure palace? The people of Kapilavastu, and all the country afflicted with grief; your father, now an old man, mindful of his son, loving him moreover tenderly; surely this determination to leave your home, this is not according to duty; it is wrong, surely, to disregard father and mother—we cannot speak of such a thing with propriety! Gotamî, too, who has nourished you so long, fed you with milk when a helpless child, such love as hers cannot easily be forgotten; it is impossible surely to turn the back on a benefactor; the highly gifted virtuous mother of a child, is ever respected by the most distinguished families; to inherit distinction and then to turn round, is not the mark of a distinguished man. The illustrious child of Yasodharâ, who has inherited a kingdom, rightly governed, his years now gradually ripening, should not thus go away from and forsake his home; but though he has gone away from his royal father, and forsaken his family and his kin, forbid it he should still drive me away, let me not depart from the feet of my master; my heart is bound to thee, as the heat is bound up in the boiling water. I cannot return without thee to my country; to return and leave the prince thus, in the midst of the solitude of the desert, then should I be like Sumanta, who left and forsook Râma; and now if I return alone to the palace, what words can I address to the king? How can I reply to the reproaches of all the dwellers in the palace with suitable words? Therefore let the prince rather tell me, how I may truly describe, and with what device, the disfigured body, and the merit-seeking condition of the hermit! I am full of fear and alarm, my tongue can utter no words; tell me then what words to speak; but who is there in the empire will believe me? If I say that the moon's rays are scorching, there are men, perhaps, who may believe me; but they will not believe that the prince, in his conduct, will act without piety; for the prince's heart is sincere and refined, always actuated with pity and love to men. To be deeply affected with love, and yet to forsake the object of love, this surely is opposed to a constant mind. O then, for pity's sake! return to your home, and thus appease my foolish longings."

The prince having listened to Kandaka, pitying his grief expressed in so many words, with heart resolved and strong in its determination, spoke thus to him once more, and said: "Why thus on my account do you feel the pain of separation? you should overcome this sorrowful mood, it is for you to comfort yourself; all creatures, each in its way, foolishly arguing that all things are constant, would influence me to-day not to forsake my kin and relatives; but when dead and come to be a ghost, how then, let them say, can I be kept? My loving mother when she bore me, with deep affection painfully carried me, and then when born she died, not permitted to nourish me. One alive, the other dead, gone by different roads, where now shall she be found? Like as in a wilderness, on some high tree, all the birds living with their mates assemble in the evening and at dawn disperse, so are the separations of the world; the floating clouds rise like a high mountain, from the four quarters they fill the void, in a moment again they are separated and disappear; so is it with the habitations of men; people from the beginning have erred thus, binding themselves in society and by the ties of love, and then, as after a dream, all is dispersed; do not then recount the names of my relatives; for like the wood which is produced in spring, gradually grows and brings forth its leaves, which again fall in the autumn-chilly-dews—if the different parts of the same body are thus divided—how much more men who are united in society! and how shall the ties of relationship escape rending? Cease therefore your grief and expostulation, obey my commands and return home; the thought of your return alone will save me, and perhaps after your return I also may come back. The men of Kapilavastu, hearing that my heart is fixed, will dismiss from their minds all thought of me, but you may make known my words, 'when I have escaped from the sad ocean of birth and death, then afterwards I will come back again; but I am resolved, if I obtain not my quest, my body shall perish in the mountain wilds.'" The white horse hearing the prince, as he uttered these true and earnest words, bent his knee and licked his foot, whilst he sighed deeply and wept. Then the prince with his soft and glossy palm, fondly stroking the head of the white horse, said, "Do not let sorrow rise within, I grieve indeed at losing you, my gallant steed—so strong and active, your merit now has gained its end; you shall enjoy for long a respite from an evil birth, but for the present take as your reward these precious jewels and this glittering sword, and with them follow closely after Kandaka." The prince then drawing forth his sword, glancing in the light as the dragon's eye, cut off the knot of hair with its jewelled stud, and forthwith cast it into space; ascending upwards to the firmament, it floated there as the wings of the phœnix; then all the Devas of the Trayastrimsa heavens seizing the hair, returned with it to their heavenly abodes; desiring always to adore the feet (offer religious service), how much rather now possessed of the crowning locks, with unfeigned piety do they increase their adoration, and shall do till the true law has died away.

Then the royal prince thought thus, "My adornments now are gone forever, there only now remain these silken garments, which are not in keeping with a hermit's life."

Then the Deva of the Pure abode, knowing the heart-ponderings of the prince, transformed himself into a hunter's likeness, holding his bow, his arrows in his girdle, his body girded with a Kashâya-colored robe, thus he advanced in front of the prince. The prince considering this garment of his, the color of the ground, a fitting pure attire, becoming to the utmost the person of a Rishi, not fit for a hunter's dress, forthwith called to the hunter, as he stood before him, in accents soft, and thus addressed him: "That dress of thine belikes me much, as if it were not foul, and this my dress I'll give thee in exchange, so please thee."

The hunter then addressed the prince, "Although I ill can spare this garment, which I use as a disguise among the deer, that alluring them within reach I may kill them, notwithstanding, as it so pleases you, I am now willing to bestow it in exchange for yours." The hunter having received the sumptuous dress, took again his heavenly body.

The prince and Kandaka, the coachman, seeing this, thought deeply thus: "This garment is of no common character, it is not what a worldly man has worn"—and in the prince's heart great joy arose, as he regarded the coat with double reverence, and forthwith giving all the other things to Kandaka, he himself was clad in it, of Kashâya color; then like the dark and lowering cloud, that surrounds the disc of the sun or moon, he for a moment gazed, scanning his steps, then entered on the hermit's grot; Kandaka following him with wistful eyes, his body disappeared, nor was it seen again. "My lord and master now has left his father's house, his kinsfolk and myself," he cried; "he now has clothed himself in hermit's garb, and entered the painful forest." Raising his hands he called on Heaven, o'erpowered with grief he could not move; till holding by the white steed's neck, he tottered forward on the homeward road, turning again and often looking back, his body going on, his heart back-hastening; now lost in thought and self-forgetful, now looking down to earth, then raising up his drooping eye to heaven, falling at times and then rising again, thus weeping as he went, he pursued his way homewards.

Entering the Place of Austerities

The prince having dismissed Kandaka, as he entered the Rishis' abode, his graceful body brightly shining, lit up on every side the forest "place of suffering"; himself gifted with every excellence, according to his gifts, so were they reflected. As the lion, the king of beasts, when he enters among the herd of beasts, drives from their minds all thoughts of common things, as now they watch the true form of their kind, so those Rishi masters assembled there, suddenly perceiving the miraculous portent, were struck with awe and fearful gladness, as they gazed with earnest eyes and hands conjoined. The men and women, engaged in various occupations, beholding him, with unchanged attitudes, gazed as the gods look on King Sakra, with constant look and eyes unmoved; so the Rishis, with their feet fixed fast, looked at him even thus; whatever in their hands they held, without releasing it, they stopped and looked; even as the ox when yoked to the wain, his body bound, his mind also restrained; so also the followers of the holy Rishis, each called the other to behold the miracle. The peacocks and the other birds with cries commingled flapped their wings; the Brahmakârins holding the rules of deer, following the deer wandering through mountain glades, as the deer coarse of nature, with flashing eyes, regard the prince with fixed gaze; so following the deer, those Brahmakârins intently gaze likewise, looking at the exceeding glory of the Ikshvâku. As the glory of the rising sun is able to affect the herds of milch kine, so as to increase the quantity of their sweet-scented milk, so those Brahmakârins, with wondrous joy, thus spoke one to the other: "Surely this is one of the eight Vasu Devas"; others, "this is one of the two Asvins"; others, "this is Mâra"; others, "this is one of the Brahmakâyikas"; others, "this is Sûryadeva or Kandradeva, coming down; are they not seeking here a sacrifice which is their due? Come let us haste to offer our religious services!"

The prince, on his part, with respectful mien addressed to them polite salutation. Then Bodhisattva, looking with care in every direction on the Brahmakârins occupying the wood, each engaged in his religious duties, all desirous of the delights of heaven, addressed the senior Brahmakârin, and asked him as to the path of true religion. "Now having just come here, I do not yet know the rules of your religious life. I ask you therefore for information, and I pray explain to me what I ask."

On this that twice-born (Brahman) in reply explained in succession all the modes of painful discipline, and the fruits expected as their result. How some ate nothing brought from inhabited places but that produced from pure water, others edible roots and tender twigs, others fruits and flowers fit for food, each according to the rules of his sect, clothing and food in each case different; some living amongst bird-kind, and like them capturing and eating food; others eating as the deer the grass and herbs; others living like serpents, inhaling air; others eating nothing pounded in wood or stone; some eating with two teeth, till a wound be formed; others, again, begging their food and giving it in charity, taking only the remnants for themselves; others, again, who let water continually drip on their heads and those who offer up with fire; others who practise water-dwelling like fish; thus there are Brahmakârins of every sort, who practise austerities, that they may at the end of life obtain a birth in heaven, and by their present sufferings afterwards obtain peaceable fruit."

The lord of men, the excellent master, hearing all their modes of sorrow-producing penance, not perceiving any element of truth in them, experienced no joyful emotion in his heart; lost in thought, he regarded the men with pity, and with his heart in agreement his mouth thus spake: "Pitiful indeed are such sufferings! and merely in quest of a human or heavenly reward, ever revolving in the cycle of birth or death, how great your sufferings, how small the recompense! Leaving your friends, giving up honorable position; with a firm purpose to obtain the joys of heaven, although you may escape little sorrows, yet in the end involved in great sorrow; promoting the destruction of your outward form, and undergoing every kind of painful penance, and yet seeking to obtain another birth; increasing and prolonging the causes of the five desires, not considering that herefrom birth and death, undergoing suffering and, by that, seeking further suffering; thus it is that the world of men, though dreading the approach of death, yet strive after renewed birth; and being thus born, they must die again. Although still dreading the power of suffering, yet prolonging their stay in the sea of pain. Disliking from their heart their present kind of life, yet still striving incessantly after other life; enduring affliction that they may partake of joy; seeking a birth in heaven, to suffer further trouble; seeking joys, whilst the heart sinks with feebleness. For this is so with those who oppose right reason; they cannot but be cramped and poor at heart. But by earnestness and diligence, then we conquer. Walking in the path of true wisdom, letting go both extremes, we then reach ultimate perfection; to mortify the body, if this is religion, then to enjoy rest, is something not resulting from religion. To walk religiously and afterwards to receive happiness, this is to make the fruit of religion something different from religion; but bodily exercise is but the cause of death, strength results alone from the mind's intention; if you remove from conduct the purpose of the mind, the bodily act is but as rotten wood; wherefore, regulate the mind, and then the body will spontaneously go right. You say that to eat pure things is a cause of religious merit, but the wild beasts and the children of poverty ever feed on these fruits and medicinal herbs; these then ought to gain much religious merit. But if you say that the heart being good then bodily suffering is the cause of further merit, then I ask why may not those who live in ease, also possess a virtuous heart? If joys are opposed to a virtuous heart, a virtuous heart may also be opposed to bodily suffering; if, for instance, all those heretics profess purity because they use water in various ways, then those who thus use water among men, even with a wicked mind, yet ought ever to be pure. But if righteousness is the groundwork of a Rishi's purity, then the idea of a sacred spot as his dwelling, being the cause of his righteousness is wrong. What is reverenced, should be known and seen. Reverence indeed is due to righteous conduct, but let it not redound to the place or mode of life."

Thus speaking at large on religious questions, they went on till the setting sun. He then beheld their rites in connection with sacrifice to fire, the drilling for sparks and the fanning into flame, also the sprinkling of the butter libations, also the chanting of the mystic prayers, till the sun went down. The prince considering these acts, could not perceive the right reason of them, and was now desirous to turn and go. Then all those Brahmakârins came together to him to request him to stay; regarding with reverence the dignity of Bodhisattva, very desirous, they earnestly besought him: "You have come from an irreligious place, to this wood where true religion flourishes, and yet, now, you wish to go away; we beg you, then, on this account, to stay." All the old Brahmakârins, with their twisted hair and bark clothes, came following after Bodhisattva, asking him as a god to stay a little while. Bodhisattva seeing these aged ones following him, their bodies worn with macerations, stood still and rested beneath a tree; and soothing them, urged them to return. Then all the Brahmakârins, young and old, surrounding him, made their request with joined hands: "You who have so unexpectedly arrived here, amid these garden glades so full of attraction, why now are you leaving them and going away, to seek perfection in the wilderness? As a man loving long life, is unwilling to let go his body, so we are even thus; would that you would stop awhile. This is a spot where Brahmans and Rishis have ever dwelt, royal Rishis and heavenly Rishis, these all have dwelt within these woods. The places on the borders of the snowy mountains, where men of high birth undergo their penance, those places are not to be compared to this. All the body of learned masters from this place have reached heaven; all the learned Rishis who have sought religious merit, have from this place and northwards found it; those who have attained a knowledge of the true law, and gained divine wisdom come not from southwards; if you indeed see us remiss and not earnest enough, practising rules not pure, and on that account are not pleased to stay, then we are the ones that ought to go; you can still remain and dwell here; all these different Brahmakârins ever desire to find companions in their penances. And you, because you are conspicuous for your religious earnestness, should not so quickly cast away their society: if you can remain here, they will honor you as god Sakra, yea! as the Devas pay worship to Brihaspati."

Then Bodhisattva answered the Brahmakârins and told them what his desires were: "I am seeking for a true method of escape, I desire solely to destroy all mundane influences; but you, with strong hearts, practise your rules as ascetics, and pay respectful attention to such visitors as may come. My heart indeed is moved with affection towards you, for pleasant conversation is agreeable to all, those who listen are affected thereby; and so hearing your words, my mind is strengthened in religious feeling; you indeed have all paid me much respect, in agreement with the courtesy of your religious profession; but now I am constrained to depart, my heart grieves thereat exceedingly: first of all, having left my own kindred, and now about to be separated from you. The pain of separation from associates, this pain is as great as the other; it is impossible for my mind not to grieve, as it is not to see others' faults. But you, by suffering pain, desire earnestly to obtain the joys of birth in heaven; whilst I desire to escape from the three worlds, and therefore I give up what my reason tells me must be rejected. The law which you practise, you inherit from the deeds of former teachers, but I, desiring to destroy all combination, seek a law which admits of no such accident. And, therefore, I cannot in this grove delay for a longer while in fruitless discussions."

At this time all the Brahmakârins, hearing the words spoken by Bodhisattva, words full of right reason and truth, very excellent in the distinction of principles, their hearts rejoiced and exulted greatly, and deep feelings of reverence were excited within them.

At this time there was one Brahmakârin, who always slept in the dust, with tangled hair and raiment of the bark of trees, his eyes bleared, preparing himself in an ascetic practice called "high-nose."[1] This one addressed Bodhisattva in the following words: "Strong in will! bright in wisdom! firmly fixed in resolve to escape the limits of birth, knowing that in escape from birth there alone is rest, not affected by any desire after heavenly blessedness, the mind set upon the eternal destruction of the bodily form, you are indeed miraculous in appearance, as you are alone in the possession of such a mind. To sacrifice to the gods, and to practise every kind of austerity, all this is designed to secure a birth in heaven, but here there is no mortification of selfish desire, there is still a selfish personal aim; but to bend the will to seek final escape, this is indeed the work of a true teacher, this is the aim of an enlightened master; this place is no right halting-place for you; you ought to proceed to Mount Pinda: there dwells a great Muni, whose name is A-lo-lam. He only has reached the end of religious aims, the most excellent eye of the law. Go, therefore, to the place where he dwells, and listen there to the true exposition of the law. This will make your heart rejoice, as you learn to follow the precepts of his system. As for me, beholding the joy of your resolve, and fearing that I shall not obtain rest, I must once more let go those following me, and seek other disciples; straighten my head and gaze with my full eyes; anoint my lips and cleanse my teeth; cover my shoulders and make bright my face, smooth my tongue and make it pliable. Thus, O excellently marked sir! fully drinking at the fountain of the water you give, I shall escape from the unfathomable depths. In the world nought is comparable to this, that which old men and Rishis have not known, that shall I know and obtain."

Bodhisattva having listened to these words, left the company of the Rishis, whilst they all, turning round him to the right, returned to their place.

[1] That is, raising his nose to look up at the sun.

The General Grief of the Palace

Kandaka leading back the horse, opening the way for his heart's sorrow, as he went on, lamented and wept: unable to disburden his soul. First of all with the royal prince, passing along the road for one night, but now dismissed and ordered to return. As the darkness of night closed on him, irresolute he wavered in mind. On the eighth day approaching the city, the noble horse pressed onwards, exhibiting all his qualities of speed; but yet hesitating as he looked around and beheld not the form of the royal prince; his four members bent down with toil, his head and neck deprived of their glossy look, whinnying as he went on with grief, he refused night and day his grass and water, because he had lost his lord, the deliverer of men. Returning thus to Kapilavastu, the whole country appeared withered and bare, as when one comes back to a deserted village; or as when the sun hidden behind Sumeru causes darkness to spread over the world. The fountains of water sparkled no more, the flowers and fruits were withered and dead, the men and women in the streets seemed lost in grief and dismay. Thus Kandaka with the white horse went on sadly and with slow advance, silent to those inquiring, wearily progressing as when accompanying a funeral; so they went on, whilst all the spectators seeing Kandaka, but not observing the royal Sâkya prince, raised piteous cries of lamentation and wept; as when the charioteer returned without Râma.

Then one by the side of the road, with his body bent, called out to Kandaka: "The prince, beloved of the world, the defender of his people, the one you have taken away by stealth, where dwells he now?" Kandaka, then, with sorrowful heart, replied to the people and said: "I with loving purpose followed after him whom I loved; 'tis not I who have deserted the prince, but by him have I been sent away; by him who now has given up his ordinary adornments, and with shaven head and religious garb, has entered the sorrow-giving grove."

Then the men hearing that he had become an ascetic, were oppressed with thoughts of wondrous boding; they sighed with heaviness and wept, and as their tears coursed down their cheeks, they spake thus one to the other: "What then shall we do?" Then they all exclaimed at once, "Let us haste after him in pursuit; for as when a man's bodily functions fail, his frame dies and his spirit flees, so is the prince our life, and he our life gone, how shall we survive? This city, perfected with slopes and woods; those woods, that cover the slopes of the city, all deprived of grace, ye lie as Bharata when killed!"

Then the men and women within the town, vainly supposing the prince had come back, in haste rushed out to the heads of the way, and seeing the horse returning alone, not knowing whether the prince was safe or lost, began to weep and to raise every piteous sound; and said, "Behold! Kandaka advancing slowly with the horse, comes back with sighs and tears; surely he grieves because the prince is lost." And thus sorrow is added to sorrow!

Then like a captive warrior is drawn before the king his master, so did he enter the gates with tears, his eyes filled so that he said nought. Then looking up to heaven he loudly groaned; and the white horse too whined piteously; then all the varied birds and beasts in the palace court, and all the horses within the stables, hearing the sad whinnying of the royal steed, replied in answer to him, thinking "now the prince has come back." But seeing him not, they ceased their cries!

And now the women of the after-palace, hearing the cries of the horses, birds, and beasts, their hair dishevelled, their faces wan and yellow, their forms sickly to look at, their mouths and lips parched, their garments torn and unwashed, the soil and heat not cleansed from their bodies, their ornaments all thrown aside, disconsolate and sad, cheerless in face, raised their bodies, without any grace, even as the feeble little morning star; their garments torn and knotted, soiled like the appearance of a robber, seeing Kandaka and the royal horse shedding tears instead of the hoped-for return, they all, assembled thus, uttered their cry, even as those who weep for one beloved just dead. Confused and wildly they rushed about, as a herd of oxen that have lost their way.

Mahâpragâpati Gotamî, hearing that the prince had not returned, fell fainting on the ground, her limbs entirely deprived of strength, even as some mad tornado wind crushes the golden-colored plantain tree; and again, hearing that her son had become a recluse, deeply sighing and with increased sadness she thought, "Alas! those glossy locks turning to the right, each hair produced from each orifice, dark and pure, gracefully shining, sweeping the earth when loose,[8] or when so determined, bound together in a heavenly crown, and now shorn and lying in the grass! Those rounded shoulders and that lion step! Those eyes broad as the ox-king's, that body shining bright as yellow gold; that square breast and Brahma voice; that you! possessing all these excellent qualities, should have entered on the sorrow-giving forest; what fortune now remains for the world, losing thus the holy king of earth? That those delicate and pliant feet, pure as the lily and of the same color, should now be torn by stones and thorns; O how can such feet tread on such ground! Born and nourished in the guarded palace, clad with garments of the finest texture, washed in richly scented water, anointed with the choicest perfumes, and now exposed to chilling blasts and dews of night, O! where during the heat or the chilly morn can rest be found! Thou flower of all thy race! Confessed by all the most renowned! Thy virtuous qualities everywhere talked of and exalted, ever reverenced, without self-seeking! why hast thou unexpectedly brought thyself upon some morn to beg thy food for life! Thou who wert wont to repose upon a soft and kingly couch, and indulge in every pleasure during thy waking hours: how canst thou endure the mountain and the forest wilds, on the bare grass to make thyself a resting-place!"

Thus thinking of her son—her heart was full of sorrow, disconsolate she lay upon the earth. The waiting women raised her up, and dried the tears from off her face, whilst all the other courtly ladies, overpowered with grief, their limbs relaxed, their minds bound fast with woe, unmoved they sat like pictured-folk.

And now Yasodharâ, deeply chiding, spoke thus to Kandaka: "Where now dwells he, who ever dwells within my mind? You two went forth, the horse a third, but now two only have returned! My heart is utterly o'erborne with grief, filled with anxious thoughts, it cannot rest. And you, deceitful man! Untrustworthy and false associate! evil contriver! plainly revealed a traitor, a smile lurks underneath thy tears! Escorting him in going; returning now with wails! Not one at heart—but in league against him—openly constituted a friend and well-wisher, concealing underneath a treacherous purpose; so thou

[8] This description of the prince's hair seems to contradict the head arrangement of the figures of Buddha, unless the curls denote the shaven head of the recluse.

hast caused the sacred prince to go forth once and not return again! No questioning the joy you feel! Having done ill you now enjoy the fruit; better far to dwell with an enemy of wisdom, than work with one who, while a fool, professes friendship. Openly professing sweetness and light, inwardly a scheming and destructive enemy. And now this royal and kingly house, in one short morn is crushed and ruined! All these fair and queen-like women, with grief o'erwhelmed, their beauty marred, their breathing choked with tears and sobs, their faces soiled with crossing tracks of grief! Even the queen (Mâyâ) when in life, resting herself on him, as the great snowy mountains repose upon the widening earth, through grief in thought of what would happen, died. How sad the lot of these —within these open lattices—these weeping ones, these deeply wailing! Born in another state than hers in heaven, how can their grief be borne!" Then speaking to the horse she said, "Thou unjust! what dulness this—to carry off a man, as in the darkness some wicked thief bears off a precious gem. When riding thee in time of battle, swords, and javelins and arrows, none of these alarmed or frighted thee! But now what fitfulness of temper this, to carry off by violence, to rob my soul of one, the choicest jewel of his tribe. O! thou art but a vicious reptile, to do such wickedness as this! to-day thy woeful lamentation sounds everywhere within these palace walls, but when you stole away my cherished one, why wert thou dumb and silent then! if then thy voice had sounded loud, and roused the palace inmates from their sleep, if then they had awoke and slumbered not, there would not have ensued the present sorrow."

Kandaka, hearing these sorrowful words, drawing in his breath and composing himself, wiping away his tears, with hands clasped together, answered: "Listen to me, I pray, in self-justification—be not suspicious of, nor blame the royal horse, nor be thou angry with me, either. For in truth no fault has been committed by us. It is the gods who have effected this. For I, indeed, extremely reverenced the king's command, it was the gods who drove him to the solitudes, urgently leading on the horse with him: thus they went together fleet as with wings, his breathing hushed! suppressed was every sound, his feet scarce touched the earth! The city gates wide opening of themselves! all space self-lighted! this was the work indeed of the gods; and what was I, or what my strength, compared with theirs?"

Yasodharâ hearing these words, her heart was lost in deep consideration! the deeds accomplished by the gods could not be laid to others' charge, as faults; and so she ceased her angry chiding, and allowed her great consuming grief to smoulder. Thus prostrate on the ground she muttered out her sad complaints, "That the two doves should be divided! Now," she cried, "my stay and my support is lost, between those once agreed in life, separation has sprung up! those who were at one as to religion are now divided! where shall I seek another mode of life? In olden days the former conquerors greatly rejoiced to see their kingly retinue; these with their wives in company, in search of highest wisdom, roamed through groves and plains. And now, that he should have deserted me! and what is the religious state he seeks! the Brahman ritual respecting sacrifice, requires the wife to take part in the offering, and because they both share in the service they shall both receive a common reward hereafter! but you O prince! art niggard in your religious rites, driving me away, and wandering forth alone! Is it that you saw me jealous, and so turned against me! that you now seek someone free from jealousy! or did you see some other cause to hate me, that you now seek to find a heaven-born nymph! But why should one excelling in every personal grace seek to practise self-denying austerities! is it that you despise a common lot with me, that variance rises in your breast against your wife! Why does not Râhula fondly repose upon your knee. Alas! alas! unlucky master! full of grace without, but hard at heart! The glory and the pride of all your tribe, yet hating those who reverence you! O! can it be, you have turned your back for good upon your little child, scarce able yet to smile! My heart is gone! and all my strength! my lord has fled, to wander in the mountains! he cannot surely thus forget me! he is then but a man of wood or stone." Thus having spoken, her mind was dulled and darkened, she muttered on, or spoke in wild mad words, or fancied that she saw strange sights, and sobbing past the power of self-restraint, her breath grew less, and sinking thus, she fell asleep upon the dusty ground! The palace ladies seeing this, were wrung with heartfelt sorrow, just as the full-blown lily, struck by the wind and hail, is broken down and withered.

And now the king, his father, having lost the prince, was filled, both night and day, with grief; and fasting, sought the gods for help. He prayed that they would soon restore him, and having prayed and finished sacrifice, he went from out the sacred gates; then hearing all the cries and sounds of mourning, his mind distressed became confused, as when heaven's thundering and lightning put to bewildering flight a herd of elephants. Then seeing Kandaka with the royal steed, after long questioning, finding his son a hermit, fainting he fell upon the earth, as when the flag of Indra falls and breaks. Then all the ministers of state, upraising him, exhort him, as was right, to calm himself. After awhile, his mind somewhat recovered, speaking to the royal steed, he said: "How often have I ridden thee to battle, and every time have thought upon your excellence! but now I hate and loathe thee, more than ever I have loved or praised thee! My son, renowned for noble qualities, thou hast carried off and taken from me; and left him 'mid the mountain forests; and now you have come back alone; take me, then, quickly hence and go! And going, never more come back with me! For since you have not brought him back, my life is worth no more preserving; no longer care I about governing! My son about me was my only joy; as the Brahman Gayanta met death for his son's sake, so I, deprived of my religious son, will of myself deprive myself of life. So Manu, lord of all that lives, ever lamented for his son; how much more I, a mortal man deprived of mine, must lose all rest! In old time the king Aga, loving his son, wandering through the mountains, lost in thought, ended life, and forthwith was born in heaven. And now I cannot die! Through the long night fixed in this sad state, with this great palace round me, thinking of my son, solitary and athirst as any hungry spirit; as one who, thirsty, holding water in his hand, but when he tries to drink lets all escape, and so remains athirst till death ensues, and after death becomes a wandering ghost; so I, in the extremity of thirst, through loss, possessed once of a son, but now without a son, still live and cannot end my days! But come! tell me at once where is my son! let me not die athirst for want of knowing this and fall among the Pretas. In former days, at least, my will was strong and firm, difficult to move as the great earth; but now I've lost my son, my mind is dazed, as was in old time the king Dasaratha's."

And now the royal teacher (Purohita), an illustrious sage, with the chief minister, famed for wisdom, with earnest and considerate minds, both exhorted with remonstrances, the king. "Pray you (they said) arouse yourself to thought, and let not grief cramp and hold your mind! in olden days there were mighty kings, who left their country, as flowers are scattered; your son now practises the way of wisdom; why then nurse your grief and misery; you should recall the prophecy of Asita, and reasonably count on what was probable! Think of the heavenly joys which you, a universal king, have inherited! But now, so troubled and constrained in mind, how will it not be said, 'The Lord of earth can change his golden-jewel-heart!' Now, therefore, send us forth, and bid us seek the place he occupies, then by some stratagem and strong remonstrances, and showing him our earnestness of purpose, we will break down his resolution, and thus assuage your kingly sorrow."

The king, with joy, replied and said: "Would that you both would go in haste, as swiftly as the Saketa bird flies through the void for her young's sake; thinking of nought but the royal prince, and sad at heart—I shall await your search!"

The two men having received their orders, the king retired among his kinsfolk, his heart somewhat more tranquillized, and breathing freely through si throat.

The Mission to Seek the Prince

The king now suppressing his grief, urged on his great teacher and chief minister, as one urges on with whip a ready horse, to hasten onwards as the rapid stream; whilst they fatigued, yet with unflagging effort, come to the place of the sorrow-giving grove; then laying on one side the five outward marks of dignity and regulating well their outward gestures, they entered the Brahmans' quiet hermitage, and paid reverence to the Rishis. They, on their part, begged them to be seated, and repeated the law for their peace and comfort.

Then forthwith they addressed the Rishis and said: "We have on our minds a subject on which we would ask for advice. There is one who is called Suddhodana râga, a descendant of the famous Ikshvâku family, we are his teacher and his minister, who instruct him in the sacred books as required. The king indeed is like Indra for dignity; his son, like Ke-yan-to, in order to escape old age, disease, and death, has become a hermit, and depends on this; on his account have we come hither, with a view to let your worships know of this."

Replying, they said: "With respect to this youth, has he long arms and the signs of a great man? Surely he is the one who, inquiring into our practice, discoursed so freely on the matter of life and death. He has gone to the abode of Arâda, to seek for a complete mode of escape."

Having received this certain information, respectfully considering the urgent commands of the anxious king, they dared not hesitate in their undertaking, but straightway took the road and hastened on. Then seeing the wood in which the royal prince dwelt, and him, deprived of all outward marks of dignity, his body still glorious with lustrous shining, as when the sun comes forth from the black cloud; then the religious teacher of the country and the great minister holding to the true law, put off from them their courtly dress, and descending from the chariot gradually advanced, like the royal Po-ma-ti and the Rishi Vasishtha, went through the woods and forests, and seeing the royal prince Râma, each according to his own prescribed manner, paid him reverence, as he advanced to salute him; or as Sukra, in company with Angiras, with earnest heart paid reverence, and sacrificed to Indra râga.

Then the royal prince in return paid reverence to the royal teacher and the great minister, as the divine Indra placed at their ease Sukra and Angiras; then, at his command, the two men seated themselves before the prince, as Pou-na and Pushya, the twin stars attend beside the moon; then the Purohita and the great minister respectfully explained to the royal prince, even as Pi-li-po-ti spoke to that Gayanta: "Your royal father, thinking of the prince, is pierced in heart, as with an iron point; his mind distracted, raves in solitude; he sleeps upon the dusty ground; by night and day he adds to his sorrowful reflections; his tears flow down like the incessant rain; and now to seek you out, he has sent us hither. Would that you would listen with attentive mind; we know that you delight to act religiously; it is certain, then, without a doubt, this is not the time for you to enter the forest wilds; a feeling of deep pity consumes our heart! You, if you be indeed moved by religion, ought to feel some pity for our case; let your kindly feelings flow abroad, to comfort us who are worn at heart; let not the tide of sorrow and of sadness completely overwhelm the outlets of our heart; as the torrents which roll down the grassy mountains; or the calamities of tempest, fiery heat, and lightning; for so the grieving heart has these four sorrows, turmoil and drought, passion and overthrow. But come! return to your native place, the time will arrive when you can go forth again as a recluse. But now to disregard your family duties, to turn against father and mother, how can this be called love and affection? that love which overshadows and embraces all. Religion requires not the wild solitudes; you can practise a hermit's duties in your home; studiously thoughtful, diligent in expedients, this is to lead a hermit's life in truth. A shaven head, and garments soiled with dirt—to wander by yourself through desert wilds—this is but to encourage constant fears, and cannot be rightly called 'an awakened hermit's life.' Would rather we might take you by the hand, and sprinkle water on your head, and crown you with a heavenly diadem, and place you underneath a flowery canopy, that all eyes might gaze with eagerness upon you; after this, in truth, we would leave our home with joy. The former kings, Teou-lau-ma, A-neou-ke-o-sa, Po-ke-lo-po-yau, Pi-po-lo-'anti, Pi-ti-o-ke-na, Na-lo-sha-po-lo, all these several kings refused not the royal crown, the jewels, and the ornaments of person; their hands and feet were adorned with gems, around them were women to delight and please, these things they cast not from them, for the sake of escape; you then may also come back home, and undertake both necessary duties; your mind prepare itself in higher law, whilst for the sake of earth you wield the sceptre; let there be no more weeping, but comply with what we say, and let us publish it; and having published it with your authority, then you may return and receive respectful welcome. Your father and your mother, for your sake, in grief shed tears like the great ocean; having no stay and no dependence now—no source from which the Sâkya stem may grow—you ought, like the captain of the ship, to bring it safely across to a place of safety. The royal prince Pi-san-ma, as also Lo-me-po-ti, they respectfully attended to the command of their father: you also should do the same! Your loving mother who cherished you so kindly, with no regard for self, through years of care, as the cow deprived of her calf, weeps and laments, forgetting to eat or sleep; you surely ought to return to her at once, to protect her life from evil; as a solitary bird, away from its fellows, or as the lonely elephant, wandering through the jungle, losing the care of their young, ever think of protecting and defending them, so you the only child, young and defenceless, not knowing what you do, bring trouble and solicitude; cause, then, this sorrow to dissipate itself; as one who rescues the moon from being devoured, so do you reassure the men and women of the land, and remove from them the consuming grief, and suppress the sighs that rise like breath to heaven, which cause the darkness that obscures their sight; seeking you, as water, to quench the fire; the fire quenched, their eyes shall open."

Bodhisattva, hearing of his father the king, experienced the greatest distress of mind, and sitting still, gave himself to reflection; and then, in due course, replied respectfully: "I know indeed that my royal father is possessed of a loving and deeply considerate mind, but my fear of birth, old age, disease, and death, has led me to disobey, and disregard his extreme kindness. Whoever neglects right consideration about his present life, and because he hopes to escape in the end, therefore disregards all precautions in the present: on this man comes the inevitable doom of death. It is the knowledge of this, therefore, that weighs with me, and after long delay has constrained me to a hermit's life; hearing of my father, the king, and his grief, my heart is affected with increased love; but yet, all is like the fancy of a dream, quickly reverting to nothingness. Know then, without fear of contradiction, that the nature of existing things is not uniform; the cause of sorrow is not necessarily the relationship of child with parent, but that which produces the pain of separation, results from the influence of delusion; as men going along a road suddenly meet midway with others, and then a moment more are separated, each one going his own way, so by the force of concomitance, relationships are framed, and then, according to each one's destiny, there is separation; he who thoroughly investigates this false connection of relationship ought not to cherish in himself grief; in this world there is rupture of family love, in another life it is sought for again; brought together for a moment, again rudely divided, everywhere the fetters of kindred are formed! Ever being bound, and ever being loosened! who can sufficiently lament such constant separations; born into the world, and then gradually changing, constantly separated by death and then born again. All things which exist in time must perish; the forests and mountains, all things that exist; in time are born all sensuous things, so is it both with worldly substance and with time. Because, then, death pervades all time, get rid of death, and time will disappear. You desire to make me king, and it is difficult to resist the offices of love; but as a disease is difficult to bear without medicine, so neither can I bear this weight of dignity; in every condition, high or low, we find folly and ignorance, and men carelessly following the dictates of lustful passion; at last, we come to live in constant fear; thinking anxiously of the outward form, the spirit droops; following the ways of men, the mind resists the right; but, the conduct of the wise is not so. The sumptuously ornamented and splendid palace I look upon as filled with fire; the hundred dainty dishes of the divine kitchen, as mingled with destructive poisons; the lily growing on the tranquil lake, in its midst harbors countless noisome insects; and so the towering abode of the rich is the house of calamity; the wise will not dwell therein. In former times illustrious kings, seeing the many crimes of their home and country, affecting as with poison the dwellers therein, in sorrowful disgust sought comfort in seclusion; we know, therefore, that the troubles of a royal estate are not to be compared with the repose of a religious life; far better dwell in the wild mountains, and eat the herbs like the beasts of the field; therefore I dare not dwell in the wide palace, for the black snake has its dwelling there. I reject the kingly estate and the five desires; to escape such sorrows I wander through the mountain wilds. This, then, would be the consequence of compliance: that I, who, delighting in religion, am gradually getting wisdom, should now quit these quiet woods, and returning home, partake of sensual pleasures, and thus by night and day increase my store of misery. Surely this is not what should be done! that the great leader of an illustrious tribe, having left his home from love of religion, and forever turned his back upon tribal honor, desiring to confirm his purpose as a leader—that he—discarding outward form, clad in religious garb, loving religious meditation, wandering through the wilds—should now reject his hermit vestment, tread down his sense of proper shame and give up his aim. This, though I gained heaven's kingly state, cannot be done! how much less to gain an earthly, though distinguished, home!

"For having spewed forth lust, passion, and ignorance, shall I return to feed upon it? as a man might go back to his vomit! such misery, how could I bear? Like a man whose house has caught fire, by some expedient finds a way to escape, will such a man forthwith go back and enter it again? such conduct would disgrace a man! So I, beholding the evils, birth, old age, and death, to escape the misery, have become a hermit; shall I then go back and enter in, and like a fool dwell in their company? He who enjoys a royal estate and yet seeks rescue, cannot dwell thus, this is no place for him; escape is born from quietness and rest; to be a king is to add distress and poison; to seek for rest and yet aspire to royal condition are but contradictions; royalty and rescue, motion and rest, like fire and water, having two principles, cannot be united. So one resolved to seek escape cannot abide possessed of kingly dignity! And if you say a man may be a king, and at the same time prepare deliverance for himself, there is no certainty in this! to seek certain escape is not to risk it thus; it is through this uncertain frame of mind that once a man gone forth is led to go back home again; but I, my mind is not uncertain; severing the baited hook of relationship, with straightforward purpose, I have left my home. Then tell me, why should I return again?"

The great minister, inwardly reflecting, thought, "The mind of the royal prince, my master, is full of wisdom, and agreeable to virtue, what he says is reasonable and fitly framed." Then he addressed the prince and said: "According to what your highness states, he who seeks religion must seek it rightly; but this is not the fitting time for you; your royal father, old and of declining years, thinking of you his son, adds grief to grief; you say indeed, 'I find my joy in rescue. To go back would be apostasy.' But yet your joy denotes unwisdom, and argues want of deep reflection; you do not see, because you seek the fruit, how vain to give up present duty. There are some who say, There is 'hereafter'; others there are who say, 'Nothing hereafter.' So whilst this question hangs in suspense, why should a man give up his present pleasure? If perchance there is 'hereafter,' we ought to bear patiently what it brings; if you say, 'Hereafter is not,' then there is not either salvation! If you say, 'Hereafter is,' you would not say, 'Salvation causes it.' As earth is hard, or fire is hot, or water moist, or wind is mobile, 'Hereafter' is just so. It has its own distinct nature.

So when we speak of pure and impure, each comes from its own distinctive nature. If you should say, 'By some contrivance this can be removed,' such an opinion argues folly. Every root within the moral world has its own nature predetermined; loving remembrance and forgetfulness, these have their nature fixed and positive; so likewise age, disease, and death, these sorrows, who can escape by strategy? If you say, 'Water can put out fire,' or 'Fire can cause water to boil and pass away,' then this proves only that distinctive natures may be mutually destructive; but nature in harmony produces living things; so man when first conceived within the womb, his hands, his feet, and all his separate members, his spirit and his understanding, of themselves are perfected; but who is he who does it? Who is he that points the prickly thorn? This too is nature, self-controlling. And take again the different kinds of beasts, these are what they are, without desire on their part; and so, again, the heaven-born beings, whom the self-existent (Isvara) rules, and all the world of his creation; these have no self-possessed power of expedients; for if they had a means of causing birth, there would be also means for controlling death, and then what need of self-contrivance, or seeking for deliverance? There are those who say, 'I' (the soul) is the cause of birth, and others who affirm, 'I' (the soul) is the cause of death. There are some who say, 'Birth comes from nothingness, and without any plan of ours we perish.' Thus one is born a fortunate child, removed from poverty, of noble family, or learned in testamentary lore of Rishis, or called to offer mighty sacrifices to the gods, born in either state, untouched by poverty, then their famous name becomes to them 'escape,' their virtues handed down by name to us; yet if these attained their happiness, without contrivance of their own, how vain and fruitless is the toil of those who seek 'escape.' And you, desirous of deliverance, purpose to practise some high expedient, whilst your royal father frets and sighs; for a short while you have essayed the road, and leaving home have wandered through the wilds, to return then would not now be wrong; of old, King Ambarîsha for a long while dwelt in the grievous forest, leaving his retinue and all his kinsfolk, but afterwards returned and took the royal office; and so Râma, son of the king of the country, leaving his country occupied the mountains, but hearing he was acting contrary to usage, returned and governed righteously. And so the king of

Sha-lo-po, called To-lo-ma, father and son, both wandered forth as hermits, but in the end came back again together; so Po-'sz-tsau Muni, with On-tai-tieh, in the wild mountains practising as Brahmakârins, these too returned to their own country. Thus all these worthies of a by-gone age, famous for their advance in true religion, came back home and royally governed, as lamps enlightening the world. Wherefore for you to leave the mountain wilds, religiously to rule, is not a crime."

The royal prince, listening to the great minister's loving words without excess of speaking, full of sound argument, clear and unconfused, with no desire to wrangle after the way of the schools, with fixed purpose, deliberately speaking, thus answered the great minister: "The question of being and not being is an idle one, only adding to the uncertainty of an unstable mind, and to talk of such matters I have no strong inclination; purity of life, wisdom, the practice of asceticism, these are matters to which I earnestly apply myself, the world is full of empty studies which our teachers in their office skilfully involve; but they are without any true principle, and I will none of them! The enlightened man distinguishes truth from falsehood; but how can truth be born from such as those? For they are like the man born blind, leading the blind man as a guide; as in the night, as in thick darkness both wander on, what recovery is there for them? Regarding the question of the pure and impure, the world involved in self-engendered doubt cannot perceive the truth; better to walk along the way of purity, or rather follow the pure law of self-denial, hate the practice of impurity, reflect on what was said of old, not obstinate in one belief or one tradition, with sincere mind accepting all true words, and ever banishing sinful sorrow (i.e. sin, the cause of grief). Words which exceed sincerity are vainly spoken; the wise man uses not such words. As to what you say of Râma and the rest, leaving their home, practising a pure life, and then returning to their country, and once more mixing themselves in sensual pleasures, such men as these walk vainly; those who are wise place no dependence on them. Now, for your sakes, permit me, briefly, to recount this one true principle of action: The sun, the moon may fall to earth, Sumeru and all the snowy mountains overturn, but I will never change my purpose; rather than enter a forbidden place, let me be cast into the fierce fire; not to accomplish rightly what I have entered on, and to return once more to my own land, there to enter the fire of the five desires, let it befall me as my own oath records." So spake the prince, his arguments as pointed as the brightness of the perfect sun; then rising up he passed some distance off.

The Purohita and the minister, their words and discourse prevailing nothing, conversed together, after which, resolving to depart on their return, with great respect they quietly inform the prince, not daring to intrude their presence on him further; and yet regarding the king's commands, not willing to return with unbecoming haste. They loitered quietly along the way, and whomsoever they encountered, selecting those who seemed like wise men, they interchanged such thoughts as move the learned, hiding their true position, as men of title; then passing on, they speeded on their way.

CHAPTER III

Bimbisâra Râga Invites the Prince

THE royal prince, departing from the court-master (i.e. the Purohita) and the great minister, Saddharma, keeping along the stream, then crossing the Ganges, he took the road towards the Vulture Peak,* hidden among the five mountains, standing alone a lovely peak as a roof amid the others. The trees and shrubs and flowers in bloom, the flowing fountains, and the cooling rills; all these he gazed upon—then passing on, he entered the city of the five peaks, calm and peaceful, as one come down from heaven. The country folk, seeing the royal prince, his comeliness and his excessive grace, though young in years, yet glorious in his person, incomparable as the appearance of a great master, seeing him thus, strange thoughts affected them, as if they gazed upon the banner of Isvara. They stayed the foot, who passed athwart the path; those hastened on, who were behind; those going before, turned back their heads and gazed with earnest, wistful look. The marks and distinguishing points of his person, on these they fixed their eyes without fatigue, and then approached with reverent homage, joining both their hands in salutation. With all there was a sense of wondrous joy, as in their several ways they offered what they had, looking at his noble and illustrious features; bending down their bodies modestly, correcting every careless or unseemly gesture, thus they showed their reverence to him silently; those who with anxious heart, seeking release, were moved by love, with feelings composed, bowed down the more. Great men and women, in their several engagements, at the same time arrested on their way, paid to his person and his presence homage: and following him as they gazed, they went not back. For the white circle between his eyebrows adorning his wide and violet-colored eyes, his noble body bright as gold,

* The distance from the place of the interview with the ministers to the Vulture Peak would be, in a straight line, about 150 miles.

his pure and web-joined fingers, all these, though he were but a hermit, were marks of one who was a holy king; and now the men and women of Râgagriha, the old and young alike, were moved, and cried, "This man so noble as a recluse, what common joy is this for us!" At this time Bimbisâra Râga, placed upon a high tower of observation, seeing all those men and women, in different ways exhibiting one mark of surprise, calling before him some man outside, inquired at once the cause of it; this one bending his knee below the tower, told fully what he had seen and heard, "That one of the Sâkya race, renowned of old, a prince most excellent and wonderful, divinely wise, beyond the way of this world, a fitting king to rule the eight regions, now without home, is here, and all men are paying homage to him."

The king on hearing this was deeply moved at heart, and though his body was restrained, his soul had gone. Calling his ministers speedily before him, and all his nobles and attendants, he bade them follow secretly the prince's steps, to observe what charity was given. So, in obedience to the command, they followed and watched him steadfastly, as with even gait and unmoved presence he entered on the town and begged his food, according to the rule of all great hermits, with joyful mien and undisturbed mind, not anxious whether much or little alms were given; whatever he received, costly or poor, he placed within his bowl, then turned back to the wood, and having eaten it and drunk of the flowing stream, he joyous sat upon the immaculate mountain. There he beheld the green trees fringing with their shade the crags, the scented flowers growing between the intervals, whilst the peacocks and the other birds, joyously flying, mingled their notes; his sacred garments bright and lustrous, shone as the sun-lit mulberry leaves; the messengers beholding his fixed composure, one by one returning, reported what they had seen; the king hearing it, was moved at heart, and forthwith ordered his royal equipment to be brought, his god-like crown and his flower-bespangled robes; then, as the lion-king, he strode forth, and choosing certain aged persons of consideration, learned men, able calmly and wisely to discriminate, he, with them, led the way, followed by a hundred thousand people, who like a cloud ascended with the king the royal mountain.

And now beholding the dignity of Bodhisattva, every outward gesture under government, sitting with ease upon the mountain crag, as the moon shining limpid in the pure heavens, so was his matchless beauty and purity of grace; then as the converting presence of religion dwelling within the heart makes it reverential, so, beholding him, he reverently approached, even as divine Sâkara comes to the presence of Mo-hi-su-ma, so with every outward form of courtesy and reverence the king approached and asked him respectfully of his welfare.

Bodhisattva, answering as he was moved, in his turn made similar inquiries. Then the king, the questioning over, sat down with dignity upon a clean-faced rock. And so he steadfastly beheld the divine appearance of the prince, the sweetness and complacency of his features revealing what his station was and high estate, his family renown, received by inheritance; the king, who for a time restrained his feelings, now wishful to get rid of doubts, inquired why one descended from the royal family of the sun-brightness having attended to religious sacrifices through ten thousand generations, whereof the virtue had descended as his full inheritance, increasing and accumulating until now, why he so excellent in wisdom, so young in years, had now become a recluse, rejecting the position of a Kakravartin's son, begging his food, despising family fame, his beauteous form, fit for perfumes and anointings, why clothed with coarse Kasâya garments; the hand which ought to grasp the reins of empire, instead thereof, taking its little stint of food; if indeed (the king continued) you were not of royal descent, and would receive as an offering the transfer of this land, then would I divide with you my empire; saying this, he scarcely hoped to excite his feelings, who had left his home and family, to be a hermit. Then forthwith the king proceeded thus: "Give just weight I pray you to my truthful words: desire for power is kin to nobleness, and so is just pride of fame or family or wealth or personal appearance; no longer having any wish to subdue the proud, or to bend others down and so get thanks from men, it were better, then, to give to the strong and warlike martial arms to wear, for them to follow war and by their power to get supremacy; but when by one's own power a kingdom falls to hand, who would not then accept the reins of empire? The wise man knows the time to take religion, wealth, and worldly pleasure. But if he obtains not the threefold profit, then in the end he abates his earnest efforts, and reverencing religion, he lets go material wealth. Wealth is the one desire of worldly men; to be rich and lose all desire for religion, this is to gain but outside wealth. But to be poor and even thus despise religion, what pleasure can indulgence give in such a case! But when possessed of all the three, and when enjoyed with reason and propriety, then religion, wealth, and pleasure make what is rightly called a great master; permit not, then, your perfectly endowed body to lay aside its glory, without reward; the Kakravartin, as a monarch, ruled the four empires of the world, and shared with Sakra his royal throne, but was unequal to the task of ruling heaven. But you, with your redoubtable strength, may well grasp both heavenly and human power; I do not rely upon my kingly power, in my desire to keep you here by force, but seeing you change your comeliness of person, and wearing the hermit's garb, whilst it makes me reverence you for your virtue, moves me with pity and regret for you as a man; you now go begging your food, and I offer you the whole land as yours; whilst you are young and lusty enjoy yourself. During middle life acquire wealth, and when old and all your abilities ripened, then is the time for following the rules of religion; when young to encourage religious fervor, is to destroy the sources of desire; but when old and the breath is less eager, then is the time to seek religious solitude; when old we should avoid, as a shame, desire of wealth, but get honor in the world by a religious life; but when young, and the heart light and elastic, then is the time to partake of pleasure, in boon companionship to indulge in gayety, and partake to the full of mutual intercourse; but as years creep on, giving up indulgence, to observe the ordinances of religion, to mortify the five desires, and go on increasing a joyful and religious heart, is not this the law of the eminent kings of old, who as a great company paid worship to heaven, and borne on the dragon's back received the joys of celestial abodes? All these divine and victorious monarchs, glorious in person, richly adorned, thus having as a company performed their religious offering, in the end received the reward of their conduct in heaven." Thus Bimbasâra Râga used every kind of winning expedient in argument. The royal prince, unmoved and fixed, remained firm as Mount Sumeru.

The Reply to Bimbasâra Râga

Bimbasâra Râga, having, in a decorous manner, and with soothing speech, made his request, the prince on his part respectfully replied, in the following words, deep and heart-stirring: "Illustrious and world-renowned! Your words are not opposed to reason, descendant of a distinguished family—an Aryan—amongst men a true friend indeed, righteous and sincere to the bottom of your heart, it is proper for religion's sake to speak thus. In all the world, in its different sections, there is no chartered place for solid virtue, for if virtue flags and folly rules, what reverence can there be, or honor paid, to a high name or boast of prowess, inherited from former generations! And so there may be in the midst of great distress, large goodness, these are not mutually opposed. This then is so with the world in the connection of true worth and friendship. A true friend who makes good use of wealth—is rightly called a fast and firm treasure, but he who guards and stints the profit he has made, his wealth will soon be spent and lost; the wealth of a country is no constant treasure, but that which is given in charity is rich in returns, therefore charity is a true friend: although it scatters, yet it brings no repentance; you indeed are known as liberal and kind, I make no reply in opposition to you, but simply as we meet, so with agreeable purpose we talk. I fear birth, old age, disease, and death, and so I seek to find a sure mode of deliverance; I have put away thought of relatives and family affection, how is it possible then for me to return to the world and not to fear to revive the poisonous snake, and after the hail to be burned in the fierce fire; indeed, I fear the objects of these several desires, this whirling in the stream of life troubles my heart, these five desires, the inconstant thieves—stealing from men their choicest treasures, making them unreal, false, and fickle—are like the man called up as an apparition; for a time the beholders are affected by it, but it has no lasting hold upon the mind; so these five desires are the great obstacles, forever disarranging the way of peace; if the joys of heaven are not worth having, how much less the desires common to men, begetting the thirst of wild love, and then lost in the enjoyment, as the fierce wind fans the fire, till the fuel be spent and the fire expires; of all unrighteous things in the world.

there is nothing worse than the domain of the five desires; for all men maddened by the power of lust, giving themselves to pleasure, are dead to reason. The wise man fears these desires, he fears to fall into the way of unrighteousness; for like a king who rules all within the four seas, yet still seeks beyond for something more, so is lust; like the unbounded ocean, it knows not when and where to stop. Mandha, the Kakravartin, when the heavens rained yellow gold, and he ruled all within the seas, yet sighed after the domain of the thirty-three heavens; dividing with Sakra his seat, and so through the power of this lust he died; Nung-Sha, whilst practising austerities, got power to rule the thirty-three heavenly abodes, but from lust he became proud and supercilious; the Rishi whilst stepping into his chariot, through carelessness in his gait, fell down into the midst of the serpent pit. Yen-lo, the universal monarch (Kakravartin), wandering abroad through the Trayastrimsas heaven, took a heavenly woman (Apsara) for a queen, and unjustly extorted the gold of a Rishi; the Rishi, in anger, added a charm, by which the country was ruined, and his life ended. Po-lo, and Sakra king of Devas, and Nung-Sha returning to Sakra; what certainty is there, even for the lord of heaven? Neither is any country safe, though kept by the mighty strength of those dwelling in it. But when one's clothing consists of grass, the berries one's food, the rivulets one's drink, with long hair flowing to the ground, silent as a Muni, seeking nothing, in this way practising austerities, in the end lust shall be destroyed. Know then, that the province of the five desires is avowedly an enemy of the religious man. Even the one-thousand-armed invincible king, strong in his might, finds it hard to conquer this. The Rishi Râma perished because of lust; how much more ought I, the son of a Kshatriya, to restrain lustful desire; but indulge in lust a little, and like the child it grows apace, the wise man hates it therefore; who would take poison for food? every sorrow is increased and cherished by the offices of lust. If there is no lustful desire, the risings of sorrow are not produced, the wise man seeing the bitterness of sorrow, stamps out and destroys the risings of desire; that which the world calls virtue, is but another form of this baneful law; worldly men enjoying the pleasure of covetous desire then every form of careless conduct results; these careless ways producing hurt, at death, the subject of them reaps perdition. But by the diligent use of means, and careful continuance therein, the consequences of negligence are avoided, we should therefore dread the non-use of means; recollecting that all things are illusory, the wise man covets them not; he who desires such things, desires sorrow, and then goes on again ensnared in love, with no certainty of ultimate freedom; he advances still and ever adds grief to grief, like one holding a lighted torch burns his hand, and therefore the wise man enters on no such things. The foolish man and the one who doubts, still encouraging the covetous and burning heart, in the end receives accumulated sorrow, not to be remedied by any prospect of rest; covetousness and anger are as the serpent's poison; the wise man casts away the approach of sorrow as a rotten bone; he tastes it not nor touches it, lest it should corrupt his teeth, that which the wise man will not take, the king will go through fire and water to obtain, the wicked sons labor for wealth as for a piece of putrid flesh, o'er which the hungry flocks of birds contend. So should we regard riches; the wise man is ill pleased at having wealth stored up, the mind wild with anxious thoughts, guarding himself by night and day, as a man who fears some powerful enemy, like as a man's feelings revolt with disgust at the sights seen beneath the slaughter post of the East Market; so the high post which marks the presence of lust, and anger, and ignorance, the wise man always avoids; as those who enter the mountains or the seas have much to contend with and little rest, as the fruit which grows on a high tree, and is grasped at by the covetous at the risk of life, so is the region of covetous desire, though they see the difficulty of getting it, yet how painfully do men scheme after wealth, difficult to acquire, easy to dissipate, as that which is got in a dream: how can the wise man hoard up such trash! Like covering over with a false surface a hole full of fire, slipping through which the body is burnt, so is the fire of covetous desire. The wise man meddles not with it. Like that Kaurava, or Pih-se-ni Nanda, or Ni-k'he-lai Danta, as some butcher's appearance, such also is the appearance of lustful desire; the wise man will have nothing to do with it; he would rather throw his body into the water or fire, or cast himself down over a steep precipice. Seeking to obtain heavenly pleasures, what is this but to remove the place of sorrow, without profit. Sün-tau, Po-sun-tau, brothers of Asura, lived together in great affection, but on account of lustful desire slew one another, and their name perished; all this then comes from lust; it is this which makes a man vile, and lashes and goads him with piercing sorrow; lust debases a man, robs him of all hope, whilst through the long night his body and soul are worn out; like the stag that covets the power of speech and dies, or the winged bird that covets sensual pleasure, or the fish that covets the baited hook, such are the calamities that lust brings; considering what are the requirements of life, none of these possess permanency; we eat to appease the pain of hunger, to do away with thirst we drink, we clothe ourselves to keep out the cold and wind, we lie down to rest to get sleep, to procure locomotion we seek a carriage, when we would halt we seek a seat, we wash to cleanse ourselves from dirt; all these things are done to avoid inconvenience; we may gather therefore that these five desires have no permanent character; for as a man suffering from fever seeks and asks for some cooling medicine, so covetousness seeks for something to satisfy its longings; foolish men regard these things as permanent, and as the necessary requirements of life, but, in sooth, there is no permanent cessation of sorrow; for by coveting to appease these desires we really increase them; there is no character of permanency therefore about them. To be filled and clothed are no lasting pleasures, time passes, and the sorrow recurs; summer is cool during the moon-tide shining; winter comes and cold increases; and so through all the eightfold laws of the world they possess no marks of permanence, sorrow and joy cannot agree together, as a person slave-governed loses his renown. But religion causes all things to be of service, as a king reigning in his sovereignty; so religion controls sorrow, as one fits on a burden according to power of endurance. Whatever our condition in the world, still sorrows accumulate around us. Even in the condition of a king, how does pain multiply, though bound to others by love, yet this is a cause of grief; without friends and living alone, what joy can there be in this? Though a man rules over the four kingdoms, yet only one part can be enjoyed; to be concerned in ten thousand matters, what profit is there in this, for we only accumulate anxieties. Put an end to sorrow, then, by appeasing desire, refrain from busy work, this is rest. A king enjoys his sensual pleasures; deprived of kingship there is the joy of rest; in both cases there are pleasures but of different kinds; why then be a king! Make then no plan or crafty expedient, to lead me back to the five desires; what my heart prays for, is some quiet place and freedom; but you desire to entangle me in relationships and duties, and destroy the completion of what I seek; I am in no fear of family hatred, nor do I seek the joys of heaven; my heart hankers after no vulgar profit, so I have put away my royal diadem; and contrary to your way of thinking, I prefer, henceforth, no more to rule. A hare rescued from the serpent's mouth, would it go back again to be devoured? holding a torch and burning himself, would not a man let it go? A man blind and recovering his sight, would he again seek to be in darkness? the rich, does he sigh for poverty? the wise, does he long to be ignorant? Has the world such men as these? then will I again enjoy my country. But I desire to get rid of birth, old age, and death, with body restrained, to beg my food; with appetites moderated, to keep in my retreat; and then to avoid the evil modes of a future life, this is to find peace in two worlds: now then I pray you pity me not. Pity, rather, those who rule as kings! their souls ever vacant and athirst, in the present world no repose, hereafter receiving pain as their meed. You, who possess a distinguished family name, and the reverence due to a great master, would generously share your dignity with me, your worldly pleasures and amusements; I, too, in return, for your sake, beseech you to share my reward with me; he who indulges in the threefold kinds of pleasure, this man the world calls 'Lord,' but this is not according to reason either, because these things cannot be retained, but where there is no birth, or life, or death, he who exercises himself in this way, is Lord indeed! You say that while young a man should be gay, and when old then religious, but I regard the feebleness of age as bringing with it loss of power to be religious, unlike the firmness and power of youth, the will determined and the heart established; but death as a robber with a drawn sword follows us all, desiring to catch his prey; how then should we wait for old age, ere we bring our mind to a religious life? Inconstancy is the great hunter, age his bow, disease his arrows, in the fields of life and death he hunts for living things as for the deer; when he can get his opportunity, he takes our life; who then would wait for age? And what the teachers say and do, with reference to matters connected with life and death, exhorting the young, mature, or middle-aged, all to contrive by any means, to prepare vast meetings for sacrifices, this they do indeed of their own ignorance; better far to reverence the true law, and put an end to sacrifice to appease the gods! Destroying life to gain religious merit, what love can such a man possess? even if the reward of such sacrifices were lasting, even for this, slaughter would be unseemly; how much more, when the reward is transient! Shall we, in search of this, slay that which lives, in worship? this is like those who practise wisdom, and the way of religious abstraction, but neglect the rules of moral conduct. It ill behooves us then to follow with the world, and attend these sacrificial assemblies, and seek some present good in killing that which lives; the wise avoid destroying life! Much less do they engage in general sacrifices, for the purpose of gaining future reward! the fruit promised in the three worlds is none of mine to choose for happiness! All these are governed by transient, fickle laws, like the wind, or the drop that is blown from the grass; such things therefore I put away from me, and I seek for true escape. I hear there is one O-lo-lam who eloquently discourses on the way of escape; I must go to the place where he dwells, that great Rishi and hermit. But in truth, sorrow must be banished; I regret indeed leaving you; may your country have repose and quiet! safely defended by you as by the divine Sakra râga! May wisdom be shed abroad as light upon your empire, like the brightness of the meridian sun! may you be exceedingly victorious as lord of the great earth, with a perfect heart ruling over its destiny! May you direct and defend its sons! ruling your empire in righteousness! Water and snow and fire are opposed to one another, but the fire by its influence causes vapor, the vapor causes the floating clouds, the floating clouds drop down rain; there are birds in space, who drink the rain, with rainless bodies.[10] Slaughter and peaceful homes are enemies! those who would have peace hate slaughter, and if those who slaughter are so hateful, then put an end, O king, to those who practise it! And bid these find release, as those who drink and yet are parched with thirst."

Then the king, clasping together his hands, with greatest reverence and joyful heart, said, "That which you now seek, may you obtain quickly the fruit thereof; having obtained the perfect fruit, return I pray and graciously receive me!"

[10] The sense of the text and context appears to be this, that as there are those who drink the rain-clouds and yet are parched with thirst, so there are those who constantly practise religious duties and yet are still unblest.

Bodhisattva, his heart inwardly acquiescing, purposing to accomplish his prayer, departing, pursued his road, going to the place where Ârâda Kâlâma dwelt; whilst the king with all his retinue, their hands clasped, themselves followed a little space, then with thoughtful and mindful heart, returned once more to Râgagriha!

Visit to Ârâda Udrarâma

The child of the glorious sun of the Ikshvâku race, going to that quiet peaceful grove, reverently stood before the Muni, the great Rishi Ârâda Râma; the dark-clad followers of the Kalam (Sanghârâma) seeing afar-off Bodhisattva approaching, with loud voice raised a joyful chant, and with suppressed breath muttered "Welcome," as with clasped hands they reverenced him. Approaching one another, they made mutual inquiries; and this being done, with the usual apologies, according to their precedence in age they sat down; the Brahmakârins observing the prince, beheld his personal beauty and carefully considered his appearance; respectfully they satisfied themselves of his high qualities, like those who, thirsty, drink the "pure dew." Then with raised hands they addressed the prince: "Have you been long an ascetic, divided from your family and broken from the bonds of love, like the elephant who has cast off restraint? Full of wisdom, completely enlightened, you seem well able to escape the poisonous fruit of this world. In old time the monarch Ming Shing gave up his kingly estate to his son, as a man who has carried a flowery wreath, when withered casts it away: but such is not your case, full of youthful vigor, and yet not enamoured with the condition of a holy king; we see that your will is strong and fixed, capable of becoming a vessel of the true law, able to embark in the boat of wisdom, and to cross over the sea of life and death. The common class, enticed to come to learn, their talents first are tested, then they are taught; but as I understand your case, your mind is already fixed and your will firm; and now you have undertaken the purpose of learning, I am persuaded you will not in the end shrink from it."

The prince hearing this exhortation, with gladness made reply: "You have with equal intention, illustrious! cautioned me with impartial mind; with humble heart I accept the advice, and pray that it may be so with me as you anticipate; that I may in my night-journey obtain a torch, to guide me safely through treacherous places; a handy boat to cross over the sea;—may it be so even now with me! But as I am somewhat in doubt and anxious to learn, I will venture to make known my doubts, and ask, with respect to old age, disease, and death, how are these things to be escaped?"

At this time O-lo-lam hearing the question asked by the prince, briefly from the various Sûtras and Sâstras quoted passages in explanation of a way of deliverance. "But thou," he said, "illustrious youth! so highly gifted, and eminent among the wise! hear what I have to say, as I discourse upon the mode of ending birth and death; nature, and change, birth, old age, and death, these five attributes belong to all; nature is (in itself) pure and without fault; the involution of this with the five elements, causes an awakening and power of perception, which, according to its exercise, is the cause of change; form, sound, order, taste, touch, these are called the five objects of sense; as the hand and foot are called the two ways, so these are called the roots of action (the five skandhas); the eye, the ear, the nose, the tongue, the body, these are named the roots (instruments) of understanding. The root of mind (manas) is two-fold, being both material, and also intelligent; nature by its involutions is the cause, the knower of the cause is I (the soul); Kapila the Rishi and his numerous followers, on this deep principle of soul, practising wisdom (Buddhi), found deliverance. Kapila and now Vâkaspati, by the power of Buddhi perceiving the character of birth, old age, and death, declare that on this is founded true philosophy; whilst all opposed to this, they say, is false. Ignorance and passion, causing constant transmigration, abiding in the midst of these (they say) is the lot of all that lives. Doubting the truth of soul is called excessive doubt, and without distinguishing aright, there can be no method of escape. Deep speculation as to the limits of perception is but to involve the soul; thus unbelief leads to confusion, and ends in differences of thought and conduct. Again, the various speculations on soul, such as 'I say,' 'I know and perceive,' 'I come' and 'I go,' or 'I remain fixed,' these are called the intricacies of soul. And then the fancies raised in different natures, some saying 'this is so,' others denying it, and this condition of uncertainty is called the state of darkness. Then there are those who say that outward things are one with soul, who say that the objective is the same as mind, who confuse intelligence with instruments, who say that number is the soul. Thus not distinguishing aright, these are called excessive quibbles, marks of folly, nature changes, and so on. To worship and recite religious books, to slaughter living things in sacrifice, to render pure by fire and water, and thus awake the thought of final rescue, all these ways of thinking are called without right expedient, the result of ignorance and doubt, by means of word or thought or deed; involving outward relationships, this is called depending on means; making the material world the ground of soul, this is called depending on the senses. By these eight sorts of speculation are we involved in birth and death. The foolish masters of the world make their classifications in these five ways: Darkness, folly, and great folly, angry passion, with timid fear. Indolent coldness is called darkness; birth and death are called folly; lustful desire is great folly; because of great men subjected to error, cherishing angry feelings, passion results; trepidation of the heart is called fear. Thus these foolish men dilate upon the five desires; but the root of the great sorrow of birth and death, the life destined to be spent in the five ways, the cause of the whirl of life, I clearly perceive, is to be placed in the existence of 'I'; because of the influence of this cause, result the consequences of repeated birth and death; this cause is without any nature of its own, and its fruits have no nature; rightly considering what has been said, there are four matters which have to do with escape, kindling wisdom—opposed to dark ignorance—making manifest—opposed to concealment and obscurity—if these four matters be understood, then we may escape birth, old age, and death. Birth, old age, and death being over, then we attain a final place; the Brahmans all depending on this principle, practising themselves in a pure life, have also largely dilated on it, for the good of the world."

The prince hearing these words again inquired of Ârâda: "Tell me what are the expedients you name, and what is the final place to which they lead, and what is the character of that pure Brahman life; and again what are the stated periods during which such life must be practised, and during which such life is lawful; all these are principles to be inquired into; and on them I pray you discourse for my sake."

Then that Ârâda, according to the Sûtras and Sâstras, spoke: "Yourself using wisdom is the expedient; but I will further dilate on this a little; first by removing from the crowd and leading a hermit's life, depending entirely on alms for food, extensively practising rules of decorum, religiously adhering to right rules of conduct; desiring little and knowing when to abstain, receiving whatever is given in food, whether pleasant or otherwise, delighting to practise a quiet life, diligently studying all the Sûtras and Sâstras; observing the character of covetous longing and fear, without remnant of desire to live in purity, to govern well the organs of life, the mind quieted and silently at rest; removing desire, and hating vice, all the sorrows of life put away, then there is happiness; and we obtain the enjoyment of the first dhyâna.[11] Having obtained this first dhyâna, then with the illumination thus obtained, by inward meditation is born reliance on thought alone, and the entanglements of folly are put away; the mind depending on this, then after death, born in the Brahma heavens, the enlightened are able to know themselves; by the use of means is produced further inward illumination; diligently persevering, seeking higher advance, accomplishing the second dhyâna, tasting of that great joy, we are born in the Kwong-yin heaven; then by the use of means putting away this delight, practising the third dhyâna, resting in such delight and wishing no further excellence, there is a birth in the Subhakritsna heaven; leaving the thought of such delight, straightway we reach the fourth dhyâna, all joys and sorrows done away, the thought of escape produced; we dwell in this fourth dhyâna, and are born in the Vrihat-phala heaven; because of its long enduring years, it is thus called Vrihat-phala (extensive-fruit); whilst in that state of abstraction rising higher, perceiving there is a place beyond any bodily condition, adding still and persevering further in practising wisdom, rejecting this fourth dhyâna, firmly resolved to persevere in the search, still contriving to put away every desire after form, gradually from every pore of the body there is perceived a feeling of empty release, and in the end this extends to every solid part, so that the whole is perfected in an apprehension of emptiness. In brief, perceiving no limits to this emptiness, there is opened to the view boundless knowledge. Endowed with in-

[11] The dhyânas are the conditions of ecstasy, enjoyed by the inhabitants of the Brahmaloka heavens.

ward rest and peace, the idea of 'I' departs, and the object of 'I'—clearly discriminating the non-existence of matter, this is the condition of immaterial life. As the Muñga (grass) when freed from its horny case, or as the wild bird which escapes from its prison trap, so, getting away from all material limitations, we thus find perfect release. Thus ascending above the Brahmans, deprived of every vestige of bodily existence, we still endure. Endued with wisdom! let it be known this is real and true deliverance. You ask what are the expedients for obtaining this escape; even as I have before detailed, those who have deep faith will learn. The Rishis Gaigîshavya, Ganaka, Vriddha Parâsara, and other searchers after truth, all by the way I have explained, have reached true deliverance."

The prince hearing these words, deeply pondering on the outline of these principles, and reaching back to the influences produced by our former lives, again asked with further words: "I have heard your very excellent system of wisdom, the principles very subtle and deep-reaching, from which I learn that because of not 'letting go' (by knowledge as a cause), we do not reach the end of the religious life; but by understanding nature in its involutions, then, you say, we obtain deliverance; I perceive this law of birth has also concealed in it another law as a germ; you say that the 'I' (i.e. the soul of Kapila) being rendered pure, forthwith there is true deliverance; but if we encounter a union of cause and effect, then there is a return to the trammels of birth; just as the germ in the seed, when earth, fire, water, and wind seem to have destroyed in it the principle of life, meeting with favorable concomitant circumstances will yet revive, without any evident cause, but because of desire; so those who have gained this supposed release, likewise keeping the idea of 'I' and living things, have in fact gained no final deliverance; in every condition, letting go the three classes and again reaching the three excellent qualities, because of the eternal existence of soul, by the subtle influences of that (influences resulting from the past), the heart lets go the idea of expedients, and obtains an almost endless duration of years. This, you say, is true release; you say 'letting go the ground on which the idea of soul rests,' that this frees us from 'limited existence,' and that the mass of people have not yet removed the idea of soul, and are therefore still in bondage. But what is this letting go gunas (cords fettering the soul); if one is fettered by these gunas, how can there be release? For gunî (the object) and guna (the quality) in idea are different, but in substance one; if you say that you can remove the properties of a thing and leave the thing by arguing it to the end, this is not so. If you remove heat from fire, then there is no such thing as fire, or if you remove surface from body, what body can remain? Thus guna is as it were surface, remove this and there can be no gunî. So that this deliverance, spoken of before, must leave a body yet in bonds. Again, you say that by clear knowledge you get rid of body; there is then such a thing as knowledge or the contrary; if you affirm the existence of clear knowledge, then there should be someone who possesses it (i.e. possesses this knowledge); if there be a possesor, how can there be deliverance from this personal 'I'? If you say there is no 'knower,' then who is it that is spoken of as 'knowing'? If there is knowledge and no person, then the subject of knowledge may be a stone or a log; moreover, to have clear knowledge of these minute causes of contamination and reject them thoroughly, these being so rejected, there must be an end, then, of the 'doer.' What Ârâda has declared cannot satisfy my heart. This clear knowledge is not universal wisdom, I must go on and seek a better explanation."

Going on then to the place of Udra Rishi, he also expatiated on this question of "I." But although he refined the matter to the utmost, laying down a term of "thought" and "no thought" taking the position of removing "thought" and "no thought," yet even so he came not out of the mire; for supposing creatures attained that state, still (he said) there is a possibility of returning to the coil, whilst Bodhisattva sought a method of getting out of it. So once more leaving Udra Rishi, he went on in search of a better system, and came at last to Mount Kia-ke (the forest of mortification), where was a town called Pain-suffering forest. Here the five Bhikshus had gone before. When then he beheld these five, virtuously keeping in check their senses, holding to the rules of moral conduct, practising mortification, dwelling in that grove of mortification; occupying a spot beside the Nairañgana river, perfectly composed and filled with contentment, Bodhisattva forthwith by them selecting one spot, quietly gave himself to thought. The five Bhikshus knowing him with earnest heart to be seeking escape, offered him their services with devotion, as if reverencing Isvara Deva.

Having finished their attentions and dutiful services, then going on he took his seat not far off, as one about to enter on a course of religious practice, composing all his members as he desired. Bodhisattva diligently applied himself to "means," as one about to cross over old age, disease, and death. With full purpose of heart he set himself to endure mortification, to restrain every bodily passion, and give up thought about sustenance, with purity of heart to observe the fast-rules, which no worldly man can bear; silent and still, lost in thoughtful meditation; and so for six years he continued, each day eating one hemp grain, his bodily form shrunken and attenuated, seeking how to cross the sea of birth and death, exercising himself still deeper and advancing further; making his way perfect by the disentanglements of true wisdom, not eating, and yet not looking to that as a cause of emancipation, his four members although exceedingly weak, his heart of wisdom increasing yet more and more in light; his spirit free, his body light and refined, his name spreading far and wide, as "highly gifted," even as the moon when first produced, or as the Kumuda flower spreading out its sweetness. Everywhere through the country his excellent fame extended; the daughters of the lord of the place both coming to see him, his mortified body like a withered branch, just completing the period of six years, fearing the sorrow of birth and death, seeking earnestly the method of true wisdom, he came to the conviction that these were not the means to extinguish desire and produce ecstatic contemplation; nor yet the means by which in former time, seated underneath the Gambu tree, he arrived at that miraculous condition, that surely was the proper way, he thought, the way opposed to this of "withered body."

"I should therefore rather seek strength of body, by drink and food refresh my members, and with contentment cause my mind to rest. My mind at rest, I shall enjoy silent composure; composure is the trap for getting ecstasy (dhyâna); while in ecstasy perceiving the true law, then the force of truth obtained, disentanglement will follow. And thus composed, enjoying perfect quiet, old age and death are put away; and then defilement is escaped by this first means; thus then by equal steps the excellent law results from life restored by food and drink."

Having carefully considered this principle, bathing in the Nairañgana river, he desired afterwards to leave the water, but owing to extreme exhaustion was unable to rise; then a heavenly spirit holding out a branch, taking this in his hand he raised himself and came forth. At this time on the opposite side of the grove there was a certain chief herdsman, whose eldest daughter was called Nandâ. One of the Suddhavâsa Devas addressing her said, " Bodhisattva dwells in the grove, go you then, and present to him a religious offering."

Nandâ Balada (or Balaga or Baladhya) with joy came to the spot, above her hands (i.e. on her wrists) white chalcedony bracelets, her clothing of a gray color; the gray and the white together contrasted in the light, as the colors of the rounded river bubble; with simple heart and quickened step she came, and, bowing down at Bodhisattva's feet, she reverently offered him perfumed rice milk, begging him of his condescension to accept it. Bodhisattva taking it, partook of it at once, whilst she received, even then, the fruits of her religious act. Having eaten it, all his members refreshed, he became capable of receiving Bodhi; his body and limbs glistening with renewed strength, and his energies swelling higher still, as the hundred streams swell the sea, or the first quartered moon daily increases in brightness. The five Bhikshus having witnessed this, perturbed, were filled with suspicious reflection; they supposed that his religious zeal was flagging, and that he was leaving and looking for a better abode, as though he had obtained deliverance, the five elements entirely removed.

Bodhisattva wandered on alone, directing his course to that " fortunate " tree,[12] beneath whose shade he might accomplish his search after complete enlightenment. Over the ground wide and level, producing soft and pliant grass, easily he advanced with lion step, pace by pace, whilst the earth shook withal; and as it shook, Kâla nâga aroused, was filled with joy, as his eyes were opened to the light. Forthwith he exclaimed: " When formerly I saw the Buddhas of old, there was the sign of an earthquake as now; the virtues of a Muni are so great in majesty, that the great earth cannot endure them; as step by step his foot treads upon the ground, so is there heard the sound of the rumbling earth-shaking; a brilliant light now illumes the world, as the shining of the rising sun; five hundred bluish-tinted birds I see, wheeling round to the right, flying through space; a gentle, soft, and cooling breeze blows around

[12] The "fortunate tree," the tree "of good omen," the Bodhi tree.

in an agreeable way; all these auspicious signs are the same as those of former Buddhas; wherefore I know that this Bodhisattva will certainly arrive at perfect wisdom. And now, behold! from yonder man, a grass cutter, he obtains some pure and pliant grass, which spreading out beneath the tree, with upright body, there he takes his seat; his feet placed under him, not carelessly arranged, moving to and fro, but like the firmly fixed and compact body of a Nâga; nor shall he rise again from off his seat till he has completed his undertaking." And so he (the Nâga) uttered these words by way of confirmation. The heavenly Nâgas, filled with joy, caused a cool refreshing breeze to rise; the trees and grass were yet unmoved by it, and all the beasts, quiet and silent, looked on in wonderment.

These are the signs that Bodhisattva will certainly attain enlightenment.

Defeats Mâra

The great Rishi, of the royal tribe of Rishis, beneath the Bodhi tree firmly established, resolved by oath to perfect the way of complete deliverance.

The spirits, Nâgas, and the heavenly multitude, all were filled with joy; but Mâra Devarâga, enemy of religion, alone was grieved, and rejoiced not; lord of the five desires, skilled in all the arts of warfare, the foe of those who seek deliverance, therefore his name is rightly given Pisuna. Now this Mâra râga had three daughters, mincingly beautiful and of a pleasant countenance, in every way fit by artful ways to inflame a man with love, highest in this respect among the Devîs. The first was named Yuh-yen, the second Neng-yueh-gin, the third Ngai-loh. These three, at this time, advanced together, and addressed their father Pisuna and said: "May we not know the trouble that afflicts you?"

The father, calming his feelings, addressed his daughters thus: "The world has now a great Muni, he has taken a strong oath as a helmet, he holds a mighty bow in his hand, wisdom is the diamond shaft he uses. His object is to get the mastery in the world, to ruin and destroy my territory; I am myself unequal to him, for all men will believe in him, and all find refuge in the way of his salvation; then will my land be desert and unoccupied. But as when a man transgresses the laws of morality, his body is then empty. So now, the eye of wisdom, not yet opened in this man, whilst my empire still has peace, I will go and overturn his purpose, and break down and divide the ridge-pole of his house."

Seizing then his bow and his five arrows, with all his retinue of male and female attendants, he went to that grove of "fortunate rest" with the vow that the world should not find peace. Then seeing the Muni, quiet and still, preparing to cross the sea of the three worlds, in his left hand grasping his bow, with his right hand pointing his arrow, he addressed Bodhisattva and said: "Kshatriya! rise up quickly! for you may well fear! your death is at hand; you may practise your own religious system, but let go this effort after the law of deliverance for others; wage warfare in the field of charity as a cause of merit, appease the tumultuous world, and so in the end reach your reward in heaven. This is a way renowned and well established, in which former saints have walked, Rishis and kings and men of eminence; but this system of penury and alms-begging is unworthy of you. Now then if you rise not, you had best consider with yourself, that if you give not up your vow, and tempt me to let fly an arrow, how that Aila, grandchild of Soma, by one of these arrows just touched, as by a fanning of the wind, lost his reason and became a madman. And how the Rishi Vimala, practising austerities, hearing the sound of one of these darts, his heart possessed by great fear, bewildered and darkened he lost his true nature; how much less can you—a late-born one—hope to escape this dart of mine. Quickly arise then! if hardly you may get away! This arrow full of rankling poison, fearfully insidious where it strikes a foe! See now! with all my force, I point it! and are you resting in the face of such calamity? How is it that you fear not this dread arrow? say! why do you not tremble?" Mâra uttered such fear-inspiring threats, bent on overawing Bodhisattva. But Bodhisattva's heart remained unmoved; no doubt, no fear was present. Then Mâra instantly discharged his arrow, whilst the three women came in front. Bodhisattva regarded not the arrow, nor considered aught the women three. Mâra râga now was troubled much with doubt, and muttered thus 'twixt heart and mouth: "Long since the maiden of the snowy mountains, shooting at Mahesvara, constrained him to change his mind; and yet Bodhisattva is unmoved, and heeds not even this dart of mine, nor the three heavenly women! nought prevails to move his heart or raise one spark of love within him. Now must I assemble my army-host, and press him sore by force;" having thought thus awhile, Mâra's army suddenly assembled round. Each assumed his own peculiar form; some were holding spears, others grasping swords, others snatching up trees, others wielding diamond maces; armed with every sort of weapon. Some had heads like hogs, others like fishes, others like asses, others like horses; some with forms like snakes or like the ox or savage tiger; lion-headed, dragon-headed, and like every other kind of beast. Some had many heads on one body-trunk, with faces having but a single eye, and then again with many eyes; some with great-bellied mighty bodies. And others thin and skinny, belly-less; others long-legged, mighty-kneed; others big-shanked and fat-calved; some with long and claw-like nails. Some were headless, breastless, faceless; some with two feet and many bodies; some with big faces looking every way; some pale and ashy-colored; others colored like the bright star rising, others steaming fiery vapor, some with ears like elephants, with humps like mountains, some with naked forms covered with hair. Some with leather skins for clothing, their faces parti-colored, crimson, and white; some with tiger skins as robes, some with snake skins over them, some with tinkling bells around their waists, others with twisted screw-like hair, others with hair dishevelled covering the body, some breath-suckers, others body-snatchers, some dancing and shrieking awhile, some jumping onwards with their feet together, some striking one another as they went. Others waving in the air, others flying and leaping between the trees, others howling, or hooting, or screaming, or whining, with their evil noises shaking the great earth; thus this wicked goblin troop encircled on its four sides the Bodhi tree; some bent on tearing his body to pieces, others on devouring it whole; from the four sides flames belched forth, and fiery steam ascended up to heaven; tempestuous winds arose on every side; the mountain forests shook and quaked. Wind, fire, and steam, with dust combined, produced a pitchy darkness, rendering all invisible. And now the Devas well affected to the law, and all the Nâgas and the spirits, all incensed at this host of Mâra, with anger fired, wept tears of blood; the great company of Suddhavâsa gods, beholding Mâra tempting Bodhisattva, free from low-feeling, with hearts undisturbed by passion, moved by pity towards him and commiseration, came in a body to behold the Bodhisattva, so calmly seated and so undisturbed, surrounded with an uncounted host of devils, shaking the heaven and earth with sounds ill-omened. Bodhisattva silent and quiet in the midst remained, his countenance as bright as heretofore, unchanged; like the great lion-king placed amongst all the beasts howling and growling round him so he sat, a sight unseen before, so strange and wonderful! The host of Mâra hastening, as arranged, each one exerting his utmost force, taking each other's place in turns, threatening every moment to destroy him. Fiercely staring, grinning with their teeth, flying tumultuously, bounding here and there; but Bodhisattva, silently beholding them, watched them as one would watch the games of children. And now the demon host waxed fiercer and more angry, and added force to force, in further conflict; grasping at stones they could not lift, or lifting them, they could not let them go. Their flying spears, lances, and javelins, stuck fast in space, refusing to descend; the angry thunderdrops and mighty hail, with these, were changed into five-colored lotus flowers, whilst the foul poison of the dragon snakes was turned to spicy-breathing air. Thus all these countless sorts of creatures, wishing to destroy the Bodhisattva, unable to remove him from the spot, were with their own weapons wounded. Now Mâra had an aunt-attendant whose name was Ma-kia-ka-li, who held a skull-dish in her hands, and stood in front of Bodhisattva, and with every kind of winsome gesture, tempted to lust the Bodhisattva. So all these followers of Mâra, possessed of every demon-body form, united in discordant uproar, hoping to terrify Bodhisattva; but not a hair of his was moved, and Mâra's host was filled with sorrow. Then in the air the crowd of angels, their forms invisible, raised their voices, saying: "Behold the great Muni; his mind unmoved by any feeling of resentment, whilst all that wicked Mâra race, besotted, are vainly bent on his destruction; let go your foul and murderous thoughts against that silent Muni, calmly seated! You cannot with a breath move the Sumeru mountain. Fire may freeze, water may burn, the roughened earth may grow soft and pliant, but ye cannot hurt the Bodhisattva! Through ages past disciplined by suffering. Bodhisattva rightly trained in thought, ever advancing in the use of 'means,' pure and illustrious for wisdom, loving and merciful to all. These four conspicuous virtues cannot with him be rent asunder, so as to make it hard or doubtful whether he gain the highest wisdom. For as the thousand rays of yonder sun must drown the darkness of the world, or as the boring wood must kindle fire, or as the earth deep-dug gives water, so he who perseveres in the 'right means,' by seeking thus, will find. The world without instruction, poisoned by lust and hate and ignorance; because he pitied 'flesh,' so circumstanced, he sought on their account the joy of wisdom. Why then would you molest and hinder one who seeks to banish sorrow from the world? The ignorance that everywhere prevails is due to false pernicious books, and therefore Bodhisattva, walking uprightly, would lead and draw men after him. To obscure and blind the great world-leader, this undertaking is impossible, for 'tis as though in the Great Desert a man would purposely mislead the merchant-guide. So 'all flesh' having fallen into darkness, ignorant of where they are going, for their sakes he would light the lamp of wisdom; say then! why would you extinguish it? All flesh engulfed and overwhelmed in the great sea of birth and death, this one prepares the boat of wisdom; say then! why destroy and sink it? Patience is the sprouting of religion, firmness its root, good conduct is the flower, the enlightened heart the boughs and branches. Wisdom supreme the entire tree, the 'transcendent law' the fruit, its shade protects all living things; say then! why would you cut it down? Lust, hate, and ignorance, are the rack and bolt, the yoke placed on the shoulder of the world; through ages long he has practised austerities to rescue men from these their fetters. He now shall certainly attain his end, sitting on this right-established throne; as all the previous Buddhas, firm and compact like a diamond. Though all the earth were moved and shaken, yet would this place be fixed and stable; him, thus fixed and well assured, think not that you can overturn. Bring down and moderate your mind's desire, banish these high and envious thoughts, prepare yourselves for right reflection, be patient in your services."

Mâra hearing these sounds in space, and seeing Bodhisattva still unmoved, filled with fear and banishing his high and supercilious thoughts, again took up his way to heaven above. Whilst all his host were scattered, o'erwhelmed with grief and disappointment, fallen from their high estate, bereft of their warrior pride, their warlike weapons and accoutrements thrown heedlessly and cast away 'mid woods and deserts. Like as when some cruel chieftain slain, the hateful band is all dispersed and scattered, so the host of Mâra disconcerted, fled away. The mind of Bodhisattva now reposed peaceful and quiet. The morning sunbeams brighten with the dawn, the dust-like mist dispersing, disappears; the moon and stars pale their faint light, the barriers of the night are all removed, whilst from above a fall of heavenly flowers pay their sweet tribute to the Bodhisattva.

O-wei-san-pou-ti (Abhisambodhi)

Bodhisattva having subdued Mâra, his firmly fixed mind at rest, thoroughly exhausting the first principle of truth, he entered into deep and subtle contemplation. Every kind of Sâmadhi in order passed before his eyes. During the first watch he entered on " right perception " and in recollection all former births passed before his eyes. Born in such a place, of such a name, and downwards to his present birth, so through hundreds, thousands, myriads, all his births and deaths he knew. Countless in number were they, of every kind and sort; then knowing, too, his family relationships, great pity rose within his heart.

This sense of deep compassion passed, he once again considered " all that lives," and how they moved within the six portions of life's revolution, no final term to birth and death; hollow all, and false and transient as the plantain tree, or as a dream, or phantasy. Then in the middle watch of night, he reached to knowledge of the pure Devas, and beheld before him every creature, as one sees images upon a mirror; all creatures born and born again to die, noble and mean, the poor and rich, reaping the fruit of right or evil doing, and sharing happiness or misery in consequence. First he considered and distinguished evil-doers' works, that such must ever reap an evil birth. Then he considered those who practise righteous deeds, that these must gain a place with men or gods; but those again born in the nether hells, he saw participating in every kind of misery; swallowing molten brass, the iron skewers piercing their bodies, confined within the boiling caldron, driven and made to enter the fiery oven dwelling, food for hungry, long-toothed dogs, or preyed upon by brain-devouring birds; dismayed by fire, then they wander through thick woods, with leaves like razors gashing their limbs, while knives divide their writhing bodies, or hatchets lop their members, bit by bit; drinking the bitterest poisons, their fate yet holds them back from death. Thus those who found their joy in evil deeds, he saw receiving now their direst sorrow; a momentary taste of pleasure here, a dreary length of suffering there. A laugh or joke because of others' pain, a crying out and weeping now at punishment received. Surely if living creatures saw the consequence of all their evil deeds, self-visited, with hatred would they turn and leave them, fearing the ruin following—the blood and death. He saw, moreover, all the fruits of birth as beasts, each deed entailing its own return; and when death ensues born in some other form (beast shape), different in kind according to the deeds. Some doomed to die for the sake of skin or flesh, some for their horns or hair or bones or wings; others torn or killed in mutual conflict, friend or relative before, contending thus; some burdened with loads or dragging heavy weights, others pierced and urged on by pricking goads. Blood flowing down their tortured forms, parched and hungry—no relief afforded; then, turning round, he saw one with the other struggling, possessed of no independent strength. Flying through air or sunk in deep water, yet no place as a refuge left from death. He saw, moreover, those, misers and covetous, born now as hungry ghosts; vast bodies like the towering mountain, with mouths as small as any needle-tube, hungry and thirsty, nought but fire and poisoned flame to enwrap their burning forms within. Covetous, they would not give to those who sought, or duped the man who gave in charity, now born among the famished ghosts, they seek for food, but cannot find withal. The refuse of the unclean man they fain would eat, but this is changed and lost before it can be eaten. Oh! if a man believes that covetousness is thus repaid, as in their case, would he not give his very flesh in charity even as Sivi râga did! Then, once more he saw, those reborn as men, with bodies like some foul sewer, ever moving 'midst the direst sufferings, born from the womb to fear and trembling, with body tender, touching anything its feelings painful, as if cut with knives. Whilst born in this condition, no moment free from chance of death, labor, and sorrow, yet seeking birth again, and being born again, enduring pain. Then he saw those who by a higher merit were enjoying heaven; a thirst for love ever consuming them, their merit ended with the end of life, the five signs warning them of death. Just as the blossom that decays, withering away, is robbed of all its shining tints; not all their associates, living still, though grieving, can avail to save the rest. The palaces and joyous precincts empty now, the Devis all alone and desolate, sitting or asleep upon the dusty earth, weep bitterly in recollection of their loves. Those who are born, sad in decay; those who are dead, belovéd, cause of grief; thus ever struggling on, preparing future pain, covetous they seek the joys of heaven, obtaining which, these sorrows come apace; despicable joys! oh, who would covet them! using such mighty efforts to obtain, and yet unable thence to banish pain. Alas, alas! these Devas, too, alike deceived—no difference is there! through lapse of ages bearing suffering, striving to crush desire and lust, now certainly expecting long reprieve, and yet once more destined to fall! in hell enduring every kind of pain, as beasts tearing and killing one the other, as Pretas parched with direst thirst, as men worn out, seeking enjoyment; although, they say, when born in heaven, "then we shall escape these greater ills." Deceived, alas! no single place exempt, in every birth incessant pain! Alas! the sea of birth and death revolving thus—an ever-whirling wheel—all flesh immersed within its waves cast here and there without reliance! thus with his pure Deva eyes he thoughtfully considered the five domains of life. He saw that all was empty and vain alike! with no dependence! like the plantain or the bubble. Then, on the third eventful watch, he entered on the deep, true apprehension; he meditated on the entire world of creatures, whirling in life's tangle, born to sorrow; the crowds who live, grow old, and die, innumerable for multitude. Covetous, lustful, ignorant, darkly-fettered, with no way known for final rescue. Rightly considering, inwardly he reflected from what source birth and death proceed. He was assured that age and death must come from birth as from a source. For since a man has born with him a body, that body must inherit pain. Then looking further whence comes birth, he saw it came from life-deeds done elsewhere; then with his Deva-eyes scanning these deeds, he saw they were not framed by Isvara. They were not self-caused, they were not personal existences, nor were they either uncaused; then, as one who breaks the first bamboo joint finds all the rest easy to separate, having discerned the cause of birth and death, he gradually came to see the truth; deeds come from upâdâna, like as fire which catches hold of grass; upâdâna comes from trishnâ, just as a little fire inflames the mountains; trishnâ comes from vedanâ, the perception of pain and pleasure, the desire for rest; as the starving or the thirsty man seeks food and drink, so " sensation " brings " desire " for life; then contact is the cause of all sensation, producing the three kinds of pain or pleasure, even as by art of man the rubbing wood produces fire for any use or purpose; contact is born from the six entrances.[1] The six entrances are caused by name and thing, just as the germ grows to the stem and leaf; name and thing are born from knowledge, as the seed which germinates and brings forth leaves. Knowledge, in turn, proceeds from name and thing, the two are intervolved leaving no remnant; by some concurrent cause knowledge engenders name and thing, whilst by some other cause concurrent, name and thing engender knowledge. Just as a man and ship advance together, the water and the land mutually involved; thus knowledge brings forth name and thing; name and thing produce the roots. The roots engender contact; contact again brings forth sensation; sensation brings forth longing desire; longing desire produces upâdâna. Upâdâna is the cause of deeds; and these again engender birth; birth again produces age and death; so does this one incessant round cause the existence of all living things. Rightly illumined, thoroughly perceiving this, firmly established, thus was he enlightened; destroy birth, old age and death will cease; destroy bhava then will birth cease; destroy " cleaving " then will bhava end; destroy desire then will cleaving end; destroy sensation then will trishnâ end. Destroy contact then will end sensation; destroy the six entrances, then will contact cease; the six entrances all destroyed, from this, moreover, names and things will cease. Knowledge destroyed, names and things will cease; names and things destroyed, then knowledge perishes; ignorance destroyed, then the constituents of individual life will die; the great Rishi was thus perfected in wisdom. Thus perfected, Buddha then devised for the world's benefit the eightfold path, right sight, and so on, the only true path for the world to tread. Thus did he complete the end of " self," as fire goes out for want of grass; thus he had done what he would have men do; he first had found the way of

[1] The six organs of sense.

perfect knowledge. He finished thus the first great lesson; entering the great Rishi's house (dreamless sleep), the darkness disappeared; light coming on, perfectly silent, all at rest, he reached at last the exhaustless source of truth; lustrous with all wisdom the great Rishi sat, perfect in gifts, whilst one convulsive throe shook the wide earth. And now the world was calm again and bright, when Devas, Nâgas, spirits, all assembled, amidst the void raise heavenly music, and make their offerings as the law directs. A gentle cooling breeze sprang up around, and from the sky a fragrant rain distilled; exquisite flowers, not seasonable, bloomed; sweet fruits before their time were ripened. Great Mandâras, and every sort of heavenly precious flower, from space in rich confusion fell, as tribute to the illustrious monk. Creatures of every different kind were moved one towards the other lovingly; fear and terror altogether put away, none entertained a hateful thought, and all things living in the world with faultless men consorted freely; the Devas giving up their heavenly joys, sought rather to alleviate the sinner's sufferings. Pain and distress grew less and less, the moon of wisdom waxed apace; whilst all the Rishis of the Ikshvâku clan who had received a heavenly birth, beholding Buddha thus benefitting men, were filled with joy and satisfaction; and whilst throughout the heavenly mansions religious offerings fell as raining flowers, the Devas and the Nâga spirits, with one voice, praised the Buddha's virtues; men seeing the religious offerings, hearing, too, the joyous hymn of praise, were all rejoiced in turn; they leapt for unrestrained joy; Mâra, the Devarâga, only, felt in his heart great anguish. Buddha for those seven days, in contemplation lost, his heart at peace, beheld and pondered on the Bodhi tree, with gaze unmoved and never wearying:—" Now resting here, in this condition, I have obtained," he said, "my ever-shifting heart's desire, and now at rest I stand, escaped from self." The eyes of Buddha then considered " all that lives," and forthwith rose there in him deep compassion; much he desired to bring about their welfare, but how to gain for them that most excellent deliverance, from covetous desire, hatred, ignorance, and false teaching, this was the question; how to suppress this sinful heart by right direction; not by anxious use of outward means, but by resting quietly in thoughtful silence. Now looking back and thinking of his mighty vow, there rose once more within his mind a wish to preach the law; and looking carefully throughout the world, he saw how pain and sorrow ripened and increased everywhere. Then Brahma-deva knowing his thoughts, and considering it right to request him to advance religion for the wider spread of the Brahma-glory, in the deliverance of all flesh from sorrow, coming, beheld upon the person of the reverend monk all the distinguishing marks of a great preacher, visible in an excellent degree; fixed and unmoved he sat in the possession of truth and wisdom, free from all evil impediments, with a heart cleansed from all insincerity or falsehood. Then with reverent and a joyful heart, great Brahma stood and with hands joined, thus made known his request:—"What happiness in all the world so great as when a loving master meets the unwise; the world with all its occupants, filled with impurity and dire confusion, with heavy grief oppressed, or, in some cases, lighter sorrows, waits deliverance; the lord of men, having escaped by crossing the wide and mournful sea of birth and death, we now entreat to rescue others—those struggling creatures all engulfed therein; as the just worldly man, when he gets profit, gives some rebate withal. So the lord of men enjoying such religious gain, should also give somewhat to living things. The world indeed is bent on large personal gain, and hard it is to share one's own with others. O! let your loving heart be moved with pity towards the world burdened with vexing cares." Thus having spoken by way of exhortation, with reverent mien he turned back to the Brahma heaven. Buddha, regarding the invitation of Brahma-deva, rejoiced at heart, and his design was strengthened; greatly was his heart of pity nourished, and purposed was his mind to preach. Thinking he ought to beg some food, each of the four kings offered him a Pâtra; Tathâgata, in fealty to religion, received the four and joined them all in one. And now some merchant men were passing by, to whom "a virtuous friend," a heavenly spirit, said: "The great Ṛishi, the venerable monk, is dwelling in this mountain-grove, affording in the world a noble field for merit; go then and offer him a sacrifice!" Hearing the summons, joyfully they went, and offered the first meal religiously. Having partaken of it, then he deeply pondered, who first should hear the law; he thought at once of Ârâda Kâlâma and Udraka Râmaputra, as being fit to accept the righteous law; but now they both were dead. Then next he thought of the five men, that they were fit to hear the first sermon. Bent then on this design to preach Nirvâna, as the sun's glory bursts through the darkness, so went he on towards Benares, the place where dwelt the ancient Rishis. With eyes as gentle as the ox king's, his pace as firm and even as the lion's, because he would convert the world he went on towards the Kâsi city. Step by step, like the king of beasts, did he advance watchfully through the grove of wisdom.

Turning the Law-wheel

Tathâgata piously composed and silent, radiant with glory, shedding light around, with unmatched dignity advanced alone, as if surrounded by a crowd of followers. Beside the way he encountered a young Brahman whose name was Upâka; struck with the deportment of the Bhikshu, he stood with reverent mien on the roadside. Joyously he gazed at such an unprecedented sight, and then, with closed hands, he spake as follows:—" The crowds who live around are stained with sin, without a pleasing feature, void of grace, and the great world's heart is everywhere disturbed; but you alone, your senses all composed, with visage shining as the moon when full, seem to have quaffed the water of the immortals' stream. The marks of beauty yours, as the great man's, the strength of wisdom, as an all-sufficient, independent king's; what you have done must have been wisely done: what then your noble tribe and who your master?" Answering he said, " I have no master; no honorable tribe; no point of excellence; self-taught in this profoundest doctrine, I have arrived at superhuman wisdom. That which behooves the world to learn, but through the world no learner found, I now myself and by myself have learned throughout; 'tis rightly called Sambodhi. That hateful family of griefs the sword of wisdom has destroyed; this then is what the world has named, and rightly named, the 'chiefest victory.' Through all Benares soon will sound the drum of life, no stay is possible—I have no name—nor do I seek profit or pleasure. But simply to declare the truth; to save men from pain, and to fulfil my ancient oath, to rescue all not yet delivered. The fruit of this my oath is ripened now, and I will follow out my ancient vow. Wealth, riches, self all given up, unnamed, I still am named 'Righteous Master.' And bringing profit to the world,

I also have the name 'Great Teacher'; facing sorrows, not swallowed up by them, am I not rightly called 'Courageous Warrior?' If not a healer of diseases, what means the name of 'Good Physician?' Seeing the wanderer, not showing him the way, why then should I be called 'Good Master-guide?' Like as the lamp shines in the dark, without a purpose of its own, self-radiant, so burns the lamp of the Tathâgata, without the shadow of a personal feeling. Bore wood in wood, there must be fire; the wind blows of its own free self in space; dig deep and you will come to water; this is the rule of self-causation. All the Munis who perfect wisdom, must do so at Gayâ; and in the Kâsi country they must first turn the Wheel of Righteousness." The young Brahman Upâka, astonished, breathed the praise of such strange doctrine, and called to mind like thoughts he had before experienced; lost in thought at the wonderful occurrence, at every turning of the road he stopped to think; embarrassed in every step he took, Tathâgata proceeding slowly onwards, came to the city of Kâsi. The land so excellently adorned as the palace of Sakradevendra; the Ganges and Baranâ, two twin rivers flowed amidst; the woods and flowers and fruits so verdant, the peaceful cattle wandering together, the calm retreats free from vulgar noise, such was the place where the old Rishis dwelt. Tathâgata, glorious and radiant, redoubled the brightness of the place; the son of the Kaundinya tribe, and next Dasabalakâsyapa, and the third Vâshpa, the fourth Asvagit, the fifth called Bhadra, practising austerities as hermits, seeing from far Tathâgata approaching, sitting together all engaged in conversation, said: "This Gautama, defiled by worldly indulgence, leaving the practice of austerities, now comes again to find us here, let us be careful not to rise in salutation, nor let us greet him when he comes, nor offer him the customary refreshments. Because he has broken his first vow, he has no claim to hospitality"—for men on seeing an approaching guest by rights prepare things for his present and his after wants. They arrange a proper resting-couch, and take on themselves care for his comfort. Having spoken thus and so agreed, each kept his seat, resolved and fixed. And now Tathâgata slowly approached, when, lo! these men unconsciously, against their vow, rose and invited him to take a seat; offering to take his robe and Pâtra. They begged to wash and rub his feet, and asked him what he required more;

thus in everything attentive, they honored him and offered all to him as teacher. They did not cease however to address him still as Gautama, after his family. Then spake the Lord to them and said: " Call me not after my private name, for it is a rude and careless way of speaking to one who has obtained Arhatship; but whether men respect or disrespect me, my mind is undisturbed and wholly quiet. But you—your way is not so courteous: let go, I pray, and cast away your fault. Buddha can save the world; they call him, therefore, Buddha. Towards all living things, with equal heart he looks as children, to call him then by his familiar name is to despise a father; this is sin." Thus Buddha, by exercise of mighty love, in deep compassion spoke to them; but they, from ignorance and pride, despised the only wise and true one's words. They said that first he practised self-denial, but having reached thereby no profit, now giving rein to body, word, and thought, how by these means, they asked, has he become a Buddha? Thus equally entangled by doubts, they would not credit that he had attained the way. Thoroughly versed in highest truth, full of all-embracing wisdom, Tagâgata on their account briefly declared to them the one true way; the foolish masters practising austerities, and those who love to gratify their senses, he pointed out to them these two distinctive classes, and how both greatly erred. " Neither of these," he said, " has found the way of highest wisdom, nor are their ways of life productive of true rescue. The emaciated devotee by suffering produces in himself confused and sickly thoughts, not conducive even to worldly knowledge, how much less to triumph over sense! For he who tries to light a lamp with water, will not succeed in scattering the darkness, and so the man who tries with worn-out body to trim the lamp of wisdom shall not succeed, nor yet destroy his ignorance or folly. Who seeks with rotten wood to evoke the fire will waste his labor and get nothing for it; but boring hard wood into hard, the man of skill forthwith gets fire for his use. In seeking wisdom then it is not by these austerities a man may reach the law of life. But to indulge in pleasure is opposed to right: this is the fool's barrier against wisdom's light. The sensualist cannot comprehend the Sûtras or the Sâstras, how much less the way of overcoming all desire! As some man grievously afflicted eats food not fit to eat, and so in ignorance aggravates his sickness, so can he get rid of lust who pampers lust? Scatter the fire amid the desert grass, dried by the sun, fanned by the wind—the raging flames who shall extinguish? Such is the fire of covetousness and lust, I, then, reject both these extremes: my heart keeps in the middle way. All sorrow at an end and finished, I rest at peace, all error put away; my true sight greater than the glory of the sun, my equal and unvarying wisdom, vehicle of insight—right words as it were a dwelling-place—wandering through the pleasant groves of right conduct, making a right life my recreation, walking along the right road of proper means, my city of refuge in right recollection, and my sleeping couch right meditation; these are the eight even and level roads by which to avoid the sorrows of birth and death. Those who come forth by these means from the slough, doing thus, have attained the end; such shall fall neither on this side or the other, amidst the sorrow-crowd of the two periods. The tangled sorrow-web of the three worlds by this road alone can be destroyed; this is my own way, unheard of before; by the pure eyes of the true law, impartially seeing the way of escape, I, only I, now first make known this way; thus I destroy the hateful company of Trishnâ's host, the sorrows of birth and death, old age, disease, and all the unfruitful aims of men, and other springs of suffering. There are those who warring against desire are still influenced by desire; who whilst possessed of body, act as though they had none; who put away from themselves all sources of true merit—briefly will I recount their sorrowful lot. Like smothering a raging fire, though carefully put out, yet a spark left, so in their abstraction, still the germ of 'I,' the source of great sorrow still surviving, perpetuates the suffering caused by lust, and the evil consequences of every kind of deed survive. These are the sources of further pain, but let these go and sorrow dies, even as the seed of corn taken from the earth and deprived of water dies; the concurrent causes not uniting, then the bud and leaf cannot be born; the intricate bonds of every kind of existence, from the Deva down to the evil ways of birth, ever revolve and never cease; all this is produced from covetous desire; falling from a high estate to lower ones, all is the fault of previous deeds. But destroy the seed of covetousness and the rest, then there will be no intricate binding, but all effect of deeds destroyed, the various degrees of sorrow then will end for good. Having this, then, we must inherit that; destroying this, then that is ended too; no birth, old age, disease, or death; no earth, or water, fire, or wind. No beginning, end, or middle; and no deceptive systems of philosophy; this is the standpoint of wise men and sages; the certain and exhausted termination, complete Nirvâna. Such do the eight right ways declare; this one expedient has no remains; that which the world sees not, engrossed by error I declare, I know the way to sever all these sorrow-sources; the way to end them is by right reason, meditating on these four highest truths, following and perfecting this highest wisdom. This is what means the 'knowing' sorrow; this is to cut off the cause of all remains of being; these destroyed, then all striving, too, has ended, the eight right ways have been assayed. Thus, too, the four great truths have been acquired, the eyes of the pure law completed. In these four truths, the equal, true or right, eyes not yet born, there is not mention made of gaining true deliverance; it is not said what must be done is done, nor that all is finished, nor that the perfect truth has been acquired. But now because the truth is known, then by myself is known 'deliverance gained,' by myself is known that 'all is done,' by myself is known 'the highest wisdom.'" And having spoken thus respecting truth, the member of the Kaundinya family, and eighty thousand of the Deva host, were thoroughly imbued with saving knowledge. They put away defilement from themselves, they got the eyes of the pure law; Devas and earthly masters thus were sure, that what was to be done was done. And now with lion-voice he joyfully inquired, and asked Kaundinya, "Knowest thou yet?" Kaundinya forthwith answered Buddha, "I know the mighty master's law." And for this reason, knowing it, his name was Âgñâta Kaundinya. Amongst all the disciples of Buddha, he was the very first in understanding. Then as he understood the sounds of the true law, hearing the words of the disciple—all the earth spirits together raised a shout triumphant, "Well done! deeply seeing the principles of the law, Tathâgata, on this auspicious day, has set revolving that which never yet revolved, and far and wide, for gods and men, has opened the gates of immortality. Of this wheel the spokes are the rules of pure conduct; equal contemplation, their uniformity of length; firm wisdom is the tire; modesty and thoughtfulness, the rubbers (sockets in the nave in which the axle is fixed); right reflection is the nave; the wheel itself the law of perfect truth; the right truth now has gone forth in the world, not to retire before another teacher."

Thus the earth spirits shouted, the spirits of the air took up the strain, the Devas all joined in the hymn of praise, up to the highest Brahma heaven. The Devas of the triple world, now hearing what the great Rishi taught, in intercouse together spoke, " The widely honored Buddha moves the world! Widespread, for the sake of all that lives, he turns the wheel of the law of complete purity! " The stormy winds, the clouds, the mists, all disappeared; down from space the heavenly flowers descended. The Devas revelled in their joys celestial, filled with unutterable gladness.

CHAPTER IV

Bimbisâra Râga Becomes a Disciple

AND now those five men, Asvagit Vâshpa, and the others, having heard that he (Kaundinya) "knew" the law, with humble mien and self-subdued, their hands joined, offered their homage, and looked with reverence in the teacher's face. Tathâgata, by wise expedient, caused them one by one to embrace the law. And so from first to last the five Bhikshus obtained reason and subdued their senses, like the five stars which shine in heaven, waiting upon the brightening moon. At this time in the town of Ku-i there was a noble's son called Yasas; lost in night-sleep suddenly he woke, and when he saw his attendants all, men and women, with ill-clad bodies, sleeping, his heart was filled with loathing; reflecting on the root of sorrow, he thought how madly foolish men were immersed in it. Clothing himself, and putting on his jewels, he left his home and wandered forth; then on the way he stood and cried aloud, "Alas! alas! what endless chain of sorrows." Tathâgata, by night, was walking forth, and hearing sounds like these, "Alas! what sorrow," forthwith replied, "You are welcome! here, on the other hand, there is a place of rest—the most excellent, refreshing, Nirvâna, quiet and unmoved, free from sorrow." Yasas hearing Buddha's exhortation, there rose much joy within his heart. And in the place of the disgust he felt, the cooling streams of holy wisdom found their way, as when one enters first a cold pellucid lake. Advancing then, he came where Buddha was—his person decked with common ornaments, his mind already freed from all defects; by power of the good root obtained in other births, he quickly reached the fruit of an Arhat. The secret light of pure wisdom's virtue enabled him to understand, on listening to the law; just as a pure silken fabric with ease is dyed a different color. Thus having attained to self-illumination, and done that which was to be done, he was converted; then looking at his person richly ornamented, his heart was filled with shame. Tathâgata knowing his inward thoughts, in gâthas spoke the following words: "Though ornamented with jewels, the heart may yet have conquered sense; looking with equal mind on all that lives, in such a case the outward form does not affect religion; the body, too, may wear the ascetic's garb, the heart, meanwhile, be immersed in worldly thoughts; dwelling in lonely woods, yet covetous of worldly show, such men are after all mere worldlings; the body may have a worldly guise, the heart mount high to things celestial. The layman and the hermit are the same, when only both have banished thought of 'self,' but if the heart be twined with carnal bonds, what use the marks of bodily attention? He who wears martial decorations, does so because by valor he has triumphed o'er an enemy—so he who wears the hermit's colored robe, does so for having vanquished sorrow as his foe." Then he bade him come, and be a member of his church; and at the bidding, lo! his garments changed! and he stood wholly attired in hermit's dress, complete; in heart and outward look, a Sramana. Now Yasas had in former days some light companions, in number fifty and four; when these beheld their friend a hermit, they, too, one by one, attained true wisdom. By virtue of deeds done in former births, these deeds now bore their perfect fruit. Just as when burning ashes are sprinkled by water, the water being dried, the flame bursts forth. So now, with those above, the disciples were altogether sixty, all Arhats; entirely obedient and instructed in the law of perfect discipleship. So perfected he taught them further:—"Now ye have passed the stream and reached 'the other shore,' across the sea of birth and death; what should be done, ye now have done! and ye may now receive the charity of others. Go then through every country, convert those not yet converted; throughout the world that lies burnt up with sorrow, teach everywhere; instruct those lacking right instruction. Go, therefore! each one travelling by himself; filled with compassion, go! rescue and receive. I too will go alone, back to yonder Kia-ke mountain; where there are great Rishis, royal Rishis, Brahman Rishis too, these all dwell there, influencing men according to their schools. The Rishi Kâsyapa, enduring pain, reverenced by all the country, making converts too of many, him will I visit and convert." Then the sixty Bhikshus respectfully receiving orders to preach,

each according to his fore-determined purpose, following his inclination, went through every land. The honored of the world went on alone, till he arrived at the Kia-ke mountain, then entering a retired religious dell, he came to where the Rishi Kâsyapa was. Now this one had a " fire grot " where he offered sacrifice, where an evil Nâga dwelt, who wandered here and there in search of rest, through mountains and wild places of the earth. The honored of the world, wishing to instruct this hermit and convert him, asked him, on coming, for a place to lodge that night. Kâsyapa, replying, spake to Buddha thus:—" I have no resting-place to offer for the night, only this fire grot where I sacrifice; this is a cool and fit place for the purpose, but an evil dragon dwells there, who is accustomed, as he can, to poison men." Buddha replied, " Permit me only, and for the night I'll take my dwelling there." Kâsyapa made many difficulties, but the world-honored one still asked the favor. Then Kâsyapa addressed Buddha, " My mind desires no controversy, only I have my fears and apprehensions, but follow you your own good pleasure." Buddha forthwith stepped within the fiery grot, and took his seat with dignity and deep reflection; and now the evil Nâga seeing Buddha, belched forth in rage his fiery poison, and filled the place with burning vapor. But this could not affect the form of Buddha. Throughout the abode the fire consumed itself, the honored of the world still sat composed: Even as Brahma, in the midst of the kalpa-fire that burns and reaches to the Brahma heavens, still sits unmoved, without a thought of fear or apprehension, so Buddha sat; the evil Nâga seeing him, his face glowing with peace, and still unchanged, ceased his poisonous blast, his heart appeased; he bent his head and worshipped. Kâsyapa in the night seeing the fire-glow, sighed:—" Ah! alas! what misery! this most distinguished man is also burnt up by the fiery Nâga." Then Kâsyapa and his followers at morning light came one and all to look. Now Buddha having subdued the evil Nâga, had straightway placed him in his pâtra, beholding which, and seeing the power of Buddha, Kâsyapa conceived within him deep and secret thoughts:—" This Gotama," he thought, " is deeply versed in religion, but still he said, 'I am a master of religion.' " Then Buddha, as occasion offered, displayed all kinds of spiritual changes, influencing Kâsyapa's heart-thoughts, changing and subduing them, making his mind pliant and yielding, until at length prepared to be a vessel of the true law, he confessed that his poor wisdom could not compare with the complete wisdom of the world-honored one. And so, convinced at last, humbly submitting, he accepted right instruction. Thus U-pi-lo Uravilva Kâsyapa, and five hundred of his followers following their master, virtuously submissive, in turn received the teaching of the law. Kâsyapa and all his followers were thus entirely converted. The Rishi then, taking his goods and all his sacrificial vessels, threw them together in the river, which floated down upon the surface of the current. Nadi and Gada, brothers, who dwelt adown the stream, seeing these articles of clothing and the rest floating along the stream disorderly, said, "Some great change has happened," and deeply pained, were restlessly concerned. The two, each with five hundred followers, going up the stream to seek their brother. Seeing him now dressed as a hermit, and all his followers with him, having got knowledge of the miraculous law—strange thoughts engaged their minds—"our brother having submitted thus, we too should also follow him." Thus the three brothers, with all their band of followers, were brought to hear the lord's discourse on the comparison of a fire sacrifice: and in the discourse he taught, "How the dark smoke of ignorance arises, whilst confused thoughts, like wood drilled into wood, create the fire. Lust, anger, delusion, these are as fire produced, and these inflame and burn all living things. Thus the fire of grief and sorrow, once enkindled, ceases not to burn, ever giving rise to birth and death; but whilst this fire of sorrow ceases not, yet are there two kinds of fire, one that burns but has no fuel left. So when the heart of man has once conceived distaste for sin, this distaste removing covetous desire, covetous desire extinguished, there is rescue; if once this rescue has been found, then with it is born sight and knowledge, by which distinguishing the streams of birth and death, and practising pure conduct, all is done that should be done, and hereafter shall be no more life." Thus the thousand Bhikshus hearing the world-honored preach, all defects forever done away, their minds found perfect and complete deliverance. Then Buddha for the Kâsyapas' sakes, and for the benefit of the thousand Bhikshus, having preached, and done all that should be done, himself with purity and wisdom and all the concourse of high qualities excellently adorned, he gave them, as in charity, rules for cleansing sense.

The great Rishi, listening to reason, lost all regard for bodily austerities, and, as a man without a guide, was emptied of himself, and learned discipleship. And now the honored one and all his followers go forward to the royal city (Râgagriha), remembering, as he did, the Magadha king, and what he heretofore had promised. The honored one when he arrived, remained within the "staff grove"; Bimbisâra Râga hearing thereof, with all his company of courtiers, lords and ladies all surrounding him, came to where the master was. Then at a distance seeing Buddha seated, with humbled heart and subdued presence, putting off his common ornaments, descending from his chariot, forward he stepped; even as Sakra, king of gods, going to where Brahmadeva-râga dwells. Bowing down at Buddha's feet, he asked him, with respect, about his health of body; Buddha in his turn, having made inquiries, begged him to be seated on one side. Then the king's mind reflected silently:—"This Sâkya must have great controlling power, to subject to his will these Kâsyapas who now are round him as disciples." Buddha, knowing all thoughts, spoke thus to Kâsyapa, questioning him:—"What profit have you found in giving up your fire-adoring law?" Kâsyapa hearing Buddha's words, rising with dignity before the great assembly, bowed lowly down, and then with clasped hands and a loud voice addressing Buddha, said:—"The profit I received, adoring the fire spirit, was this—continuance in the wheel of life, birth and death, with all their sorrows growing—this service I have therefore cast away. Diligently I persevered in fire-worship, seeking to put an end to the five desires, in return I found desires endlessly increasing: therefore have I cast off this service. Sacrificing thus to fire with many Mantras, I did but miss escape from birth; receiving birth, with it came all its sorrows, therefore I cast it off and sought for rest. I was versed, indeed, in self-affliction, my mode of worship largely adopted, and counted of all most excellent, and yet I was opposed to highest wisdom. Therefore have I discarded it, and gone in quest of the supreme Nirvâna. Removing from me birth, old age, disease, and death, I sought a place of undying rest and calm. And as I gained the knowledge of this truth, then I cast off the law of worshipping the fire."

The honored-of-the-world, hearing Kâsyapa declaring his experience of truth, wishing to move the world throughout to conceive a heart of purity and faith, addressing Kâsyapa further, said: "Welcome! great master, welcome! Rightly have you distinguished law from law, and well obtained the highest wisdom; now before this great assembly, pray you! exhibit your excellent endowments; as any rich and wealthy noble opens for view his costly treasures, causing the poor and sorrow-laden multitude to increase their forgetfulness awhile; and honor well your lord's instruction." Forthwith in presence of the assembly, gathering up his body and entering Samâdhi, calmly he ascended into space, and there displayed himself, walking, standing, sitting, sleeping, emitting fiery vapor from his body, on his right and left side water and fire, not burning and not moistening him. Then clouds and rain proceeded from him, thunder with lightning shook the heaven and earth; thus he drew the world to look in adoration, with eyes undazzled as they gazed; with different mouths, but all in language one, they magnified and praised this wondrous spectacle, then afterwards drawn by spiritual force, they came and worshipped at the master's feet, exclaiming:—"Buddha is our great teacher! we are the honored one's disciples." Thus having magnified his work and finished all he purposed doing, drawing the world as universal witness, the assembly was convinced that he, the world-honored, was truly the "Omniscient!" Buddha, perceiving that the whole assembly was ready as a vessel to receive the law, spoke thus to Bimbisâra Râga: "Listen now and understand: The mind, the thoughts, and all the senses are subject to the law of life and death. This fault of birth and death, once understood, then there is clear and plain perception. Obtaining this clear perception, then there is born knowledge of self; knowing oneself and with this knowledge laws of birth and death, then there is no grasping and no sense-perception. Knowing oneself, and understanding how the senses act, then there is no room for 'I' (soul) or ground for framing it; then all the accumulated mass of sorrow, sorrows born from life and death, being recognized as attributes of body, and as this body is not 'I,' nor offers ground for 'I,' then comes the great superlative, the source of peace unending. This thought of 'self' gives rise to all these sorrows, binding as with cords the world, but having found there is no 'I' that can be bound, then all these bonds are severed. There are no bonds indeed —they disappear—and seeing this there is deliverance. The world holds to this thought of 'I,' and so, from this, comes false apprehension. Of those who maintain the truth of it, some say the 'I' endures, some day it perishes; taking the two extremes of birth and death, their error is most grievous! For if they say the 'I' is perishable, the fruit they strive for, too, will perish; and at some time there will be no hereafter: this is indeed a meritless deliverance. But if they say the 'I' is not to perish, then in the midst of all this life and death there is but one identity as space, which is not born and does not die. If this is what they call the 'I,' then are all things living, one—for all have this unchanging self—not perfected by any deeds, but self-perfect. If so, if such a self it is that acts, let there be no self-mortifying conduct, the self is lord and master; what need to do that which is done? For if this 'I' is lasting and imperishable, then reason would teach it never can be changed. But now we see the marks of joy and sorrow, what room for constancy then is here? Knowing that birth brings this deliverance then I put away all thought of sin's defilement; the whole world, everything, endures! what then becomes of this idea of rescue? We cannot even talk of putting self away, truth is the same as falsehood; it is not 'I' that do a thing, and who, forsooth, is he that talks of 'I'? But if it is not 'I' that do the thing, then there is no 'I' that does it, and in the absence of these both, there is no 'I' at all, in very truth. No doer and no knower, no lord, yet notwithstanding this, there ever lasts this birth and death, like morn and night ever recurring. But now attend to me and listen: The senses six and their six objects united cause the six kinds of knowledge, these three united bring forth contact, then the intervolved effects of recollection follow. Then like the burning glass and tinder through the sun's power cause fire to appear, so through the knowledge born of sense and object, the lord of knowledge (self) is born. The shoot springs from the seed, the seed is not the shoot, not one and yet not different: such is the birth of all that lives." The honored of the world preaching the truth, the equal and impartial paramârtha, thus addressed the king with all his followers. Then King Bimbisâra filled with joy, removing from himself defilement, gained religious sight, a hundred thousand spirits also, hearing the words of the immortal law, shook off and lost the stain of sin.

The Great Disciple Becomes a Hermit

At this time Bimbisâra Râga, bowing his head, requested the honored of the world to change his place of abode for the bamboo grove; graciously accepting it, Buddha remained silent. Then the king, having perceived the truth, offered his adoration and returned to his palace. The world-honored, with the great congregation, proceeded on foot, to rest for awhile in the bamboo garden. There he dwelt to convert all that breathed, to kindle once for all the lamp of wisdom, to establish Brahma and the Devas, and to confirm the lives of saints and sages. At this time Asvagit and Vâshpa, with heart composed and every sense subdued, the time having come for begging food, entered into the town of Râgagriha. Unrivalled in the world were they for grace of person, and in dignity of carriage excelling all. The lords and ladies of the city seeing them, were filled with joy; those who were walking stood still, those before waited, those behind hastened on. Now the Rishi Kapila amongst all his numerous disciples had one of wide-spread fame, whose name was Sâriputra; he, beholding the wonderful grace of the Bhikshus, their composed mien and subdued senses, their dignified walk and carriage, raising his hands, inquiring, said: " Young in years, but pure and graceful in appearance, such as I before have never seen. What law most excellent have you obeyed? and who your master that has taught you? and what the doctrine you have learned? Tell me, I pray you, and relieve my doubts." Then of the Bhikshus, one, rejoicing at his question, with pleasing air and gracious words, replied: " The omniscient, born of the Ikshvâku family, the very first 'midst gods and men, this one is my great master. I am indeed but young, the sun of wisdom has but just arisen, how can I then explain the master's doctrine? Its meaning is deep and very hard to understand, but now, according to my poor wisdom, I will recount in brief the master's doctrine:—" Whatever things exist all spring from cause, the principles of birth and death may be destroyed, the way is by the means he has declared." Then the twice-born Upata, embracing heartily what he had heard, put from him all sense-pollution, and obtained the pure eyes of the law. The former explanations he had trusted, respecting cause and what was not the cause that there was nothing that was made, but was made by Isvara; all this, now that he had heard the rule of true causation, understanding the wisdom of the no-self, adding thereto the knowledge of the minute dust troubles, which can never be overcome in their completeness but by the teaching of Tathâgata, all this he now forever put away; leaving no room for thought of self, the thought of self will disappear. Who, when the brightness of the sun gives light, would call for the dimness of the lamp? for, like the severing the lotus, the stem once cut, the pods will also die. "So Buddha's teaching cutting off the stem of sorrow, no seeds are left to grow or lead to further increase." Then bowing at the Bhikshu's feet, with grateful mien, he wended homewards. The Bhikshus after having begged their food, likewise went back to the bamboo grove. Sâriputra on his arrival home rested with joyful face and full of peace. His friend, the honored Mugalin, equally renowned for learning, seeing Sâriputra in the distance, his pleasing air and lightsome step, spoke thus:—"As I now see thee, there is an unusual look I notice; your former nature seems quite changed, the signs of happiness I now observe, all indicate the possession of eternal truth: these marks are not uncaused." Answering he said: "The words of the Tathâgata are such as never yet were spoken," and then, requested, he declared what he had heard. Hearing the words and understanding them, he too put off the world's defilement, and gained the eyes of true religion, the reward of a long-planted virtuous cause; and, as one sees by a lamp that comes to hand, so he obtained an unmoved faith in Buddha; and now they both set out for Buddha's presence, with a large crowd of followers. Buddha seeing the two worthies coming, thus spoke to his disciples:—"These two men who come shall be my two most eminent followers, one unsurpassed for wisdom, the other for powers miraculous." And then with Brahma's voice, profound and sweet, he forthwith bade them "Welcome!" Here is the pure and peaceful law, he said; here the end of all discipleship! Their hands grasping the triple-staff, their twisted hair holding the water-vessel, hearing the words of Buddha's welcome, they forthwith changed into complete Sramanas; the leaders two and all their followers, assuming the complete appearance of Bhikshus, with prostrate forms fell down at Buddha's feet, then rising, sat beside him, and with obedient heart listening to the word, they all became Arhats. At this time there was a twice-born sage, Kâsyapa Shi-ming-teng, celebrated and perfect in person, rich in possessions, and his wife most virtuous. But all this he had left and become a hermit, seeking the way of salvation. And now in the way by the To-tseu tower he suddenly encountered Sâkya Muni, remarkable for his dignified and illustrious appearance, as the embroidered flag of a temple. Respectfully and reverently approaching, with head bowed down, he worshipped his feet, whilst he said: "Truly, honored one, you are my teacher, and I am your follower: much and long time have I been harassed with doubts, oh! would that you would light the lamp of knowledge." Buddha knowing that this twice-born sage was heartily desirous of finding the best mode of escape, with soft and pliant voice, he bade him come and welcome. Hearing his bidding and his heart complying, losing all listlessness of body or spirit, his soul embraced the terms of this most excellent salvation. Quiet and calm, putting away defilement, the great merciful, as he alone knew how, briefly explained the mode of this deliverance, exhibiting the secrets of his law, ending with the four indestructible acquirements. The great sage, everywhere celebrated, was called Mahâ Kâsyapa. His original faith was that "body and soul are different," but he had also held that they are the same; that there was both "I" and a place for "I"; but now he forever cast away his former faith, and considered only that "sorrow" is ever accumulating; so by removing sorrow there will be "no remains"; obedience to the precepts and the practice of discipline, though not themselves the cause, yet he considered these the necessary mode by which to find deliverance. With equal and impartial mind, he considered the nature of sorrow, for evermore freed from a cleaving heart. Whether we think "this is" or "this is not" he thought, both tend to produce a listless, idle mode of life.. But when with equal mind we see the truth, then certainty is produced and no more doubt. If we rely for support on wealth or form, then wild confusion and concupiscence result: inconstant and impure. But lust and covetous desire removed, the heart of love and equal thoughts produced, there can be then no enemies or friends, but the heart is pitiful and kindly disposed to all, and thus is destroyed the power of anger and of hate. Trusting to outward things and their relationships, then crowding thoughts of every kind are gendered. Reflecting well, and crushing out confusing thought, then lust for pleasure is destroyed. Though born in the Arûpa world he saw that there would be a remnant of life still left; unacquainted with the four right truths, he had felt an eager longing for this deliverance, for the quiet resulting from the absence of all thought. And now putting away forever covetous desire for such a formless state of being, his restless heart was agitated still, as the stream is excited by the rude wind. Then entering on deep reflection in quiet he subdued his troubled mind, and realized the truth of there being no "self," and that therefore birth and death are no realities; but beyond this point he rose not: his thought of "self" destroyed, all else was lost. But now the lamp of wisdom lit, the gloom of every doubt dispersed, he saw an end to that which seemed without an end; ignorance finally dispelled, he considered the ten points of excellence; the ten seeds of sorrow destroyed, he came once more to life, and what he ought to do, he did. And now regarding with reverence the face of his lord, he put away the three and gained the three; so were there three disciples in addition to the three; and as the three stars range around the Trayastrimsas heaven, waiting upon the three and five, so the three wait on Buddha.

Conversion of the "Supporter of the Orphans and Destitute"

At this time there was a great householder whose name was "Friend of the Orphaned and Destitute"; he was very rich and widely charitable in helping the poor and needy. Now this man, coming far away from the north, even from the country of Kosala, stopped at the house of a friend whose name was Sheu-lo. Hearing that Buddha was in the world and dwelling in the bamboo grove near at hand, understanding moreover his renown and illustrious qualities, he set out that very night for the grove. Tathâgata, well aware of his character, and that he was prepared to bring forth purity and faith, according to the case, called him by his true name, and for his sake addressed him in words of religion:—"Having rejoiced in the true law, and being humbly desirous for a pure and believing heart, thou hast overcome desire for sleep, and art here to pay me reverence. Now then will I for your sake discharge fully the duties of a first meeting. In your former births the root of virtue planted firm in pure and rare expectancy, hearing now the name of Buddha, you rejoiced because you are a vessel fit for righteousness, humble in mind, but large in gracious deeds, abundant in your charity to the poor and helpless. The name you possess widespread and famous, the just reward of former merit, the deeds you now perform are done of charity: done with the fullest purpose and of single heart. Now, therefore, take from me the charity of perfect rest, and for this end accept my rules of purity. My rules are full of grace, able to rescue from destruction, and cause a man to ascend to heaven and share in all its pleasures. But yet to seek for these is a great evil, for lustful longing in its increase brings much sorrow. Practise then the art of 'giving up' all search, for 'giving up' desire is the joy of perfect rest. Know then! that age, disease, and death, these are the great sorrows of the world. Rightly considering the world, we put away birth and old age, disease and death; but now because we see that men at large inherit sorrow caused by age, disease, and death, we gather that when born in heaven, the case is also thus; for there is no continuance there for any, and where there is no continuance there is sorrow, and having sorrow there is no 'true self.' And if the state of 'no continuance' and of sorrow is opposed to 'self,' what room is there for such idea or ground for self? Know then! that 'sorrow' is this very sorrow and its repetition is 'accumulation'; destroy this sorrow and there is joy, the way is in the calm and quiet place. The restless busy nature of the world, this I declare is at the root of pain. Stop then the end by choking up the source. Desire not either life or its opposite; the raging fire of birth, old age, and death burns up the world on every side. Seeing the constant toil of birth and death we ought to strive to attain a passive state: the final goal of Sammata, the place of immortality and rest. All is empty! neither 'self,' nor place for 'self,' but all the world is like a phantasy; this is the way to regard ourselves, as but a heap of composite qualities."

The nobleman, hearing the spoken law, forthwith attained the first degree of holiness: he emptied as it were, the sea of birth and death, one drop alone remaining. By practising, apart from men, the banishment of all desire, he soon attained the one impersonal condition, not as common folk do now-a-day who speculate upon the mode of true deliverance; for he who does not banish sorrow-causing samskâras does but involve himself in every kind of question; and though he reaches to the highest form of being, yet grasps not the one and only truth. Erroneous thoughts as to the joy of heaven are still entwined by the fast cords of lust. The nobleman attending to the spoken law the cloud of darkness opened before the shining splendor. Thus he attained true sight, erroneous views forever dissipated; even as the furious winds of autumn sway to and fro and scatter all the heaped-up clouds. He argued not that Isvara was cause, nor did he advocate some cause heretical, nor yet again did he affirm there was no cause for the beginning of the world. "If the world was made by Isvara deva, there should be neither young nor old, first nor after, nor the five ways of birth; and when once born there should be no destruction. Nor should there be such thing as sorrow or calamity, nor doing wrong nor doing right; for all, both pure and impure deeds, these must come from Isvara deva. Again, if Isvara deva made the world there should be never doubt about the fact, even as a son born of his father ever confesses him and pays him reverence. Men when pressed by sore calamity ought not to rebel against him, but rather reverence him completely, as the self-existent. Nor ought they to adore more gods than one. Again, if Isvara be the maker he should not be called the self-existent, because in that he is the maker now he always should have been the maker; but if ever making, then ever self-remembering, and therefore not the self-existent one—and if he made without a purpose then is he like the sucking child; but if he made having an ever prompting purpose, then is he not, with such a purpose, self-existent? Sorrow and joy spring up in all that lives, these at least are not the works of Isvara; for if he causes grief and joy, he must himself have love and hate; but if he loves unduly, or has hatred, he cannot properly be named the self-existent. Again, if Isvara be the maker, all living things should silently submit, patient beneath the maker's power, and then what use to practise virtue? 'Twere equal, then, the doing right or wrong: there should be no reward of works; the works themselves being his making, then all things are the same with him, the maker, but if all things are one with him, then our deeds, and we who do them, are also self-existent. But if Isvara be uncreated, then all things, being one with him, are uncreated. But if you say there is another cause beside him as creator, then

Isvara is not the 'end of all'; Isvara, who ought to be inexhaustible, is not so, and therefore all that lives may after all be uncreated—without a maker. Thus, you see, the thought of Isvara is overthrown in this discussion; and all such contradictory assertions should be exposed; if not, the blame is ours. Again, if it be said self-nature is the maker, this is as faulty as the first assertion; nor has either of the Hetuvidyâ sâstras asserted such a thing as this, till now. That which depends on nothing cannot as a cause make that which is; but all things round us come from a cause, as the plant comes from the seed; we cannot therefore say that all things are produced by self-nature. Again, all things which exist spring not from one nature as a cause; and yet you say self-nature is but one: it cannot then be cause of all. If you say that that self-nature pervades and fills all places, if it pervades and fills all things, then certainly it cannot make them too; for there would be nothing, then, to make, and therefore this cannot be the cause. If, again, it fills all places and yet makes all things that exist, then it should throughout 'all time' have made forever that which is. But if you say it made things thus, then there is nothing to be made 'in time'; know then, for certain, self-nature cannot be the cause of all. Again, they say that that self-nature excludes all modifications, therefore all things made by it ought likewise to be free from modifications. But we see, in fact, that all things in the world are fettered throughout by modifications; therefore, again, we say that self-nature cannot be the cause of all. If, again, you say that that self-nature is different from such qualities, we answer, since self-nature must have ever caused, it cannot differ in its nature from itself; but if the world be different from these qualities, then self-nature cannot be the cause. Again, if self-nature be unchangeable, so things should also be without decay; if we regard self-nature as the cause, then cause and consequence of reason should be one; but because we see decay in all things, we know that they at least are caused. Again, if self-nature be the cause, why should we seek to find 'escape'? for we ourselves possess this nature; patient then should we endure both birth and death. For let us take the case that one may find 'escape,' self-nature still will reconstruct the evil of birth. If self-nature in itself be blind, yet 'tis the maker of the world that sees. On this account, again, it cannot be the maker, because, in this case, cause and effect would differ in their character, but in all the world around us, cause and effect go hand in hand. Again, if self-nature have no aim, it cannot cause that which has such purpose. We know on seeing smoke there must be fire, and cause and result are ever classed together thus. We are forbidden, then, to say an unthinking cause can make a thing that has intelligence. The gold of which the cup is made is gold throughout from first to last, self-nature, then, that makes these things, from first to last must permeate all it makes. Once more, if 'time' is maker of the world, 'twere needless then to seek 'escape,' for 'time' is constant and unchangeable: let us in patience bear the 'intervals' of time. The world in its successions has no limits, the 'intervals' of time are boundless also. Those then who practise a religious life need not rely on 'methods' or 'expedients.' The To-lo-piu Kiu-na, the one strange Sâstra in the world, although it has so many theories, yet still, be it known, it is opposed to any single cause. But if, again, you say that 'self' is maker, then surely self should make things pleasingly; but now things are not pleasing for oneself, how then is it said that self is maker? But if he did not wish to make things so, then he who wishes for things pleasing, is opposed to self, the maker. Sorrow and joy are not self-existing, how can these be made by self? But if we allow that self was maker, there should not be, at least, an evil karman; but yet our deeds produce results both good and evil; know then that 'self' cannot be maker. But perhaps you say 'self' is the maker according to occasion, and then the occasion ought to be for good alone. But as good and evil both result from 'cause,' it cannot be that 'self' has made it so. But if you adopt the argument—there is no maker—then it is useless practising expedients; all things are fixed and certain of themselves: what good to try to make them otherwise? Deeds of every kind, done in the world, do, notwithstanding, bring forth every kind of fruit; therefore we argue all things that exist are not without some cause or other. There is both 'mind' and 'want of mind'—all things come from fixed causation; the world and all therein is not the result of 'nothing' as a cause." The nobleman, his heart receiving light, perceived throughout the most excellent system of truth. Simple, and of wisdom born; thus firmly settled in the true doctrine he lowly bent in worship at the feet of Buddha and with closed hands made his request:—

"I dwell indeed at Srâvastî, a land rich in produce, and enjoying peace; Prasenagit is the great king thereof, the offspring of the 'lion' family; his high renown and fame spread everywhere, reverenced by all both far and near. Now am I wishful there to found a Vihâra, I pray you of your tenderness accept it from me. I know the heart of Buddha has no preferences, nor does he seek a resting-place from labor, but on behalf of all that lives refuse not my request."

Buddha, knowing the householder's heart, that his great charity was now the moving cause—untainted and unselfish charity, nobly considerate of the heart of all that lives—he said:

"Now you have seen the true doctrine, your guileless heart loves to exercise its charity: for wealth and money are inconstant treasures, 'twere better quickly to bestow such things on others. For when a treasury has been burnt, whatever precious things may have escaped the fire, the wise man, knowing their inconstancy, gives freely, doing acts of kindness with his saved possessions. But the niggard guards them carefully, fearing to lose them, worn by anxiety, but never fearing 'inconstancy,' and that accumulated sorrow, when he loses all! There is a proper time and a proper mode in charity; just as the vigorous warrior goes to battle, so is the man 'able to give'—he also is an able warrior; a champion strong and wise in action. The charitable man is loved by all, well-known and far-renowned! his friendship prized by the gentle and the good, in death his heart at rest and full of joy! He suffers no repentance, no tormenting fear, nor is he born a wretched ghost or demon! this is the opening flower of his reward, the fruit that follows—hard to conjecture! In all the six conditions born there is no sweet companion like pure charity; if born a Deva or a man, then charity brings worship and renown on every hand; if born among the lower creatures, the result of charity will follow in contentment got; wisdom leads the way to fixed composure without dependence and without number, and if we even reach the immortal path, still by continuous acts of charity we fulfil ourselves in consequence of kindly charity done elsewhere. Training ourselves in the eightfold path of recollection, in every thought the heart is filled with joy; firm fixed in holy contemplation, by meditation still we add to wisdom, able to see aright the cause of birth and death; having beheld aright the cause of these, then follows in due order perfect deliverance. The charitable man discarding earthly wealth, nobly excludes the power of covetous desire; loving and compassionate now, he gives with reverence and banishes all hatred, envy, anger. So plainly may we see the fruit of charity, putting away all covetous and unbelieving ways, the bands of sorrow all destroyed: this is the fruit of kindly charity. Know then! the charitable man has found the cause of final rescue; even as the man who plants the sapling thereby secures the shade, the flowers, the fruit of the tree full grown; the result of charity is even so, its reward is joy and the great Nirvâna. The charity which unstores wealth leads to returns of well-stored fruit. Giving away our food we get more strength, giving away our clothes we get more beauty, founding religious rest-places we reap the perfect fruit of the best charity. There is a way of giving, seeking pleasure by it; there is a way of giving, coveting to get more; some also give away to get a name for charity, others to get the happiness of heaven, others to avoid the pain of being poor hereafter, but yours, O friend! is a charity without such thoughts: the highest and the best degree of charity, without self-interest or thought of getting more. What your heart inclines you now to do, let it be quickly done and well completed! The uncertain and the lustful heart goes wandering here and there, but the pure eyes of virtue opening, the heart comes back and rests!" The nobleman accepting Buddha's teaching, his kindly heart receiving yet more light.

He invited Upatishya, his excellent friend, to accompany him on his return to Kosala; and then going round to select a pleasant site, he saw the garden of the heir-apparent, Geta, the groves and limpid streams most pure. Proceeding where the prince was dwelling, he asked for leave to buy the ground; the prince, because he valued it so much, at first was not inclined to sell, but said at last:—"If you can cover it with gold then, but not else, you may possess it."

The nobleman, his heart rejoicing, forthwith began to spread his gold. Then Geta said: "I will not give, why then spread you your gold?" The nobleman replied, "Not give; why then said you, 'Fill it with yellow gold'?" And thus they differed and contended both, till they resorted to the magistrate.

Meanwhile the people whispered much about his unwonted charity, and Geta too, knowing the man's sincerity, asked more about the matter: what his reasons were. On his reply, "I wish to found a Vihâra, and offer it to the Tathâgata and all his Bhikshu followers," the prince, hearing the name of Buddha, received at once illumination, and only took one-half the gold, desiring to share in the foundation: "Yours is the land," he said, "but mine the trees; these will I give to Buddha as my share in the offering." Then the noble took the land, Geta the trees, and settled both in trust on Sâriputra. Then they began to build the hall, laboring night and day to finish it. Lofty it rose and choicely decorated, as one of the four kings' palaces, in just proportions, following the directions which Buddha had declared the right ones. Never yet so great a miracle as this! the priests shone in the streets of Srâvastî! Tathâgata, seeing the divine shelter, with all his holy ones resorted to the place to rest. No followers there to bow in prostrate service, his followers rich in wisdom only. The nobleman reaping his reward, at the end of life ascended up to heaven, leaving to sons and grandsons a good foundation, through successive generations, to plough the field of merit.

Interview between Father and Son

Buddha in the Magadha country employing himself in converting all kinds of unbelievers, entirely changed them by the one and self-same law he preached, even as the sun drowns with its brightness all the stars. Then leaving the city of the five mountains with the company of his thousand disciples, and with a great multitude who went before and came after him, he advanced towards the Ni-kin mountain, near Kapilavastu; and there he conceived in himself a generous purpose to prepare an offering according to his religious doctrine to present to his father, the king. And now, in anticipation of his coming, the royal teacher and the chief minister had sent forth certain officers and their attendants to observe on the right hand and the left what was taking place; and they soon espied him (Buddha) as he advanced or halted on the way. Knowing that Buddha was now returning to his country they hastened back and quickly announced the tidings, "The prince who wandered forth afar to obtain enlightenment, having fulfilled his aim, is now coming back." The king hearing the news was greatly rejoiced, and forthwith went out with his gaudy equipage to meet his son; and the whole body of gentry belonging to the country, went forth with him in his company. Gradually advancing he beheld Buddha from afar, his marks of beauty sparkling with splendor twofold greater than of yore; placed in the middle of the great congregation he seemed to be even as Brahma râga. Descending from his chariot and advancing with dignity, the king was anxious lest there should be any religious difficulty in the way of instant recognition; and now beholding his beauty he inwardly rejoiced, but his mouth found no words to utter. He reflected, too, how that he was still dwelling among the unconverted throng, whilst his son had advanced and become a saint; and although he was his son, yet as he now occupied the position of a religious lord, he knew not by what name to address him. Furthermore he thought with himself how he had long ago desired earnestly this interview, which now had happened unawares. Meantime his son in silence took a seat, perfectly composed and with unchanged countenance. Thus for some time sitting opposite each other, with no expression of feeling the king reflected thus, "How desolate and sad does he now make my heart, as that of a man, who, fainting, longs for water, upon the road espies a fountain pure and cold; with haste he speeds towards it and longs to drink, when suddenly the spring dries up and disappears. Thus, now I see my son, his well-known features as of old; but how estranged his heart! and how his manner high and lifted up! There are no grateful outflowings of soul, his feelings seem unwilling to express themselves; cold and vacant there he sits; and like a thirsty man before a dried-up fountain so am I."

Still distant thus they sat, with crowding thoughts rushing through the mind, their eyes full met, but no responding joy; each looking at the other, seemed as one thinking of a distant friend who gazes by accident upon his pictured form. "That you," the king reflected, "who of right might rule the world, even as that Mândhâtri râga, should now go begging here and there your food! what joy or charm has such a life as this? Composed and firm as Sumeru, with marks of beauty bright as the sunlight, with dignity of step like the ox king, fearless as any lion, and yet receiving not the tribute of the world, but begging food sufficient for your body's nourishment!"

Buddha, knowing his father's mind, still kept to his own filial purpose. And then to open out his mind, and moved with pity for the multitude of people, by his miraculous power he rose in mid-air and with his hands appeared to grasp the sun and moon. Then he walked to and fro in space, and underwent all kinds of transformation, dividing his body into many parts, then joining all in one again. Treading firm on water as on dry land, entering the earth as in the water, passing through walls of stone without impediment, from the right side and the left water and fire produced! The king, his father, filled with joy, now dismissed all thought of son and father; then upon a lotus throne, seated in space, he (Buddha) for his father's sake declared the law:—

"I know that the king's heart is full of love and recollection, and that for his son's sake he adds grief to grief; but now let the bands of love that bind him, thinking of his son, be instantly unloosed and utterly destroyed. Ceasing from thoughts of love, let your calmed mind receive from me, your son, religious nourishment such as no son has offered yet to father: such do I present to you the king, my father. And what no father yet has from a son received, now from your son you may accept, a gift miraculous for any mortal king to enjoy, and seldom had by any heavenly king! The way superlative of life immortal I offer now the Mahârâga; from accumulated deeds comes birth, and as the result of deeds comes recompense. Knowing then that deeds bring fruit, how diligent should you be to rid yourself of worldly deeds! how careful that in the world your deeds should be only good and gentle! Fondly affected by relationship or firmly bound by mutual ties of love, at end of life the soul goes forth alone—then, only our good deeds befriend us. Whirled in the five ways of the wheel of life, three kinds of deeds produce three kinds of birth, and these are caused by lustful hankering, each kind different in its character. Deprive these of their power by the practice now of proper deeds of body and of word; by such right preparation, day and night strive to get rid of all confusion of the mind and practise silent contemplation; only this brings profit in the end, besides this there is no reality; for be sure! the three worlds are but as the froth and bubble of the sea. Would you have pleasure, or would you practise that which brings it near? then prepare yourself by deeds that bring the fourth birth: but still the five ways in the wheel of birth and death are like the uncertain wandering of the stars; for heavenly beings too must suffer change: how shall we find with men a hope of constancy; Nirvâna! that is the chief rest; composure! that the best of all enjoyments! The five indulgences enjoyed by mortal kings are fraught with danger and distress, like dwelling with a poisonous snake; what pleasure, for a moment, can there be in such a case? The wise man sees the world as compassed round with burning flames; he fears always, nor can he rest till he has banished, once for all, birth, age, and death. Infinitely quiet is the place where the wise man finds his abode; no need of arms or weapons there! no elephants or horses, chariots or soldiers there! Subdued the power of covetous desire and angry thoughts and ignorance, there's nothing left in the wide world to conquer! Knowing what sorrow is, he cuts away the cause of sorrow. This destroyed, by practising right means, rightly enlightened in the four true principles, he casts off fear and escapes the evil ways of birth."

The king when first he saw his wondrous spiritual power of miracle rejoiced in heart; but now his feelings deeply affected by the joy of hearing truth, he became a perfect vessel for receiving true religion, and with clasped hands he breathed forth his praise: "Wonderful indeed! the fruit of your resolve completed thus! Wonderful indeed! the overwhelming sorrow passed away! Wonderful indeed, this gain to me! At first my sorrowing heart was heavy, but now my sorrow has brought forth only profit! Wonderful indeed! for now, to-day, I reap the full fruit of a begotten son. It was right he should reject the choice pleasures of a monarch, it was right he should so earnestly and with diligence practise penance; it was right he should cast off his family and kin; it was right he should cut off every feeling of love and affection. The old Rishi kings boasting of their penance gained no merit; but you, living in a peaceful, quiet place, have done all and completed all; yourself at rest now you give rest to others, moved by your mighty sympathy for all that lives! If you had kept your first estate with men, and as a Kakravartin monarch ruled the world, possessing then no self-depending power of miracle, how could my soul have then received deliverance? Then there would have been no excellent law declared, causing me such joy to-day; no! had you been a universal sovereign, the bonds of birth and death would still have been unsevered, but now you have escaped from birth and death; the great pain of transmigration overcome, you are able, for the sake of every creature, widely to preach the law of life immortal, and to exhibit thus your power miraculous, and show the deep and wide power of wisdom; the grief of birth and death eternally destroyed, you now have risen far above both gods and men. You might have kept the holy state of a Kakravartin monarch; but no such good as this would have resulted." Thus his words of praise concluded, filled with increased reverence and religious love, he who occupied the honored place of a royal father, bowed down respectfully and did obeisance. Then all the people of the kingdom, beholding Buddha's miraculous power, and having heard the deep and excellent law, seeing, moreover, the king's grave reverence, with clasped hands bowed down and worshipped. Possessed with deep portentous thoughts, satiated with sorrows attached to lay-life, they all conceived a wish to leave their homes. The princes, too, of the Sâkya tribe, their minds enlightened to perceive the perfect fruit of righteousness, entirely satiated with the glittering joys of the world, forsaking home, rejoiced to join his company. Ânanda, Nanda, Kin-pi, Anuruddha, Nandupananda, with Kundadana, all these principal nobles and others of the Sâkya family, from the teaching of Buddha became disciples and accepted the law. The sons of the great minister of state, Udâyin being the chief, with all the royal princes following in order became recluses. Moreover, the son of Atalî, whose name was Upâli, seeing all these princes and the sons of the chief minister becoming hermits, his mind opening for conversion, he, too, received the law of renunciation. The royal father seeing his son possessing the great qualities of Riddhi, himself entered on the calm flowings of thought, the gate of the true law of eternal life. Leaving his kingly estate and country, lost in meditation, he drank sweet dew. Practising his religious duties in solitude, silent and contemplative he dwelt in his palace, a royal Rishi. Tathâgata following a peaceable life, recognized fully by his tribe, repeating the joyful news of religion, gladdened the hearts of all his kinsmen hearing him. And now, it being the right time for begging food, he entered the Kapila country; in the city all the lords and ladies, in admiration, raised this chant of praise: "Siddhârtha! fully enlightened! has come back again!" The news flying quickly in and out of doors, the great and small came forth to see him; every door and every window crowded, climbing on shoulders, bending down the eyes, they gazed upon the marks of beauty on his person, shining and glorious! Wearing his Kashâya garment outside, the glory of his person from within shone forth, like the sun's perfect wheel; within, without, he seemed one mass of splendor. Those who beheld were filled with sympathizing joy; their hands conjoined, they wept for gladness; and so they watched him as he paced with dignity the road, his form collected, all his organs well-controlled! His lovely body exhibiting the perfection of religious beauty, his dignified compassion adding to their regretful joy; his shaven head, his personal beauty sacrificed! his body clad in dark and sombre vestment, his manner natural and plain, his unadorned appearance; his circumspection as he looked upon the earth in walking! "He who ought to have had held over him the feather-shade," they said, "whose hands should grasp 'the reins of the flying dragon,' see how he walks in daylight on the dusty road! holding his alms-dish, going to beg! Gifted enough to tread down every enemy, lovely enough to gladden woman's heart, with glittering vesture and with godlike crown reverenced he might have been by servile crowds! But now, his manly beauty hidden, with heart restrained, and outward form subdued, rejecting the much-coveted and glorious apparel, his shining body clad with garments gray, what aim, what object, now! Hating the five delights that move the world, forsaking virtuous wife and tender child, loving the solitude, he wanders friendless; hard, indeed, for virtuous wife through the long night, cherishing her grief; and now to hear he is a hermit! She inquires not now of the royal Suddhodana if he has seen his son or not! But as she views his beauteous person, to think his altered form is now a hermit's! hating his home, still full of love; his father, too, what rest for him! And then his loving child Râhula, weeping with constant sorrowful desire! And now to see no change, or heart-relenting; and this the end of such enlightenment! All these attractive marks, the proofs of a religious calling, whereas, when born, all said, these are marks of a 'great man,' who ought to receive tribute from the four seas! And now to see what he has come to! all these predictive words vain and illusive."

Thus they talked together, the gossiping multitude, with confused accents. Tathâgata, his heart unaffected, felt no joy and no regret. But he was moved by equal love to all the world, his one desire that men should escape the grief of lust; to cause the root of virtue to increase, and for the sake of coming ages, to leave the marks of self-denial behind him, to dissipate the clouds and mists of sensual desire.

He entered, thus intentioned, on the town to beg. He accepted food both good or bad, whatever came, from rich or poor, without distinction; having filled his alms-dish, he then returned back to the solitude.

Receiving the Getavana Vihâra

The lord of the world, having converted the people of Kapilavastu according to their several circumstances, his work being done, he went with the great body of his followers, and directed his way to the country of Kosala, where dwelt King Prasenagit. The Getavana was now fully adorned, and its halls and courts carefully prepared. The fountains and streams flowed through the garden which glittered with flowers and fruit; rare birds sat by the pools, and on the land they sang in sweet concord, according to their kind.

Beautiful in every way as the palace of Mount Kilas, such was the Getavana. Then the noble friend of the orphans, surrounded by his attendants, who met him on the way, scattering flowers and burning incense, invited the lord to enter the Getavana. In his hand he carried a golden dragon-pitcher, and bending low upon his knees he poured the flowing water as a sign of the gift of the Getavana Vihâra for the use of the priesthood throughout the world. The lord then received it, with the prayer that " overruling all evil influences it might give the kingdom permanent rest, and that the happiness of Anâthapindada might flow out in countless streams." Then the king Prasenagit, hearing that the lord had come, with his royal equipage went to the Getavana to worship at the lord's feet. Having arrived and taken a seat on one side, with clasped hands he spake to Buddha thus:—

" O that my unworthy and obscure kingdom should thus suddenly have met such fortune! For how can misfortunes or frequent calamities possibly affect it, in the presence of so great a man? And now that I have seen your sacred features, I may perhaps partake of the converting streams of your teaching. A town although it is composed of many sections, yet both ignoble and holy persons may enter the surpassing stream; and so the wind which fans the perfumed grove causes the scents to unite and form one pleasant breeze; and as the birds which collect on Mount Sumeru are many, and the various shades that blend in shining gold, so an assembly may consist of persons of different capacities: individually insignificant, but a glorious body. The desert master by nourishing the Rishi, procured a birth as the three leg, or foot star; worldly profit is fleeting and perishable, religious profit is eternal and inexhaustible; a man though a king is full of trouble, a common man, who is holy, has everlasting rest."

Buddha knowing the state of the king's heart—that he rejoiced in religion as Sakrarâga—considered the two obstacles that weighted him—viz., too great love of money and of external pleasures, then seizing the opportunity, and knowing the tendencies of his heart, he began, for the king's sake, to preach: "Even those who, by evil karma, have been born in low degree, when they see a person of virtuous character, feel reverence for him; how much rather ought an independent king, who by his previous conditions of life has acquired much merit, when he encounters Buddha, to conceive even more reverence. Nor is it difficult to understand, that a country should enjoy more rest and peace, by the presence of Buddha, than if he were not to dwell therein. And now, as I briefly declare my law, let the Mahârâga listen and weigh my words, and hold fast that which I deliver! See now the end of my perfected merit, my life is done, there is for me no further body or spirit, but freedom from all ties of kith or kin! The good or evil deeds we do from first to last follow us as shadows; most exalted then the deeds of the king of the law. The prince who cherishes his people, in the present life gains renown, and hereafter ascends to heaven; but by disobedience and neglect of duty, present distress is felt and future misery! As in old times Lui-'ma râga, by obeying the precepts, was born in heaven, whilst Kin-pu râga, doing wickedly, at the end of life was born in misery. Now then, for the sake of the great king, I will briefly relate the good and evil law. The great requirement is a loving heart! to regard the people as we do an only son, not to oppress, not to destroy; to keep in due check every member of the body, to forsake unrighteous doctrine and walk in the straight path; not to exalt one's self by treading down others, but to comfort and befriend those in suffering; not to exercise one's self in false theories, nor to ponder much on kingly dignity, nor to listen to the smooth words of false teachers. Not to vex one's self by austerities, not to exceed or transgress the right rules of kingly conduct, but to meditate on Buddha and weigh his righteous law, and to put down and adjust all that is contrary to religion; to exhibit true superiority by virtuous conduct and the highest exercise of reason, to meditate deeply on the vanity of earthly things, to realize the fickleness of life by constant recollection; to exalt the mind to the highest point of reflection, to seek sincere faith (truth) with firm purpose; to retain an inward sense of happiness resulting from one's self, and to look forward to increased happiness hereafter; to lay up a good name for distant ages, this will secure the favor of Tathâgata, as men now loving sweet fruit will hereafter be praised by their descendants. There is a way of darkness out of light, there is a way of light out of darkness; there is darkness which follows after the gloom, there is a light which causes the brightening of light. The wise man, leaving first principles, should go on to get more light; evil words will be repeated far and wide by the multitude, but there are few to follow good direction: It is impossible, however, to avoid result of works, the doer cannot escape; if there had been no first works, there had been in the end no result of doing—no reward for good, no hereafter joy; but because works are done, there is no escape. Let us then practise good works; let us inspect our thoughts that we do no evil, because as we sow so we reap. As when enclosed in a four-stone mountain, there is no escape or place of refuge for anyone, so within this mountain-wall of old age, birth, disease, and death, there is no escape for the world. Only by considering and practising the true law can we escape from this sorrow-piled mountain. There is, indeed, no constancy in the world, the end of the pleasures of sense is as the lightning flash, whilst old age and death are as the piercing bolts; what profit, then, in doing iniquity! All the ancient conquering kings, who were as gods on earth, thought by their strength to overcome decay; but after a brief life they too disappeared. The Kalpa-fire will melt Mount Sumeru, the water of the ocean will be dried up, how much less can our human frame, which is as a bubble, expect to endure for long upon the earth! The fierce wind scatters the thick mists, the sun's rays encircle Mount Sumeru, the fierce fire licks up the place of moisture, so things are ever born once more to be destroyed! The body is a thing of unreality, kept through the suffering of the long night pampered by wealth, living idly and in carelessness, death suddenly comes and it is carried away as rotten wood in the stream! The wise man, expecting these changes, with diligence strives against sloth; the dread of birth and death acts as a spur to keep him from lagging on the road; he frees himself from engagements, he is not occupied with self-pleasing, he is not entangled by any of the cares of life, he holds to no business, seeks no friendships, engages in no learned career, nor yet wholly separates himself from it; for his learning is the wisdom of not-perceiving wisdom, but yet perceiving that which tells him of his own impermanence; having a body, yet keeping aloof from defilement, he learns to regard defilement as the greatest evil. He knows that, though born in the Arûpa world, there is yet no escape from the changes of time; his learning, then, is to acquire the changeless body; for where no change is, there is peace. Thus the possession of this changeful body is the foundation of all sorrow. Therefore, again, all who are wise make this their aim—to seek a bodiless condition; all the various orders of sentient creatures, from the indulgence of lust, derive pain; therefore all those in this condition ought to conceive a heart, loathing lust; putting away and loathing this condition, then they shall receive no more pain; though born in a state with or without an external form, the certainty of future change is the root of sorrow; for so long as there is no perfect cessation of personal being, there can be, certainly, no absence of personal desire; beholding, in this way, the character of the three worlds, their inconstancy and unreality, the presence of ever-consuming pain, how can the wise man seek enjoyment therein? When a tree is burning with fierce flames how can the birds congregate therein? The wise man, who is regarded as an enlightened sage, without this knowledge is ignorant; having this knowledge, then true wisdom dawns; without it, there is no enlightenment. To get this wisdom is the one aim, to neglect it is the mistake of life. All the teaching of the schools should be centred here; without it is no true reason. To recount this excellent system is not for those who dwell in family connection; nor is it, on that account, not to be said, for religion concerns a man individually. Burned up with sorrow, by entering the cool stream, all may obtain relief and ease; the light of a lamp in a dark room lights up equally objects of all colors, so is it with those who devote themselves to religion—there is no distinction between the professed disciple and the unlearned. Sometimes the mountain-dweller falls into ruin, sometimes the humble householder mounts up to be a Rishi; the want of faith is the engulfing sea, the presence of disorderly belief is the rolling flood. The tide of lust carries away the world; involved in its eddies there is no escape; wisdom is the handy boat, reflection is the hold-fast. The drum-call of religion, the barrier of thought, these alone can rescue from the sea of ignorance."

At this time the king, sincerely attentive to the words of the All-wise, conceived a distaste for the world's glitter and was dissatisfied with the pleasures of royalty, even as one avoids a drunken elephant, or returns to right reason after a debauch. Then all the heretical teachers, seeing that the king was well affected to Buddha, besought the king, with one voice, to call on Buddha to exhibit his miraculous gifts. Then the king addressed the lord of the world: "I pray you, grant their request!" Then Buddha silently acquiesced. And now all the different professors of religion, the doctors who boasted of their spiritual power, came together in a body to where Buddha was; then he manifested before them his power of miracle: ascending up into the air, he remained seated, diffusing his glory as the light of the sun he shed abroad the brightness of his presence. The heretical teachers were all abashed, the people all were filled with faith. Then for the sake of preaching to his mother, he forthwith ascended to the heaven of the thirty-three gods, and for three months dwelt in heavenly mansions. There he converted the occupants of that abode, and having concluded his pious mission to his mother, the time of his sojourn in heaven finished, he forthwith returned, the angels accompanying him on wing; he travelled down a seven-gemmed ladder, and again arrived at Gambudvîpa. Stepping down he alighted on the spot where all the Buddhas return, countless hosts of angels accompanied him, conveying with them their palace abodes as a gift.

The people of Gambudvîpa, with closed hands, looking up with reverence, beheld him.

Escaping the Drunken Elephant and Devadatta

Having instructed his mother in heaven with all the angel host, and once more returned to men, he went about converting those capable of it. Gutika, Givaka, Sula, and Kûrna, the noble's son Anga and the son of the fearless king Abhaya Nyagrodha and the rest; Srîkutaka, Upâli the Nirgrantha; all these were thoroughly converted. So also the king of Gandhâra, whose name was Fo-kia-lo; he, having heard the profound and excellent law, left his country and became a recluse. So also the demons Himapati and Vâtagiri, on the mountain Vibhâra, were subdued and converted. The Brahmakârin Prayantika, on the mountain Vagana, by the subtle meaning of half a gâtha, he convinced and caused to rejoice in faith; the village of Dânamati had one Kûtadanta, the head of the twice-born Brahmans; at this time he was sacrificing countless victims; Tathâgata by means converted him, and caused him to enter the true path. On Mount Bhatika a heavenly being of eminent distinction, whose name was Pañkasikha, receiving the law, attained Dhyâna; in the village of Vainushta, he converted the mother of the celebrated Nanda. In the town of Añkavari, he subdued the powerful mahâbâla spirit; Bhanabhadra, Sronadanta, the malevolent and powerful Nâgas, the king of the country and his harem, received together the true law, as he opened to them the gate of immortality. In the celebrated Viggi village, Kina and Sila, earnestly seeking to be born in heaven, he converted and made to enter the right path. The Angulimâla, in that village of Sumu, through the exhibition of his divine power, he converted and subdued; there was that noble's son, Purigivana, rich in wealth and stores as Punavatî, directly he was brought to Buddha, accepting the doctrine, he became vastly liberal. So in that village of Padatti he converted the celebrated Patali, and also Patala, brothers, and both demons. In Bhidhavali there were two Brahmans, one called Great-age, the other Brahma-age. These by the power of a discourse he subdued, and caused them to attain knowledge of the true law; when he came to Vaisâlî, he converted all the Raksha demons, and the lion of the Likkhavis, and all the Likkhavis, Saka the Nirgrantha, all these he caused to attain the true law. Hama kinkhava had a demon Potala, and another Potalaka, these he converted.

Again he came to Mount Ala, to convert the demon Alava, and a second called Kumâra, and a third Asidaka; then going back to Mount Gaga he converted the demon Kañgana, and Kamo the Yaksha, with the sister and son. Then coming to Benares, he converted the celebrated Katyâyana; then afterwards going, by his miraculous power, to Sruvala, he converted the merchants Davakin and Nikin, and received their sandalwood hall, exhaling its fragrant odors till now. Going then to Mahîvatî, he converted the Rishi Kapila, and the Muni remained with him; his foot stepping on the stone, the thousand-spoked twin-wheels appeared, which never could be erased.

Then he came to the place Po-lo-na, where he converted the demon Po-lo-na; coming to the country of Mathurâ, he converted the demon Godama. In the Thurakusati he also converted Pindapâla; coming to the village of Vairañga, he converted the Brahman; in the village of Kalamasa, he converted Savasasin, and also that celebrated Agirivasa. Once more returning to the Srâvastî country, he converted the Gautamas Gâtisruna and Dakâtili; returning to the Kosala country, he converted the leaders of the heretics Vakrapali and all the Brahmakârins. Coming to Satavaka, in the forest retreat, he converted the heretical Rishis, and constrained them to enter the path of the Buddha Rishi. Coming to the country of Ayodhyâ, he converted the demon Nâgas; coming to the country of Kimbila, he converted the two Nâgarâgas; one called Kimbila, the other called Kâlaka. Again coming to the Vaggi country, he converted the Yaksha demon, whose name was Pisha, the father and mother of Nâgara, and the great noble also, he caused to believe gladly in the true law. Coming to the Kausâmbî country, he converted Goshira, and the two Upasîkâs, Vaguttarâ and her companion Uvarî; and besides these, many others, one after the other. Coming to the country of Gandhâra he converted the Nâga Apalâla; thus in due order all these air-going, water-loving natures he completely converted and saved, as the sun when he shines upon some dark and sombre cave. At this time Devadatta, seeing the remarkable excellences of Buddha, conceived in his heart a jealous hatred; losing all power of thoughtful abstraction he ever plotted wicked schemes, to put a stop to the spread of the true law; ascending the Gridhrakûta mount he rolled down a stone to hit Buddha; the stone divided into two parts, each part passing on either side of him. Again, on the royal highway he loosed a drunken, vicious elephant. With his raised trunk trumpeting as thunder he ran, his maddened breath raising a cloud around him, his wild pace like the rushing wind, to be avoided more than the fierce tempest; his trunk and tusks and tail and feet, when touched only, brought instant death. Thus he ran through the streets and ways of Râgagriha, madly wounding and killing men; their corpses lay across the road, their brains and blood scattered afar. Then all the men and women filled with fear, remained indoors; throughout the city there was universal terror, only piteous shrieks and cries were heard; beyond the city men were running fast, hiding themselves in holes and dens. Tathâgata, with five hundred followers, at this time came towards the city; from tops of gates and every window, men, fearing for Buddha, begged him not to advance; Tathâgata, his heart composed and quiet, with perfect self-possession, thinking only on the sorrow caused by hate, his loving heart desiring to appease it, followed by guardian angel-nâgas, slowly approached the maddened elephant. The Bhikshus all deserted him, Ânanda only remained by his side; joined by every tie of duty, his steadfast nature did not shake or quail. The drunken elephant, savage and spiteful, beholding Buddha, came to himself at once, and bending, worshipped at his feet just as a mighty mountain falls to earth. With lotus hand the master pats his head, even as the moon lights up a flying cloud. And now, as he lay crouched before the master's feet, on his account he speaks some sacred words: "The elephant cannot hurt the mighty dragon, hard it is to fight with such a one; the elephant desiring so to do will in the end obtain no happy state of birth; deceived by lust, anger, and delusion, which are hard to conquer, but which Buddha has conquered. Now, then, this very day, give up this lust, this anger and delusion! You! swallowed up in sorrow's mud! if not now given up, they will increase yet more and grow."

The elephant, hearing Buddha's words, escaped from drunkenness, rejoiced in heart; his mind and body both found rest, as one athirst finds joy who drinks of heavenly dew. The elephant being thus converted, the people around were filled with joy; they all raised a cry of wonder at the miracle, and brought their offerings of every kind. The scarcely-good arrived at middle-virtue, the middling-good passed to a higher grade, the unbelieving now became believers, those who believed were strengthened in their faith. Agâtasatru, mighty king, seeing how Buddha conquered the drunken elephant, was moved at heart by thoughts profound; then, filled with joy, he found a twofold growth of piety. Tathâgata, by exercise of virtue, exhibited all kinds of spiritual powers; thus he subdued and harmonized the minds of all, and caused them in due order to attain religious truth, and through the kingdom virtuous seeds were sown, as at the first when men began to live. But Devadatta, mad with rage, because he was ensnared by his own wickedness, at first by power miraculous able to fly, now fallen, dwells in lowest hell.

The Lady Âmra Sees Buddha

The lord of the world having finished his wide work of conversion conceived in himself a desire for Nirvâna. Accordingly proceeding from the city of Râgagriha, he went on towards the town of Pâtaliputra.

Having arrived there, he dwelt in the famous Pâtali ketiya. Now this town of Pâtaliputra is the frontier town of Magadha, defending the outskirts of the country. Ruling the country was a Brahman of wide renown and great learning in the scriptures; and there was also an overseer of the country, to take the omens of the land with respect to rest or calamity. At this time the king of Magadha sent to that officer of inspection a messenger, to warn and command him to raise fortifications in the neighborhood of the town for its security and protection. And now the lord of the world, as they were raising the fortifications, predicted that in consequence of the Devas and spirits who protected and kept the land, the place should continue strong and free from calamity or destruction. On this the heart of the overseer greatly rejoiced, and he made religious offerings to Buddha, the law, and the church. Buddha now leaving the city gate went on towards the river Ganges. The overseer, from his deep reverence for Buddha, named the gate through which the lord had passed the "Gautama gate." Meanwhile the people all by the side of the river Ganges went forth to pay reverence to the lord of the world. They prepared for him every kind of religious offering, and each one with his gaudy boat invited him to cross over. The lord of the world, considering the number of the boats, feared lest by an appearance of partiality in accepting one, he might hurt the minds of all the rest. Therefore in a moment, by his spiritual power, he transported himself and the great congregation across the river, leaving this shore he passed at once to that, signifying thereby the passage in the boat of wisdom from this world to Nirvâna: a boat large enough to transport all that lives to save the world, even as without a boat he crossed without hindrance the river Ganges. Then all the people on the bank of the river, with one voice, raised a rapturous shout, and all declared this ford should be called the Gautama ford. As the city gate is called the Gautama gate, so this Gautama ford is so known through ages; and shall be so called through generations to come. Then Tathâgata, going forward still, came to that celebrated Kuli village, where he preached and converted many; again he went on to the Nâdi village, where many deaths had occurred among the people. The friends of the dead then came to the lord and asked, "Where have our friends and relatives deceased, now gone to be born, after this life ended?" Buddha, knowing well the sequence of deeds, answered each according to his several needs. Then going forward to Vaisâlî, he located himself in the Âmrâ grove. The celebrated Lady Âmrâ, well affected to Buddha, went to that garden followed by her waiting women, whilst the children from the schools paid her respect. Thus with circumspection and self-restraint, her person lightly and plainly clothed, putting away all her ornamented robes and all adornments of scent and flowers, as a prudent and virtuous woman goes forth to perform her religious duties, so she went on, beautiful to look upon, like any Devî in appearance. Buddha seeing the lady in the distance approaching, spake thus to all the Bhikshus:—

"This woman is indeed exceedingly beautiful, able to fascinate the minds of the religious; now then, keep your recollection straight! let wisdom keep your mind in subjection! Better fall into the fierce tiger's mouth, or under the sharp knife of the executioner, than to dwell with a woman and excite in yourselves lustful thoughts. A woman is anxious to exhibit her form and shape, whether walking, standing, sitting, or sleeping. Even when represented as a picture, she desires most of all to set off the blandishments of her beauty, and thus to rob men of their steadfast heart! How then ought you to guard yourselves? By regarding her tears and her smiles as enemies, her stooping form, her hanging arms, and all her disentangled hair as toils designed to entrap man's heart. Then how much more should you suspect her studied, amorous beauty; when she displays her dainty outline, her richly ornamented form, and chatters gayly with the foolish man! Ah, then! what perturbation and what evil thoughts, not seeing underneath the horrid, tainted shape, the sorrows of impermanence, the impurity, the unreality! Considering these as the reality, all lustful thoughts die out; rightly considering these, within their several limits, not even an Apsaras would give you joy. But yet the power of lust is great with men, and is to be feared withal; take then the bow of earnest perseverance, and the sharp arrow points of wisdom, cover your head with the helmet of right-thought, and fight with fixed resolve against the five desires. Better far with red-hot iron pins bore out both your eyes, than encourage in yourselves lustful thoughts, or look upon a woman's form with such desires. Lust beclouding a man's heart, confused with woman's beauty, the mind is dazed, and at the end of life that man must fall into an 'evil way.' Fear then the sorrow of that 'evil way!' and harbor not the deceits of women. The senses not confined within due limits, and the objects of sense not limited as they ought to be, lustful and covetous thoughts grow up between the two, because the senses and their objects are unequally yoked. Just as when two ploughing oxen are yoked together to one halter and cross-bar, but not together pulling as they go, so is it when the senses and their objects are unequally matched. Therefore, I say, restrain the heart, give it no unbridled license."

Thus Buddha, for the Bhikshus' sake, explained the law in various ways. And now that Âmrâ lady gradually approached the presence of the lord; seeing Buddha seated beneath a tree, lost in thought and wholly absorbed by it, she recollected that he had a great compassionate heart, and therefore she believed he would in pity receive her garden grove. With steadfast heart and joyful mien and rightly governed feelings, her outward form restrained, her heart composed, bowing her head at Buddha's feet, she took her place as the lord bade her, whilst he in sequence right declared the law:—

"Your heart, O lady! seems composed and quieted, your form without external ornaments; young in years and rich, you seem well-talented as you are beautiful. That one, so gifted, should by faith be able to receive the law of righteousness is, indeed, a rare thing in the world! The wisdom of a master derived from former births, enables him to accept the law with joy: this is not rare; but that a woman, weak of will, scant in wisdom, deeply immersed in love, should yet be able to delight in piety, this, indeed, is very rare. A man born in the world, by proper thought comes to delight in goodness, he recognizes the impermanence of wealth and beauty, and looks upon religion as his best ornament. He feels that this alone can remedy the ills of life and change the fate of young and old; the evil destiny that cramps another's life cannot affect him, living righteously; always removing that which excites desire, he is strong in the absence of desire; seeking to find, not what vain thoughts suggest, but that to which religion points him. Relying on external help, he has sorrow; self-reliant, there is strength and joy. But in the case of woman, from another comes the labor, and the nurture of another's child. Thus then should everyone consider well, and loathe and put away the form of woman."

Amrâ, the lady, hearing the law, rejoiced. Her wisdom strengthened, and still more enlightened, she was enabled to cast off desire, and of herself dissatisfied with woman's form, was freed from all polluting thoughts. Though still constrained to woman's form, filled with religious joy, she bowed at Buddha's feet and spoke: "Oh! may the lord, in deep compassion, receive from me, though ignorant, this offering, and so fulfil my earnest vow." Then Buddha knowing her sincerity, and for the good of all that lives, silently accepted her request, and caused in her full joy, in consequence; whilst all her friends attentive, grew in knowledge, and, after adoration, went back home.

CHAPTER V

By Spiritual Power Fixing His Term of Years

AT this time the great men among the Likkhavis, hearing that the lord of the world had entered their country and was located in the Âmrâ garden, went thither riding in their gaudy chariots with silken canopies, and clothed in gorgeous robes, both blue and red and yellow and white, each one with his own cognizance. Accompanied by their body guard surrounding them, they went; others prepared the road in front; and with their heavenly crowns and flower-bespangled robes they rode, richly dight with every kind of costly ornament. Their noble forms resplendent increased the glory of that garden grove; now taking off the five distinctive ornaments, alighting from their chariots, they advanced afoot. Slowly thus, with bated breath, their bodies reverent they advanced. Then they bowed down and worshipped Buddha's foot, and, a great multitude, they gathered round the lord, shining as the sun's disc, full of radiance.

There was the lion Likkhavi, among the Likkhavis the senior, his noble form bold as the lion's, standing there with lion eyes, but without the lion's pride, taught by the Sâkya lion, who thus began: "Great and illustrious personages, famed as a tribe for grace and comeliness! put aside, I pray, the world's high thoughts, and now accept the abounding lustre of religious teaching. Wealth and beauty, scented flowers and ornaments like these, are not to be compared for grace with moral rectitude! Your land productive and in peaceful quiet—this is your great renown; but true gracefulness of body and a happy people depend upon the heart well-governed. Add but to this a reverent feeling for religion, then a people's fame is at its height! a fertile land and all the dwellers in it, as a united body, virtuous! To-day then learn this virtue, cherish with carefulness the people, lead them as a body in the right way of rectitude, even as the ox-king leads the way across the river-ford. If a man with earnest recollection ponder on things of this world and the next, he will consider how by right behavior right morals he prepares, as the result of merit, rest in either world. For all in this world will exceedingly revere him, his fame will spread abroad through every part, the virtuous will rejoice to call him friend, and the outflowings of his goodness will know no bounds forever. The precious gems found in the desert wilds are all from earth engendered; moral conduct, likewise, as the earth, is the great source of all that is good. By this, without the use of wings, we fly through space, we cross the river needing not a handy boat; but without this a man will find it hard indeed to cross the stream of sorrow or stay the rush of sorrow. As when a tree with lovely flowers and fruit, pierced by some sharp instrument, is hard to climb, so is it with the much-renowned for strength and beauty, who break through the laws of moral rectitude! Sitting upright in the royal palace, the heart of the king was grave and majestic; with a view to gain the merit of a pure and moral life, he became a convert of a great Rishi. With garments dyed and clad with hair, shaved, save one spiral knot, he led a hermit's life, but, as he did not rule himself with strict morality, he was immersed in suffering and sorrow. Each morn and eve he used the three ablutions, sacrificed to fire and practised strict austerity, let his body be in filth as the brute beast, passed through fire and water, dwelt amidst the craggy rocks, inhaled the wind, drank from the Ganges' stream, controlled himself with bitter fasts—but all! far short of moral rectitude. For though a man inure himself to live as any brute, he is not on that account a vessel of the righteous law; whilst he who breaks the laws of right behavior invites detraction, and is one no virtuous man can love; his heart is ever filled with boding fear, his evil name pursues him as a shadow. Having neither profit nor advantage in this world, how can he in the next world reap content? Therefore the wise man ought to practise pure behavior; passing through the wilderness of birth and death, pure conduct is to him a virtuous guide. From pure behavior comes self-power, which frees a man from many dangers; pure conduct, like a ladder, enables us to climb to heaven. Those who found themselves on right behavior, cut off the source of pain and grief; but they who by transgression destroy this mind, may mourn the loss of every virtuous principle. To gain this end first banish every ground of 'self'; this thought of 'self' shades every lofty aim, even as the ashes that conceal the fire, treading on which the foot is burned. Pride and indifference shroud this heart, too, as the sun is obscured by the piled-up clouds; supercilious thoughts root out all modesty of mind, and sorrow saps the strongest will. As age and disease waste youthful beauty, so pride of self destroys all virtue; the Devas and Asuras, thus from jealousy and envy, raised mutual strife. The loss of virtue and of merit which we mourn, proceeds from 'pride of self' throughout; and as I am a conqueror amid conquerors, so he who conquers self is one with me. He who little cares to conquer self, is but a foolish master; beauty, or earthly things, family renown and such things, all are utterly inconstant, and what is changeable can give no rest of interval. If in the end the law of entire destruction is exacted, what use is there in indolence and pride? Covetous desire is the greatest source of sorrow, appearing as a friend in secret 'tis our enemy. As a fierce fire excited from within a house, so is the fire of covetous desire: the burning flame of covetous desire is fiercer far than fire which burns the world. For fire may be put out by water in excess, but what can overpower the fire of lust? The fire which fiercely burns the desert grass dies out, and then the grass will grow again; but when the fire of lust burns up the heart, then how hard for true religion there to dwell! for lust seeks worldly pleasures, these pleasures add to an impure karman; by this evil karman a man falls into perdition, and so there is no greater enemy to man than lust. Lusting, man gives way to amorous indulgence, by this he is led to practise every kind of lustful longing; indulging thus, he gathers frequent sorrow. No greater evil is there than lust. Lust is a dire disease, and the foolish master stops the medicine of wisdom. The study of heretical books not leading to right thought, causes the lustful heart to increase and grow, for these books are not correct on the points of impermanency, the non-existence of self, and any object ground for 'self.' But a true and right apprehension through the power of wisdom, is effectual to destroy that false desire, and therefore our object should be to practise this true apprehension. Right apprehension once produced then there is deliverance from covetous desire, for a false estimate of excellency produces a covetous desire to excel, whilst a false view of demerit produces anger and regret; but the idea of excelling and also of inferiority (in the sense of demerit) both destroyed, the desire to excel and also anger (on account of inferiority) are destroyed. Anger! how it changes the comely face, how it destroys the loveliness of beauty! Anger dulls the brightness of the eye, chokes all desire to hear the principles of truth, cuts and divides the principle of family affection, impoverishes and weakens every worldly aim. Therefore let anger be subdued, yield not to the angry impulse; he who can hold his wild and angry heart is well entitled 'illustrious charioteer.' For men call such a one 'illustrious team-breaker' who can with bands restrain the unbroken steed; so anger not subdued, its fire unquenched, the sorrow of repentance burns like fire. A man who allows wild passion to arise within, himself first burns his heart, then after burning adds the wind thereto which ignites the fire again, or not, as the case may be. The pain of birth, old age, disease, and death, press heavily upon the world, but adding 'passion' to the score, what is this but to increase our foes when pressed by foes? But rather, seeing how the world is pressed by throngs of grief, we ought to encourage in us love, and as the world produces grief on grief, so should we add as antidotes unnumbered remedies." Tathâgata, illustrious in expedients, according to the disease, thus briefly spoke; even as a good physician in the world, according to the disease, prescribes his medicine. And now the Likkhavis, hearing the sermon preached by Buddha, arose forthwith and bowed at Buddha's feet, and joyfully they placed them on their heads. Then they asked both Buddha and the congregation on the morrow to accept their poor religious offerings. But Buddha told them that already Âmrâ had invited him. On this the Likkhavis, harboring thoughts of pride and disappointment, said: "Why should that one take away our profit?" But, knowing Buddha's heart to be impartial and fair, they once again regained their cheerfulness. Tathâgata, moreover, nobly seizing the occasion, appeasing them, produced within a joyful heart; and so subdued, their grandeur of appearance came again, as when a snake subdued by charms glistens with shining skin. And now, the night being passed, the signs of dawn appearing, Buddha and the great assembly go to the abode of Âmrâ, and having received her entertainment, they went on to the village of Pi-nau, and there he rested during the rainy season; the three months' rest being ended, again he returned to Vaisâli, and dwelt beside the Monkey Tank; sitting there in a shady grove, he shed a flood of glory from his person; aroused thereby, Mâra Pisuna came to the place where Buddha was, and with closed palms exhorted him thus: "Formerly, beside the Nairañganâ river, when you had accomplished your true and steadfast aim, you said, 'When I have done all I have to do, then will I pass at once to Nirvâna'; and now you have done all you have to do, you should, as then you said, pass to Nirvâna."

Then Buddha spake to Pisuna: "The time of my complete deliverance is at hand, but let three months elapse, and I shall reach Nirvâna." Then Mâra, knowing that Tathâgata had fixed the time for his emancipation, his earnest wish being thus fulfilled, joyous returned to his abode in heaven. Tathâgata, seated beneath a tree, straightway was lost in ecstasy, and willingly rejected his allotted years, and by his spiritual power fixed the remnant of his life. On this, Tathâgata thus giving up his years, the great earth shook and quaked through all the limits of the universe; great flames of fire were seen around, the tops of Sumeru were shaken, from heaven there rained showers of flying stones, a whirling tempest rose on every side, the trees were rooted up and fell, heavenly music rose with plaintive notes, whilst angels for a time were joyless. Buddha rising from out his ecstasy, announced to all the world: "Now have I given up my term of years; I live henceforth by power of faith; my body like a broken chariot stands, no further cause of 'coming' or of 'going'; completely freed from the three worlds, I go enfranchised, as a chicken from its egg."

The Differences of the Likkhavis

The venerable Ânanda, seeing the earth shaking on every side, his heart was fearful and his hair erect; he asked the cause thereof of Buddha.

Buddha replied: "Ânanda! I have fixed three months to end my life, the rest of life I utterly give up; this is the reason why the earth is greatly shaken."

Ânanda, hearing the instruction of Buddha, was moved with pity and the tears flowed down his face, even as when an elephant of mighty strength shakes the sandal-wood tree. Thus was Ânanda shaken and his mind perturbed, whilst down his cheeks the tears, like drops of perfume, flowed; so much he loved the lord his master, so full of kindness was he, and, as yet, not freed from earthly thoughts. Thinking then on these four things alone, he gave his grief full liberty, nor could he master it, but said, "Now I hear the lord declare that he has fixed for good his time to die, my body fails, my strength is gone, my mind is dazed, my soul is all discordant, and all the words of truth forgotten; a wild deserted waste seems heaven and earth. Have pity! save me, master! perish not so soon! Perished with bitter cold, I chanced upon a fire—forthwith it disappeared. Wandering amid the wilds of grief and pain, deceived, confused, I lost my way—suddenly a wise and prudent guide encountered me, but hardly saved from my bewilderment, he once more vanished. Like some poor man treading through endless mud, weary and parched with thirst, longs for the water, suddenly he lights upon a cool refreshing lake, he hastens to it—lo! it dries before him. The deep blue, bright, refulgent eye, piercing through all the worlds, with wisdom brightens the dark gloom, the darkness for a moment is dispelled. As when the blade shoots through the yielding earth, the clouds collect and we await the welcome shower, then a fierce wind drives the big clouds away, and so with disappointed hope we watch the dried-up field! Deep darkness reigned for want of wisdom, the world of sentient creatures groped for light, Tathâgata lit up the lamp of wisdom, then suddenly extinguished it—ere he had brought it out."

Buddha, hearing Ânanda speaking thus, grieved at his words, and pitying his distress, with soothing accents and with gentle presence spake with purpose to declare the one true law:—

"If men but knew their own nature, they would not dwell in sorrow; everything that lives, whate'er it be, all this is subject to destruction's law; I have already told you plainly, the law of things 'joined' is to 'separate'; the principle of kindness and of love is not abiding, 'tis better then to reject this pitiful and doting heart. All things around us bear the stamp of instant change; born, they perish; no self-sufficiency; those who would wish to keep them long, find in the end no room for doing so. If things around us could be kept for aye, and were not liable to change or separation, then this would be salvation! where then can this be sought? You, and all that lives, can seek in me this great deliverance! That which you may all attain I have already told you, and tell you, to the end. Why then should I preserve this body? The body of the excellent law shall long endure! I am resolved; I look for rest! This is the one thing needful. So do I now instruct all creatures, and as a guide, not seen before, I lead them; prepare yourselves to cast off consciousness, fix yourselves well in your own island. Those who are thus fixed mid-stream, with single aim and earnestness striving in the use of means, preparing quietly a quiet place, not moved by others' way of thinking, know well, such men are safe on the law's island. Fixed in contemplation, lighted by the lamp of wisdom, they have thus finally destroyed ignorance and gloom. Consider well the world's four bounds, and dare to seek for true religion only; forget 'yourself,' and every 'ground of self,' the bones, the nerves, the skin, the flesh, the mucus, the blood that flows through every vein; behold these things as constantly impure, what joy then can there be in such a body? every sensation born from cause, like the bubble floating on the water. The sorrow coming from the consciousness of birth and death and inconstancy, removes all thought of joy—the mind acquainted with the law of production, stability, and destruction, recognizes how again and once again things follow or succeed one another with no endurance. But thinking well about Nirvâna, the thought of endurance is forever dismissed; we see how the samskâras from causes have arisen, and how these aggregates will again dissolve, all of them impermanent. The foolish man conceives the idea of 'self,' the wise man sees there is no ground on which to build the idea of 'self,' thus through the world he rightly looks and well concludes, all, therefore, is but evil; the aggregate amassed by sorrow must perish in the end! if once confirmed in this conviction, that man perceives the truth. This body, too, of Buddha now existing soon will perish: the law is one and constant, and without exception." Buddha having delivered this excellent sermon, appeased the heart of Ânanda.

Then all the Likkhavis, hearing the report, with fear and apprehension assembled in a body; devoid of their usual ornaments, they hastened to the place where Buddha was. Having saluted him according to custom, they stood on one side, wishing to ask him a question, but not being able to find words. Buddha, knowing well their heart, by way of remedy, in the right use of means, spake thus:—

"Now I perfectly understand that you have in your minds unusual thoughts, not referring to worldly matters, but wholly connected with subjects of religion; and now you wish to hear from me, what may be known respecting the report about my resolve to terminate my life, and my purpose to put an end to the repetition of birth. Impermanence is the nature of all that exists, constant change and restlessness its conditions; unfixed, unprofitable, without the marks of long endurance. In ancient days the Rishi kings, Vasishtha Rishi, Mândhâtri, the Kakravartin monarchs, and the rest, these and all others like them, the former conquerors, who lived with strength like Îsvara, these all have long ago perished, not one remains till now; the sun and moon, Sakra himself, and the great multitude of his attendants, will all, without exception, perish; there is not one that can for long endure; all the Buddhas of the past ages, numerous as the sands of the Ganges, by their wisdom enlightening the world, have all gone out as a lamp; all the Buddhas yet to come will also perish in the same way; why then should I alone be different? I too will pass into Nirvâna; but as they prepared others for salvation, so now should you press forward in the path; Vaisâlî may be glad indeed, if you should find the way of rest! The world, in truth, is void of help, the 'three worlds' not enough for joy—stay then the course of sorrow, by engendering a heart without desire. Give up for good the long and straggling way of life, press onward on the northern track, step by step advance along the upward road, as the sun skirts along the western mountains."

At this time the Likkhavis, with saddened hearts, went back along the way; lifting their hands to heaven and sighing bitterly: "Alas! what sorrow this! His body like the pure gold mountain, the marks upon his person so majestic, ere long and like a towering crag he falls; not to live, then why not, 'not to love'? The powers of birth and death, weakened awhile, the lord Tathâgata, himself the fount of wisdom appeared, and now to give it up and disappear! without a saviour now, what check to sorrow? The world long time endured in darkness, and men were led by a false light along the way—when lo! the sun of wisdom rose; and now, again, it fades and dies—no warning given. Behold the whirling waves of ignorance engulfing all the world! Why is the bridge or raft of wisdom in a moment cut away? The loving and the great physician king came with remedies of wisdom, beyond all price, to heal the hurts and pains of men—why suddenly goes he away? The excellent and heavenly flag of love adorned with wisdom's blazonry, embroidered with the diamond heart, the world not satisfied with gazing on it, the glorious flag of heavenly worship! Why in a moment is it snapped? Why such misfortune for the world, when from the tide of constant revolutions a way of escape was opened—but now shut again! and there is no escape from weary sorrow! Tathâgata, possessed of fond and loving heart, now steels himself and goes away; he holds his heart so patient and so loving, and, like the Wai-ka-ni flower, with thoughts cast down, irresolute and tardy, he goes depressed along the road. Or like a man fresh from a loved one's grave, the funeral past and the last farewell taken, comes back with anxious look.

Parinirvâna

When Buddha went towards the place of his Nirvâna, the city of Vaisâlî was as if deserted, as when upon a dark and cloudy night the moon and stars withdraw their shining. The land that heretofore had peace, was now afflicted and distressed; as when a loving father dies, the orphan daughter yields to constant grief. Her personal grace unheeded, her clever skill but lightly thought of, with stammering lips she finds expression for her thoughts; how poor her brilliant wit and wisdom now! Her spiritual powers ill regulated without attractiveness, her loving heart faint and fickle, exalted high but without strength, and all her native grace neglected; such was the case at Vaisâlî; all outward show now fallen, like autumn verdure in the fields bereft of water, withered up and dry; or like the smoke of a half-smouldering fire, or like those who having food before them yet forget to eat, so these forgot their common household duties, and nought prepared they for the day's emergencies. Thinking thus on Buddha, lost in deep reflection, silent they sat nor spoke a word. And now the lion Likkhavis manfully enduring their great sorrow, with flowing tears and doleful sighs, signifying thereby their love of kindred, destroyed forever all their books of heresy, to show their firm adherence to the true law. Having put down all heresy, they left it once for all; severed from the world and the world's doctrines, convinced that non-continuance was the great disease. Moreover thus they thought: "The lord of men now enters the great quiet place (Nirvâna), and we are left without support, and with no saviour; the highest lord of 'means' is now about to extinguish all his glory in the final place of death. Now we indeed have lost our steadfast will, as fire deprived of fuel; greatly to be pitied is the world, now that the lord gives up his world-protecting office, even as a man bereft of spiritual power throughout the world is greatly pitied. Oppressed by heat we seek the cooling lake, nipped by the cold we use the fire; but in a moment all is lost, the world is left without resource; the excellent law, indeed, is left, to frame the world anew, as a metal-caster frames anew his work. The world has lost its master-guide, and, men bereaved of him, the way is lost; old age, disease, and death, self-sufficient, now that the road is missed, pervade the world without a way. What is there now throughout the world equal to overcome the springs of these great sorrows? The great cloud's rain alone can make the raging and excessive fire, that burns the world, go out. So only he can make the raging fire of covetous desire go out; and now he, the skilful maker of comparisons, has firmly fixed his mind to leave the world! And why, again, is the sword of wisdom, ever ready to be used for an uninvited friend, only like the draught of wine given to him about to undergo the torture and to die? Deluded by false knowledge the mass of living things are only born to die again; as the sharp knife divides the wood, so constant change divides the world. The gloom of ignorance like the deep water, lust like the rolling billow, sorrow like the floating bubbles, false views like the Makara fish, amidst all these the ship of wisdom only can carry us across the mighty sea. The mass of ills are like the flowers of the sorrow-tree, old age and all its griefs, the tangled boughs; death the tree's tap-root, deeds done in life the buds, the diamond sword of wisdom only strong enough to cut down the mundane tree! Ignorance the burning-glass, covetous desire the scorching rays, the objects of the five desires the dry grass, wisdom alone the water to put out the fire. The perfect law, surpassing every law, having destroyed the gloom of ignorance, we see the straight road leading to quietness and rest, the end of every grief and sorrow. And now the loving one, converting men, impartial in his thoughts to friend or foe, the all-knowing, perfectly instructed, even he is going to leave the world! He with his soft and finely modulated voice, his compact body and broad shoulders, he, the great Rishi, ends his life! Who then can claim exemption? Enlightened, now he quickly passes hence! let us therefore seek with earnestness the truth, even as a man meets with the stream beside the road, then drinks and passes on. Inconstancy, this is the dreaded enemy—the universal destroyer—sparing neither rich nor poor; rightly perceiving this and keeping it in mind, this man, though sleeping, yet is the only ever-wakeful."

Thus the Likkhavi lions, ever mindful of the Buddha's wisdom, disquieted with the pain of birth and death, sighed forth their fond remembrance of the man-lion. Retaining in their minds no love of worldly things, aiming to rise above the power of every lustful quality, subduing in their hearts the thought of light or trivial matters, training their thoughts to seek the quiet, peaceful place; diligently practising the rules of unselfish, charitable conduct; putting away all listlessness, they found their joy in quietness and seclusion, meditating only on religious truth. And now the all-wise, turning his body round with a lion-turn, once more gazed upon Vaisâlî, and uttered this farewell verse:—

"Now this, the last time this, I leave Vaisâlî—the land where heroes live and flourish! Now am I going to die." Then gradually advancing, stage by stage he came to Bhoga-nagara, and there he rested in the Sâla grove, where he instructed all his followers in the precepts:—

"Now having gone on high I shall enter on Nirvâna: ye must rely upon the law—this is your highest, strongest, vantage ground. What is not found in Sûtra, or what disagrees with rules of Vinaya, opposing the one true system of my doctrine, this must not be held by you. What opposes Dharma, what opposes Vinaya, or what is contrary to my words, this is the result of ignorance: ye must not hold such doctrine, but with haste reject it. Receiving that which has been said aright, this is not subversive of true doctrine, this is what I have said, as the Dharma and Vinaya say. Accepting that which I, the law, and the Vinaya declare, this is to be believed. But words which neither I, the law, nor the Vinaya declare, these are not to be believed. Not gathering the true and hidden meaning, but closely holding to the letter, this is the way of foolish teachers, but contrary to my doctrine and a false way of teaching. Not separating the true from false, accepting in the dark without discrimination, is like a shop where gold and its alloys are sold together, justly condemned by all the world. The foolish masters, practising the ways of superficial wisdom, grasp not the meaning of the truth; but to receive the law as it explains itself, this is to accept the highest mode of exposition. Ye ought, therefore, thus to investigate true principles, to consider well the true law and the Vinaya, even as the goldsmith does who melts and strikes and then selects the true. Not to know the Sûtras and the Sâstras, this is to be devoid of wisdom; not saying properly that which is proper, is like doing that which is not fit to see. Let all be done in right and proper order, according as the meaning of the sentence guides, for he who grasps a sword unskilfully, does but inflict a wound upon his hand. Not skilfully to handle words and sentences, the meaning then is hard to know; as in the night-time travelling and seeking for a house, if all be dark within, how difficult to find. Losing the meaning, then the law is disregarded, disregarding the law the mind becomes confused; therefore every wise and prudent master neglects not to discover the true and faithful meaning."

Having spoken these words respecting the precepts of religion, he advanced to the town of Pâvâ, where all the Mallas prepared for him religious offerings of every kind. At this time a certain householder's son whose name was Kunda, invited Buddha to his house, and there he gave him, as an offering, his very last repast. Having partaken of it and declared the law, he onward went to the town of Kusi, crossing the river Tsae-kieuh and the Hiranyavatî. Then in that Sâla grove, a place of quiet and seclusion, he took his seat: entering the golden river he bathed his body, in appearance like a golden mountain. Then he spake his bidding thus to Ânanda: "Between those twin Sâla trees, sweeping and watering, make a clean space, and then arrange my sitting-mat. At midnight coming, I shall die."

Ânanda hearing the bidding of his master, his breath was choked with heart-sadness; but going and weeping he obeyed the instruction, and spreading out the mat he came forthwith back to his master and acquainted him. Tathâgata having lain down with his head towards the north and on his right side, slept thus. Resting upon his hand as on a pillow with his feet crossed, even as a lion-king; all grief is passed, his last-born body from this one sleep shall never rise. His followers round him, in a circle gathered, sigh dolefully: "The eye of the world is now put out!" The wind is hushed, the forest streams are silent, no voice is heard of bird or beast. The trees sweat out large flowing drops, flowers and leaves out of season singly fall, whilst men and Devas, not yet free from desire, are filled with overwhelming fear. Thus were they like men wandering through the arid desert, the road full dangerous, who fail to reach the longed-for hamlet; full of fear they go on still, dreading they might not find it, their heart borne down with fear they faint and droop. And now Tathâgata, aroused from sleep, addressed Ânanda thus: "Go! tell the Mallas, the time of my decease is come; they, if they see me not, will ever grieve and suffer deep regret." Ânanda listening to the bidding of his master, weeping went along the road. And then he told those Mallas all—"The lord is near to death." The Mallas hearing it, were filled with great, excessive grief. The men and women hurrying forth, bewailing as they went, came to the spot where Buddha was; with garments torn and hair dishevelled, covered with dust and sweat they came. With piteous cries they reached the grove, as when a Deva's day of merit comes to an end, so did they bow weeping and adoring at the feet of Buddha, grieving to behold his failing strength. Tathâgata, composed and quiet, spake: "Grieve not! the time is one for joy; no call for sorrow or for anguish here; that which for ages I have aimed at, now am I just about to obtain; delivered now from the narrow bounds of sense, I go to the place of never-ending rest and peace. I leave these things, earth, water, fire, and air, to rest secure where neither birth nor death can come. Eternally delivered there from grief, oh! tell me! why should I be sorrowful? Of yore on Sîrsha's mount, I longed to rid me of this body, but to fulfil my destiny I have remained till now with men in the world; I have kept this sickly, crumbling body, as dwelling with a poisonous snake; but now I am come to the great resting-place, all springs of sorrow now forever stopped. No more shall I receive a body, all future sorrow now forever done away; it is not meet for you, on my account, for evermore, to encourage any anxious fear."

The Mallas hearing Buddha's words, that he was now about to die, their minds confused, their eyes bedimmed, as if they saw before them nought but blackness, with hands conjoined, spake thus to Buddha: " Buddha is leaving now the pain of birth and death, and entering on the eternal joy of rest; doubtless we ought to rejoice thereat. Even as when a house is burnt a man rejoices if his friends are saved from out the flames; the gods! perhaps they rejoice—then how much more should men! But—when Tathâgata has gone and living things no more may see him, eternally cut off from safety and deliverance—in thought of this we grieve and sorrow. Like as a band of merchants crossing with careful steps a desert, with only a single guide, suddenly he dies! Those merchants now without a protector, how can they but lament! The present age, coming to know their true case, has found the omniscient, and looked to him, but yet has not obtained the final conquest; how will the world deride! Even as it would laugh at one who, walking o'er a mountain full of treasure, yet ignorant thereof, hugs still the pain of poverty."

So spake the Mallas, and with tearful words excuse themselves to Buddha, even as an only child pleads piteously before a loving father. Buddha then, with speech most excellent, exhibited and declared the highest principle of truth, and thus addressed the Mallas:—

" In truth, 'tis as you say; seeking the way, you must exert yourselves and strive with diligence—it is not enough to have seen me! Walk, as I have commanded you; get rid of all the tangled net of sorrow; walk in the way with steadfast aim; 'tis not from seeing me this comes—even as a sick man depending on the healing power of medicine, gets rid of all his ailments easily without beholding the physician. He who does not do what I command sees me in vain, this brings no profit; whilst he who lives far off from where I am, and yet walks righteously, is ever near me! A man may dwell beside me, and yet, being disobedient, be far away from me. Keep your heart carefully—give not place to listlessness! earnestly practise every good work. Man born in this world is pressed by all the sorrows of the long career, ceaselessly troubled—without a moment's rest, as any lamp blown by the wind!" The Mallas all, hearing Buddha's loving instruction, inwardly composed, restrained their tears, and, firmly self-possessed, returned.

Mahâparinirvâna

At this time there was a Brahmakârin whose name was Su-po-to-lo; he was well-known for his virtuous qualities, leading a pure life according to the rules of morality, and protecting all living things. When young he had adopted heretical views, and become a recluse among unbelievers—this one, wishing to see the lord, spake to Ânanda thus:—

"I hear that the system of Tathâgata is of a singular character and very profound, and that he has reached the highest wisdom in the world, the first of all horse-tamers. I hear moreover that he is now about to die, it will be difficult indeed to meet with him again, and difficult to see those who have seen him with difficulty, even as it is to catch in a mirror the reflection of the moon. I now desire respectfully to see him the greatest and most virtuous guide of men, because I seek to escape this mass of sorrow and reach the other shore of birth and death. The sun of Buddha now about to quench its rays, O! let me for a moment gaze upon him." The feelings of Ânanda now were much affected, thinking that this request was made with a view to controversy, or that he felt an inward joy because the lord was on the eve of death. He was not willing therefore to permit the interview with Buddha. Buddha, knowing the man's earnest desire and that he was a vessel fit for true religion, therefore addressed Ânanda thus: "Permit that heretic to advance; I was born to save mankind, make no hindrance therefore, or excuse!"

Subhadra, hearing this, was overjoyed at heart, and his religious feelings were much enlarged, as with increased reverence he advanced to Buddha's presence. Then, as the occasion required, he spoke becoming words and with politeness made his salutation, his features pleasing and with hands conjoined he said:—

"Now I desire to ask somewhat from thee; the world has many teachers of religion, those who know the law as I am myself; but I hear that Buddha has attained a way which is the end of all complete emancipation. O that you would, on my account, briefly explain your method, moisten my empty, thirsty soul! not with a view to controversy or from a desire to gain the mastery, but with sincerity I ask you so to do."

Then Buddha, for the Brahmakârin's sake, in brief recounted the eight "right ways"—on hearing which, his empty soul accepted it, as one deceived accepts direction in the right road. Perceiving now, he knew that what he had before perceived was not the final way of salvation, but now he felt he had attained what he had not before attained, and so he gave up and forsook his books of heresy. Moreover, now he rejected the gloomy hindrances of doubt, reflecting how by his former practices, mixed up with anger, hate, and ignorance, he had long cherished no real joy. For if, he argued, the ways of lust and hate and ignorance are able to produce a virtuous karman, then "hearing much" and "persevering wisdom," these, too, are born from lust, which cannot be. But if a man is able to cut down hate and ignorance, then also he puts off all consequences of works, and these being finally destroyed, this is complete emancipation. Those thus freed from works are likewise freed from subtle questionings, such as what the world says "that all things, everywhere, possess a self-nature." But if this be the case and therefore lust, hate, and ignorance, possess a self-implanted nature, then this nature must inhere in them; what then means the word "deliverance"? For even if we rightly cause the overthrow of hate and ignorance, yet if lust remains, then there is a return of birth; even as water, cold in its nature, may by fire be heated, but when the fire goes out then it becomes cold again, because this is its constant nature; so we may ever know that the nature which lust has is permanent, and neither hearing wisdom nor perseverance can alter it. Neither capable of increase or diminution, how can there be deliverance? I held aforetime that birth and death resulted thus, from their own innate nature; but now I see that such a belief excludes deliverance; for what is born by nature must endure so, what end can such things have? Just as a burning lamp cannot but give its light; the way of Buddha is the only true one, that lust, as the root-cause, brings forth the things that live; destroy this lust then there is Nirvâna; the cause destroyed then the fruit is not produced. I formerly maintained that "I" was a distinct entity, not seeing that it has no maker. But now I hear the right doctrine preached by Buddha, there is no "self" in all the world, for all things are produced by cause, and therefore there is no creator. If then sorrow is produced by cause, the cause may likewise be destroyed; for if the world is cause-produced, then is the view correct, that by destruction of the cause, there is an end. The cause destroyed, the world brought to an end, there is no room for such a thought as permanence, and therefore all my former views are " done away," and so he deeply " saw " the true doctrine taught by Buddha.

Because of seeds well sown in former times, he was enabled thus to understand the law on hearing it; thus he reached the good and perfect state of quietness, the peaceful, never-ending place of rest. His heart expanding to receive the truth, he gazed with earnest look on Buddha as he slept, nor could he bear to see Tathâgata depart and die; " ere yet," he said, " Buddha shall reach the term I will myself first leave the world;" and then with hands close joined, retiring from the holy form, he took his seat apart, and sat composed and firm. Then giving up his life, he reached Nirvâna, as when the rain puts out a little fire. Then Buddha spake to all his followers: " This my very last disciple has now attained Nirvâna, cherish him properly."

Then Buddha, the first night watch passed, the moon bright shining and all the stars clear in their lustre, the quiet grove without a sound, moved by his great compassionate heart, declared to his disciples this his bequeathed precepts: " After my Nirvâna, ye ought to reverence and obey the Pratimoksha, as your master, a shining lamp in the dark night, or as a great jewel treasured by a poor man. These injunctions I have ever given, these you ought to obey and follow carefully, and treat in no way different from myself. Keep pure your body, words, and conduct, put from you all concerns of daily life, lands, houses, cattle, storing wealth or hoarding grain. All these should be avoided as we avoid a fiery pit; sowing the land, cutting down shrubs, healing of wounds or the practice of medicine, star-gazing and astrology, forecasting lucky or unfortunate events by signs, prognosticating good or evil, all these are things forbidden. Keeping the body temperate, eat at proper times; receive no mission as a go-between; compound no philteries; abhor dissimulation; follow right doctrine, and be kind to all that lives; receive in moderation what is given; receive but hoard not up; these are, in brief, my spoken precepts. These form the groundwork of my rules, these also are the ground of full emancipation. Enabled thus to live this is rightly to receive all other things. This is true wisdom which embraces all, this is the way to attain the end; this code of rules, therefore, ye should hold and keep, and never let it slip or be destroyed. For when pure rules of conduct are observed then there is true religion; without these, virtue languishes; found yourselves therefore well on these my precepts; grounded thus in rules of purity, the springs of feeling will be well controlled, even as the well-instructed cow-herd guides well his cattle. Ill-governed feelings, like the horse, run wild through all the six domains of sense, bringing upon us in the present world unhappiness, and in the next, birth in an evil way. So, like the horse ill-broken, these land us in the ditch; therefore the wise and prudent man will not allow his senses license. For these senses are, indeed, our greatest foes, causes of misery; for men enamoured thus by sensuous things cause all their miseries to recur. Destructive as a poisonous snake, or like a savage tiger, or like a raging fire, the greatest evil in the world, he who is wise, is freed from fear of these. But what he fears is only this—a light and trivial heart, which drags a man to future misery—just for a little sip of pleasure, not looking at the yawning gulf before us; like the wild elephant freed from the iron curb, or like the ape that has regained the forest trees, such is the light and trivial heart; the wise man should restrain and hold it therefore. Letting the heart go loose without restraint, that man shall not attain Nirvâna; therefore we ought to hold the heart in check, and go apart from men and seek a quiet resting-place. Know when to eat and the right measure; and so with reference to the rules of clothing and of medicine; take care you do not by the food you take, encourage in yourselves a covetous or an angry mind. Eat your food to satisfy your hunger and drink to satisfy your thirst, as we repair an old or broken chariot, or like the butterfly that sips the flower destroying not its fragrance or its texture. The Bhikshu, in begging food, should beware of injuring the faithful mind of another; if a man opens his heart in charity, think not about his capabilities, for 'tis not well to calculate too closely the strength of the ox, lest by loading him beyond his strength you cause him injury. At morning, noon, and night, successively, store up good works. During the first and after-watch at night be not overpowered by sleep, but in the middle watch, with heart composed, take sleep and rest—be thoughtful towards the dawn of day. Sleep not the whole night through, making the body and the life relaxed and feeble; think! when the fire shall burn the body always, what length of sleep will then be possible? For when the hateful brood of sorrow rising through space, with all its attendant horrors, meeting the mind o'erwhelmed by sleep and death, shall seize its prey, who then shall waken it?

"The poisonous snake dwelling within a house can be enticed away by proper charms, so the black toad that dwells within his heart, the early waker disenchants and banishes. He who sleeps on heedlessly without plan, this man has no modesty; but modesty is like a beauteous robe, or like the curb that guides the elephant. Modest behavior keeps the heart composed, without it every virtuous root will die. Who has this modesty, the world applauds; without it, he is but as any beast. If a man with a sharp sword should cut the body bit by bit, let not an angry thought, or of resentment, rise, and let the mouth speak no ill word. Your evil thoughts and evil words but hurt yourself and not another; nothing so full of victory as patience, though your body suffer the pain of mutilation. For recollect that he who has this patience cannot be overcome, his strength being so firm; therefore give not way to anger or evil words towards men in power. Anger and hate destroy the true law; and they destroy dignity and beauty of body; as when one dies we lose our name for beauty, so the fire of anger itself burns up the heart. Anger is foe to all religious merit, he who loves virtue let him not be passionate; the layman who is angry when oppressed by many sorrows is not wondered at. But he who has 'left his home' indulging anger, this is indeed opposed to principle, as if in frozen water there were found the heat of fire. If indolence arises in your heart, then with your own hand smooth down your head, shave off your hair, and clad in sombre garments, in your hand holding the begging-pot, go ask for food; on every side the living perish, what room for indolence? the worldly man, relying on his substance or his family, indulging in indolence, is wrong; how much more the religious man, whose purpose is to seek the way of rescue, who encourages within an indolent mind; this surely is impossible!

"Crookedness and straightness are in their nature opposite and cannot dwell together more than frost and fire; for one who has become religious, and practises the way of straight behavior, a false and crooked way of speech is not becoming. False and flattering speech is like the magician's art; but he who ponders on religion cannot speak falsely. To 'covet much,' brings sorrow; desiring little, there is rest and peace. To procure rest, there must be small desire—much more in case of those who seek salvation. The niggard dreads the much-seeking man lest he should filch away his property, but he who loves to give has also fear, lest he should not possess enough to give; therefore we ought to encourage small desire, that we may have to give to him who wants, without such fear. From this desiring-little-mind we find the way of true deliverance; desiring true deliverance we ought to practise knowing-enough contentment.

"A contented mind is always joyful, but joy like this is but religion; the rich and poor alike, having contentment, enjoy perpetual rest. The ill-contented man, though he be born to heavenly joys, because he is not contented would ever have a mind burned up by the fire of sorrow. The rich, without contentment, endures the pain of poverty; though poor, if yet he be contented, then he is rich indeed! That ill-contented man, the bounds of the five desires extending further still, becomes insatiable in his requirements, and so through the long night of life gathers increasing sorrow. Without cessation thus he cherishes his careful plans, whilst he who lives contented, freed from anxious thoughts about relationships, his heart is ever peaceful and at rest. And so because he rests and is at peace within, the gods and men revere and do him service. Therefore we ought to put away all cares about relationship.

"For like a solitary desert tree in which the birds and monkeys gather, so is it when we are cumbered much with family associations; through the long night we gather many sorrows. Many dependents are like the many bands that bind us, or like the old elephant that struggles in the mud. By diligent perseverance a man may get much profit; therefore night and day men ought with ceaseless effort to exert themselves; the tiny streams that trickle down the mountain slopes by always flowing eat away the rock. If we use not earnest diligence in drilling wood in wood for fire, we shall not obtain the spark, so ought we to be diligent and persevere, as the skilful master drills the wood for fire. A 'virtuous friend' though he be gentle is not to be compared with right reflection—right thought kept well in the mind, no evil thing can ever enter there.

"Wherefore those who practise a religious life should always think about 'the body'; if thought upon one's self be absent, then all virtue dies. For as the champion warrior relies for victory upon his armor's strength, so 'right thought' is like a strong cuirass, able to withstand the six sense-robbers. Right faith enwraps the enlightened heart, so that a man perceives the world throughout is liable to birth and death; therefore the religious man should practise faith.

"Having found peace in faith, we put an end to all the mass of sorrows, wisdom then can enlighten us, and so we put away the rules by which we acquire knowledge by the senses. By inward thought and right consideration following with gladness the directions of the 'true law,' this is the way in which both laymen of the world and men who have left their homes should walk.

"Across the sea of birth and death, 'wisdom' is the handy bark; 'wisdom' is the shining lamp that lightens up the dark and gloomy world. 'Wisdom' is the grateful medicine for all the defiling ills of life; 'wisdom' is the axe wherewith to level all the tangled forest trees of sorrow. 'Wisdom' is the bridge that spans the rushing stream of ignorance and lust—therefore, in every way, by thought and right attention, a man should diligently inure himself to engender wisdom. Having acquired the threefold wisdom, then, though blind, the eye of wisdom sees throughout; but without wisdom the mind is poor and insincere; such things cannot suit the man who has left his home.

"Wherefore let the enlightened man lay well to heart that false and fruitless things become him not, and let him strive with single mind for that pure joy which can be found alone in perfect rest and quietude.

"Above all things be not careless, for carelessness is the chief foe of virtue; if a man avoid this fault he may be born where Sakra-râga dwells. He who gives way to carelessness of mind must have his lot where the Asuras dwell. Thus have I done my task, my fitting task, in setting forth the way of quietude, the proof of love. On your parts be diligent! with virtuous purpose practise well these rules, in quiet solitude of desert hermitage nourish and cherish a still and peaceful heart. Exert yourselves to the utmost, give no place to remissness, for as in worldly matters when the considerate physician prescribes fit medicine for the disease he has detected, should the sick man neglect to use it, this cannot be the physician's fault, so I have told you the truth, and set before you this the one and level road. Hearing my words and not with care obeying them, this is not the fault of him who speaks; if there be anything not clearly understood in the principles of the 'four truths,' you now may ask me, freely; let not your inward thoughts be longer hid." The lord in mercy thus instructing them, the whole assembly remained silent.

Then Anuruddha, observing that the great congregation continued silent and expressed no doubt, with closed hands thus spake to Buddha:—

"The moon may be warm, the sun's rays be cool, the air be still, the earth's nature mobile; these four things, though yet unheard of in the world, may happen; but this assembly never can have doubt about the principles of sorrow, accumulation, destruction, and the incontrovertible truths, as declared by the lord. But because the lord is going to die, we all have sorrow; and we cannot raise our thoughts to the high theme of the lord's preaching. Perhaps some fresh disciple, whose feelings are yet not entirely freed from other influences might doubt; but we, who now have heard this tender, sorrowful discourse, have altogether freed ourselves from doubt. Passed the sea of birth and death, without desire, with nought to seek, we only know how much we love, and, grieving, ask why Buddha dies so quickly?"

Buddha regarding Anuruddha, perceiving how his words were full of bitterness, again with loving heart, appeasing him, replied:—

"In the beginning things were fixed, in the end again they separate; different combinations cause other substances, for there is no uniform and constant principle in nature. But when all mutual purposes be answered, what then shall chaos and creation do! the gods and men alike that should be saved, shall all have been completely saved! Ye then! my followers, who know so well the perfect law, remember! the end must come; give not way again to sorrow!

"Use diligently the appointed means; aim to reach the home where separation cannot come; I have lit the lamp of wisdom, its rays alone can drive away the gloom that shrouds the world. The world is not forever fixed! Ye should rejoice therefore! as when a friend, afflicted grievously, his sickness healed, escapes from pain. For I have put away this painful vessel, I have stemmed the flowing sea of birth and death, free forever now, from pain! for this you should exult with joy! Now guard yourselves aright, let there be no remissness! that which exists will all return to nothingness! and now I die. From this time forth my words are done, this is my very last instruction."

Then entering the Samâdhi of the first Dhyâna, he went successively through all the nine in a direct order; then inversely he returned throughout and entered on the first, and then from the first he raised himself and entered on the fourth. Leaving the state of Samâdhi, his soul without a resting-place, forthwith he reached Nirvâna. And then, as Buddha died, the great earth quaked throughout. In space, on every hand, was fire like rain, no fuel, self-consuming. And so from out the earth great flames arose on every side.

Thus up to the heavenly mansions flames burst forth; the crash of thunder shook the heavens and earth, rolling along the mountains and the valleys, even as when the Devas and Asuras fight with sound of drums and mutual conflict. A wind tempestuous from the four bounds of earth arose—whilst from the crags and hills, dust and ashes fell like rain. The sun and moon withdrew their shining; the peaceful streams on every side were torrent-swollen; the sturdy forests shook like aspen leaves, whilst flowers and leaves untimely fell around, like scattered rain. The flying dragons, carried on pitchy clouds, wept down their tears; the four kings and their associates, moved by pity, forgot their works of charity. The pure Devas came to earth from heaven, halting mid-air they looked upon the changeful scene, not sorrowing, not rejoicing. But yet they sighed to think of the world, heedless of its sacred teacher, hastening to destruction. The eightfold heavenly spirits, on every side filled space: cast down at heart and grieving, they scattered flowers as offerings. Only Mâra-râga rejoiced, and struck up sounds of music in his exultation. Whilst Gambudvîpa shorn of its glory, seemed to grieve as when the mountain tops fall down to earth, or like the great elephant robbed of its tusks, or like the ox-king spoiled of his horns; or heaven without the sun and moon, or as the lily beaten by the hail; thus was the world bereaved when Buddha died!

Praising Nirvâna

At this time there was a Devaputra, riding on his thousand white-swan palace in the midst of space, who beheld the Parinirvâna of Buddha. This one, for the universal benefit of the Deva assembly, sounded forth at large these verses on impermanence:—

"Impermanency is the nature of all things, quickly born, they quickly die. With birth there comes the rush of sorrows, only in Nirvâna is there joy. The accumulated fuel heaped up by the power of karman, this the fire of wisdom alone can consume. Though the fame of our deeds reach up to heaven as smoke, yet in time the rains which descend will extinguish all, as the fire that rages at the kalpa's end is put out by the judgment of water."

Again there was a Brahma-Rishi-deva, like a most exalted Rishi, dwelling in heaven, possessed of superior happiness, with no taint in his bliss, who thus sighed forth his praises of Tathâgata's Nirvâna, with his mind fixed in abstraction as he spoke:

"Looking through all the conditions of life, from first to last nought is free from destruction. But the incomparable seer dwelling in the world, thoroughly acquainted with the highest truth, whose wisdom grasps that which is beyond the world's ken, he it is who can save the worldly-dwellers. He it is who can provide lasting escape from the destructive power of impermanence. But, alas! through the wide world, all that lives is sunk in unbelief."

At this time Anuruddha, "not stopped" by the world, "not stopped" from being delivered, the stream of birth and death forever "stopped," sighed forth the praises of Tathâgata's Nirvâna:—

"All living things completely blind and dark! the mass of deeds all perishing, even as the fleeting cloud-pile! Quickly arising and as quickly perishing! the wise man holds not to such a refuge, for the diamond mace of inconstancy can overturn the mountain of the Rishi hermit. How despicable and how weak the world! doomed to destruction, without strength! Impermanence, like the fierce lion, can even spoil the Nâga-elephant-great-Rishi. Only the diamond curtain of Tathâgata can overwhelm inconstancy! How much more should those not yet delivered from desire, fear and dread its power? From the six seeds there grows one sprout, one kind of water from the rain, the origin of the four points is far removed: five kinds of fruit from the two 'Koo'—the three periods, past, present, future, are but one in substance; the Muni-great-elephant plucks up the great tree of sorrow, and yet he cannot avoid the power of impermanence. For like the crested bird delights within the pool to seize the poisonous snake, but when from sudden drought he is left in the dry pool, he dies; or as the prancing steed advances fearlessly to battle, but when the fight has passed goes back subdued and quiet; or as the raging fire burns with the fuel, but when the fuel is done, expires; so is it with Tathâgata, his task accomplished he returns to find his refuge in Nirvâna: just as the shining of the radiant moon sheds everywhere its light and drives away the gloom, all creatures grateful for its light, it disappears concealed by Sumeru; such is the case with Tathâgata, the brightness of his wisdom lit up the gloomy darkness, and for the good of all that lives drove it away, when suddenly it disappears behind the mountain of Nirvâna. The splendor of his fame throughout the world diffused, had banished all obscurity, but like the stream that ever flows, it rests not with us; the illustrious charioteer with his seven prancing steeds flies through the host and disappears.

"The bright-rayed Sûrya-deva, entering the Yen-tsz' cave, was, with the moon, surrounded with fivefold barriers; 'all things that live,' deprived of light, present their offerings to heaven; but from their sacrifice nought but the blackened smoke ascends; thus it is with Tathâgata, his glory hidden, the world has lost its light. Rare was the expectancy of grateful love that filled the heart of all that lives; that love, reached its full limit, then was left to perish! The cords of sorrow all removed, we found the true and only way; but now he leaves the tangled mesh of life, and enters on the quiet place! His spirit mounting through space, he leaves the sorrow-bearing vessel of his body! the gloom of doubt and the great darkness all dispelled, by the bright rays of wisdom! The earthy soil of sorrow's dust his wisdom's water purifies! no more, no more, returns he here! forever gone to the place of rest!

"The power of birth and death destroyed, the world instructed in the highest doctrine! he bids the world rejoice in knowledge of his law, and gives to all the benefit of wisdom! Giving complete rest to the world, the virtuous streams flow forth! his fame known throughout the world, shines still with increased splendor! How great his pity and his love to those who opposed his claims, neither rejoicing in their defeat nor exulting in his own success. Illustriously controlling his feelings, all his senses completely enlightened, his heart impartially observing events, unpolluted by the six objects of sense! Reaching to that unreached before! obtaining that which man had not obtained! with the water which he provided filling every thirsty soul! Bestowing that which never yet was given, and providing a reward not hoped for! his peaceful, well-marked person, perfectly knowing the thoughts of all.

"Not greatly moved either by loving or disliking! overcoming all enemies by the force of his love! the welcome physician for all diseases, the one destroyer of impermanency! All living things rejoicing in religion, fully satisfied! obtaining all they need, their every wish fulfilled! The great master of holy wisdom once gone returns no more! even as the fire gone out for want of fuel! Declaring the eight rules without taint; overcoming the five senses, difficult to compose! with the three powers of sight seeing the three precious ones; removing the three robbers (i.e. lust, anger, ignorance); perfecting the three grades of a holy life, concealing the one (himself) and obtaining the one saintship—leaping over the seven 'bodhyangas' and obtaining the long sleep; the end of all, the quiet, peaceful way; the highest prize of sages and of saints!

"Having himself severed the barriers of sorrow, now he is able to save his followers, and to provide the draught of immortality for all who are parched with thirst! Armed with the heavy cuirass of patience, he has overcome all enemies! by the subtle principles of his excellent law to satisfy every heart. Planting a sacred seed in the hearts of those practising virtue; impartially directing and not casting off those who are right or not right in their views! Turning the wheel of the superlative law! received with gladness through the world by those who have in former conditions implanted in themselves a love for religion, these all saved by his preaching! Going forth among men converting those not yet converted; those who had not seen the truth, causing them to see the truth! All those practising a false method of religion, delivering to them deep principles of his religion! preaching the doctrines of birth and death and impermanency; declaring that without a master teacher there can be no happiness! Erecting the standard of his great renown, overcoming and destroying the armies of Mâra! advancing to the point of indifference to pleasure or pain, caring not for life, desiring only rest! Causing those not yet converted to obtain conversion! those not yet saved to be saved! those not yet at rest to find rest! those not yet enlightened to be enlightened!

"Thus the Muni taught the way of rest for the direction of all living things! alas! that any transgressing the way of holiness should practise impure works. Even as at the end of the great kalpa, those holding the law who die, when the rolling sound of the mysterious thunder-cloud severs the forests, upon these there shall fall the rain of immortality. The little elephant breaks down the prickly forest, and by cherishing it we know that it can profit men; but the cloud that removes the sorrow of the elephant old-age, this none can bear. He by destroying systems of religion has perfected his system, in saving the world and yet saving! he has destroyed the teaching of heresy, in order to reach his independent mode of doctrine.

"And now he enters the great quiet place! no longer has the world a protector or saviour! the great army host of Mâra-râga, rousing their warrior, shaking the great earth, desired to injure the honored Muni! but they could not move him, whom in a moment now the Mâra 'inconstancy' destroys. The heavenly occupants everywhere assemble as a cloud! they fill the space of heaven, fearing the endless birth and death! their hearts are full of grief and dread! His Deva eyes clearly behold, without the limitations of near or distant, the fruits of works discerned throughout, as an image perceived in a mirror! His Deva ears perfect and discriminating throughout, hear all, though far away, mounting through space he teaches all the Devas, surpassing his method of converting men! He divides his body still one in substance, crosses the water as if it were not weak (to bear)! remembers all his former births, through countless kalpas none forgotten! His senses wandering through the fields of sense, all these distinctly remembered; knowing the wisdom learned in every state of mind, all this perfectly understood! By spiritual discernment and pure mysterious wisdom equally surveying all things! every vestige of imperfection removed! thus he has accomplished all he had to do. By wisdom rejecting other spheres of life, his wisdom now completely perfected, lo! he dies! let the world, hard and unyielding, still, beholding it, relent!

"All living things though blunt in sense, beholding him, receive the enlightenment of wisdom! their endless evil deeds long past, as they behold, are cancelled and completely cleansed! In a moment gone! who shall again exhibit qualities like his? no saviour now in all the world—our hope cut off, our very breath is stopped and gone! Who now shall give us life again with the cool water of his doctrine? his own great work accomplished, his great compassion now has ceased to work for long: has long ceased or stopped! The world ensnared in the toils of folly, who shall destroy the net? who shall, by his teaching, cause the stream of birth and death to turn again? Who shall declare the way of rest to instruct the heart of all that lives, deceived by ignorance? Who will point out the quiet place, or who make known the one true doctrine?

"All flesh suffering great sorrow, who shall deliver, like a loving father? Like the horse changing his master loses all gracefulness, as he forgets his many words of guidance! as a king without a kingdom, such is the world without a Buddha! as a disciple with no power of dialectic left, or like a physician without wisdom, as men whose king has lost the marks of royalty, so, Buddha dead, the world has lost its glory! the gentle horses left without a charioteer, the boat without a pilot left! The three divisions of an army left without a general! the merchantman without a guide! the suffering and diseased without a physician! a holy king without his seven insignia. The stars without the moon! the loving years without the power of life! such is the world now that Buddha, the great teacher, dies!"

Thus spake the Arhat, all done that should be done, all imperfections quite removed, knowing the meed of gratitude, he was grateful therefore. Thus thinking of his master's love he spake! setting forth the world's great sorrow; whilst those, not yet freed from the power of passion, wept with many tears, unable to control themselves. Yet even those who had put away all faults, sighed as they thought of the pain of birth and death. And now the Malla host hearing that Buddha had attained Nirvâna, with cries confused, wept piteously, greatly moved, as when a flight of herons meet a hawk. In a body now they reach the twin trees, and as they gaze upon Tathâgata dead, entered on his long sleep, those features never again to awake to consciousness, they smote their breasts and sighed to heaven; as when a lion seizing on a calf, the whole herd rushes on with mingled sounds.

In the midst there was one Malla, his mind enamoured of the righteous law, who gazed with steadfastness upon the holy law-king, now entered on the mighty calm, and said: "The world was everywhere asleep, when Buddha setting forth his law caused it to awake; but now he has entered on the mighty calm, and all is finished in an unending sleep. For man's sake he had raised the standard of his law, and now, in a moment, it has fallen; the sun of Tathâgata's wisdom spreading abroad the lustre of its 'great awakening,' increasing ever more and more in glory, spreading abroad the thousand rays of highest knowledge, scattering and destroying all the gloom of earth, why has the darkness great come back again? His unequalled wisdom lightening the three worlds, giving eyes that all the world might see, now suddenly the world is blind again, bewildered, ignorant of the way; in a moment fallen the bridge of truth that spanned the rolling stream of birth and death, the swelling flood of lust and rage and doubt, and all flesh overwhelmed therein, forever lost."

Thus all that Malla host wept piteously and lamented; whilst some concealed their grief nor spoke a word; others sank prostrate on the earth; others stood silent, lost in meditation; others, with sorrowful heart, groaned deeply. Then on a gold and silver gem-decked couch richly adorned with flowers and scents, they placed the body of Tathâgata; a jewelled canopy they raised above, and round it flags and streamers and embroidered banners; then using every kind of dance and music, the lords and ladies of the Mallas followed along the road presenting offerings, whilst all the Devas scattered scents and flowers, and raised the sound of drums and music in the heavens. Thus men and Devas shared one common sorrow, their cries united as they grieved together. Entering the city, there the men and women, old and young, completed their religious offerings. Leaving the city, then, and passing through the Lung-tsiang gate, and crossing over the Hiranyavatî river, they repaired to where the former Buddhas, having died, had Kaityas raised to them. There collecting ox-head sandal-wood and every famous scented wood, they placed the whole above the Buddha's body, pouring various scented oils upon the pyre; then placing fire beneath to kindle it, three times they walked around; but yet it burned not. At this time the great Kâsyapa had taken his abode at Râgagriha, and knowing Buddha was about to die was coming thence with all his followers; his pure mind, deeply moved, desired to see the body of the lord; and so, because of that his sincere wish, the fire went out and would not kindle. Then Kâsyapa and his followers coming, with piteous sighs looked on the sight and reverenced at the master's feet; and then, forthwith, the fire burst out. Quenched the fire of grief within; without, the fire has little power to burn. Or though it burn the outside skin and flesh, the diamond true-bone still remains. The scented oil consumed, the fire declines, the bones they place within a golden pitcher; for as the mystic world is not destroyed, neither can these, the bones of Buddha, perish; the consequence of diamond wisdom, difficult to move as Sumeru. The relics which the mighty golden-pinioned bird cannot remove or change, they place within the precious vase, to remain until the world shall pass away; ana wonderful! the power of men can thus fulfil Nirvâna's laws, the illustrious name of one far spread, is sounded thus throughout the universe; and as the ages roll, the long Nirvâna, by these, the sacred relics, sheds through the world its glorious light, and brightens up the abodes of life. He perished in a moment! but these relics, placed within the vase, the imperishable signs of wisdom, can overturn the mount of sorrow; the body of accumulated griefs this imperishable mind can cause to rest, and banish once forever all the miseries of life. Thus the diamond substance was dealt with at the place of burning. And now those valiant Mallas, unrivalled in the world for strength, subduing all private animosities, sought escape from sorrow in the true refuge. Finding sweet comfort in united love, they resolved to banish every complaining thought. Beholding thus the death of Tathâgata, they controlled their grieving hearts, and with full strength of manly virtue dismissing every listless thought, they submitted to the course of nature. Oppressed by thoughts of grievous sorrow, they entered the city as a deserted wild: holding the relics thus they entered, whilst from every street were offered gifts. They placed the relics then upon a tower for men and Devas to adore.

Division of the Sariras

Thus those Mallas offered religious reverence to the relics, and used the most costly flowers and scents for their supreme act of worship. Then the kings of the seven countries, having heard that Buddha was dead, sent messengers to the Mallas asking to share the sacred relics of Buddha. Then the Mallas reverencing the body of Tathâgata, trusting to their martial renown, conceived a haughty mind: "They would rather part with life itself," they said, "than with the relics of the Buddha"—so those messengers returned from the futile embassage. Then the seven kings, highly indignant, with an army numerous as the rain-clouds, advanced on Kusinagara; the people who went from the city filled with terror soon returned and told the Mallas all: that the soldiers and the cavalry of the neighboring countries were coming, with elephants and chariots, to surround the Kusinagara city. The gardens, lying without the town, the fountains, lakes, flower and fruit-trees were now destroyed by the advancing host, and all the pleasant resting-places lay in ruins.

The Mallas, mounting on the city towers, beheld the great supports of life destroyed; they then prepared their warlike engines to crush the foe without: balistas and catapults and "flying torches," to hurl against the advancing host. Then the seven kings entrenched themselves around the city, each army host filled with increasing courage; their wings of battle shining in array as the sun's seven beams of glory shine; the heavy drums rolling as the thunder, the warlike breath rising as the full cloud mist. The Mallas, greatly incensed, opening the gates command the fray to begin; the aged men and women whose hearts had trust in Buddha's law, with deep concern breathed forth their vow, "Oh! may the victory be a bloodless one!" Those who had friends used mutual exhortations not to encourage in themselves a desire for strife.

And now the warriors, clad in armor, grasping their spears and brandishing their swords 'midst the confused noise and heavy drums advanced. But ere the contest had begun, there was a certain Brahman whose name was Drona, celebrated for penetration, honored for modesty and lowliness, whose loving heart took pleasure in religion. This one addressed those kings and said: "Regarding the unequalled strength of yonder city, one man alone would be enough for its defence; how much less when with determined heart they are united, can you subdue it! In the beginning mutual strife produced destruction, how now can it result in glory or renown? The clash of swords and bloody onset done, 'tis certain one must perish! and therefore whilst you aim to vanquish those, both sides will suffer in the fray. Then there are many chances, too, of battle: 'tis hard to measure strength by appearances; the strong, indeed, may overcome the weak, the weak may also overcome the strong; the powerful champion may despise the snake, but how will he escape a wounded body? there are men whose natures bland and soft, seem suited for the company of women or of children, but when enlisted in the ranks, make perfect soldiers. As fire when it is fed with oil, though reckoned weak, is not extinguished easily, so when you say that they are weak, beware of leaning overmuch on strength of body; nought can compare with strength of right religion. There was in ancient times a Gina king, whose name was Kârandhama, his graceful upright presence caused such love in others that he could overcome all animosity; but though he ruled the world and was high renowned, and rich and prosperous, yet in the end he went back and all was lost! So when the ox has drunk enough, he too returns. Use then the principles of righteousness, use the expedients of good will and love. Conquer your foe by force, you increase his enmity; conquer by love, and you will reap no after-sorrow. The present strife is but a thirst for blood, this thing cannot be endured! If you desire to honor Buddha, follow the example of his patience and long-suffering!" Thus this Brahman with confidence declared the truth; imbued with highest principles of peace, he spake with boldness and unflinchingly.

And now the kings addressed the Brahman thus: "You have chosen a fitting time for giving increase to the seed of wisdom: the essence of true friendship is the utterance of truth. The greatest force of reason lies in righteous judgment. But now in turn hear what we say: The rules of kings are framed to avoid the use of force when hatred has arisen from low desires, or else to avoid the sudden use of violence in trifling questions where some trifling matter is at stake. But we for the sake of law are about to fight. What wonder is it! Swollen pride is a principle to be opposed, for it leads to the overthrow of society;

no wonder then that Buddha preached against it, teaching men to practise lowliness and humility. Then why should we be forbidden to pay our reverence to his body-relics? In ancient days a lord of the great earth, Pih-shih-tsung and Nanda, for the sake of a beautiful woman fought and destroyed each other; how much more now, for the sake of religious reverence to our master, freed from passion, gone to Nirvâna, without regard to self, or careful of our lives, should we contend and assert our rights! A former king, Kaurava, fought with a Pândava king, and the more they increased in strength the more they struggled, all for some temporary gain; how much more for our not-coveting master should we contend, coveting to get his living relics? The son of Râma, too, the Rishi, angry with King Dasaratha, destroyed his country, slew the people, because of the rage he felt; how much less for our master, freed from anger, should we be niggard of our lives! Râma, for Sita's sake, killed all the demon-spirits; how much more for our lord, heaven-received, should we not sacrifice our lives! The two demons A-lai and Po-ku were ever drawn into contention; in the first place, because of their folly and ignorance, causing wide ruin among men; how much less for our all-wise master should we begrudge our lives! Wherefore if from these examples we find others ready to die for no real principle, how shall we for our teacher of gods (Devas) and men, reverenced by the universe, spare our bodies or begrudge our lives, and not be earnest in desire to make our offerings! Now then, if you desire to stay the strife, go and for us demand within the city that they open wide the relics, and so cause our prayer to be fulfilled. But because your words are right ones, we hold our anger for a while; even as the great, angry snake, by the power of charms is quieted."

And now the Brahman, having received the kings' instruction, entering the city, went to the Mallas, and saluting them, spoke these true words: "Without the city those who are kings among men grasp with their hands their martial weapons, and with their bodies clad in weighty armor wait eagerly to fight; glorious as the sun's rays, bristling with rage as the roused lion. These united are, to overthrow this city. But whilst they wage this religious war, they fear lest they may act irreligiously, and so they have sent me here to say what they require: 'We have come, not for the sake of territory, much less for money's sake, nor on account of any insolent feeling, nor yet from any thought of hatred; but because we venerate the great Rishi, we have come on this account. You, noble sirs! know well our mind! Why should there be such sorrowful contention! You honor what we honor, both alike, then we are brothers as concerns religion. We both with equal heart revere the bequeathed spiritual relics of the lord. To be miserly in hoarding wealth, this is an unreasonable fault; how much more to grudge religion, of which there is so little knowledge in the world! The exclusive and the selfishly inclined, should practise laws of hospitality; but if ye have not rules of honor such as these, then shut your gates and guard yourselves.' This is the tenor of the words, be they good or bad, spoken by them. But now for myself and my own feelings, let me add these true and sincere words:—Let there be no contention either way; reason ought to minister for peace, the lord when dwelling in the world ever employed the force of patience. Not to obey his holy teaching, and yet to offer gifts to him, is contradiction. Men of the world, for some indulgence, some wealth or land, contend and fight, but those who believe the righteous law should obediently conform their lives to it; to believe and yet to harbor enmity, this is to oppose 'religious principle' to 'conduct.' Buddha himself at rest, and full of love, desired to bestow the rest he enjoyed on all. To adore with worship the great merciful, and yet to gender wide destruction, how is this possible? Divide the relics, then, that all may worship them alike; obeying thus the law, the fame thereof widespread, then righteous principles will be diffused; but if others walk not righteously, we ought by righteous dealing to appease them, in this way showing the advantage of religion, we cause religion everywhere to take deep hold and abide. Buddha has told us that of all charity 'religious charity' is the highest; men easily bestow their wealth in charity, but hard is the charity that works for righteousness."

The Mallas hearing the Brahman's words with inward shame gazed at one another; and answered the Brahmakârin thus: "We thank you much for purposing to come to us, and for your friendly and religious counsel—speaking so well, and reasonably. Yours are words which a Brahman ought to use, in keeping with his holy character; words full of reconciliation, pointing out the proper road; like one recovering a wandering horse brings him back by the path which he had lost. We then ought to adopt the plan of reconciliation such as you have shown us; to hear the truth and not obey it brings afterwards regretful sorrow."

Then they opened out the master's relics and in eight parts equally divided them. Themselves paid reverence to one part, the other seven they handed to the Brahman; the seven kings having accepted these, rejoiced and placed them on their heads; and thus with them returned to their own country, and erected Dâgobas for worship over them. The Brahmakârin then besought the Mallas to bestow on him the relic-pitcher as his portion, and from the seven kings he requested a fragment of their relics, as an eighth share. Taking this, he returned and raised a Kaitya, which still is named "the Golden Pitcher Dâgoba." Then the men of Kusinagara collecting all the ashes of the burning, raised over them a Kaitya, and called it "the Ashes Dâgoba." The eight Stûpas of the eight kings, "the Golden Pitcher" and "the Ashes Stûpa."

Thus throughout Gambudvîpa there first were raised ten Dâgobas. Then all the lords and ladies of the country holding gem-embroidered canopies, paid their offerings at the various shrines, adorning them as any golden mountain. And so with music and with dancing through the day and night they made merry, and sang. And now the Arhats numbering five hundred, having forever lost their master's presence, reflecting there was now no ground of certainty, returned to Gridhrakûta mount; assembling in King Sakra's cavern, they collected there the Sûtra Pitaka; all the assembly agreeing that the venerable Ânanda should say, for the sake of the congregation, the sermons of Tathâgata from first to last: "Great and small, whatever you have heard from the mouth of the deceased Muni."

Then Ânanda in the great assembly ascending the lion throne, declared in order what the lord had preached, uttering the words "Thus have I heard."

The whole assembly, bathed in tears, were deeply moved as he pronounced the words "I heard"; and so he announced the law as to the time, as to the place, as to the person; as he spoke, so was it written down from first to last, the complete Sûtra Pitaka. By diligent attention in the use of means, practising wisdom, all these Arhats obtained Nirvâna; those now able so to do, or hereafter able, shall attain Nirvâna in the same way.

King Asoka born in the world when strong, caused much sorrow; when feeble, then he banished sorrow; as the Asoka-flower tree, ruling over Gambudvîpa, his heart forever put an end to sorrow, when brought to entire faith in the true law; therefore he was called "the King who frees from sorrow." A descendant of the Mayûra family, receiving from heaven a righteous disposition, he ruled equally over the world; he raised everywhere towers and shrines, his private name the "violent Asoka," now called the "righteous Asoka."

Opening the Dâgobas raised by those seven kings to take the Sarîras thence, he spread them everywhere, and raised in one day eighty-four thousand towers; only with regard to the eighth pagoda in Râmagrama, which the Nâga spirit protected, the king was unable to obtain those relics; but though he obtained them not, knowing they were spiritually bequeathed relics of Buddha which the Nâga worshipped and adored, his faith was increased and his reverent disposition. Although the king was ruler of the world, yet was he able to obtain the first holy fruit; and thus induced the entire empire to honor and revere the shrines of Tathâgata.

In the past and present, thus there has been deliverance for all. Tathâgata, when in the world; and now his relics—after his Nirvâna; those who worship and revere these, gain equal merit; so also those who raise themselves by wisdom, and reverence the virtues of the Tathâgata, cherishing religion, fostering a spirit of almsgiving, they gain great merit also. The noble and superlative law of Buddha ought to receive the adoration of the world. Gone to that undying place, those who believe his law shall follow him there; therefore let all the Devas and men, without exception, worship and adore the one great loving and compassionate, who mastered thoroughly the highest truth, in order to deliver all that lives. Who that hears of him, but yearns with love! The pains of birth, old age, disease and death, the endless sorrows of the world, the countless miseries of "hereafter," dreaded by all the Devas, he has removed all these accumulated sorrows; say, who would not revere him? to escape the joys of after life, this is the world's chief joy! To add the pain of other births, this is the world's worst sorrow! Buddha, escaped from pain of birth, shall have no joy of the "hereafter"!

And having shown the way to all the world, who would not reverence and adore him? To sing the praises of the lordly monk, and declare his acts from first to last, without self-seeking or self-honor, without desire for personal renown, but following what the scriptures say, to benefit the world, has been my aim.